The Campaign of 1815

The Campaign of 1815

Ligny : Quatre-Bras : Waterloo

BY

WILLIAM O'CONNOR MORRIS

SOMETIME SCHOLAR OF ORIEL COLLEGE, OXFORD

' Ac nescio, an mirabilior adversis quam
secundis rebus fuerit.'
LIVY, XXVIII. 12.

The Naval & Military Press Ltd

Published by

The Naval & Military Press Ltd

Unit 5 Riverside, Brambleside,
Bellbrook Industrial Estate,
Uckfield, East Sussex,
TN22 1QQ England

Tel: +44 (0) 1825 749494
Fax: +44 (0) 1825 765701

www.naval-military-press.com
www.nmarchive.com

I DEDICATE THIS BOOK

TO

CAPTAIN A. T. MAHAN, U.S.N.,

THE GREATEST LIVING AUTHORITY ON

NAVAL WARFARE,

WITH MANY EXPRESSIONS OF ADMIRATION

AND ESTEEM

PREFACE

MY object in this work has been to combine a succinct but complete narrative of the campaign of 1815 with a careful running commentary on its military operations, and thus to satisfy, as well as I could, the requirements of the general reader and of the real and scientific student of war. It is not for me to say how I have accomplished my purpose; but I think there is no book exactly of this character in English literature, and the very favourable reception accorded to my 'Napoleon' in the 'Heroes Series,' and to other writings of mine on the grand passage of arms of which Waterloo was the consummation, has induced me to hope that this volume will be not unacceptable to the public. For many reasons I offer no apology for making an attempt to elucidate and to criticise the memorable events of the campaign of 1815. Our knowledge on some points in this great drama of war is still, and perhaps will always remain, imperfect; for example, the conduct of Wellington on the night of June 15 has not been fully explained; the same remark applies to the relations between Napoleon and Grouchy on the 17th and the 18th. An effort to arrive at the truth on these most important subjects can hardly be without some value. Again, our information respecting the campaign has of late years been largely increased. The history of Ollech has thrown a good deal of fresh light on some of its incidents; the 'Memoirs' of Marbot have directed atten-

tion, more fully than was the case before, to the ideas of
Napoleon with regard to Grouchy's operations; and this
volume, unlike nearly all other works, is at all events
up to date on these subjects.   It is, perhaps, even more
important to bear in mind that until quite recently it
has been almost impossible to examine the series of events
that ended at Waterloo with strict impartiality, apart
from the blinding influences of national prejudice and
passion, and to place them in their true proportions
and real historical aspect.   Most French writers have
exaggerated the Napoleonic legend of 1815; a certain
number have made the reverse that befell the Emperor's
arms an occasion for clever and brilliant, but unjust and
mendacious, detraction from the renown of the greatest
of the masters of modern war.   A large majority of English
writers have followed the Wellingtonian legend, far more
untrue than the Napoleonic, though it is only fair to
observe that this misrepresentation of plain and incontrovertible facts has of late years found little favour in
England.   German writers have been at least equally
biassed and carried away; in addition many parts of
the campaign, as, for instance, the D'Erlon incident on
June 16, and, above all, the conduct and the movements
of Grouchy on the 17th and the 18th—passages of supreme
importance—have not been treated in this country, or in
Germany, with the fulness and the accuracy these subjects
require; indeed, they have usually been slurred over or
misdescribed, without regard to historical truth.   I have
done what in me lay, even though it be a little, to dis-
sipate all these false conceptions, and to supply these
omissions; to arrive, with a strict regard to impartiality
and to truth, at sound and reasonable conclusions with
respect to Ligny, Quatre Bras, and Waterloo; and to add
something to the sum of the real knowledge we possess
with reference to the events of the campaign of 1815.

To understand the military events of 1815, it is necessary to understand the political events of the time, were it only clearly to perceive how a great nation, which rose superior to Blenheim and Ramillies, and which, after Metz and Sedan, resisted invaders in overwhelming strength with heroic energy, suddenly collapsed after the defeat of Waterloo. With regard to this subject, the general reader may be referred to the nearly contemporaneous histories of Capefigue, Thibaudeau, and Lamartine, and to the later histories of Thiers, Alison, and H. Houssaye. For the more thorough student of the period the sources of primary information are various and amply sufficient. The conduct and the policy of the allies, as regards France, at the Congress of Vienna, and after Napoleon had regained his throne, are fully illustrated in the Despatches and Supplementary Despatches of Wellington for the years 1814 and 1815; in the Parliamentary Debates of 1815; in the Correspondence of Castlereagh; in the 'Memoirs' of Metternich; and in the Correspondence of Gentz and of Pozzo di Borgo. The foreign policy of Louis XVIII. will be found in his correspondence with Talleyrand, in the Talleyrand 'Memoirs'; as regards Napoleon's overtures for peace, when he had returned from Elba, his correspondence for the year 1815 may be consulted, and also the pseudo 'Memoirs' of Fouché, to a great extent truthful and valuable; there are, besides, the 'Memoirs' of Metternich, and several despatches of Caulaincourt contained or referred to in different histories. With respect to the internal government of Louis XVIII., and the state of France and of French opinion, large and often curious information is afforded in the 'Memoirs' of Vitrolles and Pasquier, of Villèle, Villemain, Hyde de Neuville, Barante, Marmont, Chateaubriand, Lafayette, Benjamin Constant, Carnot, Lavallette, Savary, Mollien, and others; and in the 'Mémoires' of Blacas and of Carnot, the Souvenirs of Macdonald, and the Journal of the Duke of Orleans. Most of these authorities throw light on the internal government of Napoleon during the Hundred Days, and on the condition of France ; but we may add to these the ' Memoirs' of Benjamin Constant during the Hundred Days ; parts of the Correspondence of Davoût and of Napoleon himself; the reports of Grouchy and other French Generals employed in putting down risings in the South and elsewhere ; the ' Memoirs' of Lamarque ; passages from Madame de Staël's work on the French Revolution ; Lucien Bonaparte's ' La Vérité sur les Cent Jours,' the letters of Sir J. C. Hobhouse, and the very interesting narrative of Miss Helena Williams. As regards the intrigues relating to Marie Louise at Vienna, see the touching Souvenirs of Méneval ; and as regards the designs to deport and perhaps to get rid of Napoleon by violence, consult the authorities cited by H. Houssaye. With respect to Napoleon's return from Elba, the reader may be referred to the Napoleon Correspondence in 1814-1815 ; to Sir N. Campbell's ' Napoleon at Elba'; to the ' L'Île d'Elbe et les Cent Jours' in the Napoleon Correspondence ; to the valuable ' Memoirs' of Fleury de Chaboulon reviewed by Napoleon at St. Helena ; to a very curious publication, ' L'Itinéraire de Buonaparte de l'Île d'Elbe et St. Hélène'; and to the reports of the trials of Ney, Labédoyère, and Cambronne. The French press of this whole period reflects the violence, the animosities, and the divisions of the nation in 1814 and 1815.

Passing to the military events of 1815, the secondary sources of information are very abundant. I may refer again to the narratives of Thiers and Alison, both valuable, though in different degrees ; to the elaborate and very able but unjust and partisan history of Charras ; to the careful and well-informed résumé of Prince La Tour d'Auvergne, which contains nearly all the original documents ; and especially to the recent and admirable work of H. Houssaye, a model of industrious research, and, as a rule, marked by an impartial judgment. On the Prussian side the volumes of Wagner contain the Prussian official account; those of Damitz are well informed but rather one-sided; the work of Clausewitz is brilliant and even masterly, but in several places very uncandid; Ollech's history is, on the whole, a good book; and Muffling's 'History of the Campaign' is not without importance and merit. The best narrative from an English pen is that of Siborne; it is well written and rich in instructive details, but it wants breadth of view and insight, and it is especially deficient as regards the conduct and the operations of Grouchy. The 'Campaign of Waterloo,' by Mr. Ropes, an American writer, is excellent as a commentary; the criticism it contains is, as a rule, judicious and well conceived; this is notably the case as regards the movements of Grouchy on the 17th and the 18th of June; but the learned author scarcely attempts to describe the course of events consecutively and in their completeness; his book can hardly be called a history in the full sense of the word. The 'Waterloo' of Hooper faithfully reproduces the Wellingtonian legend; it is well written, but utterly one-sided, and is now obsolete. As regards the Dutch-Belgian operations, and, indeed, the campaign generally, the work of Van Loben Sels is remarkable for its impartiality and good information; and Brialmont's 'Life of Wellington' contains some valuable remarks on the campaign of 1815. Mr. Dorsey Gardner's book 'Ligny, Quatre Bras, and Waterloo' is not without merit; it adds something to our knowledge respecting the state of Napoleon's health in 1815, a consideration of no little importance.

Besides these more elaborate works, I may refer to a great number of minor works on the campaign and its incidents. Foremost, perhaps, of these is Jomini's 'Précis de la Campagne de 1815,' a tract, in places not well informed, and not always judicious, but on the whole marked with true insight, especially as regards the opera-

tions of Grouchy.   Other French publications of more or
less value are : 'Napoléon à Waterloo, par un Officier de
la Garde Impériale'; Baudus' 'Études sur Napoléon,'
very useful as respects the D'Erlon incident, and now
completed by H. Houssaye; Quinet's 'Histoire de la
Campagne de 1815,' really a review of Charras; Vaudon-
court's 'Histoire des Campagnes de 1814 et 1815';
Rogniat's criticism of Napoleon's conduct in 1815, de-
molished by the Emperor at St. Helena; the apology
made for Grouchy by his son, the Marquis de Grouchy;
Berton's 'Précis des Batailles de Fleurus et Waterloo';
'Le Général Pajol,' by his son; and 'Le Général Vandamme' and 'Le Général Drouet d'Erlon.'   As to
Prussian literature of this class, Muffling's 'Passages from
my Life' is a work of some importance, and reference
may be made to a few other German publications.   The
English works in this category are numerous and some
very valuable; I may mention Lord Ellesmere's comments on Waterloo, written under the eye of Wellington;
General Shaw Kennedy's 'Notes on the Battle of
Waterloo,' a very careful analysis; General Hamley's
chapter on the Waterloo Campaign in his 'Operations of
War,' and his 'Life and Career of Wellington'; the Life
of Lord Hill; Chesney's 'Waterloo Lectures,' far from
impartial or correct, but still useful; a series of articles by
General Maurice in the *United Service Magazine* for the
years 1890 and 1891 called 'Waterloo,' abounding in
paradox, but containing some good comments; and, last
but not least, Lord Wolseley's too brief sketch of the
campaign in his 'Decline and Fall of Napoleon.'   The
reader must judge for himself of my contributions to this
passage of military history, 'The Campaign of 1815' in
my 'Great Commanders of Modern Times,' and 'Disputed
Passages of the Campaign of 1815' in the *English
Historical Review* for January, 1895.   The 'Relation
Belge' of the campaign may be studied with profit.

The true student of war, of course, seeks the primary sources of information on the campaign of 1815; he ascends to the fountain-head, he does not merely follow the stream. I refer, in the first instance, to these sources as they have been supplied to us by the principal actors in the great drama. The writings of Napoleon, especially the twenty-eighth volume of his Correspondence, and the Correspondence of Davoût, give us a full account of the preparations made by the Emperor for his last conflict with Europe; the Despatches of Wellington, and his correspondence with Blucher and Schwartzenberg, contain an account of the preparations of the allies. Napoleon has written two narratives of the campaign; the first a sketch published under the name of General Gourgaud, the second originally appearing in his ' Mémoires,' but now forming a part of the fifth volume of his ' Commentaries '—these are referred to in the text by this title ; and he has besides made additional remarks on the subject in his ' Notes on the Art of War ' in the sixth volume. These compositions, written at St. Helena without sufficient or proper books of reference, are in places incorrect, and abound in errors of detail. With respect to some passages of the campaign, notably to the D'Erlon incident, they are unsatisfactory and even disingenuous. But I agree with Thiers, a great historian, many as are his faults, they describe often accurately, and always with great power of insight and expression, the broad features of the campaign; they are admirable and unanswerable on most of the questions of strategy it suggests; the tendency of modern research and inquiry has been to confirm the views and the conclusions of their renowned author; nothing can be more contemptible than the paltry and carping criticism to which they have been subjected. Wellington has written very little on the campaign; his report of Waterloo and of the events that preceded the battle is a mere official narrative, dashed off on the spur of the moment; and his reply to the strictures of Clausewitz, composed in his old age and when he was in bad health, is not trustworthy, and abounds in mistakes. Interesting remarks of the Duke, however, on Waterloo will be found in the first volume of the Greville Memoirs, when the event was recent. Wellington's high estimate of the first operations of Napoleon is sufficiently known. As regards what Blucher has left on the subject, little remains but a few characteristic letters of no permanent importance; but Gneisenau's correspondence with the King of Prussia is of some value, and his letters referred to by his biographer, Delbruck, if not of much historical worth, are significant as showing his dislike and distrust of Wellington, a sentiment that on the 18th of June was very dangerous to the cause of the allies.

A good deal has been written on the campaign of 1815 by Generals and officers not in supreme command. Ney died and left no sign, except that he wrote a letter to Fouché reflecting on Napoleon, which he ought not to have written. Soult, perhaps wisely, was reticent about himself; in conversations with Sir William Napier he rightly attributed the failure of the Emperor's operations largely to Ney, but he has not vindicated himself as chief of the French staff. The son of Ney collected in 1840 a series of papers called 'Documents Inédits sur la Campagne de 1815,' which in no sense exculpate his ill-fated parent, but are of much value. The 'Relation' of Heymès, Ney's aide-de-camp, deserves little credence. Grouchy has laboured hard to make apologies for his conduct on June 17 and 18, but his 'Observations sur la Relation de la Campagne de 1815,' and his 'Relation Succincte' abound in erroneous statements. He has garbled documents; he actually suppressed the all-important Bertrand letter on June 17 until he was confronted by it as late as 1842. Such contrivances require no comment. History has vindicated Gérard; his 'Observations' in reply to Grouchy

are somewhat exaggerated and incorrect, but he has substantially made out his case. Had he commanded in
Grouchy's place, Waterloo would not have been a
disaster for France—nay, might have been a victory.
The Life and the Correspondence of Davoût contain some
references to the campaign and more to the events immediately preceding the capitulation of Paris. Vandamme
and D'Erlon have left some papers on those subjects;
D'Erlon especially has tried to excuse himself, but with
little regard to truth, for his false movement on June 16.
I am not aware of anything of value written by the subordinate Prussian commanders, but a controversy was
maintained for some time between Gneisenau and Bulow
with reference to the absence of Bulow from Ligny. We
possess some instructive and very interesting papers and
documents from the pens of British officers relating to the
campaign. By far the most important of these are 'The
Waterloo Letters,' a collection compiled by Siborne;
these are excellent materials for history, not, of course,
accurate, but truthful in intention and often very graphic.
They are instinct with the chivalrous, manly, and generous
spirit which has always been characteristic of British
officers. The 'Journal' of the late General Mercer is also
important, especially as regards the British artillery at
Waterloo. We may refer besides to the letters and
correspondence of the late Sir William Gomm, and to
the collection of original papers in Jones's 'Waterloo.'

April 30, 1900.

CONTENTS

CHAPTER I

FRANCE UNDER THE BOURBONS IN 1814-15—NAPOLEON'S
DESCENT FROM ELBA

PAGES

State of France and of French opinion at the Restoration of
Louis XVIII.—Hopes of an auspicious future—Monarchic
and revolutionary France widely opposed—The émigrés, the
noblesse, the priesthood, the people, the army — Unwise
policy of the Government, especially as regards the confiscated lands and the army—General discontent—A great
change felt to be imminent—Napoleon at Elba—The first
months of his exile—He resolves to return to France—How
he was treated by the allies—He escapes from Elba—His
triumphant march to Paris — Fall of the Government of
Louis XVIII.—Napoleon at the Tuileries   -   - 1—18

CHAPTER II

THE HUNDRED DAYS UNTIL HOSTILITIES BEGIN

The Empire quickly restored in France—The allies proclaim
Napoleon an outlaw—Europe again in arms against him
—Large parts of France fall away from the Emperor—His
Government necessarily weak—He could not, and would not,
make himself a Jacobin dictator—His military preparations
—Formation of a field and an auxiliary army—His efforts
astonishing, and worthy of him, considering the difficulties
in which he is placed—The plans of the coalition for the war
—Alternative plans of Napoleon—He resolves to attack the

PAGES

northern column of the allies in Belgium, while it is separated
from the eastern column—Ruin and fall of Murat—Rising in
La Vendée disastrous to Napoleon—The Acte Additionnel—
The Champ de Mai—Napoleon leaves Paris to join his army

19—46

CHAPTER III

THE ADVANCE OF NAPOLEON—THE BELLIGERENT ARMIES
AND THEIR LEADERS

Sketch of the theatre of war in Belgium—The positions of the
armies of Wellington and Blucher—The arrangements of
the allied chiefs to resist attack defective—The true reason
of this—Napoleon resolves to attack the allied centre—
Reasons for this project—His forces considerably less than
he had expected—Concentration of the French army on the
verge of Belgium—Admirable skill shown in effecting this
operation—Positions of the French army on June 14, 1815—
Numbers and characteristics of the French and the allied
armies—Napoleon, Wellington, Blucher, and their lieutenants

47—71

CHAPTER IV

THE OPERATIONS OF JUNE 15, 1815

Napoleon at Beaumont—His address to his army—His orders
for the march into Belgium—Advance of the French army—
Delays—Vandamme—The desertion of Bourmont—The
French army crosses the Sambre—Napoleon at Charleroy—
His orders—The loss of time caused by delays and accidents
unfavourable to the French—The retreat of Zieten—Arrival
of Ney—Napoleon's orders to the Marshal—Ney does not
occupy Quatre Bras—Combat at Gilly—Positions of the
French army on the evening of the 15th—Great advantage
already secured by Napoleon—Dispositions of Blucher and
Wellington—The Prussian army directed to Sombreffe—
Bulow cannot join it—Delays and hesitations of Wellington
—Part of his army directed to Quatre Bras, but very late—
Examination of the allied strategy—The allied armies in a
critical position -   -   -   -   -   - 72—102

CHAPTER V

THE OPERATIONS OF JUNE 16—LIGNY AND QUATRE BRAS

PAGES

The French army on the morning of June 16—Alleged inaction
of Napoleon—His orders to Ney and Grouchy—Conduct of
Ney since the evening of the 15th—His delays and remissness—March of the main French army to Fleurus—Positions
of the Prussian army—Arrangements of Blucher, and his
faults—Interview between Blucher and Wellington—Skilful
arrangements of Napoleon—His letter of 2 p.m. to Ney—
The Battle of Ligny, attack on Blucher's right and right
centre—Desperate fighting—Napoleon's order to Ney of
3.15 p.m.—Order to D'Erlon to march to the field—Continuation of the battle — Apparition of D'Erlon towards
Fleurus — He retires from the field — Napoleon breaks
Blucher's centre and defeats the Prussians—Battle of Quatre
Bras—Conduct of Ney and Reille—Ney's attack late—
Progress of the battle—Different attacks of Ney—He recalls
D'Erlon—Wellington compels Ney to retreat to Frasnes—
Napoleon's success on the 16th great, but not decisive,
chiefly owing to Ney's conduct—Reille and D'Erlon gravely
to blame—The position of the allies very critical   · 103—152

CHAPTER VI

THE OPERATIONS OF JUNE 17

Retrospect of the operations since the beginning of the campaign
—Advantages obtained by Napoleon—Great opportunities
presented to him on the morning of June 17—The two alternative movements he might have made, of which either
should have secured him decisive success—Authorities cited
on the subject—Napoleon at Fleurus the night of the 16th
—Exultation of the French army after the victory of Ligny—
Overconfidence and negligence—The retreat of the Prussians
not followed or observed—Conduct of Ney and of Soult—
No communication between them—Letter of Soult to Ney
on the morning of the 17th—Intention that the French army
was to halt for that day—The state of his health the real

PAGES

cause of the inaction of Napoleon—He proceeds to Ligny—
Review of his army—He resolves to pursue Blucher with
Grouchy, and to attack Wellington — This combination
correct, but very late—Orders to Grouchy—The Bertrand
despatch—Its great importance—Retreat of the Prussian
army to Wavre— Napoleon reaches Quatre Bras and follows
Wellington—Character of the pursuit—Napoleon halts before
Waterloo—Movements of Grouchy—He reaches Gembloux
—His letter of 10 p.m. to Napoleon—His faulty dispositions
—Napoleon on the night of the 17th—His dispositions and
confidence—Dispositions of Blucher and Wellington—The
prospect for June 18   -   -   -   -   - 153—198

CHAPTER VII

THE OPERATIONS OF JUNE 18—THE PRELUDE TO WATERLOO

The night of June 17—The condition of the two armies—Confidence of the French—Ominous symptoms—Feelings that
prevailed in the allied army—Wellington prepares for battle
at an early hour—Overconfidence of Napoleon—He postpones the attack—This unfortunate for him—The position of
Waterloo—Its great natural strength—Disposition of Wellington's forces to resist Napoleon's attack — Blucher at
Wavre—Hesitation of Gneisenau—The Prussian army begins
its march on Waterloo—It is dangerously and unnecessarily
delayed—Blucher sets off to join Wellington—Grouchy—He
misdirects his army—He marches towards Wavre, very late,
and slowly—Magnificent appearance of Napoleon's army
before the attack—The Emperor—Soult—Grouchy   - 199—226

CHAPTER VIII

THE BATTLE OF WATERLOO TO THE DEFEAT OF D'ERLON'S CORPS

Napoleon's reliance on his lieutenants—This very marked on
the day of Waterloo—Description of Hougoumont and its
enclosures—The feint converted into a real attack—Advance
of the division of Jerôme—Bold and persistent attacks—

PAGES

Stubborn and successful defence—Waste of the strength of
the French—The apparition of the advanced guard of Bulow
—Soult's letter of 1 p.m.—His postscript—Grouchy directed
to march to the field of Waterloo—His movement on Walhain—His despatch of 11 a.m.—With other officers he hears
the cannon of Waterloo—Admirable advice of Gérard to
march and join the main army—This rejected by Grouchy,
who continues to march directly on Wavre—Napoleon's first
grand attack—Advance of D'Erlon's corps—Vicious formation of its columns—Attack on La Haye Sainte—Stubborn
defence—The charge of Somerset and Ponsonby—Defeat of
cuirassiers—Complete defeat of D'Erlon—State of the battle
at 3 p.m.   ·   ·   ·   ·   ·   - 227—250

CHAPTER IX

THE BATTLE OF WATERLOO TO THE REPULSE OF
BULOW AND HIS CORPS

Napoleon receives the news of Grouchy's tardy and false movement, and of Bulow's advance from St. Lambret towards
the Bois de Paris—The Emperor's plan of attack profoundly
modified—His orders to Ney—Intense cannonade—Ney
masters La Haye Sainte probably about 4 p.m.—Disregarding Napoleon's orders, he projects a grand cavalry attack
against the allied right centre—Extreme imprudence of this
conduct—The attacks of Milhaud and Lefebvre-Desnoëttes
—The French cavalry fail—Napoleon not aware of the
attacks until it was too late—Renewal of the cavalry attacks
by Milhaud, Lefebvre-Desnoëttes, Kellermann, and Guyot—
Why the Emperor gave his sanction to them—Attack of
Bulow on the French right—It becomes very dangerous—
Napoleon compelled to strengthen Lobau by the Young
Guard—Magnificent resistance made to the cavalry attacks
—They ultimately fail—Ney and Wellington—Part of the
Old Guard sent to retake Plancenoit—Bulow repulsed—
Fresh attacks made on the allied line—The position of Wel-
lington still critical—State of the battle ; this is still undecided
251—279

CHAPTER X

THE ATTACK AND DEFEAT OF THE IMPERIAL GUARD—
IRRUPTION OF ZIETEN AND PIRCH—ROUT AND FLIGHT
OF THE FRENCH ARMY—GROUCHY AT WAVRE

PAGE

State of the battle before the final attack—Views of Napoleon
and Wellington—Pirch approaches to support Bulow, and
Zieten to assist Wellington's left—Dangerous position of the
allied army at about 7 p.m.—Advance of part of the Imperial
Guard—Brilliant efforts made by D'Erlon—Reille and the
cavalry backward — Ney conducts the attack — He again
makes mistakes—Struggle between the Imperial Guard and
the troops defending the allied right centre—Defeat of the
Imperial Guard—Advance of Wellington's army—Irruption
of Zieten on Napoleon's extreme right—Irruption of Pirch
and Bulow on Napoleon's right flank and rear—Flight and
rout of the French army—Pursuit by part of the Prussian
army—Hideous scenes of terror and despair—The operations
of Grouchy on June 18, after he had rejected the counsels of
Gérard - - - - - - - 280—306

CHAPTER XI

REFLECTIONS ON WATERLOO, AND ON THE CAMPAIGN
OF 1815

Faulty tactics of the French at Waterloo—Four distinct mistakes
were made—How far Napoleon is to be held responsible—
Excellence of Wellington's tactics—His strength of character
was conspicuously seen—The result of Waterloo was due to
the junction of Blucher and Wellington—Consideration of
the question whether Grouchy could have prevented this—
Position of the Prussian army on the morning of June 18
—Position of Grouchy and his army—Grouchy could have
arrested the march of the Prussians, and interposed between
the allied armies, had he marched to the Dyle and crossed
at Moustier and Ottignies by the early forenoon—He could
have attained the same end had he followed the advice of
Gérard and marched towards Napoleon at noon—Examination of reasoning to the contrary—Grouchy the main cause

PAGES

of the defeat of Waterloo—Napoleon not wholly free from
blame—The strategy of the allied Generals on June 17 and 18
essentially faulty—They ought, having regard to the chances,
to have lost the Battle of Waterloo—Review of the campaign
of 1815 generally—Napoleon and his lieutenants—Wellington
and Blucher—The belligerent armies -   -   - 307—344

CHAPTER XII

THE RETREAT OF GROUCHY—THE SECOND FALL OF
NAPOLEON

Grouchy, as yet ignorant of the result of Waterloo, makes preparation to attack Thielmann and march on Brussels—
Thielmann, who had heard of the victory, attacks Grouchy,
but is repulsed—Grouchy receives the news of the complete
defeat of Napoleon—He retreats to Namur, and thence to
Givet—This movement was rapid and judicious, but has
been unduly extolled—Partial success of the French armies
on the frontier and in La Vendée—The intelligence of the
rout of Waterloo reaches Paris—Unwise attitude of the
Chambers and their foolish expectations—Perfidious conduct
of Fouché—He schemes for the restoration of Louis XVIII.
—Napoleon returns to Paris and proposes to defend France
if assisted by the Chambers—These, under the influence of
Fouché and Lafayette, usurp power—Napoleon abdicates—
Fouché at the head of a Provisional Government — He
goes on with his treacherous policy, and prevents any real
efforts to make a national defence—His negotiations with
Wellington, who seconds him and indicates the conditions of
peace—Fouché exposed to danger—Proposal of Napoleon to
attack Blucher rejected by Fouché—Indignation of the army
and the population of Paris—Imprudence of Blucher—Wise
and statesmanlike conduct of Wellington—The capitulation
of Paris and the restoration of Louis XVIII.—Fouché's
policy triumphs, but only for a short time—Great position of
Wellington—The service he does to France—Reflections—
Conclusion   -   -   -   -   -   - 345—366

APPENDIX   -   -   -   -   -   -   - 367—406

INDEXES   -   -   -   -   -   -   - 407—421

THE CAMPAIGN OF 1815

CHAPTER I

FRANCE UNDER THE BOURBONS IN 1814-15— NAPOLEON'S DESCENT FROM ELBA

State of France and of French opinion at the Restoration of
Louis XVIII.—Hopes of an auspicious future—Monarchic and
revolutionary France widely opposed—The émigrés, the noblesse,
the priesthood, the people, the army—Unwise policy of the
Government, especially as regards the confiscated lands and the
army—General discontent—A great change felt to be imminent—
Napoleon at Elba—The first months of his exile—He resolves to
return to France—How he was treated by the allies—He escapes
from Elba—His triumphant march to Paris—Fall of the Government of Louis XVIII.—Napoleon at the Tuileries.

THE Restoration of Louis XVIII., accomplished, so to
speak, by a miracle, seemed established in the summer of
1814. France, like Ilium, had been in some measure
relieved from the long agony of sufferings and woes which
had been her lot for three disastrous years. She had been
deprived, indeed, of her 'natural frontiers,' and almost
brought within her limits of 1790; the hosts of the invaders had devastated many of her fairest provinces.
From the Rhine to the Seine, and from the Pyrenees to
the Garonne, the signs of misery and desolation were to
be seen everywhere. But the Teutonic and Muscovite
hordes were on their way to the Elbe and the Niemen; the

I

ravages of war had ceased to spread; peasant conscripts were no longer torn from their homes to be 'forced,' as the phrase was, 'to the shambles'; the nation was not racked and convulsed by a hopeless struggle with the multitudinous hosts of embattled Europe. Agriculture and industry had begun to revive, the tiller of the soil was safe in his fields, the trader could apply himself to the pursuits of commerce, the country was recovering from its misfortunes with the energy and speed it has so often shown in its ever-changing annals.

Nor were hopes wanting that the Bourbon monarchy would rally the majority of Frenchmen around the throne, and would inaugurate an era of content and of well-ordered liberty. Paris had welcomed the King with general acclaim; the heads of the army, the great bodies of the State, the magistracy, and the class of the bourgeoisie had loyally declared for the Restoration; and though the attitude of many of the provinces was very different, these were, for the present at least, quiescent. There was a good prospect, too, that the ancient régime was not even thought of in the royal councils, and that the aspirations of the great and growing Liberal party of France for constitutional freedom would be satisfied. The Comte d'Artois had bowed to the will of the Senate when he had been made Lieutenant-General of the King; Louis XVIII. had bestowed a charter upon his subjects which, restricted as it was, was of happy promise, and had pledged himself to rule through two Chambers; his Ministry was partly composed of men of the revolutionary age. Spite, too, of occasional murmurs of discontent rising ominously in several districts and towns, the authority of the Government was nowhere challenged; the old Republican party and the adherents of the fallen Empire had well-nigh shrunk out of sight; the army, immensely reduced by desertion, and without the chiefs it had had at its head, was unable for the moment to stir, or even to show its feelings. A rainbow of hope shone over the still troubled waters; it was generally believed in France, and even in Europe, that the new order of things would take root and flourish.

Grave elements of disorder and peril lurked, nevertheless, under this attractive surface; it was ere long to appear that the France of the monarchy was widely separated from the France of 1789-1814. Louis XVIII., indeed, and many of his Ministers, although they committed fatal mistakes, and, as a Government, were weak and divided in mind, were not false to the professions they had made, and endeavoured, on the whole, to rule, not without regard to what seemed to them the national interests. But the great body of the genuine adherents of the House of Bourbon formed factions that stood aloof from the nation, and, in different degrees, were even hostile to it; they became a danger to the State and to the public welfare. The extreme émigré party clamoured for a return to the old order of things, which the Revolution had swept away; even the more moderate Royalists looked askance at a throne based on constitutional right, and really dependent on the popular will. At the same time, the heads of the Church and a majority of the clergy denounced the Concordat, which had reconciled France with Rome; and they were loud in their complaints of the conforming priesthood, and against the religious liberty which the Concordat had secured.

These murmurs, however, would have had little effect had they not been seconded by movements which outraged the feelings and threatened the well-being of the greatest part of the nation. The noblesse had regained its dignities; in hundreds of parishes proud and unknown gentlemen claimed the feudal homage which had once been their due, but had been abolished since the days of Louis XVI.; and a cry went forth from every part of France that this was but a prelude to the resumption of

the vast tracts of land which had passed into the hands
of the cultivators of the soil and the lower middle classes
in the great confiscations of 1792-94, but which were now
to revert to a detested order of men.   The peasantry, and
even the inhabitants of many towns, became thoroughly
alarmed in almost every province ; and their terrors were
increased by what they heard from their priests in most
places — that the tithes and the exactions of the old
Church would be again imposed on them, and that it was
a crime to resist the demands of the noblesse.   Simultaneously, the army was enormously swelled in numbers
by the return of the garrisons of fortresses in foreign
countries, and of prisoners of war in tens of thousands.
These masses seethed with angry discontent, which an
injudicious policy was to make infinitely worse; and thus
the most numerous and widely-extended parts of the
nation, and the force which in a revolutionary state must
form the chief and the best support of a government,
became gradually more and more opposed to the
monarchy.   Nor were dissatisfaction and even ill-will
absent among the classes most attached to the constitutional throne.   Disenchantment had soon followed illusions.   Liberal France quickly discovered that the Charter
fell far short of what it had expected, and it resented that
this had been made a concession by the 'special favour'
of the King.   The bourgeoisie, too, of the capital and of
the chief towns were irritated at the arrogance of the
noblesse, and disliked the pretensions of the émigrés and
the Court; and the keen wit of the Parisians scoffed at
the forgotten etiquette of Versailles paraded at the
Tuileries with costly pomp, and at the claims of the
champions of ruling by right Divine.

The difficulties in the way of the Government were
immense, as this state of things developed itself by
degrees; it would have required the genius of Henry IV.,
backed by the power of Richelieu at its height, to have

overcome, or really to cope with, them. For example, the finances were well administered, but the Treasury was unable to meet the demands made on it by ruined provinces and towns; and it could not support even half of the ever-growing army, though the attitude of this had become most threatening. The King and his Ministers, besides, were hampered and thwarted, and repeatedly placed in a false position by the conduct of the Bourbon Princes around the throne. The Comte d'Artois had put himself at the head of the émigrés, who wildly denounced the constitutional régime; the Pavillon Marsan echoed the cries of Coblentz, and condemned Louis XVIII. as a crowned time-server. The Duc d'Angoulême was a mere princely nullity, the Duchesse not unnaturally hated the Revolution which had destroyed her parents; the Duc de Berri was a braggart who aped the soldier, and earned the contempt of the army he courted. Nevertheless, after making every allowance, the Government of the Restoration was a bad Government, infirm of purpose, and, in notable instances, the instrument of an evil and most disastrous policy. The King was a scholar, a wit, and, in a sense, a statesman; but he was indolent, and carelessly let things drift. He boasted that he held his throne from God, but little heeded that it was treated with contempt by man. He was ever stickling for prerogatives he was afraid to maintain; his chief thought was of his personal ease and comfort. More than one of the Ministers were really able men, but in Wellington's phrase 'they were Ministers, not a Ministry'; they had no fixed or well-settled policy, they were divided, vacillating, unequal to rule. Their measures were thus usually weak and half-hearted, when they were not thoroughly unwise—nay, deplorable. Their first task should have been to keep the émigrés down, to put an end to the ruinous pretensions of the noblesse, especially as to the possessions they had lost, and to bring the Church under

the control of the law and the Crown; but they only
trifled with orders of men who were a most formidable
danger to the State.   Some, indeed, secretly espoused
their cause.

On one subject of the very greatest moment the Government quickened and exasperated the discontent and fear
already pervading the mass of the nation, and heaped fuel
recklessly on a devouring flame.   The Charter, the King,
and both Chambers had declared that the confiscated
lands were not to be restored to their former owners; but
these professions had had little effect, regard being had to
the claims made by the noblesse and the clergy.   In an
evil hour the Ministry proposed to give back the domains
which had not been sold by the State to those who had
forfeited them, but had been their possessors; incautious
language was most unwisely used; and rumour, multiplied
by thousands of tongues, spread far and wide that the
confiscations of the past were to be followed by a confis-
cation more unjust and grievous.   The heart of the nation
was stirred to its depths; thenceforward probably five-
sixths of Frenchmen became completely estranged from
the monarchy.

The policy of the Government was even worse as regards
the army which it should have made the mainstay of its
power.   It was inevitable, indeed, in the existing state of
the finances, that a large part of this force should be disbanded; but no effort should have been spared to make
the part that remained loyal to the existing order of things.
Exactly a contrary course was adopted; not only were
the soldiery cast adrift in multitudes, without a thought
as to what was to be their fate, but those who were left to
form the diminished armed strength of France were degraded, nay, insulted, in every conceivable way.   The old
organisation of the army was broken up; it lost the
revered eagles, long the signs of conquest; the tricolour
was replaced by the white flag, unknown, or seen only in

the ranks of the enemy; the Imperial Guard was not
permitted to attend the King; the most famous regiments
were recklessly dispersed. But what was most galling
and cruelly unjust was that, while the veterans of the past
were dismissed in thousands, and the troops who were
retained were ill-paid and treated with neglect, a great
force of Household soldiery was arrayed, which engrossed
every good appointment and place, and literally starved
the whole of the rest of the service. These ' lackeys of
the antechamber,' as they were called, were solely entrusted with the guard of the King; they were splendidly
accoutred, and had the rank of officers; they had a lion's
share of promotion in every grade, and they drove from
the ranks thousands of trained officers, who were abandoned to poverty on a miserable half-pay. From this
moment the army became the bitter enemy of the Restoration and its heads.

The policy and conduct of the men in power were also
in other respects unfortunate. The Comte d'Artois, in
the heyday of his first coming, had pledged himself that
taxes should be largely remitted. It would have been
impossible, perhaps, to redeem this pledge, but it was
contemptuously broken amidst general discontent. The
liberty of the press had been guaranteed by the Charter,
but it had been deemed necessary to set this guarantee at
naught. This increased the ill-will of those who complained that this compact was a mere gift which the
Sovereign could withdraw, especially as it bore the date
of the nineteenth year of his reign, as if the Revolution
and the Empire had been blotted out from history. The
spirit of the administration, too, of the State was irritat-
ing, unpopular, provoked distrust and suspicion. Many
of the functionaries of the Empire, indeed, were retained
in their posts, for the centralised system of government
could not otherwise work; but these were regarded at
Court with dislike and aversion. Royalist functionaries

alone were in real favour. The administration of the army, besides, only made worse the exasperation due to the disastrous changes which had been made in it. It was not only that Marmont—Marshal Judas, as he was called—was singled out for distinction at the Tuileries, and that other Marshals were loaded with wealth and honours, while the mass of the soldiery were left in discredit and indigence. Dupont, the disgraced General of Baylen, was made Minister of War. The suspicions of corruption which his surrender had caused were at least augmented by his conduct in office. He was succeeded by Soult, no doubt an able man, but a courtier of fortune utterly without principle. The extravagant loyalty of which he made a parade, the recompenses he lavished on the Chouans of the North, the extreme severity he showed to officers on half-pay, and to Excelmans, an old companion in arms, made him the most hated of the military chiefs.

Other instances of want of official sense and tact were exhibited, and had the natural results. The observance of Sundays after the English fashion—Puritan strictness hitherto unknown in France—was made compulsory by a Court in part foolishly devout. This bitterly vexed Paris, fond of her holidays, and since the Revolution given a free rein to license. The religious ceremonies which were seen in the half-infidel capital aroused cries against the superstitions of the old régime ; the refusal of a priest to give an actress burial provoked a popular demonstration for a moment dangerous. So, too, if it was not unbecoming solemnly to inter the remains of Louis XVI. and of Marie Antoinette, the violent addresses that were made were of evil omen. It was shameful to give a public funeral to Georges Cadoudal, a plotter against the life of the First Consul ; and the anniversary of the death of Louis XVI. was made an occasion of scenes of loyalist excesses which provoked angry murmurs and threatened

the public peace.   Instances of extravagances of this kind
were but too frequent; as was said, indeed, commemora-
tions that ought to have raised altars of concord only
raised altars of revenge and hatred.

An immense majority of Frenchmen and the whole
army had thus become alienated from the Bourbons and
their government.   Even the Liberal party had little
sympathy with them, nor were the classes held in special
favour by the reigning powers contented with their position in the State and their prospects.   The Ministers
flattered the émigrés, the noblesse, and, as a rule, the
Royalists.   They lavished decorations and bestowed
places; but while they succeeded in terrifying the holders
of the forfeited lands, they did not dare to restore these
to their old owners.   France was filled with needy and
discontented gentlemen, who angrily contrasted the magnificence of the Court with the indigence which was their
bitter lot.   'If he entered his own château, he should let
us enter ours,' was a phrase current on the Faubourg
Saint Germains.   'The King, with his bloated civil list,
has left us starving,' was the cry of many an indigent
seigneur returning hopelessly to England to eat the scanty
bread of exile.

Nor were the petted Marshals and Generals of the
Empire satisfied with the existing régime and what it
had brought with it.   They felt that they were in a false
position, and had deserted their great master.   They were
humiliated at the degraded state of the army; they were
vexed that they had been deprived of their dotations, the
spoils of conquest.   They were irritated, too, at the con-
descending courtesy and half-veiled sarcasms of the old
noblesse, which treated them as the grandees of Spain
treated the aristocracy of inferior rank; they resented the
ostracism to which their wives and daughters were subjected by the fine ladies of the Court.   The foreign policy
of the Government, besides, had given occasion to grave,

if far from just, complaints on the part of many thought-
ful, though hardly impartial, Frenchmen.   The Ministers,
as a condition of a coveted peace, had surrendered fortresses which France had held on the Scheldt, the Rhine,
the Oder, and the Po.   This party now insisted that these
should have been retained, in order to obtain better terms
from the conquering League of Europe.   Though France,
too, had been nearly confined to her former limits, the
idea was widespread that by some means she might be
aggrandised at the Congress of Vienna ; and there was a
strong feeling of resentment that, instead of this, that
assembly showed that one of its main objects was to place
solid barriers against French ambition and conquest.   Nor
was it contrary to human nature that hundreds of patriotic
Frenchmen felt indignant that France, but yesterday the
Queen of the Continent, had become a vanquished and
almost a second-rate Power.   Nor can we wonder that
they laid this to the charge of the Government.

The prospect, therefore, so bright in the summer of
1814, had become ominously darkened before the close of
the year ; the sounds of a coming tempest were heard in
the air.   It had become evident that the France of the
Bourbons and the France of the Revolution and the
Empire were in fierce antagonism, and would not
coalesce ; their interests, their aspirations, their sentiments were opposed.   This rapid change, doubtless, was
partly due to the variableness of the French national
character ; but it must chiefly be ascribed to deep-seated
causes.   Whatever excuses may be made for them, the
King and his Ministers had contrived to make the people
and the army hostile to the throne ; they were not popular
with any part of the nation ; their rule was felt to be
weak and ignoble.   The precariousness of their position
was shown by a wide expression of opinion, in Paris and
elsewhere, that the present order of things could not last ;
the King, it was common talk, was tottering to his fall.

One of the symptoms of a revolution dimly foreseen was that the Republican and the Imperialist parties, deadly enemies under the rule of Napoleon, lifted again their heads, and joined hands to assail the Government; and the air was thick with rumours of plots and deeds of blood, of wild movements and of *coups d'état*, signs of the restlessness and discontent that prevailed everywhere.

In this position of affairs the army naturally turned its eyes to its great chief on his Mediterranean rock, the object of its passionate devotion for years. There were numerous petty military revolts; the soldiery displayed in a thousand ways their contempt of the Bourbons and their love of Napoleon. The peasantry, too, were deeply moved. They dreaded, indeed, the memory of ruinous wars, and the despotism of the tyrannous Empire; but Napoleon, they felt, would save their farms from the spoiler, would keep the noblesse and the priests under, and was a champion of a cause essentially their own. Yet the only real conspiracy formed at this time had not as its object the restoration of the fallen Emperor. It was a military conspiracy of no importance; but its master-spirit was the base intriguer Fouché. His aim was to set up a Regency under Marie Louise, or to place the Duke of Orleans on the throne, in either case making himself supreme in the State. It is a proof how completely the monarchy was undermined that such a project was thought of by a man vile indeed, but most able. 'Louis XVIII. is falling; put anyone in his place,' was the remark of one of the minor agents in the plot.*

Napoleon, meanwhile, had in his little island been contemplating the state of France and of Europe. For some time he had devoted himself to the administration and the improvement of the speck in the sea left to him out of the

---

* 'Moi, tout ça m'est bien égal pourvu que le gros cochon s'en aille,' a general officer exclaimed.—'1815,' H. Houssaye, i. 120.

wreck of his colossal Empire.   He placed the government of Elba on a new basis, enlarged and fortified Porto
Ferrajo, opened the rural districts with excellent roads,
built houses, drained marshes, encouraged the production
of silk, planted vineyards, and laid out avenues of mul-
berry-trees—in short, gave proof of his organising genius
in the arts of peace.   And he especially took care of the
handful of troops, for the most part veterans of his Old
Guard, who had followed their loved chief to his retreat in
exile.   By degrees, however, the disorders and troubles of
France, the evident failure of the Bourbon régime, the
attitude of the mass of the people and the discontented
army, and notably the discords of the coalition, which had
begun to quarrel at Vienna over the spoils of Europe, re-
awakened in his mind the thoughts of Empire, and
inspired him with a hope that he might again appear a
commanding figure on the stage of events.

His purpose, however, was slowly formed, and was carefully concealed from all around him.   It was not until the
month of February, 1815, that he determined to effect
his escape from Elba, and, at the head of a few hundred
men, to overthrow the throne of Louis XVIII., and to
restore the fallen Empire in the face of his late conquerors.
His decision appears to have been fixed by the visit of an
emissary, sent by his faithful Bassano, who informed him
of the position of affairs in France, of the discredit in
which the Bourbons were held, of the plot which had
been arranged by Fouché, of the hopes of the army and
five-sixths of the people—that the Emperor would come to
support their cause.   It is not improbable, whatever had
happened, that Napoleon would have undertaken his
daring enterprise.   A favourable opportunity presented
itself, and it had become impossible for him to maintain
his state at Elba.   But if he had resolved to break the
pledges he had given to Europe, and to run the risk of
defying a world in arms, the conduct of the allies to him

had been simply shameful, and they had placed terrible temptations in his way. The Bourbon Government had withheld the funds secured to him by a solemn treaty, and without which he could not remain at Elba. Marie Louise had been cut off from him by an odious intrigue, and lured into adulterous arms; his infant son—the Astyanax of the House of Bonaparte—had been kept a hostage among his enemies; his family had been deprived of rights they had been promised; at the Congress of Vienna it had been seriously discussed whether he should not be deported from Elba by force, and imprisoned at St. Helena or one of the Azores. Projects of assassinating him, too, had been certainly formed, though the Bourbons and the allies were not privy to these; and Talleyrand seems to have agreed to a scheme to carry him off and shut him up in one of the St. Marguerites, where a prison would have been but the portal to a grave.*

On February 26, 1815, the Emperor set off on his wonderful venture. His military preparations, as was nearly always the case with him, had been carefully matured and skilfully masked; his departure was kept secret until the last moment. A flotilla of a few petty vessels, with about eleven hundred troops on board, bore the modern Cæsar and his fortunes over the Mediterranean wastes. The voyage was slow, and more than one enemy's sail was descried; but Fate smiled treacherously on her old favourite. Napoleon showed the calm and serene confidence he had shown fifteen years before, on his return from Egypt. The little expedition landed near Cannes on March 1, but the experiences of the adventurers at first were of evil omen. Provence had cordially disliked the Empire; the garrison of Antibes arrested a few men of the Old Guard; the attitude of Cannes and Grasse was, at best, doubtful. Napoleon, however, with true

* See the conclusive evidence as to these foul machinations accumulated by H. Houssaye, ' 1815,' i. 169-172.

instinct had resolved from the outset to advance through Dauphiné, a province attached to the Revolution and himself. He was soon threading his way with extra- ordinary speed through the rugged hills and defiles which lead to the Durance, the peasantry gradually surrounding his little band, and welcoming a deliverer with joyous acclaim.

The descent was kept a secret for about two days; but Masséna, in command at Marseilles, received the intelli- gence on March 3. The telegraph sent it to the Tuileries on the 5th. The first impression on the mind of the veteran Marshal, and of the officers and Ministers around the King, was that the enterprise was either wholly a myth, or that it was the despairing effort of a disordered intellect. Proclamations were issued denouncing Napoleon as 'a mad bandit.' That of Soult was in outrageous language; a hired press teemed with ferocious invec- tives. Preparations for resistance, however, were made on a great scale when it was known that Napoleon was on his way through Dauphiné; they seemed to assure certain and immediate success. At the instance of Talley- rand, Soult had set on foot an army nearly 30,000 strong to support the claims of France at Vienna; and as most of these troops were in the Southern provinces, it was confi- dently expected that 'the usurper and his handful of brigands' would meet a speedy fate. At the same time, Masséna, who, like all the Marshals, thought the enter- prise one of audacious foolishness, despatched a column to arrest the march of Napoleon—at least, to follow him, and to close on his rear. 'He will soon be in a mouse- trap,' the old chief exclaimed; 'this will be the end of his insensate venture.' The same ideas, though mingled with those of hatred and fear, prevailed at Vienna for some time; it was the general conviction, in Pozzo di Borgo's words, that 'Napoleon would soon be strung up on a tree.'

The Emperor, however, had reckoned on the spell of

his name, and had rightly estimated the overwhelming power of the moral forces arrayed against the House of Bourbon. For some days he was not joined by half a dozen soldiers; but as he passed through Sisteron and Gap, on his way to Grenoble, the inhabitants of the neighbouring districts crowded from all sides to greet him; his march became a triumphant popular progress. A single incident determined the course of events. Part of a regiment had been sent to La Mure to stop the adventurer on his path; but Napoleon, calmly advancing to the edge of the ranks, bared his breast and said, ' Who will slay his father ?'* The effect was instantaneous, and almost past belief. The soldiery, who hitherto had appeared faithful, broke away from their astounded officers, gathered around their old master with enthusiastic shouts; the lilies of the Bourbons were trampled in the dust; the tricolour reappeared as if by enchantment; the exulting band, preceding the column of Elba, sped on to Grenoble, now not distant. Another regiment, led by the ill-fated Labédoyère, rallied around the Emperor with the same passionate delight; and as the little army approached Grenoble, the garrison and the mass of the townsmen bore Napoleon within the fortress, its gates having been broken open by the peasantry outside the ramparts.

On March 10 the already victorious chief had reached Lyons, at the head of some 8,000 men. It was in vain that the Comte d'Artois, the Duke of Orleans, and Marshal Macdonald had assembled a body of troops, and endeavoured to recall them to a sense of duty; the scenes of Grenoble were repeated; the soldiery of either side gave Napoleon the same welcome; the authority of the Bourbons, without a hostile effort, suddenly disappeared in the second city of France. The Emperor now assumed the tone of a Sovereign. He issued a series of decrees from Lyons, almost breathing the spirit of the

---

* This striking scene took place at Laffray, near La Mure.

Convention of 1793; the monarchy, the noblesse, and feudal rights were declared abolished; the two Chambers were summarily dissolved; the Household troops were disbanded; the white flag proscribed; the émigrés ordered to quit the territory of France.* The Emperor left Lyons on March 13. He disposed of fully 14,000 armed men; his march through Burgundy into the Valley of the Yonne was a succession of ever - increasing triumphs. One notable defection from the Bourbons took place. Ney, impetuous and unreflecting, had promised the King that ' he would bring Bonaparte back in an iron cage.' He remained loyal for several days, but the contagion of events was too strong for him. ' He was swept away,' he said, ' by a sea which he could not stop with his hands.' He assembled the few thousand troops he commanded, told them ' that the cause of the Bourbons was lost,' and hastily joined his old master at Auxerre, his agitation betraying the anguish that tortured his soul.†

From this time forward the advance of the Emperor was like that of some mighty influence impossible to resist. Nearly all the Eastern provinces had pronounced for him; town, village, and country sent their delighted multitudes; his army was clamouring for vengeance, and breaking out into joy. The Emperor on his way had skilfully aroused the passions and the sentiments which swayed the people and the troops. The old phrases of despotism were dropped; he had come to vindicate the rights of French citizens; he would make short work of disloyal nobles and priests; he would establish his throne on the national will; he was the protector of the interests the Revolution had made. To the army he appealed in the magical language which he well knew would go to

* Only one of these decrees will be found in the Napoleon Correspondence, xxviii. 7, 8.
† The disdain shown to Ney's wife at Court, especially by the Duchesse d'Angoulême, had also influence on him.

their hearts: 'They had not been conquered, but had been betrayed. Would the émigrés bear the sight of their eagles? Were they not the soldiers of Marengo, ol Jena, and Austerlitz?' For the rest, 'the Eagle and the Tricolour would fly from steeple to steeple until they appeared on the towers of Nôtre Dame.'

The falling Government attempted for a few days to make head against this overwhelming movement. One circumstance gave a moment of hope; the conspiracy planned by Fouché failed; it ended in a petty demonstration which came to nothing. The bourgeoisie of Paris, too, out of temper as they were, but feeling that the return of Napoleon meant war with Europe, proclaimed their loyalty to Louis XVIII.; the Chambers, meeting in solemn session, pledged themselves to resist the usurper to the last. Renewed efforts were made to bring together troops still believed to be loyal to the Bourbon throne; edicts were made to array a huge force of National Guards; Soult, suspected of treachery, was dismissed from his post; appeals were made to volunteers to 'defend the country.' All these efforts, however, were of no avail; an army, indeed, rather imposing on paper, was brought together on the Seine to cover Paris, but the bourgeoisie, tongue valiant as they were, did not venture to appear in arms; the National Guards proved of no use; only a few hundred volunteers took up arms; authority had deserted the perishing monarchy.

Meanwhile, Napoleon, his forces swelled by auxiliaries of all kinds, had advanced rapidly into the valley of the Seine; every obstacle to his progress seemed to vanish, or became a means to increase his power. On the night of March 19, the King left the Tuileries accompanied only by a few faithful servants; the army on the Seine either melted away or joined the ranks of the imperial army; the Household troops were soon the only armed force that remained loyal to the sinking House of Bourbon.

2

Louis XVIII. sadly made his way to Lille, and thence took his departure for Ghent; he was surrounded by a petty Court of émigrés of his late Ministers, and of exiles of the noblesse. Napoleon had in the meantime left Fontainebleau and pushed on to the capital, finding simply no one to oppose him on his path. Paris was left without a Government on March 20, but the great functionaries of the Empire had filled the Tuileries, and the Tricolour floated on all public buildings. Night had closed before a shouting cavalcade, lost in the flood of an exulting populace, made its way into the court adjoining the palace; Napoleon was dragged out of his carriage by his enthusiastic followers, and was almost stifled amidst their passionate greetings. This, he afterwards said, was the happiest hour of his life; he had successfully performed the most astonishing feat of his career.*

* This striking historical scene is admirably described by H. Houssaye, '1815,' i. 361-363. See also Thiers, 'Histoire du Consulat et de l'Empire,' vi. 286, 289, 1862 edition. In the case of this, as of the subsequent chapters, the principal authorities and sources of information to which a reader may be referred will be found in the list at the beginning of this book.

CHAPTER II

THE HUNDRED DAYS UNTIL HOSTILITIES BEGIN

The Empire quickly restored in France — The allies proclaim
Napoleon an outlaw — Europe again in arms against him —
Large parts of France fall away from the Emperor—His Government necessarily weak—He could not, and would not, make himself a Jacobin dictator—His military preparations—Formation of
a field and an auxiliary army—His efforts astonishing, and worthy
of him, considering the difficulties in which he is placed—The
plans of the coalition for the war—Alternative plans of Napoleon
—He resolves to attack the northern column of the allies in
Belgium, while it is separated from the eastern column—Ruin
and fall of Murat—Rising in La Vendée disastrous to Napoleon
—The Acte Additionnel—The Champ de Mai—Napoleon leaves
Paris to join his army.

NAPOLEON having seized the helm of the State, after the
most audacious effort recorded, perhaps, in history, had
well-nigh formed his Government before the Tuileries had
ceased to shake with the acclaim which greeted his return.
With one notable exception, his Ministry was composed of
high-placed servitors of the former Empire, Cambacérès,
Caulaincourt, Davoût, Savary, Gaudin, Mollien, and others;
but it was an ominous symptom that several of these men,
fearing the signs of the times, were disinclined to take
office.   The stern Republican Carnot, however, who had
' organised victory ' in the tremendous upheaval of 1793-94,
who had kept aloof from Napoleon in the day of his power,
but had rallied to his cause in the disasters of 1814, became

Minister of the Interior; he was to give valuable assistance
to his new master, but it was maliciously remarked that
he had to accept the title of Count, to don the imperial
trappings, and to shed off the slough of the Jacobin Committee of Public Safety. Fouché, for many years almost
proscribed and disgraced by Napoleon, returned to the
post he had long held at the head of the police; it was
a sign of the diseased and demoralised state of France,
and of the difficulties already in the Emperor's way, that
he was induced to make an appointment really against his
will. But Fouché had, a few days before, been arrested
by the order of the Bourbon Government; his unquestionable ability could not be denied, and he had the credit of
having made himself the master-spirit of a secret conspiracy, pervading the chiefs of the army, to place
Napoleon again on the throne. This rumour, however,
was wholly untrue; the heads of the army had had no
relations with him. Fouché had plotted, indeed, against
the Bourbons, but he had plotted in the interest of Marie
Louise and of the Duke of Orleans; the plot, such as it
was, had, we have seen, failed. The triumph of Napoleon,
in fact, was due, not, as some writers have falsely supposed,
to a military conspiracy in any real sense: the Marshals
and chief officers, discontented as they were, dreaded the
return of their old master, and were faithful to the
Bourbons for a time. It was due to an enthusiastic
popular movement, backed by the soldiery almost to a
man, and the officers of inferior rank; and it was as
unpremeditated and spontaneous as it was widespread.
Fouché at his post was to go on with the game of
tortuous intrigues, but on a larger and more ambitious
scale, which had been the business and pastime of his
life; he was to justify Napoleon's contemptuous phrase,
‘ That dog puts his dirty foot into every shoe which he
thinks will fit him.’

Within less than five weeks after March 20 the Empire

was restored in all parts of France; the Tricolour floated
from the shores of Brittany to the shores of Provence.
Few events, indeed, have been more surprising than the
sudden collapse of the government of the Bourbons in
every part of the country, however distant from the scenes
of Napoleon's march, and the speedy re-establishment of
the imperial power; this recalled the days of Brumaire
and the Consulate. But the adherents of the Bourbons
and all classes opposed to the Empire were affrighted by
the astonishing revolution they beheld; and France in
every age has been ready to bow to triumphant force. The
Household troops, when disbanded, fled to their homes,
tracked out, in many places, by peasants in wrath; the
bourgeoisie accepted facts that seemed, for the time, accomplished; the Liberals, numerous and really powerful as
they were, kept away from the capital, and made no real
effort to protest against the imperial régime until it had
prevailed everywhere.

Faint attempts, indeed, at armed resistance were made
in provinces still at heart loyal; but they had soon sub-
sided and come to nothing. The Duc de Bourbon tried
to arouse the population of La Vendée, but the peasantry
showed little of the enthusiasm of twenty years before;
their chiefs, willing to wound, but afraid to strike, bade
them bide their time until aid from abroad should come.
The Duchesse d'Angoulême, 'the one man of the family,'
Napoleon called her, made an earnest and really a noble
effort to retain the great city of Bordeaux for the King;
but the soldiery of the garrison fell away: she was obliged
to take refuge under the British flag. Vitrolles, one of
the most active partisans of the Bourbons, endeavoured to
take possession of the tracts around Toulouse and to stir
up Royalist movement in the South; but he was soon
a prisoner, and the rising instantly collapsed. The Duc
d'Angoulême was more successful, for a few short days;
he assembled bodies of volunteers in Languedoc and

Provence, provinces always hostile to Napoleon's rule; he assumed the command of two or three regiments given him by Masséna, and supposed to be still faithful. He marched upon Lyons, two of his columns advancing into Dauphiné and Auvergne; but he was discomfited in some slight skirmishes; nearly all the regular troops declared for Napoleon; he was surrounded as he fell back, and compelled to surrender. This petty rising was the only approach to civil war at the moment; it afforded the one instance in which a regiment obeyed the command of its officers, and actually fired on the Tricolour; and it gained for Grouchy, the chief of an imperial detachment, the great prize of the staff of a Marshal of France, with what results was ere long to appear. Napoleon gave proof of extraordinary clemency in these passages of arms; he did not take vengeance on one of the House of Bourbon; he permitted his prisoner, the Duc d'Angoulême, to leave France. Meanwhile, nearly all the military leaders, if some of these were far from sincere, had again surrounded the imperial throne; they were lavish of professions, in several cases mere lip-service.

But if the Empire had been easily restored in France, it was threatened from abroad by appalling dangers. Napoleon had hoped before he left Elba that the Congress of Vienna would have been dissolved, and this league of his enemies broken up; but this expectation had proved fruitless. He had scarcely landed in France before he sent a message to the Emperor of Austria giving a pledge of peace. He promised, after he had regained the throne, that he would respect the treaties of 1814, which had reduced France within greatly narrowed limits. He wrote to the allied Sovereigns, assuring them that his last thought was of war. In these professions he was, doubtless, sincere; but, remembering what his career had been, we cannot be surprised that he was not believed, and history would not have blamed the allies had they taken the most stringent precautions against him.

But they were carried away by passion or terror; they feared they might have to disgorge the spoils of Europe which they had been dividing among themselves. Some saw in imagination the conqueror of 1800 to 1809 bestriding once more a subdued Continent; their conduct must be almost unreservedly condemned. Having already really broken faith with Napoleon, they issued a furious proclamation when he was on his way to Paris, denouncing him as an outlaw and a public enemy; he was a filibustering pirate who had no title to exist. At the same time their Embassies were withdrawn from Paris; the emissaries, avowed and secret, despatched by Napoleon to attempt to negotiate were arrested; his letters were not answered, or were left unopened; the Ruler of France, and France herself, were placed under the ban of the civilised world. Cruel insult was added to wrong that cannot be justified. Marie Louise, weak and worthless, was compelled to declare that she had no part in her husband's fortunes; the infant King of Rome was torn from his French attendants, and taken to Vienna a captive in all but the name, his mother having sold her son to obtain an interest for life in Parma secured to her in full possession by a solemn treaty.* Meanwhile, another coalition against France was formed; every Power in Europe was invited to join it. England, as always, promised enormous subsidies. Austria, Prussia, and Russia were to take the field, each with an army not less than 150,000 strong, if necessary to be indefinitely increased; and England was to make up in money for any deficiency in her contingent of men. War to the knife, deadly and universal, was to be waged against the usurper, who had made France his own. The allies did

* For a description of this pathetic scene see Ménéval, ' Mémoires,' ii. 325-327.

not reflect, in their savage temper, how they had violated
the pledges they had made to him, and how terrible was
the contrast between their vindictive fury and the mag-
nanimity he had shown to Bourbons, whom he might
have made his victims.

While Europe was rising up in arms against Napoleon,
France had ceased to be enthusiastic in his cause; large
parts of the nation were falling away from him. This
change of sentiment and opinion was partly due to the
fickleness of the French character, and partly, as had
happened in the case of the Bourbons, to the reaction
from illusions when found to be false; but it is mainly to
be ascribed to more potent causes. Napoleon, in his
progress from Cannes to Paris, announced himself as an
apostle of peace; his military career was for ever ended.
The multitudes which gave him welcome believed in his
words. This conviction spread far and wide through the
country. But the hopes of the nation were quickly dispelled when the proclamation of the allies was circulated
far and near, when hosts of invaders were on their way
to the Rhine and the Scheldt, when it was evident that a
tremendous conflict was at hand. The peasantry and the
humbler classes felt themselves deceived. In the general
alarm coming war inspired they became intimidated, and
began to dread that the restored Empire would bring
with it the horrors of the past. The Liberals and the
bourgeoisie, too enlightened from the first not to perceive
that a frightful struggle was at hand, shared in and encouraged these sentiments; and the Royalist party, still
with much influence, though for the moment unable to
rise, held up Napoleon to execration as the scourge of
France in countless publications artfully diffused.

Special causes, too, concurred to estrange from the
Emperor the classes which at first had given him their
hearts. The soldiery, indeed, and the officers of the lower
grades, remained devoted to their old chief. Their loyalty

to the death is the one noble feature which history recognises in the France of 1815. But the Emperor had, we have seen, in his triumphant march appealed to the passions of angry masses, filled with hatred of the émigrés, the noblesse, and most of the priesthood; he had declared himself the deliverer of the people from their worst enemies. There was a general expectation, when he had regained the throne, that he would take vengeance on these orders of men. He was adjured in addresses, speeches, and writings of all kinds to put down once for all the adherents of the House of Bourbon, and to save France and himself from traitorous factions dangerous to both. But Napoleon, always at heart detesting popular movements, had no notion, when he had become the head of the State, to give a free rein to the vindictiveness he saw around him. He would be 'the Ruler of France,' he said, 'not of a jacquerie.' He showed studious moderation towards the very classes which, as an adventurer, he had exposed to the odium of mobs. When, therefore, the peasantry and the populace of the towns saw that the émigrés were left alone if they did not take part against the Government, that the noblesse were neither proscribed nor banished, that priests were not molested if they did not preach sedition—that, in a word, they could not wreak the vengeance on which they had set their hearts—hundreds of thousands of Frenchmen who had pronounced for the Empire became indifferent to it, or even hostile. The circumstance that the men in office were nearly all instruments of the old despotism increased greatly these adverse sentiments.

A dictatorship, placed in the hands of Napoleon, was obviously at this tremendous crisis the one hope for the safety, perhaps the existence, of France, nor can history doubt that the Roman people would have made this choice in a trial of the kind, as it did when Hannibal was within a few marches from Rome. But France, enervated by revolution and years of war, split into hostile and reckless factions, sick of a despotism which had proved a curse to her, though she had long glorified and bowed down to it, had no thought of making a dictator at this time, still less of giving Napoleon power without control. It might have been expected, however, that a nation which had made Napoleon once more its chief, with full knowledge of the almost inevitable results, would have given him, for its own sake, loyal support—at least have secured him a strong Government.   But within a few weeks after the Empire had been restored it had become evident that France was a house divided against itself, and that she would not even unite against the common foreign enemy.   The Royalists began to plot and intrigue, and to some extent to paralyse the arm of the State ; the great Liberal party, and the higher middle classes, disliking and dreading Napoleon's return, and unfriendly to the Empire from the first moment, had ceased to conceal their aversion to it ; the nation, we have seen, was in part lukewarm, in part was becoming almost hostile. Treason, distrust, suspicion, even widespread ill-will, were conspiring to impair Napoleon's hold on France.   Under these conditions his Government could not be strong. ' Where,' he once bitterly remarked, ' is the arm of the old Emperor ?'

Peculiar circumstances, besides, increased the weakness of the authority of the State at this conjuncture.   The feeling was almost universal in France that no attempt should be made, in any event, to recur to the hated despotism of the past; that France must be under a constitutional régime; that the Emperor could only rule as a constitutional Sovereign ; that the nation must have political liberty, though the invasion of the hosts of Europe was near the frontier.   The men in office, and even Napoleon himself, felt the influence of this overmastering sentiment.   They hesitated to do acts and to adopt a policy perhaps necessary to the public weal at the time; they were unduly lenient to offenders against the State; they spared in several instances in which they ought perhaps to have struck. The Government was, therefore, an essentially feeble Government, when it ought to have possessed the greatest energy; Napoleon was hampered and thwarted, when he ought to have had a free hand. Another circumstance worked in the same direction. The provincial and local administration in France, so effective when in the hands of men loyal to existing powers, was largely composed of functionaries of the Bourbons; and these men did much to weaken and cross the central Government, especially when they found that comparative impunity followed their acts.

It has been said by well-informed and real thinkers—by Benjamin Constant, Madame de Staël, and Jomini—that had Napoleon, at this crisis of his fate, yielded to the revengeful passions of the multitude in France, and especially of the masses of peasants; had he carried out unflinchingly measures of proscription and blood, revived the evil days of the Reign of Terror, and acted the part of the Committee of Public Safety, he would have rallied the nation in patriotic fervour to his cause, have made every Frenchman a devoted soldier, and have triumphed over the coalition of 1815, as the Convention had triumphed in 1792-95.* This view, however, we believe is wholly erroneous. It disregards the essential facts of the time, and ignores elements of the situation of supreme importance. Had Napoleon let loose the fury of the mob, and hounded it on even against the émigrés, nobles, and priests — that is, ultimately, against social order and property—he might have gained momentary and partial success; but he would have had Liberal France and every other class against him; he would have been

* See the list of authorities quoted at length in H. Houssaye, ' 1815,' i. 489, 490.

repudiated by his own Government; the Robespierre of 1815 would soon have found his Thermidor. Nor could he certainly, without provoking civil war, and causing a revolution of the most frightful kind, have made himself a Jacobin tyrant of France. The attempt, in all probability, would alone have led to his ruin.

But even if he could have succeeded in this desperate policy, he could not have aroused the enthusiasm of twenty years before, and united France in arms against the foreign invader. The nation was hopelessly divided, enfeebled, and exhausted by protracted wars; the days of the fourteen armies of the Republic had passed away for ever; the bright visions of 1789-92 had vanished; apathy, listlessness, and a desire for ease and peace had, in the minds of hundreds of thousands of Frenchmen, replaced the aspirations which had secured victory in 1793-94.* It is unnecessary, too, to remark how very different was the feeble coalition of 1792-95, with its Yorks, its Coburgs, and its Brunswicks at its head, from the armed League of Europe in 1815, directed by Generals, some of a very high order. Napoleon could never have had the time to make France ready for the field given the Convention by the allies of that day. A dictatorship really backed by the nation might perhaps have saved France, but a Jacobin dictatorship would have been fatal; and, in fact, any dictatorship, especially that of Napoleon, was simply out of the question. For the rest, this kind of speculation is vain. Napoleon would never have been a mere revolutionary chief; he would be the Cæsar of France, or nothing. Even at St. Helena he did not regret that he had not staked his fortunes on a venture hateful to his mind.†

* This is well pointed out by Hooper, ' Waterloo,' 27, 1890 edition.

† His words recorded by Las Cases, ' Mémoires,' vi. 93-95, are significant : ' Une révolution est le plus grand des fléaux. Tous les avantages qu'elle procure ne sauraient égaler le trouble dont elle remplie la vie de ceux qui en sont les auteurs.'

France was thus largely forsaking Napoleon, while he had been proclaimed the outlaw of Europe. Nevertheless, gravely as the allies were to be blamed, and whatever may be laid to the charge of Frenchmen, he had to thank himself for much that he beheld around him. Nemesis had commended the poisoned chalice to his lips; he was paying the penalty for the excesses of conquest, and of despotism unrestrained and above law. Yet he was not wanting to himself in these terrible straits. The efforts he made to restore the military power of France, and to enable her to confront the hosts of Europe, were in the circumstances wonderful, and worthy of him. He did not, indeed, summon the nation to arms, and the summons would in a great measure have failed; but, within the limits of the resources available to him, he effected all, and more than all, that could be expected from such a man. France, doubtless, at this juncture contained elements of strength adapted to war, of immense value, in veterans, prisoners of the late wars, and trained officers; but these were as yet dispersed and unorganised; time was required to fashion them into armies able to take the field.

When Napoleon became head of the State in 1815, the military force of France was not more than from 180,000 to 200,000 men, allowing for troops in depots and strong places; there were hardly 50,000 that could be employed in active service. Of this force, the cavalry was little more than 20,000 sabres; the artillery only about 12,000 strong; the infantry, as the least expensive arm, was out of due proportion, the most numerous. The National Guards only existed on paper; they were no more than a police for the protection of towns. The material of the army was in a deplorable state; there were only about 200,000 muskets in reserve, and nearly a third of these were worn out; and if there was a sufficient supply of guns, there was a great lack of projectiles. The supplementary services, too, were out of joint and neglected. The accoutrements of many regiments were in rags; the store of gunpowder, of clothing, of a hundred other things of the kind, was lamentably deficient, even for a small force. Metternich had said a short time before, with no less truth than malice, that the army of the Bourbons was the mere shadow of a name.

Napoleon probably did not believe* that the allies would take heed of his pacific overtures; he made preparations from the outset for a conflict with Europe. One of his first measures was to break up and recast the organisation of the royal army. The regiments received their former numbers; their loved eagles were soon to be restored to them; the Imperial Guard was placed on its old footing. Within a week after the reins were in his hands, he arrayed and sent towards the frontier the skeletons of eight corps d'armée—four in station between Lille and Metz, one holding the tract around Soissons, one covering Alsace and the borders of the Middle Rhine, one observing the French Alps, the last the Pyrenees— these bodies being the centres to which the troops who were to raise them to their full force were to move. At the same time, he left nothing undone to strengthen and improve his trusted Guard; and though this noble array could not be what it once had been, the veteran Tenth Legion of the Cæsar of France, he composed it for the most part of picked men, including some thousands of choice volunteers, and he made it not unworthy of its old renown.

Meanwhile he addressed himself, as early as the close of March, though his orders were deferred for a time, for he did not wish prematurely to alarm France, to gathering together the materials of military power abounding in the country, but not combined, which would make his

* See his remarkable conversation with Davoût on the night of March 20: Thiers, vi. 294.

armies capable of appearing in strength in the field. Had he had the authority of 1800 to 1812, he would doubtless have summoned into the ranks all his old soldiers, have compelled late prisoners of war to serve, have called out the conscription of 1815, and even of 1816; nay, though this is unlikely, he might have adjured the nation to rally around him for the defence of France. All this, however, had become out of the question. Napoleon felt that he must act strictly within the law, for he well knew that his power was jealously watched; he could only make use of the forces available under these conditions. These were about 33,000 men on long leave, and about 85,000 who had deserted, but were of course liable to serve again. This contingent, added to 180,000 or 200,000 under the flag, would make up an army perhaps 260,000 strong—making allowance for losses and absent men—150,000 being probably all that could be opposed to an enemy in the field. This obviously was a quite inadequate force. There remained the resource of the National Guards, who could be raised to very large numbers—Carnot actually calculated to 2,000,000; of the conscription of 1815, which might yield 120,000 men; and of volunteers, veterans, seamen, and foreign soldiers, who might be induced to join the ranks. By these means a really imposing force might be arrayed; but it was uncertain to what extent this could be forthcoming, and Napoleon hesitated for some weeks to call the conscription out, for it had been declared abolished by Louis XVIII.

The object of Napoleon was to increase and strengthen the army intended to take the field, and to supplement it by a great auxiliary army, which would enable the first to cope with the enemy with a prospect of success, and would be available for operations of a less active kind. Recollecting his position, he achieved wonders. Within the space of a little more than two months he had assembled nearly 500,000 armed men, and within three more he would have assembled 800,000, an array which he said 'would have made the frontiers of the Empire a wall of brass.' We may glance at the condition of the armed strength of France as it existed in the first week of June, 1815. About 53,000 of the men on leave and of the deserters had rejoined the colours ; some 23,000 were on the march. The National Guards had furnished 150,000 men, all in the flower and vigour of life, to be employed with the regular army ; some thousands of these had entered the ranks, and proved themselves to be very good soldiers. The veterans did not supply more than 25,000 men, the volunteers only 15,000 ; but several regiments were drawn from Corsica ; and to these should be added four or five regiments of foreign troops, for the most part of excellent quality. Besides these forces there was an immense array of National Guards, of worn-out soldiers, of seamen from the fleets, gendarmes, partisans, even Custom-house officers ; this was to support the regular army, to strengthen or form the garrisons of strong places, to undertake subordinate services of many kinds—in short, to set the regular army free to act with all its power in the field. The combined masses, taking the grand total, were formed into a field army about 284,000 strong, some 198,000 men being under arms and present with their corps, and into an auxiliary army of about 222,000 men, which, we have said, was to sustain the regular army, and to perform much of its ordinary work. These forces, we repeat, would in a short time have been increased by 300,000 men, for Napoleon resolved at last to call the conscription out, though he gave the levy a different name. The young soldiers had proved themselves willing to join the army, and 200,000 more National Guards could have been collected. Napoleon's efforts, as affairs stood, had been astonishing ; he had raised France out of a state of impotence, and made her ready to undertake a great war.*

* For the numbers of the field and auxiliary army of France in the beginning of June, 1815, see H. Houssaye, ' 1815,' ii. 37. The able

France did not earnestly second, at first, the efforts of Napoleon to increase her military power. The provinces of the East, indeed, which had felt the effects of the terrible invasion of 1814, sent from the outset their tale of National Guards to the standards; but the South, the West, and large parts of the North held back. By degrees, however, the martial spirit of the people awoke; the vindictive and insolent attitude of the allies provoked resentment almost universally felt; the publication of the proclamation declaring Napoleon an outlaw, and of the overtures he had made for peace, disseminated by the Government far and wide, aroused multitudes of Frenchmen to take up arms. There were few signs of the exulting fervour of 1792-93, or of the prodigious effort made in 1813; but there was not the general despondency of 1814, and France, divided and alarmed as she was, did enable Napoleon to assemble the masses he had collected in June, 1815. The large numbers of officers on half-pay and of veteran officers to be found in the country gave him the means of organising his levies with comparative success; even the newly-formed regiments of National Guards seem to have had capable men at their heads.

It was a gigantic task, however, to find the material required to arm and prepare the bodies of men being brought together; this, indeed, proved to be in many respects deficient. The supplies of small arms, we have seen, were far from sufficient, but through extraordinary exertions of many kinds about 370,000 muskets were fabricated, repaired, or purchased; these added to those of the former royal army were nearly adequate—at least, for the moment. Munitions of war and projectiles for cannon were manufactured in large quantities, but spite of every effort there was here a deficiency. The chief

---

and conscientious author has studied the subject with the greatest care; his figures do not widely differ from those of Thiers, and may be accepted. The estimate of the partisan Charras is quite false.

3

difficulty, however, consisted in finding the means for procuring clothing and uniforms for the National Guards, and even the army. The Bourbon Government, we have seen, had been culpably remiss in this matter; few contractors had received orders, and many had failed; and though Napoleon contrived to obtain funds for the purpose, a most essential requirement could not be made good in a few weeks. Some regiments of the regular army, and even, it has been said, of the Imperial Guard, were not properly accoutred when hostilities began;* and more than half the National Guards were without the uniform, which alone would entitle them to rank as soldiers. The forces, therefore, arrayed by Napoleon—apart from the defects inherent in hasty organisations of the kind—were to a great extent ill prepared for the severest trials of war; but they were formidable in numbers, and a large part of them possessed military qualities of a high order.

The field army, about 198,000 strong, was composed almost wholly of regular troops, especially along the frontier of the North. The Imperial Guard was the best part of this fine force; it had been raised, by extraordinary exertions, to 28,000 men. The cavalry, too, had been increased to 40,000 sabres, the artillery to nearly 17,000 men; these two arms were well supplied with horses, which had been obtained by requisitions, purchases, and dismounting the gendarmerie. As to the distribution of the field army, the eight original corps d'armée had been left in their stations—that is, four along the borders of Belgium, one on the Aisne, two in the East, and one on the Pyrenees; but the numbers of these had been largely increased, especially of the four corps in the North. To these, however, should be added four new corps, one observing the defiles of the Jura, another Provence and the line of the Var, a third watching the region of La

* Part of the Imperial Guard had not its full uniform at Ligny : H. Houssaye, 'Waterloo,' ii. 180.

Vendée, a fourth the Western Pyrenees and the adjoining country;* and the great array of the Imperial Guard was, for the most part, assembled in and around Paris.

But, besides the field army, Napoleon had to provide for the security of the triple barrier of the fortresses of France. These had suffered little from the invasion of 1814, but in some instances they were strengthened and improved. They were supplied with sufficient stores of provisions; they were given garrisons mainly composed of National Guards and veterans, but with a small admixture of regular soldiers. The value of the arrangements of the Emperor was here distinctly seen. These strong places were held by forces able to defend ramparts, but were not permitted to absorb the real army; this was for the most part left free to encounter the enemy in the field. Napoleon, too, especially addressed himself to the defence of Lyons, at this time almost an open town. Redoubts were constructed, and armed lines made; the passages of the Rhone were fortified; a large body of National Guards was thrown into the place. His chief attention, however, in this province was given to shielding Paris from attack. The city had been unprotected since the day of Louis XIV., though Vauban had wished to surround it with walls; and this had been Napoleon's intention likewise, if he had never had time to carry it into effect. He remembered that had the capital held out, even for a few days, in 1814, he might have compelled the allies to withdraw from it, perhaps have placed them in the gravest straits. He resolved to fortify it as far as was now possible.† Paris was placed, to some extent, in a state of defence along the northern bank of the Seine;

---

* It will be remarked that three, at least, of these corps were employed in observing the far from obedient southern and western provinces. All the subsidiary corps were weak.

† For the admirable remarks of Napoleon on the defence of Paris, see 'Comment.,' v. 104-108, 1867 edition.

but the work was begun late, not to alarm the citizens.
By June little had been done along the southern bank.
The garrison was formed partly of regular troops, partly
of nearly 40,000 National Guards, and partly of irregular
levies, these last, however, being not yet armed, if it was
ever really meant to give them arms. It remains to add
that the immense expenditure required for all these preparations for war was defrayed either from funds left by
the Bourbon Government — the administration of its
finances, we have said, had been good—or from taxation,
loans, and other fiscal devices.

The allies, meanwhile, had been making gigantic exertions to overwhelm Napoleon and to invade France.
Their armies had been on their way homewards when
the intelligence arrived of the escape from Elba. Part of
the forces of England were across the Atlantic; the hosts
of Germany were spread from the Danube to the Oder;
the Russian hordes had approached the Vistula. But the
decision for war was no sooner taken than immense efforts
were made to combine these masses, and to direct them
as speedily as possible against the common enemy. Peace
with America set thousands of British soldiers free. Wellington had reached Brussels in the first days of April,
and was soon in command of a considerable force; his
colleague, Blucher, was ere long on his way from the
Rhine with a Prussian army; large bodies of troops, increasing in numbers, were assembled in the Low Countries
between the Lys and the Meuse.

The more distant armies were, meantime, advancing.
By the first days of June, from 600,000 to 750,000 men
were brought together to avenge Europe on France and
her ruler. Wellington and Blucher were now at the
head of 220,000 men, Barclay de Tolly of about 150,000
Russians, Schwartzenberg of some 250,000 Austrians and
Germans of the Lesser States, and an Austrian and Sar-
dinian force, perhaps 80,000 or 100,000 strong, was being

directed from Italy upon Dauphiné and Provence. It deserves notice that Wellington desired to take the offensive as quickly as possible. As early as April he proposed to invade France with 300,000 men,* who could be on the frontier in a few weeks; but the other chiefs of the coalition, if we except Blucher, recollecting the events of 1813-14, rejected the bold counsels of the English commander, the only one of the allied Generals who had not felt the terrible strokes of Napoleon, and resolved to advance only when apparently irresistible strength promised to render decisive success certain. Their plan was to march into France with four great armies, extending from the edge of the Channel to the Mediterranean; these, which may be broadly described as the columns of the North and the East, were to converge on Paris, and in much lesser force on Lyons, the march beginning about July 1; and as they would be three or four fold superior in numbers to any army which Napoleon could place in the field, scarcely a doubt seemed possible but that he would be overwhelmed and crushed.† But even this enormous array of force was to be seconded by other means. La Vendée was incited to rise against the Emperor, and Metternich set on foot an intrigue with Fouché in order to increase the divisions of France, an intrigue, however, which had no immediate results, save to irritate Napoleon against his false-hearted Minister.

Two plans of operations offered themselves to Napoleon, confronted as he was by the armed hosts of Europe. Assuming that some 600,000 men would invade France between the Belgian and the Swiss frontiers, 150,000

* The Wellington Despatches, xii. 295 *et seq.*, 304 *et seq.*

† For the numbers of the forces of the coalition, Alison, ' History of Europe,' xii. 207, 1854 edition, followed by Siborne and Hooper, may be compared with Thiers, ' Histoire du Consulat et de l'Empire,' vi. 333; with Charras, ' Campagne de 1815,' i. 14, 1858 edition; with Napoleon, ' Comment.,' v. 115, 116, 1867 edition; and with H. Houssaye, ' 1815,' ii. 91-94.

would be required to mask the French fortresses; 450,000 only, therefore, could appear before Paris, and they could not reach the capital before the end of July. If Napoleon chose to act on the defensive, and to await the enemy outside the city, he would have an army by this time more than 200,000 strong; Paris would be armed with at least 600 cannon, and would possess a garrison of about 70,000 men behind completed works of considerable strength. The conditions, therefore, of the contest would be much better than they were in the campaign of 1814; and if we bear in mind what the Emperor achieved in that magnificent passage of arms, he certainly would have had many chances of success. In the same way, if 100,000 more men were to cross the south-eastern borders of France, not more than 60,000 or 70,000 could reach Lyons. Suchet, the one fortunate French General in Spain, would command around the city and its fortified lines at the head of 30,000 or 40,000 men; it might be reasonably expected that he could hold the enemy in check. This plan, therefore, was not without real promise. Excellent judges have thought it much the best; but in the circumstances in which France was placed, divided and disheartened, torn by faction, there were objections insuperable, perhaps, to it. The nation, in a word, would not endure a repetition of the scenes of 1814.

Another plan presented itself, no doubt daring in the extreme and perilous, but in conformity with the true principles of war, and exactly the same in conception as those which led to the operations of 1800 and 1805, and had as their results Marengo and Ulm and Austerlitz. The allies, we have seen, were divided into two great masses, separated from each other by immense distances; the column of the North was in Belgium in June, the column of the East approaching the Rhine, the French Alps, and the Var. It might be possible, therefore, to make a sudden spring on the most isolated part of the huge front of invasion—the two armies of Blucher and Wellington—to attack, separate, and beat these in detail; and though they were 220,000 strong, their position, we shall see, made them dangerously exposed to defeat even by a largely inferior force. Napoleon resolved to adopt this project. He calculated that he could have 150,000 men in hand to advance into Belgium by the middle of June, and subsequent events show that had he possessed this force, in all probability he would have emerged victorious from the strife. Having overcome the column of the North, the Emperor would march against the eastern column and encounter it on the Rhine and the Moselle.*

Two events at this juncture threw a grievous weight into the scales of fortune against the Emperor. Napoleon had been reconciled with Murat, who had abandoned his benefactor in 1814; he had entreated his brother-in-law, when he was leaving Elba, to assure the Austrian Government of his pacific intentions; and at the same time he advised Murat, if necessary, to prepare himself for war, but in no event prematurely to march into Northern Italy. The triumphant progress of Napoleon through France, however, turned the head of the ill-fated King of Naples; from whatever motives he advanced to the Po, at the head of about 50,000 men, an ambiguous letter of Joseph Bonaparte seemed to approve of the movement. He made a bold effort to cross the great river, and to carry the war into the Austrian Italian States. The invasion was, without difficulty, repelled. An Austrian army, in superior force, had soon compelled Murat hastily to retreat. After a fruitless display of his characteristic valour, he was routed, near Tolentino, in a decisive battle. The King escaped in disguise from his enemies; he

---

* The best account of Napoleon's celebrated plans of operations in 1815 will be found in 'Comment.,' v. 114, 118, 1867 edition.

landed a helpless fugitive in Provence. He vainly entreated Napoleon, justly incensed, to give him a command in the French army. The only result of his insensate venture was to deprive France of an ally who might have been of use had he conducted himself with the simplest prudence, and to set free a large Austrian force to take part in the crusade against the Emperor.

The other event was even more disastrous in view of the operations in Belgium planned by Napoleon. The allies, we have seen, had designed a rising in La Vendée against the Ruler of France; this proved to a certain extent successful, though the peasantry had apparently been quiescent for some weeks. Their chiefs, however, having received some help from England, and promises of aid on a much greater scale, were able to stir up a considerable population to revolt. The movement seemed for a time to threaten civil war. Napoleon felt it necessary to send a powerful detachment to support his corps in the West, and to keep La Vendée down. The rising had before long collapsed, mainly perhaps owing to the machinations of Fouché, who contrived to persuade the Royalist leaders that it was useless for them to shed their blood in a quarrel soon to be decided elsewhere. In this way he seemed to serve Napoleon and the Bourbons alike, for he was perfectly ready to assist and to deceive both, and, whatever the event, to hedge with Fortune. La Vendée was in a few weeks at peace, but in the meantime from 15,000 to 20,000 excellent troops, including two regiments of the Imperial Guard, had been prevented from joining the French army on the Belgian frontier.*

* Napoleon, ' Comment.,' v. 119, 1867 edition, makes the number 20,000 men, and is followed by Alison, ' History of Europe,' xii. 217, and by Thiers, ' Histoire du Consulat et de l'Empire,' vi. 200. H. Houssaye, ' 1815,' seems to make the figures less ; but the detachment sent to the Army of the West is perhaps not included. The immense importance of this diversion in favour of the allies is hardly noticed by most English commentators. Napoleon properly describes it as ' un événement bien funeste.'

Meanwhile Napoleon had been addressing himself to an attempt to reconcile Liberal France to his rule, and to gain the loyal support of the great mass of the nation, for some weeks partly estranged from him. In the decrees he had issued from Lyons he had pledged himself to a reform of the institutions of France, and to assemble the electorate from all parts of the country, in a solemn convention to be held in Paris, in order to assist him in this great work, and to witness—a vain hope—the coronation of Marie Louise.* He felt that he must redeem this pledge. The Liberals, a powerful and the most energetic party in the State, which regarded the Empire with alarm and dislike, would otherwise remain a real danger to his throne; the great body of the people would have cause for complaint; and, besides, Napoleon knew that he must establish a régime as constitutional, at least, as that formed by the Charter, and was desirous to prove to Europe that he was not a mere despot, the author of a revolution of sheer military force, accomplished against the will of the people, a reproach common in the mouths of the Royalists and the allies.

He adopted a course which had the semblance, at least, of conspicuous frankness and an honest purpose; he summoned Benjamin Constant, one of the heads of the Liberal party, supposed to be the constitutional Sieyès of the day, and a bitter enemy of Napoleon up to this moment; and he entrusted him with the task of framing a new Constitution for France, on a broad and even a popular basis. Benjamin Constant found the Emperor generally willing to accept his views; he applied himself sincerely to his work, and in a short time he had sketched out a series of institutions for France, certainly more liberal than those of the Charter, and securing, on paper at least, a large measure of social and political liberty. The freedom of the press, before withheld, was conceded

* 'Correspondence,' xxviii. 7, 8.

almost without restriction; the freedom of worship, a gift
of the Concordat, indeed, but lately threatened by the
Bourbon Government, was declared the heritage of every
Frenchman; the electorate was increased sixfold; the
special tribunals which had been the disgrace of French
justice for ages were abolished wellnigh without exception; the scope of trial by jury was largely extended.
The Constitution, in its strictly political aspect, was
fashioned, in the main, on the model of that of England.
There was to be a House of Hereditary Peers and a House
of Deputies; the responsibility of Ministers was assured by
law; the right of taxation and of raising troops—in short,
the power of the purse, and nearly that of the sword—was
confined to the Legislature, and the Legislature alone.*

For three reasons, however, the new polity, contemptuously called 'La Benjamine,' found little favour in the
sight of the greater part of the nation. The Liberals,
and even the electorate, looked forward to a Constituent
Assembly like that of 1789, charged to make the Constitution itself; they resented that this had been the work of
Napoleon and a subordinate. The name, too, of Acte
Additionnel given to the Constitution, liberal as it was,
savoured too much of the Actes of the Empire; it was
generally thought that the Constitution was a mere piece
of the furniture of the old despotism furbished up and
given an attractive look. The prevalent distrust of
Napoleon was here distinctly seen; but Napoleon had
insisted upon the title: he would no more forego the rights
he had gained by genius and his sword than Louis XVIII.
would abandon his right Divine. The hereditary peerage
was also regarded with dislike, and the Executive Government—that is, the Emperor—retained the power of confis-

* See a copy of the Acte Additionnel, Napoleon Correspondence,
xxviii. 122, 129; and the admirable analysis of H. Houssaye, '1815,'
i. 542, 543. See also Thiers, 'Histoire du Consulat et de l'Empire,'
vi. 353-356, 1862 edition.

cation in his hands, which, with other Sovereigns of France, he had often abused. The Constitution therefore was from the first unpopular; 'opinion,' Napoleon acknowledged, ' had turned against it '; and when it was put to the vote for acceptance, the votes for it were little more than a third of the votes for the Consulate and for the Empire in 1804.

The Emperor, on the advice of Benjamin Constant, backed by Lafayette and other chiefs of the Liberals, was induced to bring the Constitution into being at once, and to summon the Chambers without delay, though this was against his real wishes. He dreaded, and rightly dreaded, what such assemblies, newly formed, and without experience in affairs of State, might do in the presence of the coalition and its hosts. The Chambers, however, were quickly convened; they represented to a considerable extent, at least, the feelings uppermost in the middle and lower middle classes, if not in the army and the mass of the peasantry. In the House of Deputies, composed of more than 600 members, little more than eighty were friends of Napoleon at heart; there were thirty or forty of a revolutionary type; the immense majority were Liberals inspired with the new ideas. As to the House of Peers, it was, for the most part, formed of ennobled functionaries of the Empire, and of a few members of the old noblesse; but it was also pervaded by the prevailing sentiment; it was jealous of its own rights and of constitutional freedom; it was completely different from the late servile Senate. The spirit of both assemblies was very much the same : both were averse to the Bourbons and the fallen Government; both really wished to support Napoleon, while victorious at least, and to continue the war until an honourable peace was made; both were loud in eager professions of loyalty. But both betrayed symptoms of the profound distrust which at this juncture Napoleon inspired; both were not fully alive to the perils of a tremendous crisis. The Chamber of Deputies echoed with babble about reforms in the law when the hostile League of Europe was upon the frontier. Napoleon censured this unreflecting and unwise attitude in characteristically grave and dignified language; but his remarks gave offence and provoked ill-will; the rift in the lute was even now manifest.

The Emperor had abandoned the project of summoning the electorate to Paris,* announced at Lyons; but he had resolved to inaugurate the Empire of the Acte Additionnel by an imposing ceremony within the capital. This celebrated pageant was held on June 1; the Champ de Mai, as it was called, was remembered for years as the farewell of Napoleon to the French people. A vast structure was erected by the École Militaire; a throne and an altar were placed in the midst; on either side spread an amphitheatre filled with the Court, with the great bodies of the State, with the magistracy, newly-elected deputies, and representatives of the electorate; beyond, in rank upon rank, were the long lines of 50,000 men of the army and the National Guards; in the near distance was an immense assemblage crowding the Champ de Mars. The ceremony was opened by a solemn Mass, for Napoleon, as was his wont, felt the power of religious effect. The Emperor received a loyal address from the deputies of the electorate, who had recorded their votes; then, rising from the throne, he made a characteristic answer, identifying the rights and interests of France with his own, and calling on Frenchmen to unite and to second his efforts.

As the ceremony proceeded, Napoleon took an oath to observe the Constitution lately established. It closed with a really heart-stirring sight: the Emperor, amidst the thunder of cannon, the deafening cheers of the armed masses on the spot, and the acclamations of the great

* The electorate under the Charter of Louis XVIII. comprised only some 30,000 men.

audience, presented eagles to the soldiery and the National Guards, and adjured them to defend these sacred emblems to the death. This feature of the scene was grand and noble, for it corresponded with the facts and the feelings of the hour. But there were other features of a different kind. The imperial mantle on Napoleon seemed out of place; it was a sign of despotism and of lost conquests; he would have appeared more becomingly in the garb of a soldier. His family of discrowned Kings and Princes sitting by his side was also unwelcome; the absence of Marie Louise and the young King of Rome was significant of the conflict with Europe at hand. Fouché, too, like a bird of evil omen hovered about; he poured base and evil counsels into many ears; the Emperor should abdicate, and make a noble self-sacrifice; the coalition would accept a constitutional France under Marie Louise or the Duke of Orleans. But the most sinister symptom of all, perhaps, was seen in the attitude of the soldiery and the Imperial Guard: they had the look of men nerved to fight to the death; but care and anxiety sat on their faces; they were the 'Ave, Cæsar, morituri!' as they defiled before their chief.

Within a few days Napoleon's arrangements were complete for his venturous spring against the allies in Belgium. The four corps stationed along this frontier had been gradually brought near each other; the corps around Soissons and the Imperial Guard were on the march to effect their junction with these; the combined masses were being directed against the point deemed by their great leader the most favourable for his attack. Napoleon left the capital at daybreak on June 12. He let drop the words, 'I am going to rub myself against Wellington.' He had abandoned for the moment the torturing cares of State; something of the confidence and high spirit of the past had revived as he saw himself within reach of his true empire, the camp. He had not lost all faith in his genius and his sword; but the perils of the situation were fully before his mind, and the burden of these was almost unbearable. He was about to struggle against a world in arms; the Generals and the army of 1815 were not the Generals and the army of the days of victory; he was leaving a divided and a revolutionary France behind him. Nor was he himself the man he had been: his physical strength had been long in decline; he was subjected to diseases occasionally giving severe pain, and making him almost prostrate for hours. And though his intellect retained its splendour and force, his energy and moral power had been impaired. Years of defeat and disaster had told on Napoleon; the prodigious and disheartening toil of the last few months—above all, his consciousness of the appalling dangers around him—had weakened the faculties most required in the terrible stress of war.* He might have exclaimed, like Richard before Bosworth:

> ' I have not that alacrity of spirit
> And cheer of heart that I was wont to have ;'

and he has told us himself that he had sad forebodings, and 'an instinct of failure,' in the contest before him.† Genius, all the more thoroughly because it was genius, knew that it was battling with supreme fact; Prometheus had defied the rule of Zeus; the Titan already felt the approach of Force.

---

* For an account of the state of Napoleon's health at this time, see the striking narrative of H. Houssaye, ' 1815,' i. 614, and the remarkable description of the Emperor's worn, unnerved, and almost woe-begone aspect in the ' Memoirs of General Thiébault,' v. 341, 342. We shall recur to this subject in considering the operations of the campaign.

† ' Je n'avais plus en moi le sentiment du success definitif. Ce n'était plus ma confiance première. Je sentais la fortune m'aban-donner. . . . J'avais l'instinct d'une issue malheureuse.'—Las Cases, vii. 179-183.

CHAPTER III

THE ADVANCE OF NAPOLEON—THE BELLIGERENT
ARMIES AND THEIR LEADERS

Sketch of the theatre of war in Belgium—The positions of the armies of Wellington and Blucher — The arrangements of the allied chiefs to resist attack defective — The true reason of this — Napoleon resolves to attack the allied centre—Reasons for this project—His forces considerably less than he had expected—Concentration of the French army on the verge of Belgium—Admirable skill shown in effecting this operation — Positions of the French army on June 14, 1815—Numbers and characteristics of the French and the allied armies—Napoleon, Wellington, Blucher, and their lieutenants.

It is necessary to have a distinct idea of the theatre of war, and of the positions of the hostile armies upon it, in order to understand the great contest of 1815, and the operations that led to the final issue. Belgium, nearly identical with the old Spanish Netherlands, is in its main features a land of plains, here and there broken by short ranges of hills, intersected by large and numerous streams, dotted over with ancient and flourishing towns, and rich with manufacturing and agricultural wealth. On its southern borders, enlarged since 1815, it meets the northern frontier of France, which, mainly owing to the exploits of Turenne, had been extended from Picardy over Burgundian Artois, and over parts of Spanish Flanders and Hainault, and which forms its boundary from the North

Sea to the verge of Lorraine. The whole tract is divided by a series of rivers, forming in most instances military lines, the Lys, the Scheldt, the Dender, the Senne, the Dyle, and others, flowing from the South northwards; but the Sambre, joining the Meuse at Namur, their united waters reaching the mouths of the Rhine, runs, with the Meuse, in a general way, from the south eastwards, and makes a defensive barrier in that direction.

The territory of Belgium, notably to the west and the south-west, is protected by a succession of strong places, rising, nearly all, along the watercourses they guard— Courtray, Tournay, Oudenarde, Ath, Mons, and several others; along this region they confront the French fortresses of Lille, Valenciennes, Maubeuge, Avesnes, and three or four more constructed to cover the borders of France to the north. To the south and east the fortresses are less numerous; but Charleroy,* Namur, Huy, Liége, and Maastricht—the last a place belonging to the Dutch— extend along the course of the Sambre or of the two rivers, and increase the natural defensive strength of parts of this district. In 1815, as at the present time, several main roads led from France into Belgium, especially to the west and the south-west: one from Lille, along the valley of the Lys to Ghent; three from Lille, Valenciennes, and Maubeuge, along the valleys of the Dender or the Senne, and by the fortresses on these lines to Brussels. To the east there were only two principal roads, one by Givet down the valley of the Meuse, the other far to the right by Sedan to Liége; but neither of these was of much importance, or easily available for the march of large armies. Due south, however, a great main road extended from Charleroy to Brussels—that is, ran nearly through the midst of Belgium; but in 1815 it was not connected with any main road leading from Charleroy to the French frontier; the communications were here by roads of an

* Charleroy in 1815 was almost an open town.

inferior kind.*   Excellent lateral roads ran along the borders of France and Belgium, uniting the fortresses on either side, and facilitating the march, by these, of masses of troops.

The two armies of Wellington and Blucher, some 220,000 strong, we have said, and forming, as we have called it, the northern column of the huge invasion, were disseminated, in June, 1815, over nearly three-fourths of the territory we have described, and were spread on a front of about a hundred miles in breadth, from near Ghent, on the west, to Liége, eastwards, and of from thirty to forty miles in depth, from Brussels near to the fortresses on the French frontier.   The forces of Wellington held the right and the right centre of this great space, those of Blucher the left centre and the left ; the middle distance was certainly the least carefully guarded.   The army of the Duke was divided into three corps d'armée, the 2nd under the command of the skilful Hill, the 1st under that of the young Prince of Orange, the 3rd, or the reserve, under that of Wellington himself, assisted by some of his best lieutenants.   The 2nd corps, Wellington's right and right centre, was rather more than 27,000 strong ; it was encamped in the valleys of the Scheldt and the Dender, a few detachments being in the valley of the Lys ; it was covered by the fortresses along this front— Tournay, Ath, Oudenarde, Lens, Leuze, and one or two others ; it observed the main roads, leading from the west and the south-west by Lille and Valenciennes, across the Belgian frontier.   The 1st corps, Wellington's left centre and left, was composed of nearly 32,000 men ; it lay, to a large extent, in the valley of the Senne, holding Braine le Comte, Soignies, Enghien, Nivelles, and other places ; it had a small detachment on the main road from Charleroy to Brussels, to which we have before referred ; it had the great fortress of Mons in its front ; and, similarly to

* This is important, and should be carefully kept in mind.

4

the 2nd corps, it watched the main roads running from Valenciennes and Maubeuge to Brussels. The 3rd corps, otherwise the reserve, about 23,000 strong, was for the most part in cantonments around Brussels; it was somewhat in the rear of the corps it supported, but its advanced divisions approached both of these; and it was aggregated in or near the Belgian capital, to the possession of which Wellington attached the greatest importance. Besides these forces there was a large corps of cavalry, commanded by Uxbridge, and about 10,500 sabres; this was mainly in the valley of the Dender, with the 2nd corps; but detachments were in the valley of the Lys, to the extreme right.

As for the army of Blucher, it comprised four corps d'armée, the 1st corps with *Z*ieten as its chief, the 2nd and 3rd under Pirch and Thielmann, the 4th led by the experienced Bulow. As we have said, it formed the left centre and the left of the two allied armies. The 1st corps, Blucher's right wing, more than 32,000 men, extended almost along the course of the Sambre—that is, not far from the French frontier, from Marchiennes by Charleroy, towards Fleurus. It came nearly in contact with part of Wellington's left near Fontaine l'Évêque, and other places to the west of the main road from Charleroy to Brussels. *Z*ieten's corps, and a portion of that of the Prince of Orange, thus formed the centre of the allies, but did not occupy this front at any point in force. The 2nd corps, to the east of the 1st of Blucher, was also more than 32,000 strong. This, too, was placed along the Sambre, and thence to the Meuse, but further from France, from Namur to Huy; and it had detachments extending to Hottomont and Hannut. The 3rd corps was considerably to the south of the 2nd; it numbered some 24,500 men. It was encamped, for the most part, around Ciney and Dinant, observing the road leading from Givet along the Meuse, and ending at the great stronghold of Namur. The 4th corps, rather more than 31,000 strong, formed the left wing of the army of Blucher; it was in cantonments northwards around Liége. It was separated by a wide distance from the three other corps.

This far-spreading dispersion of the allied armies might obviously expose them, if assailed, to really grave dangers. Four or five days or more were required to enable them to concentrate on their right or their left, two at least to concentrate upon their centre. They were thus liable to perilous attack on the part of an enemy of resource and skill, and the excuse that it was necessary widely to scatter the troops because otherwise they could not find subsistence in one of the richest countries of Europe has long ago been dismissed as scarcely worthy of notice. This faulty disposition, however, was only a part of the faulty dispositions to be ascribed to the allied chiefs. Their armies were weakest at the centre of their front, the points where their inner flanks met. This was traversed from south to north by the main road from Charleroy to Brussels, an avenue into the heart of Belgium. Could this line, therefore, be seized and held by an enemy in force, they might be rent asunder and defeated in detail, with disastrous, possibly fatal, results. Nor was this all, or even nearly all. Wellington was convinced that, should he be attacked, he would be attacked on his right or his right centre*; he had thus, not reckoning the reserve around Brussels, accumulated the largest part of his forces in the valleys of the Scheldt and the Dender, and thence towards the Senne. His left wing was comparatively—nay, very—weak at the points where it reached Blucher's right, both forming, we have said, the allied centre on both sides of the main road from Charleroy to Brussels, and he clung to the idea that

* Wellington's Despatches, xii. 337 *et seq.*, April 30, 1815. See also Charras, i. 67, 68.

he might be attacked on his right or his right centre until it was all but too late—nay, to the last moment.

As respects Blucher's army, the 1st corps was dangerously near the French frontier from Marchiennes to Charleroy along the Sambre, and was exposed to attack in that direction. The 2nd and 3rd corps were chiefly engaged in observing and covering the approaches to Namur, in view of the possible advance of an enemy, as was far from probable, by the road from Givet. The 4th corps was far from its supports, and Blucher's right wing, like Wellington's left, parts of both being, we repeat, the allied centre, was not in nearly sufficient strength on the points traversed by the main road from Charleroy to Brussels. In addition to this, Wellington had his headquarters at Brussels; the head-quarters of Blucher were at Namur; the intervening distance was upwards of thirty miles. The communication between the two commanders could not, therefore, be very easy or rapid, especially if they were suddenly attacked, a circumstance which might have unfortunate results.*

The real cause of these defective arrangements was that Wellington and Blucher, knowing well that their armies must be largely superior in numbers to any army Napoleon could oppose to them, did not at heart believe they would be assailed in Belgium; they thought they would securely march into France when the eastern column of the allies had passed her frontiers. They had contemplated, indeed, the possibility of being attacked, and they had agreed, should their adversary fall on their

---

* For the positions of the allied armies, and their distribution on the theatre of operations, now all but universally recognised as having been ill-conceived, see Napoleon, 'Comment.,' v. 204-206 ; Charras, i. 67-71 ; La Tour d'Auvergne, 'Waterloo,' 35-37 ; Shaw Kennedy, 'The Battle of Waterloo,' 169-173 ; Chesney, 'Waterloo Lectures,' 47-50 ; and Wolseley, 'The Decline and Fall of Napoleon,' 143, 144. The reasoning of Hooper, to the contrary, still followed by a very few writers, 'Waterloo,' 40-47, only proves the weakness of his case.

centre, that they would unite forces to defend this front, though it is not probable that, as has been alleged, they had chosen beforehand the points on which they subsequently tried to carry out their purpose.* But, we say again, they did not thoroughly grasp the idea that they might be attacked in formidable force, pressed home. Their correspondence at the moment when hostilities began places this beyond question.†

The positions of the allied armies in Belgium did not escape the far-reaching eye of Napoleon, who, we have said, had resolved to take the offensive. With characteristic attention to details, he had considered every line on which he could advance; but his resolution, it would appear, was quickly made. Were he to march against Wellington's right or right centre, he might sever the communications of the Duke, and force him away from Brussels; but he could not prevent him joining hands with Blucher, and both would almost certainly drive him back into France, perhaps would overwhelm him with their superior numbers. Were he to advance, on the other hand, against the left centre or the left of Blucher, he would have to move through a difficult and intricate country. At best, the issue would probably be the same as that which reasonably might be expected in the case of an attack on the right or the right centre of Wellington. An attack on the allied centre remained. Many considerations showed that this was the only movement that promised well, or could have decisive effects. Napoleon was well aware that the allied armies were very much larger than his own in numbers. His one solid chance of success, therefore, was to separate and defeat them in

* See, on this point, the judicious remarks of Ropes, ' The Campaign of Waterloo,' 71, 72, and of H. Houssaye, ' 1815,' 114, 115.
† See Wellington's Despatches, xii. 462, 470 ; and Blucher to his wife, cited by H. Houssaye, ' 1815,' ii. 107. These letters were written in June.

detail, and the only means through which he could attain this end was to fall on their centre and strike them when apart, as he had fallen on Beaulieu and Colli in 1796, and on other adversaries in his wonderful career.

There were reasons, too, to suppose that, in this instance, an attack upon the hostile centre would have very great results. The allied armies rested on divergent bases—that of Wellington ultimately on Ostend and the sea, that of Blucher ultimately on the Rhine and Cologne. Their centre, therefore, where their inner flanks met, would probably be the weakest part of their front, for it would be the most distant from their sources of supply. Napoleon had perhaps ascertained that this was actually the case, and should their centre be pierced through, it might fairly be hoped that they would divide, and recoil towards their bases, and they would expose themselves to the terrible strokes by which their adversary had often struck down enemies severed from each other in rapid succession. Besides, Wellington and Blucher were allied chiefs with perhaps dissimilar views and aims. They were certainly men of different natures — Blucher impetuous, and even rash to a fault; Wellington, in Napoleon's judgment, overcircumspect and cautious. It was probable, therefore, that, were they assailed on their centre, Blucher would advance hastily and offer battle, and Wellington would at least be slow in moving to join his colleague. An opportunity of beating both in detail was thus here presented. In addition to this, the 1st corps of Blucher, that of Zieten, formed the principal part of the allied centre, and was in a dangerous position near the French frontier. This circumstance, doubtless, had its effect on Napoleon's mind, and contributed to inspire his purpose.*

* The reasons that made Napoleon resolve to attack the centre of the allies are set forth in 'Comment.,' v. 130, 198. See also Charras, i. 81.

The centre of the allies, therefore, their most vulnerable point, was to be assailed, pierced through, and mastered by the French; and incidentally the exposed corps of Zieten was to be caught and, if possible, overwhelmed and crushed. The forces, however, available for the enterprise were, we have seen, less than Napoleon had expected to have; the rising in La Vendée had made a large deduction from the 150,000 men on whom he had reckoned; he was unable to assemble even 130,000; and it was a perilous, if a daring, venture to attack enemies not far from twofold in numbers. But the great gambler with Fortune had thrown the die; it was now too late to abandon the mighty hazard.

The operations of Napoleon in bringing his army together, and placing it in positions from which it could spring into Belgium, were as brilliant and admirable as any of his life. The four corps d'armée, which, we have seen, had been in station between Lille and Metz, had been approaching each other by degrees. They were rapidly concentrated in the first days of June; by the 14th they had all but effected their junction. The long march near the edge of the frontier of France, though made quickly on the good lateral roads, and behind the screen of many a fortress, was not far from the allied outposts, and was thus difficult to conceal, and dangerous; but it was masked by that consummate skill in stratagem in which Napoleon has no equal among leaders of modern war. The French troops advanced behind detachments of National Guards placed near the frontier at different points; offensive demonstrations were made against Wellington's right in order to deceive the British commander; communication with Belgium was prevented along the whole line. Meanwhile, the single corps originally placed at Soissons had been moved from Laon to the verge of Belgium; the Imperial Guard and a great body of cavalry followed, and by June 14 these masses were in line with the four corps which had marched from between Lille and Metz.

The positions chosen for this great concentration of force had been indicated by Napoleon with characteristic skill. A strip of territory, now Belgian, but at that time French, extended beyond the fortresses of Maubeuge and Philippeville, from a centre, Beaumont, to within a few miles from Charleroy; this small tract, therefore, was opposite the great main road from Charleroy to Brussels, dividing the allied centre, and approached the camps of the corps of Zieten. It was crossed by lateral roads from Maubeuge to Philippeville, but it was separated from Charleroy by the stream of the Sambre. It was in part covered by woodland and forest, and it was connected with Charleroy by country roads only, which, we have seen, then alone existed on this part of the frontier. The whole French army, except a small detachment to the right, 128,000 strong all told, was aggregated on this strip by the night of June 14, on a front of some twenty miles in breadth by six or eight in depth; it was not more than half a day's march from Charleroy, and was almost within reach of part of the corps of Zieten; and it approached the weak allied centre on either side of the great main road from Charleroy to Brussels. This operation was one of the finest ever accomplished in war. By this time Blucher's army was in part in motion, but Wellington's army had not stirred, and the allies were still extended on their immense front, while their enemy was concentrated well-nigh within striking distance.*

The French army thus assembled, close to the edge of Belgium, with extraordinary celerity, secrecy, and skill,

* The concentration of the French army has been admired by all historians and commentators. It would be superfluous to multiply authorities. Napoleon remarks, 'Comment.,' v. 108, 'Ce plan fut conçu et executé avec audace et sagesse.' Wellington said to Greville, 'Memoirs,' i. 40, 'Bonaparte's march upon Belgium was the finest thing ever done.'

consisted of five corps d'armée, of nearly all the Imperial Guard,* and of four corps of the cavalry of the reserve—the usual organisation of this arm in the wars of the French Empire. The 1st corps, commanded by D'Erlon, was very nearly 20,000 strong; by the night of June 14 it was on the verge of the Sambre, between Solre and Solre-sur-Sambre, its advanced divisions but a short distance from Zieten's outposts. The 2nd corps, more than 24,000 men, and with Reille, an experienced chief, at its head, was also close to the Sambre, at Leers, a few miles to the right, and was even nearer Zieten's outposts, now at Lobbes and Thuin. The 3rd corps, rather more than 19,000 strong, was under the able but quarrelsome Vandamme, and was farther to the right, but not far from the Sambre. Behind Vandamme was the 6th corps of Lobau, about 10,500 strong; and, again, at a little distance in the rear was the Imperial Guard, almost 21,000 men, directly under the Emperor's orders, but with well-known lieutenants in command, both corps being just north of Beaumont—the centre, we have seen, of the whole army's position. Some miles to the right was the 4th corps, not quite 16,000 strong, with the brilliant and ambitious Gérard at its head; it was nearly all assembled around Philippeville, but one of its detachments was not yet in line—the single body that had not completely fulfilled its mission. In the rear of the five corps and the Guard were the four corps of the cavalry reserve, with Grouchy, for the present, General in chief, but having Pajol, Excelmans, Kellermann, and Milhaud —names of distinction in many a campaign—as subordinate leaders; they were composed of more than 13,000 men; they lay south of Beaumont, in the rear of the Imperial Guard.

The corps of D'Erlon and Reille, together nearly

* Part of the Imperial Guard, we have seen, had been sent into La Vendée.

45,000 strong, formed the left wing of the French army; the corps of Vandamme, Lobau, the Imperial Guard, and Grouchy's cavalry, in all about 64,000 men, were the centre; the corps of Gérard, almost 16,000 strong, was the right wing; and the whole army, reckoning some 3,500 non-combatants, made up, we have seen, a total of 128,000 men, with from 340 to 350 guns. The allied armies, we have said, were 220,000 strong. They had about 500 guns in the field, against 340 or 350; the disproportion between the forces of the belligerents was thus very great. But the disproportion was much greater in the memorable campaign of 1814, and even in other passages of Napoleon's career, and the Emperor had already gained a distinct advantage through the admirable concentration that had just been accomplished.*

* The numbers of the French army are those given by Charras, who has studied the subject with great care. The estimates of other writers are not widely different.

FIRST CORPS, D'ERLON :   Men.
    Infantry   16,885
    Cavalry   1,506
    Artillery, etc.   ...   . 1,548 and 46 guns.

        Total   19,939

SECOND CORPS, REILLE :
    Infantry   20,635
    Cavalry   1,865
    Artillery, etc.   ...   . 1,861 and 46 guns.

        Total   24,361

THIRD CORPS, VANDAMME :
    Infantry   16,851
    Cavalry   1,017
    Artillery, etc.   ...   . 1,292 and 38 guns.

        Total   19,160

SIXTH CORPS, LOBAU :
    Infantry   9,218
    Artillery, etc.   ...   . 1,247 and 32 guns.

        Total   10,465

We may now offer a few remarks on the qualities and the characteristics of the three armies soon to encounter each other in a terrible conflict. English and German writers have, not unnaturally, described the French army of 1815 as, perhaps, the finest ever led by Napoleon. This, however, is a complete mistake. This army was not to be compared as an instrument of war with the old Grand Army of Austerlitz, Jena and Friedland, by many degrees the best of the imperial armies. It was, indeed, composed, with scarcely an exception, of good regular troops, many veterans, nearly all having had years of service. It was animated by a fierce—nay, an heroic—spirit; it burned to meet enemies it regarded with deadly hatred; it deemed itself the avenger of France for many, and prolonged disasters. But its organisation was quite

FOURTH CORPS, GÉRARD :					Men.
Infantry	...	...	...	...	12,800
Cavalry	...	...	...	...	1,628
Artillery, etc.		...	...	...	1,567 and 38 guns.
Total			...	...	15,995

IMPERIAL GUARD, NAPOLEON :					
Infantry	...	...	...	...	13,026
Cavalry	...	...	...	...	3,795
Artillery, etc.		...	...	...	4,063 and 96 guns.
Total	...		...	...	20,884

RESERVE OF CAVALRY, GROUCHY :

FOUR CORPS UNDER PAJOL, EXCELMANS, KELLERMANN, AND MILHAUD (Sabres and Artillerymen) :

			Men.
Pajol and 12 guns	...	...	3,046
Excelmans and 12 guns		...	3,515
Kellermann and 12 guns		...	3,679
Milhaud and 12 guns		...	3,544
Total	...	...	13,784
Non-combatants	...	...	3,500

Grand total (in round numbers) 128,000 and 344 guns.

new, and was hastily made. Men and officers in the regiments scarcely knew each other, and had not been accustomed to act together; they had not the noble freemasonry of comrades in the field. The army, therefore, wanted stability, coherence, and power of endurance. The staff, seldom of real excellence in the army of France, was in this instance weak in numbers and ill-trained; the cavalry and artillery arms were, in the main, very good; but the infantry, except that of the Guard, was not equal in quality.

The material defects of the army, however, were less grave than those of a moral kind, and these greatly impaired its military strength and value. The soldiery had been shifted from one flag to another; they had been demoralised by the events of the last few months; their discipline had been much injured; the return from Elba had, so to speak, turned their heads, made them violent, disobedient, not easy to command. Worse than all, they had lost confidence in most of the highest chiefs, even in many officers at the head of regiments; they had seen these men abandon Napoleon in 1814, abandon the Bourbons a short time afterwards, and then return to Napoleon again. They looked on several Generals and Marshals with profound distrust. Their faith in the Emperor, indeed, remained unbounded; he was the god of their idolatry, perhaps more than ever; but they had learned from him the fatal lesson that treason had been the real cause of their defeats. They had laid this evil teaching to heart, and they were ready to believe that treason was, as it were, in the air around them. It has been truly said that this army was at once a most formidable but a most fragile instrument of war.*

The army of Wellington, all told, was about 106,000

---

* For an admirable and exhaustive description of the French army of 1815, the reader may be referred to H. Houssaye, ' 1815,' ii. 72-83. The sketch, too, of Charras (i. 59) is good. The English and German accounts are refuted by evidence that cannot be gainsaid.

men, with very nearly 200 guns; but more than 10,000 were left in garrisons. The field army was some 95,500 strong, with 186 pieces, a few heavy guns having been rather unaccountably not made use of. This army hardly deserved the angry reproach of its chief; it was not 'an infamous and very weak' army, but as a whole it was much the worst army he ever commanded. It was a motley array of many races and tongues, exhibiting the defects and mischiefs this necessarily involves, different modes of organisation and equipment, and differences in command. In the field army there were only about 34,000 British troops. Some regiments were Peninsular veterans, who 'could go anywhere and do anything'; but others were only second battalions, and had had little or no experience of the realities of war. The King's German Legion, more than 6,000 strong, was not inferior to the best British soldiers; but the Hanoverian and Brunswick contingents, not less than 22,500 men, were young levies, to a great extent landwehr; the Dutch, Belgians, and Nassauers, together more than 32,000, were largely composed of mere militia. The regular troops had served under the imperial eagles; the fidelity of this whole contingent was in some degree suspected. On the whole Wellington had not 50,000 thoroughly good troops, and though many of his auxiliaries did excellent service, they were not the men of the invincible Peninsular army. The Duke greatly complained of his staff, and it certainly failed him once or twice, and some of his subordinate officers had not much experience.

Turning to the three arms, the British cavalry was the best in the three armies, in some respects, especially in the shock of battle; but the rest of Wellington's cavalry was not very good; part of it, indeed, was of little value. The artillery, British and German, was an excellent force, but this can hardly be said of the artillery of the other contingents; as for the British infantry, and that of the

German Legion, it was incomparable for the precision and the power of its fire, for its steadiness, constancy, and stern endurance. Even the young British infantry had the same high qualities; the other infantry were not the 'robur peditum' of Roman story. On the whole, though Wellington's composite army was very imperfect as an instrument of war, it contained many elements of the very best kind, and it was held together by the orderly and strict discipline characteristic of every army under Wellington's command.*

* See, for a very fair and impartial account of Wellington's army, Chesney, 'Waterloo Lectures,' 67, 71 ; and also Charras, i. 73, 75. The subjoined estimate of its numbers is that of Charras, not widely different from that of Siborne, Hooper, and other writers :

FIRST CORPS, THE PRINCE OF ORANGE :

		Men.
Infantry ...	...	25,942
Cavalry ...	...	3,405
Artillery ...	...	2,198 and 64 guns.
Total ...	...	31,545

SECOND CORPS, HILL :

Infantry	...	24,499
Cavalry	...	1,277
Artillery	...	1,472 and 40 guns.
Total	...	27,248

RESERVE, WELLINGTON :

Infantry	...	20,315
Cavalry	...	822
Artillery	...	1,900 and 52 guns.
Total	...	23,037

CORPS OF CAVALRY, UXBRIDGE :

22 squadrons heavy ...	...	2,605
49 squadrons light	...	7,908
Artillery	...	1,300 and 30 guns.
Total ...	...	11,813
Non-combatants ...	...	1,860
Grand total ...	...	95,503 and 186 guns, and 1 rocket battery.

The army of Blucher, according to the best estimate—
this is, however, higher than that of most German writers
—was just more than 124,000 strong, with, it is said, 312
guns.   This great force was partly composed of landwehr,
and had had a mutinous Saxon contingent, which had
certainly set a bad example, but had been severely
punished and sent away from the theatre of war.   It had
the defects of the admixture of a militia with regular
troops; but it was on the whole a formidable military
array.   Napoleon certainly underrated its intense moral
energy; perhaps, owing to the memories of Jena, Montmirail and Vauchamps, he thought it immeasurably inferior to the army he led.   But it had nothing in common
with the serf-like levies of Hohenlohe and Brunswick; it
was the living incarnation of the hatred Prussia bore
towards France; it was animated by fierce resentment
for the oppression of years, for the wrongs of a nation
trodden down by a despot.   In 1814 it had risen superior
to defeat; it was to prove that it was capable of most
remarkable efforts.

Of its arms the cavalry was not equal to the French;
the artillery was distinctly inferior; but the regular
infantry were probably better, always excepting the footmen of the Imperial Guard, foemen worthy of the steel of
the best British and German infantry.   In one respect, of
supreme importance, the Prussian army had a decided
advantage over its enemy.   The French soldiery, we have
seen, had become in some degree demoralised—deficient,
at least, in coherence and staying power; above all, they
had little confidence in most of their chiefs, and even in
many of their regimental leaders.   It was exactly the contrary in the case of the Prussian soldiery; they had the
passion for vengeance, but also the steady Teutonic constancy; they looked up to their Generals and officers with
implicit trust, and followed their bidding with eager and
loyal obedience.   As for their aged Commander-in-Chief—
their beloved " Marshal Vorwarts '—whether in victory or

in disaster—they had known both—they were as devoted to him as his Guard was to Napoleon; they had done, and were to do, great things under his inspiring guidance.*

* The reader may be referred to Charras (i. 75) for an accurate and vivid description of the Prussian army of 1815. This corresponds to that of some German writers; and see Hooper (39) and Chesney's 'Waterloo Lectures,' 67. It may be remarked here that Ropes ('The Campaign of Waterloo,' 25) thus fairly sums up his estimate of the three armies: 'It is not correct to say that the army which Napoleon led into Belgium was the finest he had ever commanded, but it is quite certain it was the best of the three armies then in the field.' With respect to the numbers of the Prussian armies, the estimate of Charras has been followed, as in the case of the two others; it is probably accurate, but certainly, as before observed, it exceeds the estimate of some German commentators. See, as to the authorities relied on by Charras, the notes A, B, C, at the end of the work (ii. 214-216). No writer seems to have so thoroughly studied this part of the subject.

FIRST CORPS, ZIETEN: Men.
  Infantry   27,887
  Cavalry   1,925
  Artillery, etc.   ...   ...   2,880 and 96 guns.
                                       ————
        Total   32,692

SECOND CORPS, PIRCH:
  Infantry   25,836
  Cavalry   4,468
  Artillery, etc.   ...   ...   2,400 and 80 guns.
                                       ————
        Total   32,704

THIRD CORPS, THIELMANN:
  Infantry   20,611
  Cavalry   2,405
  Artillery, etc.   ...   ...   1,440 and 48 guns.
                                       ————
        Total   24,456

FOURTH CORPS, BULOW:
  Infantry   25,381
  Cavalry   3,081
  Artillery, etc.   ...   ...   2,640 and 88 guns.
                                       ————
        Total   31,102

Non-combatants   3,120
                                       ————
        Grand total ...   . 124,074 and 312 guns.

From the belligerent armies we turn to their chiefs, and first to the Napoleon of 1815. Spite of the malice of petty detractors, history has long ago marked out this extraordinary man as foremost among the masters of modern war. His powerful imagination, his supreme faculty of seeing what is essential to be done in a sphere of action, his penetration, his intense application to details, made him unrivalled in the grand domain of strategy; in forming the combinations on which the issue of large military operations so often depends, he has had no equal, if, perhaps, we may except Hannibal. Nor was he less admirable as a strategist on the field of manœuvre; in his fine movements between divided enemies, in reaching the communications, the flank, and the rear of a hostile army, he was pre-eminent among the commanders of all time. The most distinctive of his excellences, perhaps, as a strategist was his power in perceiving and occupying the decisive points on a theatre of war; this was exhibited over and over again—never more clearly than in his last and fatal campaign. As a tactician Napoleon was less conspicuous; he commanded in chief at too early an age to have perfectly understood the uses of the three arms; he was often too ardent and obstinate in the stress of battle; but in the domain of the greater tactics, where strategy and tactics run into each other, his superiority almost, if not altogether, reappears. He has been surpassed in tenacity and perseverance in war; but in dexterity, in the gift of stratagem, of concealing his operations to the latest moment, of extricating himself from surrounding dangers, scarcely any commander can be compared to him. Nevertheless—for humanity is not

---

This estimate is considerably higher than that of Wagner, who has composed the official Prussian account of the campaign of 1815, and of Damitz, also a Prussian writer. Siborne ('The Waterloo Campaign,' 76, 1895 edition), makes the numbers 116,807 men and 312 guns; Ropes ('The Campaign of Waterloo,' 32, 33) follows Charras.

5

perfect—the great master was sometimes untrue to his art; errors and extravagances may be seen in much that he accomplished in it. Overconfidence was Napoleon's distinctive fault; his conceptions and projects were occasionally too ambitious; no General has run such tremendous risks, or has so boldly played double or quits with Fortune. We see this in his career from Montenotte to Waterloo. This defect, too, was increased, not diminished, by long experience; it was aggravated by success that has never had a parallel.

Napoleon defied Nature and space in the campaign of 1812; in that of 1813 he attempted what was far beyond his power; even in his magnificent campaign of 1814 he struck for an Empire already lost, and threw away resources that might have saved his throne. It was a kindred fault that he was given to underrate his enemies: in 1813 he thought he could conquer Europe with newly-raised levies; he undervalued Wellington and Blucher in 1815; it was unfortunate for him that he had never beheld a British army, save in a disastrous retreat, and would not acknowledge its best qualities until it was too late. As age advanced, too, Napoleon became almost obstinate in the convictions he had once formed in the field; he had been so often right that he believed he could never be wrong; he grew fixed in ideas he would not give up; he had lost the nimbleness, so to speak, of the General of 1796. In 1815, however, what was most wanting in him was, we have seen, physical health and moral energy; these failings became manifest in several passages of the campaign.

As for Napoleon's lieutenants, for many reasons they were not very good subordinate chiefs; they were inferior to their predecessors in the old Grand Army, inferior to what they had been in the day of success. Nearly all, indeed, had had large experience in the field; all were in the vigour and prime of manhood; several had a military reputation of a high order. But they were ill-fitted in many respects for the positions they held; this was the more unfortunate because Napoleon, though his superiority and despotism bowed them to his will, expected great things from them when in independent command. Soult, the new chief of the staff, a post of the first importance, was a very able but an indolent man; he had had no experience in the office so well filled by Berthier; he was disliked—nay, detested—throughout the army; he was to prove himself unequal to his task in 1815.* Grouchy was a good—nay, a brilliant—cavalry officer; but he had failed at Bantry in 1796; he had never been at the head of a large separate force; his name since Waterloo has become a byword.† As for Ney, the third of the Marshals in the present campaign, he was an heroic soldier of the best type; but he had not the qualities of a General-in-Chief; he was heady, impetuous, easily carried away; in 1815 he was the prey of remorse caused by the consciousness of a double treason; he was to fight, so to speak, with a halter around his neck; his companions in arms—nay, the Emperor—regarded him with distrust.

The commanders of corps d'armée, as a rule, were capable men; but D'Erlon had been a laggard in Spain; Vandamme had not forgotten the disaster of Culm; Reille had Vittoria deeply engraved in his mind. All these chiefs were bad successors of men like Desaix, Kléber, Masséna, Lannes, Davoût, and others; and, with the exception of Gérard, who ought to have had the place of Grouchy, they were to be inferior to their former selves. Nevertheless, personal defects and failings like these were not the only, or perhaps the principal, causes of the inefficiency, in the higher commands, in the French army. The

* Soult had neglected, a bad beginning, to send orders to the cavalry reserves, when the march to the frontier was made: H. Houssaye, ' 1815,' ii. 100.

† Pasquier ('Mémoires,' iii. 232) relates that Soult and other Generals warned Napoleon beforehand not to give Grouchy an independent command in 1815.

Marshals and Generals, better informed than the soldiery, knew that Europe was in arms against their master, were terrified and unnerved at the prospect before them. A few, too, regretted, at least, the fall of the Bourbons, who had secured for them a season of repose; sighed that they could not enjoy their riches and honours in peace; saw in Napoleon an assurance of internecine war, of disaster for France, of ruin for themselves. Nearly all, besides, felt that they did not possess the full confidence of their troops, as had been the case in the years of victory; that they were looked upon with more or less suspicion; that they were not at the head of devoted followers. These things all concurred with evil effects to demoralise and impair the worth of most of Napoleon's lieutenants in 1815.*

Passing on to the leaders of the allied armies, Wellington properly demands our first attention. This great General, greater still as a man, was not a strategist of the first order; in the great combinations of war he is not to be named with Napoleon. He was to give conspicuous proof of this in the campaign of 1815. Even in his admirable and triumphant career in Spain he did not shine in the sphere of strategy, though the Emperor was utterly in the wrong in describing him as 'incapable and unwise.' His advance on Talavera, excuse it as we may, very nearly involved him in a great disaster. It was well that Napoleon was not in his front when, at Busaco, he offered Masséna battle, for in all probability he would have had his left flank turned, and could hardly have reached the celebrated lines. He was outmanoeuvred by Marmont before Salamanca. But Wellington had in the highest degree quick and clear perception, and a thoroughly sound judgment. He was well acquainted

* H. Houssaye ('1815,' ii. 70-75) has given us an admirable description of the French Generals of the campaign of 1815. See also Napoleon, 'Comment.,' v. 198, 199, and Charras, i. 59, 60.

with the uses of every arm, especially of the great arm of infantry. He was a tactician of the very first quality, brilliant and energetic when on the offensive, in defence giving proof of real genius. His supreme excellence, however, was tenacity and strength of character. No commander in the great struggle of 1793 to 1815 presented a grander or more imposing spectacle than when he hung to a rock in Portugal, defying the gigantic military power of France, and, spite of neglect in England and a prostrate Continent, confident that success would ultimately attend his efforts; and in all his campaigns we see in him this master-faculty, the best Napoleon has said that a soldier can have. Wellington had not encountered Napoleon before. He had had to deal only with French Generals immeasurably inferior to their great master, and divided besides by jealous discords; and there can be no doubt that in 1815 he not only did not fathom his mighty adversary's designs, but was disconcerted by his splendid and well-concealed movements. He was to be out-generalled in the first instance, he was to commit unquestionable strategic mistakes; but his best qualities were to appear in complete fulness on the great day of Waterloo. For the rest, Wellington's lieutenants, if we except Hill and Picton, were not Generals of a high order; but many were tried and excellent soldiers. Two, Perponcher and Chassé, in the Dutch service, were on critical occasions to stand him in the best stead.*

---

* Charras has given in i. 77 this discriminating and striking portrait of Wellington: ' Il n'était qu'un général de talent, mais d'un talent, si complet, enté sur de si fortes qualités, qu'il atteignait presque au génie. Doué d'un bon sens extrême ; politique profond ; religieux observateur des lois de son pays ; excellent appreciateur des hommes ; instruit à fond de tout ce qui constitue la science et le métier des armes ; faisant parfois des fautes, mais sachant ne pas s'y obstiner après les avoir reconnues, soigneux du bien être de ses soldats, menager de leur sang ; dur au désordre, impitoyable aux déprédateurs ; habile à concevoir et à exécuter ; prudent ou hardi, temporiseur ou actif selon la circonstance ; inébranlable dans la mauvaise

The master-spirit of the Prussian army differed widely
from Wellington in many respects, yet the two chiefs had
several points in common. Blucher was a veteran of the
school of Frederick. He had been a fighting man from
his first youth ; but if, as a soldier, he had heroic qualities,
he had no knowledge of the highest parts of war. He
was sometimes imprudent—nay, reckless—in the field. He
had over and over again been struck down by Napoleon,
whose skill, resource, craft, and strategic genius had
turned his faults to the best account, and had inflicted on
him terrible defeats ; but he had always risen superior to
adverse fortune, and more than once, even after a grave
reverse, he had baffled his great adversary by his bold
movements, and by the energy and vigour of his strokes.

Blucher was not a tactician of a high order ; he too
often threw away his troops to little purpose. His
arrangements on the field were sometimes very faulty.
But he had one advantage which Wellington did not
possess : long and bitter experience had made him familiar
with Napoleon's methods in war. However unable he
was to cope with these, he perfectly understood how
promptitude was required to deal with the antagonist he
had met from Jena to Montmirail. In tenacity and
endurance Blucher resembled his colleague. It was said
of him that 'he never knew when he was beaten,' a
phrase since applied to the British soldier ; and, like
Wellington, he was not afraid of Napoleon, here very
different from the Archduke Charles, who, though a
better strategist than either, could not overcome his
dread of his great enemy, which had something to do
with the result at Wagram. Blucher was superior to
Wellington in one great quality : his officers and men

---

fortune rebelle aux enivrements du succès ; âme de fer dans un
corps de fer ; Wellington avec une petite armée avait fait de grandes
choses ; et cette armée était son ouvrage. Il devait rester ; et il
restera une des grandes figures militaires de ce siècle.'

were passionately attached to him, and he obtained from them astonishing efforts. The British General, unlike Marlborough, was here wanting; he was respected as a commander, not loved. This was one reason that he was never supreme in victory. As for Blucher's lieutenants, his chief of the staff, Gneisenau, was a learned and scientific officer; but he was suspicious, irritable, and disliked Wellington. The one great movement he was to make in 1815, extolled as it has been by the worshippers of success, was a dangerous half-measure that ought to have been fatal, and he was to be irresolute at the moment of extreme trial. Apart from Bulow, who, however, was to do little in this campaign, Blucher's other subordinates were not remarkable men, but all were to prove themselves to be good soldiers. Their chief, nevertheless, towered over all his fellows; he was to exhibit in the impending contest his defects, indeed, but his very best qualities. In a deadly encounter the rude but undaunted swordsman was to deceive, and finally to pierce through, the perfect fencer.*

---

* Charras has also described Blucher well (ii. 76) : 'Esprit peu cultivé, nature rude, passioné pour le plaisir autant que pour la guerre, Blucher n'atteignait pas au premier rang ; mais un caractère indomptable, un patriotisme ardent, une activité extrême, en dépit de la viellesse, une persévérance que rien ne laissait, une grande audace et une grande habitude de la tactique et de la strategie de Napoléon, en faîsait un adversaire de réelle valeur.'

CHAPTER IV

THE OPERATIONS OF JUNE 15, 1815

Napoleon at Beaumont—His address to his army—His orders for the
march into Belgium—Advance of the French army—Delays—
Vandamme—The desertion of Bourmont—The French army
crosses the Sambre—Napoleon at Charleroy—His orders—The
loss of time caused by delays and accidents unfavourable to the
French—The retreat of Zieten—Arrival of Ney—Napoleon's
orders to the Marshal—Ney does not occupy Quatre Bras—
Combat at Gilly—Positions of the French army on the evening
of the 15th—Great advantage already secured by Napoleon—
Dispositions of Blucher and Wellington — The Prussian army
directed to Sombreffe—Bulow cannot join it—Delays and hesitations of Wellington—Part of his army directed to Quatre Bras,
but very late—Examination of the allied strategy—The allied
armies in a critical position.

HAVING left Paris, we have seen, at the earliest dawn,
Napoleon made a halt at Laon on June 12; he stayed at
Avesnes, near the frontier, on the following day; he had
reached his camp at Beaumont by the fourteenth. The
army welcomed its chief with frenzied acclaim; 'it was
maddening,' an eye-witness wrote, 'to come to blows with
the enemy.' Every precaution had been taken to conceal
the positions it held; it lay behind woodlands stretching
towards the Sambre; the fires of the bivouacs had been
lit in folds of the ground. The Emperor had spoken to
his troops in an address despatched from Avesnes; he
reminded them of the glories of the past, but let them

know that a tremendous struggle was at hand, and that everything must depend on their efforts. In the impassioned and magical language he had made his own, ' This,' he said, ' is the anniversary of Marengo and Friedland, which had twice decided the fortunes of Europe; but then, as after Austerlitz, as after Wagram, we had been too generous . . . to the Kings we had left on their thrones.' These men ' had now formed a league to subvert the most sacred rights of France; they had set the most unjust of aggressions on foot; let us therefore march forward to meet them; are not we and they the same men ? . . . At Jena, the Prussians, so arrogant to-day, were three to one against you; at Montmirail you were one to six; as for the English, let those who have been their prisoners tell the tale of the miseries and tortures of their hulks !' Napoleon then held out hopes that the League of Europe would break up. ' The Saxons, the Belgians, the men of Hanover, the soldiers of the Confederation of the Rhine, are groaning that they are forced to lend their arms to the cause of Princes, foes of justice and of the rights of nations; they know that this coalition will never have enough. . . . Madmen ! a moment of good fortune has blinded their eyes. The oppression and the humiliation of France is above their power; let them enter her borders, they will find a grave. Soldiers, we have forced marches to make, to fight battles, to encounter perils, but with perseverance victory will be ours; the rights, the honour, the happiness of our country will be regained. For every Frenchman who has a heart the time has come to conquer or to die.'*

Within a few hours Napoleon had issued his orders for the leap into Belgium on which he had staked his fortunes. The whole army, converging on a narrowing front, was to cross the Sambre, and, assembling in or near Charleroy, to take possession of the town, and thus to reach the

* See the address at length, Napoleon Correspondence, xxviii. 288.

southern end of the great main road from Charleroy to
Brussels. The dispositions of the great master, admirably
designed, were arranged to assure celerity, certainty, and
regularity in this fine movement.* Reille, on the left,
was to break up his camp at three in the morning; he
was to march down the southern bank of the Sambre,
to seize any bridges on the river in his way, to be at
Marchiennes, a small town two or three miles from
Charleroy, and to take possession of the bridge at that
place, where 'he was probably to arrive by nine in the
forenoon.' D'Erlon was to follow the movement from
Solre and Solre-sur-Sambre, leaving his camp at the same
hour as Reille, but keeping some distance in his rear;
he was to occupy Thuin, a few miles to the west of
Marchiennes, and he was to send small detachments
across the Sambre towards Mons and Binche, where it
was known that a part of Wellington's left was in station.
At the centre Vandamme was to be on the march at three
in the morning, preceded by Pajol and a body of light
cavalry; Lobau and his corps were to be on the track of
Vandamme at an hour's interval. The Imperial Guard
was to be in motion at five and six; Grouchy and most of
his cavalry were to cover the flanks of the columns. This
great mass was to make straight, from around Beaumont,
for Charleroy—a distance of from ten to fifteen miles—and
to become master of the town as quickly as possible. To
the right, Gérard was to begin the movement also at
three, if practicable, having called in his detachment; he,
too, was to advance with his corps on Charleroy, and
therefore to come into line with the centre, which was
thus to be in very great force. The Emperor announced
that it was his purpose 'that the army should have got
over the Sambre before noon,' at the two points of
Marchiennes and Charleroy; and admirable precautions

* For these orders, see Napoleon Correspondence, xxviii. 281, 286.
They have been praised by all historians and critics.

had been taken to ensure in all respects the success of
the movement. The sappers of every corps were to be
close to the front, and the materials for bridging the river
at these places were ready, for Napoleon evidently expected that he would find the bridges on the Sambre
broken down, and had made provision for this contingency. At the same time the impedimenta of the whole
army were to be left in the rear, in order that the march
should be made with extreme rapidity; any vehicles found
on the line of the movement, in contravention of this
order, were to be instantly burnt.

The objects of Napoleon in designing this march are
evident to a certain extent, but some have been questioned
by different writers, though little doubt can now exist on
the subject. His first intention was, if possible, to destroy
the corps of Zieten, which, we have said, was dangerously
exposed; one of its divisions, that of Pirch II.,* being
along the Sambre, from beyond Marchiennes to the east
of Charleroy; another, that of Steinmetz, being around
Fontaine l'Évêque; and further, in communication with
the left of Wellington, a third, at Fleurus, rather distant
from the other two; a fourth, still at a greater distance,
at Moustier-sur-Sambre. It might be practicable, therefore, to attack this corps—to cut off and overwhelm its
two first divisions, and, not improbably, to strike down
the third by making a rapid movement across the Sambre,
and reaching the enemy at an early hour; and this was
primarily, so to speak, Napoleon's purpose.† It may be,
too, he hoped that Blucher, so often rash, would hastily
advance to support Zieten, and thus would lay himself open
to defeat, though this would seem to be hardly probable.

But Napoleon, we believe, had a deeper ulterior object,
which seems to be established by clear evidence, if a few

* This general is not to be confounded with Pirch, the chief of
Blucher's 2nd corps.

† Napoleon Correspondence, xxviii. 286 : letter to Davoût.

critics remain sceptical. His great aim in his operations, we have said, was to pierce through the weak centre of the allies, and thus to gain an opportunity of defeating them in detail; this was the calculation on which his hopes rested. But to attain this end it was essential, if he was not to run great risks, to secure a position on the allied centre, from whence he could strike the heads of the enemy's columns, should these converge against him from either side, and where he could safely maintain his ground, until he could successfully throw back their forces and fall on their armies when fully apart. Such a position existed, and was well known to the Emperor; it extended upon a wide lateral road running from Namur to Nivelles, and thence to Brussels, and forming the main communication between Blucher and Wellington in their headquarters at Namur and Brussels. At Quatre Bras it crossed the great main road from Charleroy to Brussels, and at Sombreffe, about seven miles from Quatre Bras, it reached a point, on the lateral road, not far from Namur. Could Napoleon, therefore, occupy the two places of Quatre Bras and Sombreffe, in force, he would be able to confront either Blucher or Wellington, or both —their armies being widely dispersed, they would, in all human probability, be very inferior in numbers to his own—with the prospect of almost assured success, and then he would have every chance of separating and beating them in detail. The main and paramount object of the Emperor was, accordingly, to advance to Quatre Bras and Sombreffe on June 15, to seize and to occupy both points, and this was the true reason why he was to make a forced march of extreme celerity on the first day of the campaign. Quatre Bras and Sombreffe are considerably more than twenty miles distant from the encampments of the French army on the night of the 14th.*

* Mr. Ropes is much the ablest of the writers who have argued that it was not Napoleon's intention to take possession of Quatre Bras and

The execution of Napoleon's projects for June 15 was, from different causes, unequal to the design. Reille, on the left, was on the march by the appointed time; he advanced along the edge of the Sambre by difficult roads; but he had soon mastered the bridge at Thuin, had driven in the Prussian outposts and made prisoners—the troops of Pirch II. steadily fell back before him—and had reached Marchiennes by about ten in the forenoon, having effected his movement rapidly and with success. He found the bridge at Marchiennes intact, a circumstance very favourable to the French. He proceeded to cross the river with his troops, an operation, however, which necessarily took some time. His colleague, D'Erlon, had been much less active; he had not left his camp

---

Sombreffe on June 15. In a learned and exhaustive note ('The Campaign of Waterloo,' 8-15), he contends that Napoleon's real purpose was only to fight the Prussians on that day, and that he did not aim at Quatre Bras or Sombreffe. He cites Napoleon, Wellington and Clausewitz as authorities. Now, it is true that Napoleon, in a controversy with Rogniat ('Comment.,' vi. 146), did assert that he did not mean to occupy Sombreffe on the 15th; but in his elaborate narrative of the campaign ('Comment.,' v. 199) he has declared that his intention 'was to have his headquarters at Fleurus on that day,' which necessarily implied the occupation of Sombreffe. And Charras very properly remarks that a statement in a mere literary dispute may be rejected. As for Wellington, writing through Lord Ellesmere, and Clausewitz, they only point out that it could not have been Napoleon's only object to interpose at Quatre Bras and Sombreffe between the hostile armies; and this is really a truism. But that Napoleon had resolved to occupy Quatre Bras and Sombreffe on the 15th is proved by overwhelming evidence. The *Moniteur* of June 18 and Napoleon Correspondence (xxviii. 288) expressly state that Ney was at Quatre Bras on the evening of the 15th, of course by Napoleon's orders; and Grouchy, cited by H. Houssaye ('Waterloo,' 120, 121), positively says that he was directed to occupy Sombreffe, and Ney to occupy Quatre Bras, on that day. Jomini, too, a contemporaneous writer, who knew the opinions prevailing in the French army, has no doubt on the subject ('Précis de la Campagne de 1815,' 153); and he is followed by Charras and many other authorities. On the whole, the evidence seems conclusive that Quatre Bras and Sombreffe were to be held by the French on June 15.

until after four, and he did not reach the Sambre at Marchiennes until the early afternoon, a circumstance not without untoward results afterwards. At the centre Pajol had with his horsemen made for Charleroy; he was in the saddle at three in the morning, and had approached the town by about nine. He tried ineffectually to seize the bridge on the Sambre, but he was compelled to make a halt and to wait for infantry. Like Reille, he, too, had taken a few hundred prisoners, and the Prussians had shown a disposition to retreat. Vandamme ought to have been in the immediate rear of Pajol, but Soult had sent the Emperor's orders by a single officer, who had not delivered them owing to a severe hurt.* Vandamme and his corps were still in their bivouacs by seven in the morning; in fact, he had heard nothing of the intended movement until Lobau and his troops had come into line with him, these having not left their camp until four, as had been directed, and being a considerable distance behind. The advance of Napoleon's centre had been thus retarded; unfortunate occurrences also had kept back his right. Gérard had been unable to move until five in the morning, his detachment having taken some time to join him. He also had to march by bad roads through an intricate country. It was after seven before he reached Florennes, a village only a few miles from his camp at Philippeville. His advance had besides been checked by an incident of inauspicious omen. One of his subordinates, Bourmont, an old émigré, had suddenly deserted with two or three officers, and gone over to the enemy's camp; Gérard was compelled to halt and to address the infuriated troops, suspicious, restless, wanting

---

* We know from the 'Souvenirs' of the Duc de Fezensac that the staff service in the French army, even at its best, was far from perfect. But it was bad in the campaign of 1815, and Soult was not up to his work. See, as to Soult, Thiébault, 'Mémoires,' v. 354. Thiébault, however, disliked Soult.

in strict discipline, and this had detained him for some time.

The march of the French army had thus been delayed, in different degrees, along the whole line; the success of the Emperor's plans was already threatened. Napoleon made an effort at once to repair the mischief done; he pushed forward a part of the Imperial Guard,* taking a road by the left to support Pajol; he directed Vandamme to advance as quickly as possible; he ordered Gérard not to march upon Charleroy, but to reach Châtelet, a few miles to the east of Charleroy, and to cross the Sambre by the bridge at that place. The Emperor then pressed onwards to Charleroy, at the head of his central column. He found the bridge on the Sambre, as at Marchiennes, unbroken; Pajol's cavalry and the detachment of the guard defiled, as rapidly as they could, through the narrow streets of the old town, the Prussians having evacuated the place. It was now about noon. Napoleon passed through Charleroy, the soldiery and the population greeting him with enthusiastic shouts. He took his station just outside the town, at the end of the great main road from Charleroy to Brussels, having thus gained the first move in his memorable game. To his right were the soldiery of Pirch II. in retreat; in his front, but at a distance, was the division of Steinmetz, falling back from its positions around Fontaine l'Évêque and beyond, at the intelligence of the advance of Reille. To the northwards, from twelve to fourteen miles away, were the two important points of Quatre Bras and Sombreffe, the first on the great main road from Charleroy to Brussels, the second near a main road from Charleroy, by Fleurus, the Emperor, we have said, having resolved to reach and occupy both. Had the French army—as had been Napoleon's purpose, and as, indisputably, was quite

* This was part of the Young Guard, composed, to some extent, of picked volunteers.

possible—been in force across the Sambre 'before noon,'
it is difficult to see how the two exposed divisions, at least,
of Zieten could have escaped destruction, and Quatre
Bras and Sombreffe could have been mastered before the
evening had closed.

But invaluable time had been unfortunately lost.
D'Erlon, on the left, and Gérard, on the right, were still
far from the positions they had been expected to hold.
The centre had been long kept back by the misadventure
of Vandamme; some hours were required before Vandamme and the other corps of the centre could be at or
near Charleroy. Napoleon was, therefore, compelled to
pause; but he made preparations for a forward movement, intending, no doubt, to carry out his object. The
troops of Pajol had been already despatched to observe
the enemy on the great main-road from Charleroy to
Brussels so often mentioned, and on the road from
Charleroy to Sombreffe by Fleurus; the Emperor sent
Lefebvre-Desnoëttes with the light cavalry of the Guard
and one regiment to support Pajol on the first road, and
a small part of the infantry of the Guard on the second,
for the same purpose. A short time afterwards he
directed Reille and D'Erlon to advance from Marchiennes
to occupy Gosselies, a village upon the great main-road,
and 'to attack the enemy, who seemed to be making a
stand at that place.'* This enemy was the division of
Steinmetz in retreat; it had been joined by part of the
division from Fleurus sent on by Zieten.

It was now between three and four in the afternoon.
Part of the Guard in the rear and the corps of Vandamme
were issuing from the streets of Charleroy,† but Lobau
had not as yet come up. To the left Reille was on the
march to Gosselies, but D'Erlon had hardly reached

* See Soult's letters to D'Erlon, 3 and 4.30 p.m., on the 15th :
La Tour d'Auvergne, 'Waterloo,' 63, 66.
  † Charras, i. 88.

Marchiennes. The heads of Gérard's columns had only attained Châtelet, where, too, the bridge on the Sambre had not been broken. Five, or even six, hours had thus been lost. This delay, we repeat, had probably saved half, at least, of the corps of Zieten; but Zieten not the less deserves praise for his skilful operations on June 15. He had long before informed his chief that the French were at hand. Blucher had ordered him to fall back on Fleurus, but to hold the enemy in check as long as was possible. He had very ably fulfilled his mission. One great mistake had, no doubt, been made—the bridges on the Sambre had not been broken, as Napoleon expected would have been the case, and this had facilitated the Emperor's march; but the very same mistake, we shall see, was made in the campaign on a greater occasion, and Zieten may have acted on superior orders.* Zieten had, on the whole, admirably performed his task; his two divisions of Pirch II. and Steinmetz had retreated with comparatively little loss. The first was safe, for the moment, beyond Charleroy, on the way to Fleurus, its point of assembly; the second was near Gosselies, also on the march to Fleurus, and it was to escape an attack without much injury. Zieten had judiciously sent reinforcements to both, and he was not to lose more than 2,000 men in the day.† He had also in some measure retarded the enemy, and he had now placed the division of Pirch II., supported by detachments from the rear, in a position of vantage a few miles east of Charleroy, where he was to delay for a time the advance of Napoleon. Few operations of the kind have been better conducted in war.‡

* Charras (i. 71, 104) implies this. See also some remarks of Colonel (now General) Maurice, *United Service Magazine*, ' Waterloo,' October, 1890.

† The Prussian official account only makes the loss of Zieten 1,200 men, but nearly all writers make it 2,000. See Chesney, ' Waterloo Lectures,' 94, 95.

‡ General Hamley (' Operations of War,' 133, 134, 1889 edition)

6

While Napoleon had been pressing forwards the advance of his troops—that is, between three and four in the afternoon*—Ney joined the Emperor at his station outside Charleroy. The Marshal had not as yet obtained a command; he had been summoned to the scene at the very last moment; he had hurried from Paris, without a staff, without orders, and with only one aide-de-camp. Napoleon bade him welcome, and gave him directions, the import of which can be no longer doubtful. Ney was to take the command of the corps of Reille and D'Erlon— that is, of the left wing of the army; he was also to have in his hands the light cavalry of the Guard, sent forward, we have said, a short time before; but he was not to make use of this choice force, because he would be supported on the following day by Kellermann's body of heavy cavalry; and with the troops at present under his orders—that is, about 45,000 men—he was to occupy the position of Quatre Bras, and to drive back any enemy he might find on the great main road from Charleroy to Brussels.† The Marshal set off at once to perform his

---

singles out Zieten's operations as a fine specimen of the value of a 'retarding force.' See also General Maurice, *ante*. It seems to be not exactly known where Zieten was on the 15th. Charras also highly praises Zieten.

* The time—a matter of some importance—is fixed by H. Houssaye ('1815,' ii. 119) beyond dispute, by conclusive evidence. The only statement to the contrary is that of Heymès, Ney's single aide-de-camp; but Heymès wrote to exculpate his chief, and his work, too easily credited by many writers, abounds in errors, and even falsehoods, and is not in any sense trustworthy.

† The substance of this order is that which is found in the narrative of Heymès, with the exception of the direction to occupy Quatre Bras, which Heymès—from an obvious motive—Charras, and other writers have omitted. But, as has been pointed out *ante*, the *Moniteur* of June 18, the Napoleon Correspondence, and Grouchy — contemporaneous evidence—prove that Ney was ordered to occupy Quatre Bras on June 15, 1815. The reader should refer to the statements of Grouchy, who had no interest here not to tell the truth : ' Observations sur la Campagne de 1815,' 1818 edition, p. 32 ; and ' Relation

task; but in this, as in all the passages of the campaign, he was to be utterly inferior to his old self. As we have said, he had been demoralised by his late flagrant treason; he knew that even Napoleon viewed him with distrust; he stood ill in the opinion of the army and of the public; he detested Soult, the new chief of the staff; he was unnerved by remorse and conflicting passions. He had been so injudicious, too, as to repeat to his master the unhappy phrase about the iron cage; he had been relegated to a kind of obscurity during weeks, after the return from Elba; his discomposure had been noticed at the Champ de Mai; the Emperor had abstained from giving him a command until the army had passed the frontier, and he had received his command under the very worst conditions. Ney was to show that he was a different being from the warrior of Elchingen, and of the retreat from Moscow; and it should be added that, if he was still 'the bravest of the brave,' he had never exhibited the powers of a General-in-Chief.

Ney had reached Gosselies—some five or six miles from Charleroy—by about half after four in the afternoon; he found Reille engaged with the division of Steinmetz, in retreat, we have said, from Fontaine l'Évéque, and still further, on Fleurus. The Prussians effected their escape without much loss—they had been admirably led by Steinmetz* — and they made their way to Heppignies,

---

Succincte de la Campagne de 1815,' p. 12, and appendices. Heymès, indeed, says in his work that Napoleon, he infers, did not give this part of the order; and Soult said, many years after the event, that he did not recollect its being given. But Heymès is not a faithworthy witness, and Thiers ('Histoire du Consulat et de l'Empire,' vi. 436, 437) has proved that Soult acknowledged the order was made. Jomini, again ('Précis de la Campagne de 1815,' 153, and see 265 *et seq.*), has no doubts on the subject. That the order was given is established as certainly as anything in the campaign.

* This distinguished soldier survived to see the war of 1870, and held an important command at Gravelotte.

whence they reached, without difficulty, the point where they were to assemble. Ney was now in command of the whole corps of Reille, composed of four divisions of infantry and of a body of light horsemen; the corps of D'Erlon from Marchiennes was, in part, not far off; the great main-road from Charleroy to Brussels had been laid open by the enemy's retreat; it was hardly more than five in the afternoon; Quatre Bras was not more than seven or eight miles distant. It might have been supposed that the Marshal would push forward a considerable part, at least, of the corps of Reille, to carry out the Emperor's orders and seize Quatre Bras; but at this point the hesitations and delays began, which he was to exhibit on many occasions in the campaign. He detached, probably by Napoleon's directions, one of Reille's divisions, that of Girard, to follow and to observe Steinmetz; but he left two, those of Jerôme Bonaparte and Foy, at Gosselies. He marched the fourth, that of Bachelu, only to Mellet, about two miles on the road to Quatre Bras, and he advanced with the light cavalry of the Guard, which, it will be borne in mind, he was not to engage, and perhaps with the light cavalry of the corps of Reille, under Piré.

On reaching Frasnes, rather more than two miles from Quatre Bras, the Marshal found an enemy in his path; this was a single battalion of Nassau troops, which young Bernhard of Saxe-Weimar, an illustrious name, had, on hearing the news of the advance of the French, moved forward very judiciously from Genappe, anticipating his orders by several hours; and he had supported this small force by four battalions, the five about 4,000 strong, which he had kept in reserve at Quatre Bras. The battalion at Frasnes, threatened by the French cavalry, had soon fallen back on the battalions in its rear. Infantry was required to attack this force. Ney sent orders to Bachelu to hurry forward a single battalion, it would appear, only, which was to come to his assistance at Frasnes. This reinforcement was in line at perhaps seven in the evening; but if it was only one battalion, it was not strong enough, even with the aid of the cavalry, to over-throw an enemy very superior in numbers; and Ney, after making demonstrations to no purpose, placed his troops in camp for the night at Frasnes. Had he em-ployed even two of the divisions of Reille, he could have crushed Saxe-Weimar's detachment, and have seized the important point of Quatre Bras, as he had been directed to do by Napoleon.*

Sombreffe, like Quatre Bras, was not occupied on the other side of the field of manœuvre. Zieten, ably carrying out his preconcerted plan, had, we have seen, placed Pirch II. and his division, partly reinforced, in a strong position east of Charleroy. Pirch had very skilfully arrayed his troops behind a marshy stream just beyond Gilly, three or four miles only from Charleroy, his flanks covered by woodland and broken ground, his left observing the heads of Gérard's columns, beginning, at Chatelet, to cross the Sambre. The line was extended as far as pos-sible, in order to deceive the enemy as to the strength of this force. The Prussians were, in all, about 10,000 men. Grouchy, who had ridden to the front with Excelmans' horsemen, in order to support the squadrons of Pajol, believed that he had 20,000 before him, and returned to

---

* This skirmish at Frasnes was not without importance, but writers differ widely with respect to the numbers on both sides. We have followed the narrative of H. Houssaye (' 1815,' ii. 127-129), founded on a careful study of the original reports and documents. It might be inferred from Charras (i. 90, 91) that certainly Piré and his cavalry accompanied the light cavalry of the Guard, and that perhaps more than a single battalion of Bachelu's reached Frasnes. Thiers ('Histoire du Consulat et de l'Empire,' vi. 438) gives Ney 9,000 men at Frasnes, but this is an error. H. Houssaye specifies the names of the five Nassau battalions (p. 129). It may be that the first-named battalion was not sent forward by Saxe-Weimar (p. 27), but this is most im-probable.

Charleroy to ask Napoleon to give him the help of infantry. The Emperor, having reconnoitred the position in person, went back and pressed forward the corps of Vandamme. The attack began at about half-past five in the afternoon. Pirch, as before, fell back, having made a brief resistance, losing only 500 or 600 men.   Napoleon was so irritated at the escape of the enemy that he launched his personal escort against the retreating columns, and Letort, one of his best officers, received a fatal wound.

The Prussians, excellently handled, made their way to Fleurus, only a short distance from Sombreffe ; but had Gérard been on the Sambre in force, they either could not have made a stand, or if they did would probably have been cut off.*   Grouchy now advanced, and requested Vandamme to march on Fleurus, and take possession of Sombreffe, according to his master's directions ; but Van-damme, surly and discontented at the events of the morn-ing, and jealous of a man he deemed his inferior raised over his head, gave a positive refusal, and placed his corps in camps, at a distance of a few miles from Fleurus.† Sombreffe, therefore, was not occupied by the French. Napoleon had gone back to Charleroy; yet he had more than sufficient forces at hand to seize and hold this point ; and possibly he might even now have caught Zieten, who, at Fleurus, had only a comparatively small force. Already, however, the physical decline, which was to prove so disastrous in the campaign, was telling upon Napoleon's powers; he had fallen asleep during part of the day‡ ; he went to rest at Charleroy ' overwhelmed

* Charras has given us the best account of this combat (i. 91-93). The road from Charleroy to Fleurus was obstructed by a stockade by Pirch's orders.   Chesney (' Waterloo Lectures,' 87) notices the results of the absence of Gérard's corps in force.

† See Grouchy, 'Relation Succincte,' 12, 13, and Appendix.

‡ See H. Houssaye, '1815,' ii. 118, and Napoleon Correspondence, xxviii. 286 : letter of Fain, Napoleon's private secretary.   We repeat we shall recur to this important subject.

with fatigue.' We miss the General of 1796 at the close of June 15.

The French army, when night had fallen, was in position, as on the 14th, in three masses. On the left Ney had his detachment at Frasnes; the greater part of the corps of Reille lay around Gosselies, Gérard and his division being at Wangenies, not far from Fleurus; the corps of D'Erlon was, for the most part, between Marchiennes and Gosselies, one division not having crossed the Sambre. At the centre the corps of Vandamme had approached Fleurus, covered by the horsemen of Pajol* and Excelmans; the Imperial Guard was at Gilly and Charleroy, at no great distance; but the corps of Lobau was still beyond the Sambre, and so was the heavy cavalry of Milhaud and Kellermann. To the right, about half of the corps of Gérard had marched beyond Châtelet, and was drawing near the centre; but about the other half had not got over the river, Gérard's movement having been very difficult. The day, therefore, Charras has truly said, ' had been incomplete'; the exposed corps of Zieten had not been destroyed; Quatre Bras and Sombreffe had not been reached; not only had the army failed 'to be over the Sambre before noon,' but about a fourth part of it was still south of the river.

Nevertheless, Napoleon had gained most important strategic success; his prospects for the next day were of the brightest promise. He had broken through the weak allied centre, left open by the retreat of Zieten; he had mastered the great main road from Charleroy to Brussels up to Frasnes; he had made his way far into Belgium, and was close to the line of the communications of his adversaries between Namur and Brussels; Quatre Bras and Sombreffe were almost within his reach; should he encounter his enemies at these points, all the chances

* All the cavalry of Pajol seem to have been assembled in front of Vandamme.

were that they would meet defeat; his army was concentrated upon a narrow space, and nearly stood between hostile armies, scattered widely apart.*   A few hours would carry all his forces across the Sambre.   He would have 124,000 fighting men to oppose to Wellington and Blucher, who, large as was the superiority of their numbers were they once united, would now be almost certainly inferior on the immediate scene of action.   Unquestionably he regretted the delays of the 15th, especially the delay of the central column;† but he rightly observed that 'his manœuvres had been successful; he had the means of defeating his enemies in detail.'‡

From Napoleon we turn to his antagonists, and to their operations on June 15.   Blucher had probably heard that French corps were in movement along the frontier as early as the 10th; but on the 13th the fires of the invaders' bivouacs, concealed as they had been, were descried by Zieten's troops, and this intelligence was sent to the old Prussian Marshal.   Up to this time Blucher had not stirred; but on the 14th, it would appear by nightfall, he despatched the orders to Zieten before referred to; and he directed Pirch, Thielmann, and Bulow, with the 2nd, the 3rd, and the 4th corps, to make a general movement towards Sombreffe, where he had long before resolved to assemble his army.   Pirch and Thielmann, from their headquarters at Namur and Ciney—the first place about fifteen miles from Sombreffe, the second more than thirty

---

* Napoleon had, in fact, secured the position which he thus described ('Correspondence,' i. 520) with reference to his famous operations against Wurmser in 1796: 'Si mon armée était trop faible pour faire face aux deux divisions de l'ennemi, elle pouvait battre chacune d'elles séparément.'

† 'Comment.,' v. 199. Heymès says that Napoleon did not complain that Ney had not occupied Quatre Bras when the Marshal went back to the Emperor's headquarters at Charleroy; but it is probable that Ney did not go there at all.   See H. Houssaye, '1815, ii. 186.

‡ 'Comment.,' v. 136.

—brought their troops together with extreme activity. By the early morning of June 16 the greatest part of their forces was not far from Sombreffe, while the corps of Zieten, drawn back from Fleurus, with the exception of a small advanced guard, was not far from Sombreffe, at St. Amand and Ligny.

Owing to a mistake made by the Chief of the Prussian Staff, the movement of Bulow had been retarded. Bulow received two orders upon the 15th, enjoining him only to march on Hannut—that is, to a point twenty-five miles from Sombreffe, and with no reference to an enemy at hand; and Bulow was not on the march from his head-quarters at Liége until an early hour on June 16. An angry controversy raged for years on the subject. Gneisenau and Bulow seem to have been both to blame; but Liége is upwards of fifty miles from Sombreffe.* Bulow could not possibly have reached that place in time on the 16th, whatever was done; the mistake in the orders could make no difference. Blucher, therefore, could have had no right to expect that his lieutenant, in any event, could have reached the point of assembly on the 16th, and could come to his support, should, as was the Marshal's purpose, Sombreffe be the scene of a great battle on that day. Bulow, indeed, fairly informed his chief that he could not be at Hannut until mid-day on the 16th—that is, twenty-five miles from Sombreffe.†

* Several of Bulow's detachments, too, were north of Liége—that is, still further from Sombreffe.

† For the time when Zieten's outposts discovered the presence of the French army, see Prussian official account, pp. 7-9, and Chesney's 'Waterloo Lectures,' 71. As to the directions given by Blucher on the 14th, and the movements of Pirch, Thielmann and Bulow, the reader may be referred to Charras, i. 105, 106 ; to Ropes, 'Campaign of Waterloo,' 69-73; and to Chesney's 'Waterloo Lectures,' 82. With respect to the controversy about Gneisenau and Bulow, see the same authorities *in loco*. This dispute is really beside the question ; whatever orders were given, Bulow could not be at Sombreffe in time on the 16th.

Blucher was thus assembling his forces at Sombreffe, and was about to offer Napoleon battle, with the certainty that three-fourths of his army only could be gathered together on the spot in time, and that a fourth must necessarily be absent from the field. This was characteristic of the impetuous, often reckless, haste which was the great fault of the old warrior, and which his mighty adversary had calculated, from long experience, that he might be expected to display. German writers, indeed, have declared that Blucher would not have directed his army to Sombreffe had he not been assured of the support of Wellington, but this is an error designed to excuse the Marshal. It is true, we have seen, that Blucher and Wellington had agreed, several weeks before this time, that, should Napoleon assail their centre, they would concentrate forces to repel his attack; but Sombreffe was not referred to as the point of junction; this was to be at points nearer the Belgian frontier.* It is true also that very probably Blucher expected Wellington to come to his aid, perhaps by the early morning of June 16; but he had received no promise to that effect; the operations of the Duke on the 15th give a distinct negative to this conclusion. On the other hand, abundant proof exists that Blucher had determined to assemble his army at Sombreffe of his own set purpose, and without having had any message from his colleague upon the subject. He wrote to the King of Prussia on the 15th that 'he would concentrate his army at Sombreffe next day, and that he had not received any news from Wellington.'†

We pass on to the conduct of Wellington on the 15th, to this day not completely explained. The Duke's army,

* See *ante*, Ropes, 'The Campaign of Waterloo,' 71, 72, and H. Houssaye, '1815,' ii. 114, 115. See also especially Muffling, 'Passages from my Life,' 231, 232.

† See Blucher, 90 *et seq.*; and H. Houssaye, '1815,' ii. 142, and the authorities collected in the note.

we have seen, had been widely extended, with a special view to the protection of his right and right centre, but with comparatively little regard for his left, the 2nd corps holding the valleys of the Scheldt and the Dender, the 1st being largely in the valley of the Senne, at Braine le Comte, Soignies, Enghien, Nivelle and other places, with one detachment alone reaching the great main-road from Charleroy to Brussels, the reserve being in and around the chief town of Belgium. The Duke had been in correspondence with Fouché and other traitors, and certainly as early as the first week of June had been informed that an attack was impending; between the 9th and the 13th of the month he had learned that French corps were upon the frontier.* Like Blucher, however, he made no movement for a time; but on the 15th he received an express from Zieten, perhaps at nine in the morning, more probably about three in the afternoon,† announcing that his outposts had been driven in near Charleroy. The Prince of Orange, at Brussels, gave the same intelligence, referring, however, to the attack in Thuin; and similar reports came in afterwards, all indicating a movement against Charleroy.

Wellington, nevertheless, refused to stir. The reasons of this immobility have long been known. He thought that his right and right centre might be attacked; he was convinced that Napoleon could not advance by the bad roads leading from Beaumont to Charleroy, that his left was, accordingly, secure, a signal proof of his adversary's skill in selecting this line. He had been apprised, it is said, that a false attack would be made from the Sambre

---

* Supp. Despatches, x. 451, 465, 471, 476, 478 ; and see especially 523 *et seq.*

† The evidence preponderates that the Duke did not receive this despatch until three; but see his letter to Clarke, Despatches, xii. 473. Zieten sent the despatch at four in the morning : Prussian official account, p. 17 ; and see Chesney, 'Waterloo Lectures,' 83.

upon his left.*   He therefore had resolved to see how
things would develop themselves, not reflecting, perhaps,
what the loss of time might involve 'against a man
dangerous to neglect for an hour'; but later in the afternoon a despatch from Zieten, announcing that Charleroy
had been attacked, caused him to issue orders for his first
movement on June 15.   These orders were despatched
between five and seven, or, as the Dutch archives report,
about nine.†   The purpose of Wellington was not doubtful.
The 2nd corps was practically to remain where it was—at
least, to make nothing like a decided movement; but a
large part of the reserve was to make ready to march
from Brussels; the 1st corps was to make a change in its
stations.   Its first division, the British Guards of Cooke,
was to advance to Ath; its third division, that of Alten,
British, was to march to Braine le Comte, and thence to
Nivelles, 'should that point have been attacked'; its two
Dutch Belgian divisions, under Perponcher and Chassé,
were to assemble at Nivelles.   But Alten's division was
not to move to Nivelles 'until it is quite certain that the
enemy's attack is upon the right of the Prussian army,
and the left of the British army'‡—in other words, upon
the allied centre.

These dispositions very clearly show what was passing
in Wellington's mind at this time.   The virtual immobility of his 2nd corps, and even the arrangements he was
making for the 1st—that is, placing it between Ath, Braine
le Comte, and Nivelles—prove that he was anxious about
his right and his right centre, and was not in much
apprehension for his left.   He directed, indeed, a partial

* See Supp. Despatches, x. 523 *et seq.*, and Ollech, 73.   See also
Greville, 'Memoirs,' i. 41, written in 1820.

† See Ropes, 'Campaign of Waterloo,' 77; Chesney, 83; and, to the
contrary, Charras, i. 109.   Charras seems right here.

‡ Wellington Despatches, xii. 472.   It is unnecessary to say that
every line of these despatches relating to the campaign should be
carefully studied.

concentration of the 1st corps towards his left; his two Dutch Belgian divisions were to assemble at Nivelles; Alten's division was to march to that place, but only when the left and the allied centre were assailed. But Nivelles is about seven miles to the west of the great main-road from Charleroy to Brussels; the Duke, therefore, could not have been convinced that his left and the allied centre were in immediate danger; and this, though he had been informed for some time that the French army had attacked Charleroy; and though, as a matter of fact, a powerful French force had advanced to Gosselies, with a detachment to Frasnes, had mastered the great main-road up to these points, and even might easily have occupied Quatre Bras! Nor was this all. The order to assemble the Dutch Belgian divisions at Nivelles involved the withdrawal from the great main-road of the detachment which up to this had held it, and the retreat of Saxe-Weimar from Quatre Bras; that is, it completely exposed the left of Wellington, and completely uncovered the allied centre! The order, therefore, was founded on false assumptions, and directed a movement which in some respects would have been utterly false, and pregnant with danger.*

Some time afterwards, probably after nine at night, a despatch from Blucher was placed in Wellington's hands —the first he had received upon the 15th, the head-quarters were so widely distant—announcing that the Prussian army was being assembled at Sombreffe. The Duke told Muffling, the Prussian Commissioner in his camp, that, as had been requested, he would concentrate his own army, but that he could not fix the points until he had heard from Mons, showing thus that he was still thinking of his right centre.† At ten at night new or

---

* This is very ably shown by Charras, i. 109.

† Muffling, 'Passages,' 229. The solicitude of the Duke about Mons may indicate that D'Erlon had made the demonstration against

'after' orders were issued; these also plainly indicate their author's purpose. The 2nd corps was now to be set in motion, and to advance eastwards from the valleys of the Scheldt and the Dender, in a general way, into the valley of the Senne; it was largely to assemble around Enghien; it was thus to approach Wellington's left, but still at a distance. As to the 1st corps, Cooke's Guards were to march on Braine le Comte; Alten's division was to move on Nivelles; Perponcher's and Chasse's divisions, it was assumed, were being assembled at that place. Nothing was said expressly about the reserve, but it was, of course, implied that, according to the previous orders, a large part of it was to be prepared to make a march from Brussels.*

These orders also prove that, even by this time, Wellington was chiefly solicitous for his right centre, and was not thinking much about his left and the allied centre; they certainly indicate that he had not made up his mind. Had they been carried into effect, his 2nd and 1st corps would have held positions between Enghien, Braine le Comte, and Nivelles—that is, on a curved line some eighteen miles in extent, in front especially of the fortress of Mons; the reserve, though ready, was not to move from Brussels; the chief part of the 1st corps would have been concentrated around Nivelles; in other words, the great main-road from Charleroy to Brussels would not have been occupied by a single man; the Duke's left and the allied centre would have been without protection, and wholly exposed; the wide space between Nivelles and Sombreffe—a distance of about fourteen miles—would have divided Wellington and Blucher's armies. Napoleon, already near Quatre Bras and Sombreffe, could easily have

Binche and Mons before referred to. See Maurice, *United Service Magazine*, May, 1890.
* See order, Wellington Despatches, xii. 474.

moved against either, or both, and in all probability could have gained most important success.*

But 'the intelligent disobedience,' as it has rightly been called, of a subordinate of the Duke averted, in some measure at least, the peril of dispositions that might have proved fatal. Saxe-Weimar, we have seen, had advanced some 4,000 men to Quatre Bras and Frasnes, and had held the detachment of Ney in check; he sent a report of the skirmish to Perponcher, his chief, in command of one of the Dutch-Belgian divisions of the 1st corps. Perponcher, having received this news, and having also, perhaps, learned that Charleroy was occupied by the enemy in force, took boldly on himself to direct his whole division on Quatre Bras, in order at once to support Saxe Weimar, and to retain possession, at that point, of the great main-road from Charleroy to Brussels, and of the lateral road from Nivelles to Namur, the principal link between Blucher and Wellington. He acted, no doubt, upon instructions from the Chief of the Staff of the Prince of Orange, but he disobeyed the positive commands of Wellington, directing him to assemble his division at Nivelles; and in adopting this course he gave proof of no common insight, and of undertaking a great but necessary responsibility at the gravest risks. 'Quatre Bras was thus occupied on the evening and night of the fifteenth, not only without orders from Wellington, but against his orders;'† the gap was closed for a moment against Napoleon. But Quatre Bras was held by a very small force, which ought to have been overwhelmed the next day.‡

---

* This, too, is admirably explained by Charras, i. 110.

† Ropes, 'Campaign of Waterloo,' 122.

‡ General Maurice (*United Service Magazine*, July, 1890) has argued that Wellington was right in concentrating a very large part of his army at Nivelles—at least, in giving orders to that effect—on the principle that you should not expose your forces piecemeal to the blows of a concentrated enemy. Now, it is quite true that, as

The dispositions of Wellington, therefore, had up to this time been unworthy of him. From the outset his army had been too dispersed. Though made aware that an attack was being threatened, he had done nothing to assemble it until late on the 15th; he held to a fixed idea that his right and right centre were aimed at, if, indeed, an attack was to be made at all. Being separated from Blucher by a wide distance, he had no information from him until very late; at his headquarters at Brussels he could not easily ascertain what was going on, even in his own front; and when he gave orders for the movement on Enghien, Braine le Comte, and Nivelles, these exposed Blucher and himself to defeat, perhaps to disaster.* At some time, however—we should infer about midnight— that is, after the orders made two hours before,† the Duke issued a new set of orders, which certainly point to a great movement of his army to his left, and of a considerable part of it to Quatre Bras, and upon the great main-road from Charleroy to Brussels.

These orders, it is alleged, have been lost, owing to the

Napoleon has conclusively shown ('Comment.,' v. 205-207), Blucher ought not to have concentrated at Sombreffe, and Wellington ought not, as he afterwards did, to have tried to concentrate at Quatre Bras; both ought to have fallen back. But, as Blucher did concentrate at Sombreffe, Wellington was bound to concentrate, not at Nivelles, but, as he afterwards attempted to do, though very late, at Quatre Bras. The argument of General Maurice, which has found no supporters, is fully disposed of by Mr. Ropes, 'Campaign of Waterloo,' 93-95. For much the same reasons General Maurice condemns the advance of Saxe-Weimar, and the admirable movement by Perponcher, of his division to Quatre Bras, which may have saved the campaign for the allies. But he is contradicted by every authority, and, in fact, this whole argument is mere paradox.

* See the bitter remarks of Gneisenau, who, however, disliked Wellington: letter to the King of Prussia, cited by Van Loben Sels; 'Précis de la Campagne de 1815,' 225; and see 97.

† Mr. Ropes ('Campaign of Waterloo') makes the hour much later; but Charras (i. 110) seems to have most of the evidence on his side. He gives the time at 'about eleven.'

death of Wellington's Chief of the Staff, on June 18;* but their purport has been made manifest, to some extent, if by no means conclusively proved. In the report made by Wellington of the events of the campaign, dated on the 19th, the day after Waterloo, he wrote that ' on the evening of the 16th he ordered the troops to march to their left,' and that he ' directed the whole army to march upon Quatre Bras,' at an hour not specified, but which probably was on the night of the 15th, or the early morning of the next day.† Muffling states that ' towards midnight,' on the 15th, the Duke ' entered his room and said ' that he had ' given orders for the concentration of his army at Nivelles and Quatre Bras,' and that this was while the ball of the Duke of Richmond was in full swing.‡ This is fully confirmed by a well-authenticated report of a conversation between Wellington and his host at the ball. The Duke, with other particulars of much interest, said ' that he had ordered the army to concentrate at Quatre Bras.'§   Lastly, Wellington wrote to Blucher on the morning of the 16th—the letter has been discovered not very long ago—that a considerable part of the army, at least, was at Quatre Bras and Nivelles, and that the greatest part of the army was not distant ; and we know for certain that most of the reserve had been directed at a very early hour on the 16th to march from Brussels towards Nivelles and Quatre Bras.‖   It is true that the letter to Blucher was far from accurate ; it magnified the extent of the movement on Quatre Bras and Nivelles,

---

* Search should be carefully made for these orders, for they are of the greatest importance. Mr. Ropes (' Campaign of Waterloo,' p. 2) rightly says they may, possibly, be yet found.

† Wellington Despatches, xii. 478. The report is not quite correct.

‡ Muffling, ' Passages,' 230.

§ ' Letters of the First Earl of Malmesbury,' i. 445.

‖ Letter of Wellington to Blucher, in French, Ollech, opposite p. 124.

owing probably to mistakes made by Wellington's staff. But this body of evidence distinctly shows that at some time in the night of the 15th-16th he had directed a great part of his army to move towards his left, and especially a certain part to Quatre Bras. These orders, however, were issued at a very late hour; time was needed to carry them into effect, notably for the 2nd corps of Wellington's army; and, as a matter of fact, only Perponcher's corps was in line at Quatre Bras until the afternoon of the 16th. Could this weak force stop an attack made by Ney, already at Frasnes, and in command of the whole left wing of the French army? had not Wellington's left and the allied centre been left uncovered and exposed, so that it had become impossible to turn aside for any length of time the blows of Napoleon?*

* The question of the disposition of Wellington's army after the orders of ten at night, and all the evidence relating to the subject, are very ably and exhaustively considered by Mr. Ropes, 'Campaign of Waterloo,' 80 *et seq.* The letter of the Duke to Blucher, which, no doubt, represented the Duke's army to be nearer Quatre Bras than it actually was, became the foundation of the charge made by Delbruck, the biographer of Gneisenau, to the effect that Wellington deceived his colleague, and induced him to stand and fight on the 16th in order to extricate himself from the difficulties in which his bad strategy had involved him. The charge has been well examined by Mr. Ropes, 'Campaign of Waterloo,' 109, 110, and by General Maurice, *United Service Magazine*, June, 1890, and is certainly false. The mistake made by Wellington was probably caused by his having had before him a most misleading and scarcely intelligible document, prepared by some officer on his staff, and called 'Dispositions of the British Army at 7 a.m., on June 16,' and which grossly misrepresented the real facts. At the same time, the charge was not unnaturally made, for the letter of the Duke was very incorrect, and the inference, if strained, was not without apparent foundation. The Duke's staff in the campaign was not good; he had reason to complain of it on June 15 and 16, both on account of the imperfect intelligence sent from the frontier (see Siborne, 1844 edition, i. 164), and especially of the document referred to. It should be added here that the Duke's reply to Clausewitz (Supp. Despatches, x. 523), dealing with these events, is full of errors. It was written when Wellington was more than seventy-two, and in bad health.

Let us now glance for a moment at the positions of the belligerent armies after the movements of the 15th, and in the early morning of the following day. The corps of Zieten, reduced by some 2,000 men, was, we have seen, at St. Amand and Ligny, near Sombreffe; Pirch and Thielmann were hastening to join Zieten; but some hours were required before they could come into line.* Bulow could not reach Sombreffe on the 16th in time. On the other side of the theatre of events, Perponcher's single division alone held the important point of Quatre Bras. Though Wellington's army was upon the march, it could not be at Quatre Bras, even in part, for a considerable time—as it happened, not until the afternoon—and the allied armies were widely apart. Napoleon, on the other hand, had a powerful force near Sombreffe, and another powerful force near Quatre Bras; he had broken and all but laid hold of the allied centre; he had 100,000 men within easy reach of his enemy, if part of his army had not yet crossed the Sambre. In this position of affairs he probably had the means of falling on the isolated corps of Zieten, and defeating it, after a rapid movement, before it could receive its supports; in that event, three-fourths of the Prussian army could hardly have escaped a very grave disaster. At the same time, the Emperor certainly had the means of overwhelming, by Ney, the corps of Perponcher; he then could turn against Wellington or Blucher, or both; indisputably, he could have caught and · routed the Prussian chief.

He had gained, in a word, a position of vantage, in which he could strike down the heads of his enemy's columns, and could afterwards, in all probability, defeat one or both, attacking Blucher and subsequently Wellington in detail. And if accidents of war, and the fact that

* Thielmann was not at Sombreffe until noon. As to Pirch the authorities differ: H. Houssaye, ' 1815,' ii. 141 ; Chesney, ' Waterloo Lectures,' 82.

a large part of the French army was still beyond the
Sambre, and the fatigues of a harassing march on the
15th, were to prevent him accomplishing all this, the
Emperor, nevertheless, had wellnigh secured a considerable measure at least of success. He could hardly fail,
were his operations reasonably well conducted, to crush
Perponcher, to keep Wellington back, and to fall on
Blucher in preponderating force. His adversaries, in fact,
had been outmanœuvred;* inferior in numbers as his army
was, all the chances were that he would be superior to
them at the decisive points on the immediate scene of
action.

   The strategy of Napoleon on June 15 was as admirably
designed as in any passage of his career, if not as well
carried out as it might have been; few will defend the
strategy of his foes. It should be observed, however, that
the grave dangers in which Blucher and Wellington were
now involved are largely to be ascribed to the faulty
arrangements they had made before hostilities broke out.
Their armies were disseminated over much too wide a
space; the concentration of these was therefore difficult,
were they suddenly attacked; their centre was weak
where their inner flanks met; Napoleon successfully
assailed and pounced down on it. Wellington had so
placed his army as to cover his right and right centre,
thinking little of his left; he held obstinately to this
belief; he was scarcely able, therefore, to assemble forces
in time to protect in any real sense his left and to give
sufficient support to the Prussian army. Blucher and the
Duke, too, were too far from each other at their headquarters at Namur and Brussels; their means of communication were accordingly bad; Wellington did not

---

   * Wellington frankly acknowledged this. His celebrated remark
to the Duke of Richmond at the ball : ' Napoleon has humbugged me ;
by God ! he has gained twenty-four hours' march on me,' speaks
volumes. See ' Letters of the First Earl of Malmesbury,' ii. 445.

hear that his colleague was assembling at Sombreffe until late in the evening of the 15th. Both chiefs, no doubt, had to complain of their staffs; but it is confounding lesser with greater causes to attribute faults to subordinates and to pass over their own; they ought not to have been so widely apart.

All this accounts for much that took place, but Blucher and Wellington each committed mistakes, even after the campaign had really begun. Napoleon has argued with conclusive logic that even as early as the middle of May Blucher and his army ought to have been near Fleurus, Wellington and his army around Brussels, but with detachments upon the frontier; that is, their forces and themselves should have been nearer each other than they actually were.* However this may have been, both Blucher and Wellington had been made aware days before they were attacked that a great French army was upon the frontier; they ought, therefore, to have begun to concentrate at once, and assuredly ought to have approached each other; they remained motionless, and waited upon their enemy. In addition, Blucher ought not to have advanced to Sombreffe when Napoleon had seized Charleroy and was on the allied centre; this was violating the well-known principle that an army should not be assembled within an adversary's reach; and though Blucher's movement, so to speak, compelled Wellington to march towards Quatre Bras, if he was not to desert his ally, both commanders certainly ought to have fallen back and united their forces at points in the rear, so that Napoleon could not have an opportunity to strike either at once, and fall on them with forces not yet drawn together.† Owing to all these mistakes and short-comings, Blucher and Wellington were now in no doubt-ful peril. It was only through a mere accident, we shall

* ' Comment.,' v. 204-206.   † *Ibid.*, v. 205-207.

see, that Blucher was not completely routed upon the
16th, in which event Wellington could have scarcely
escaped.*

* Impartial and competent judges have long ago, with scarcely an
exception, found fault with the operations of Blucher and Wellington
on June 15. Without referring to French and German invectives,
Charras, a great admirer of Wellington, remarks (i. 3): 'Dans cette
journée du 15 Juin, si mal employée, on ne reconnait ni sa perspicacité
si profonde, ni son coup d'œil si sur, ni son activité habituelle.'
English commentators, too, are severe on the British Chief. Lord
Wolseley ('Decline and Fall of Napoleon,' 143) dryly says: 'Had
the Duke been beaten at Waterloo, history would surely have condemned the position of his army on June 13, 14, and 15, and also his
decision to maintain it until the French attack had been fully developed, instead of at once concentrating when he first learned that
the enemy's columns had reached Maubeuge.' Chesney, another
admirer of Wellington, and a detractor of Napoleon, remarks,
'Waterloo Lectures,' 101, that Wellington's inaction during the 15th
'can hardly escape notice in the most cursory view of the strategy of
this campaign. . . . The balance of strategy was, up to this point,
on Napoleon's side.' Shaw Kennedy ('The Battle of Waterloo,'
148) observes with truth: 'Wellington and Blucher determined to
continue in their cantonments until they knew positively the line of
attack. Now, it may safely be predicted that this determination will
be considered by future and dispassionate historians as a great mistake, for, in place of waiting to see when the blow actually fell, the
armies should have been instantly put in motion to assemble. Nor
was this the only error. The line of cantonments occupied by the
Anglo-allied and Prussian armies was greatly too extended.' Napoleon's comments are severe, and no doubt are partial; but it is
impossible to see how they can be answered ('Comment.,' v. 204-207).

CHAPTER V

THE OPERATIONS OF JUNE 16—LIGNY AND QUATRE BRAS

The French army on the morning of June 16—Alleged inaction of Napoleon—His orders to Ney and Grouchy—Conduct of Ney since the evening of the 15th—His delays and remissness—March of the main French army to Fleurus—Positions of the Prussian army—Arrangements of Blucher, and his faults—Interview between Blucher and Wellington—Skilful arrangements of Napoleon—His letter of 2 p.m. to Ney—The Battle of Ligny, attack on Blucher's right and right centre—Desperate fighting—Napoleon's order to Ney of 3.15 p.m.—Order to D'Erlon to march to the field—Continuation of the battle—Apparition of D'Erlon towards Fleurus—He retires from the field—Napoleon breaks Blucher's centre and defeats the Prussians—Battle of Quatre Bras—Conduct of Ney and Reille—Ney's attack late—Progress of the battle—Different attacks of Ney—He recalls D'Erlon—Wellington compels Ney to retreat to Frasnes—Napoleon's success on the 16th great, but not decisive, chiefly owing to Ney's conduct—Reille and D'Erlon gravely to blame—The position of the allies very critical.

VERY differently from what had happened on June 15, the French army made scarcely any movement on the 16th until between nine and ten in the forenoon. D'Erlon, indeed, who, we have seen, had been backward, and had been urged more than once to effect his junction with Reille,* seems to have marched his last division across

---

* See letters of Soult, 3 p.m. and 4.30 p.m., on the 15th : 'Documents inédits,' collected by the son of Ney in 1840, Nos. 5 and 6. These letters are in La Tour d'Auvergne's 'Waterloo,' 63, 66.

the Sambre at a very early hour on the morning of the
16th; his whole corps was assembled around Jumet, a
village about two miles from Gosselies, the headquarters
of Reille and the 2nd corps, at probably from ten to
eleven o'clock.* But the rest of the French army had
not stirred; Reille, as in the evening, lay around
Gosselies, with a detachment at Frasnes, and Girard at
Wangenies; Vandamme, Excelmans and Pajol were near
Fleurus; the Imperial Guard between Gilly and Charleroy; Lobau, Milhaud and Kellermann beyond the
Sambre; Gérard, half of his corps north, half south, of
the river. None of these Generals had received orders
from headquarters until between eight and ten.

Napoleon has been severely censured for this seeming
inaction by many able critics.† These charges cannot be
lightly passed over. Napoleon, we have seen, had he
marched forward at an early hour on June 16, was, all
but certainly, assured of important success. A few
remarks must be made on the subject. It may be that
the Emperor was still suffering from the effects of the
fatigue of the 15th—he was no longer the man he once
had been—and required a somewhat protracted rest before
he could send out his orders. It may be, too, he thought
he should have his whole army in hand, and across the
Sambre, before he attacked enemies, divided indeed, but

---

* This, which is important, has been conclusively established by
H. Houssaye, 'Waterloo,' ii. 130, 199.

† Jomini (' Précis de la Campagne de 1815,' 157) remarks : ' Mal-
heureusement pour Napoléon elle ne se fit pas avec l'activité inouie
qui le distinguait ordinairement. On est forcé de l'avouer, l'emploi
qu'il fit de cette matinée du 16 restera toujours un problême pour ceux
qui le connaissent bien.' Jomini's authority is, of course, of the very
highest; he perfectly well knew what could be done by Napoleon and
a French army. Lord Wolseley (' Decline and Fall of Napoleon,'
158) says : ' No movement or advance was made until near 11 a.m.
Between seven and eight hours was thus lost.' See also Clausewitz,
cited by Ropes, 'Campaign of Waterloo,' 163, and Charras, i. 114,
118, 149. Charras is very bitter, but he is a libeller of Napoleon.

formidable in numbers, even though apart ; and Wellington has sagaciously observed that, after the exertions they
had made the day before, the French may have been
unable on the 16th to march until comparatively late.*
The delay of Napoleon, however, such as it was, was, it
would appear, mainly due to quite different reasons.   The
retreat of the Prussians from Marchiennes and Charleroy
on Fleurus seemed to point to a movement towards the
north-east and Liége—that is, far away from their British
allies ; not a British regiment had been seen on the 15th.
It seemed improbable, as affairs now stood, that Blucher
and Wellington would attempt to assemble their forces
around Sombreffe and Quatre Bras, within reach of a
concentrated enemy.   Napoleon, therefore, appears to
have inferred that his adversaries were falling back before
him, according to true strategic principles, perhaps retiring
in the direction of their respective bases.   His orders for
the 16th confirm this view, and on this supposition there
was no necessity for his army making a very early movement.   Besides, his inaction, if inaction there was, was
much less than has commonly been supposed.   He sent
an aide-de-camp to Ney soon after daybreak ; he had let
the Marshal know, by half-past six in the morning, that
Kellermann's horsemen would soon reach Gosselies ; he
desired to learn exactly where D'Erlon was, and by seven
at least he had made his arrangements for his operations
on the 16th.†

These arrangements were set forth in two pairs of
despatches, one pair directed to Ney, the other to Grouchy,
one letter in each pair being from the pen of Soult, the
other, written somewhat later, by the Emperor himself.

---

* Ellesmere, 296, 297.

† See H. Houssaye, ' Waterloo,' ii. 133, 136, 187.   The letter sent
to Ney at 5.30 in the morning, or thereabouts, is No. 7 of ' Documents inédits,' and will be found in La Tour d'Auvergne, ' Waterloo,'
94, 95.

As regards Ney first—he had been placed in command,
we must recollect, of the entire French left—the orders of
Napoleon were of no doubtful import. The Emperor
assumed, as he had reason to expect, that his lieutenant
had, or ere long would have, the whole of the 2nd and
1st corps in hand, and in addition Kellermann's corps of
cavalry ; he explained in detail how these forces were to
be disposed. One division, should no difficulty arise, was
to be placed four or five miles beyond Quatre Bras, on the
great main-road from Charleroy to Brussels ; another was
to be directed on Marbais, a village to the south-east of
Quatre Bras, and not quite five miles from that place, but
close to the lateral road from Nivelles to Namur, the
natural link between Blucher and Wellington ; the whole
of the rest of the 2nd and the 1st corps—Girard at
Wangenies was still under Ney's orders — was to be
assembled in force around Quatre Bras. As for Kellermann's cavalry, this was to stand on an ancient Roman
road called the Chaussée of Brunehaut, which crosses the
great main road from Charleroy to Brussels, and thence
reaches the road from Nivelles to Namur.   In this position
it would be near Frasnes and Quatre Bras, and yet could
easily attain Fleurus should the Emperor be in need of it.
The light cavalry of the Guard was to remain with Ney ;
the prohibition to employ it was not continued, but it
was to be 'spared' should there be an 'affair' with the
English, and to be 'covered' by the horsemen of Reille
and D'Erlon.   Napoleon proceeded to inform the Marshal
as to the disposition of the remaining parts of the army,
and as to the intentions of its chief for the day.   Grouchy
was to march on Sombreffe with the corps of Vandamme
and Gérard ; Napoleon was to advance with the Guard on
Fleurus ; no reference was made to the corps of Lobau ;
and the Emperor announced that it was his purpose to
attack the enemy should 'he happen to meet him,' and to
send a detachment as far as Gembloux, a small town six

or seven miles beyond Sombreffe. Napoleon then made
his lieutenant aware that he hoped to be able 'to be at
Brussels on the 17th,' and that Ney ought to have his
whole army in hand in order to second this great forward
movement.

Turning to the other side of the theatre of events,
Napoleon gave Grouchy the command of the whole
French right—that is, of the corps of Vandamme and
Gérard, with the cavalry of Pajol, Excelmans and Milhaud
—and directed him to advance on Sombreffe according
to what had been written to Ney. The Emperor added
that he would march to Fleurus with the Guard, and
that he would attack the enemy should he be on the spot
at Sombreffe or Gembloux ; he distinctly wrote that from
all that he had heard 'the Prussians could not oppose to
him more than 40,000 men.'*

The despatches of Soult corresponded, of course, in
nearly all respects with those of his master, except that
he placed Kellermann's cavalry entirely at the disposal of
Ney, and he expressed an opinion that the enemy had
probably retired from the great main-road from Charleroy
to Brussels, and even from the country around Nivelles.†
From these important papers we can collect, with
certainty, what were Napoleon's views on the 16th, and
what objects he hoped to accomplish. He evidently
believed that Ney could not encounter much opposition
on the part of Wellington, and that he—that is, the
Emperor—would be able to defeat or to thrust aside
Blucher. He was convinced that he could easily master
the two strategic points of Quatre Bras and Sombreffe,
which he had expected to master the day before. He

---

* These most important despatches will be found in Napoleon
Correspondence, xxviii. 289, 292. They require close study.

† The corresponding despatches of Soult are in 'Documents
inédits,' No. 8, and La Tour d'Auvergne, 'Waterloo,' 99, 102, and in
a work by a son of Grouchy.

hoped that probably he would enter Brussels on the 17th. He was plainly, therefore, convinced that the allies would not be in force at Quatre Bras and Sombreffe ; that they were not moving their armies to these places, their centre having been broken through, and their enemy being in strength, within easy reach ; and that they were falling back, possibly behind Brussels, no doubt at a distance, perhaps increasing. The Emperor's calculations for the day were accordingly based on false assumptions ; his anticipations were quite incorrect, though in conformity with the true principles of the art of war.

But it deserves special notice, and this is of the first importance, that the arrangements he made for the 16th were perfectly combined to meet all that might happen ; and, in the events that actually occurred, they secured him success that ought to have been decisive. Ney, on the left, should he do his duty—nay, should he simply obey his orders—would be easily able to hold Quatre Bras against any forces Wellington could bring up ; would probably crush Perponcher's weak division, perhaps defeat reinforcements sent to his aid ; would certainly keep Wellington far away from Blucher should the allied chiefs endeavour to unite. Nor was this all, or even nearly all. The division Ney was to send to Marbais would help to separate Blucher from Wellington ; it would be on the flank and rear of Blucher, should Blucher offer battle between Sombreffe and Fleurus, and, if it was even slightly reinforced, might involve the Prussian chief in a great disaster ; and Kellermann's cavalry would be admirably placed to second, as the case might be, either Ney or Napoleon. On the opposite side of the operations to take place, Napoleon and Grouchy would, in any event, be more than able to make head against Blucher, who could not have his four corps in hand, that of Bulow having been stationed at Liége ; and very probably, with the assistance of Ney, a few miles only

away at Quatre Bras, they would be the means of in-
flicting on Blucher a great defeat. Whatever might take
place, it was thus made certain that Blucher and Wellington could not join hands, should they attempt to meet on
Sombreffe or Quatre Bras; and all the chances were that
either or both, if they made the attempt, would heavily
suffer.*

The Emperor's orders, carried by one of his best aide-
de-camps—all commentators agree as regards the time—
left Charleroy between eight and nine in the morning, and
reached Ney at Frasnes between ten and eleven. The
movements of the Marshal since the brush with Saxe-
Weimar have not even now been fully explained; but
there is ample evidence that they gave proof of the
indecision shown on the evening of the 15th, and that
with considerably less excuse. His single aide-de-camp
has told us that Ney left Frasnes late on the 15th, passed
through Gosselies, and had an interview with his master
at Charleroy. The Emperor received him well, though
Quatre Bras had not been seized, gave him his orders,
and sent him back to Gosselies. But the aide-de-camp
alone has made this statement; he is in no sense a
trustworthy witness; there is much reason to believe that
Ney remained at Gosselies during the night of the 15th,
and until the early morning of the next day, and only
sent a report to Napoleon, without having exchanged a
word with him.†

Be this as it may, the course to be taken by Ney, after
the first hours of the 16th, ought to have been evident to
him. The Marshal had been directed on the previous

* The arrangements of Napoleon for June 16 should be carefully
studied upon a good map. Though founded on a false hypothesis,
they showed characteristic strategic insight, and, in fact, met all the
circumstances of the situation.

† H. Houssaye, 'Waterloo,' ii. 186, very able on this point.

afternoon to press forward and occupy Quatre Bras ;* he
had not succeeded in accomplishing this; but the order
of Napoleon remained in full force; he should have carried
it into effect as quickly as possible.   In addition Ney
knew that he was to have Kellermann's horsemen, and
that orders had long been given to accelerate the march
of D'Erlon; all this pointed to a forward movement early
on the 16th.   What he ought to have done cannot be,
therefore, doubtful.   He should have taken care that
Reille's three divisions should be ready to advance on
Quatre Bras in the morning of the 16th; that D'Erlon
and Kellermann should be close at hand; in short, that
the French left should be easily in his power, and near
him.   Had he done this, and it was not the least difficult,
the fortunes of Europe might have been changed for a
time.   Ney, however, simply did nothing of the kind;
he left Gosselies for Frasnes at an early hour; he did not
make the slightest attempt to assemble the corps of
Reille, D'Erlon, and Kellermann, or even to call D'Erlon
and Kellermann up; he merely told Reille to send the
Emperor's orders to Frasnes.   This remissness and negligence, inexcusable in themselves, were to be followed by
disregard of positive orders — conduct which was to
frustrate, to a great extent, the fine combinations made
by Napoleon, and to be attended with most untoward
results.†

* See *ante*, *Moniteur* of June 18, 1815, and Napoleon Correspondence, xxviii. 288.   The present writer is perhaps the first, certainly
the first English, writer who has furnished this conclusive proof of
Napoleon's orders to Ney to occupy Quatre Bras on the 15th ('Great
Commanders of Modern Times,' 327, and 'Disputed Passages of
the Campaign of 1815,' *English Historical Review*, January, 1895,
59).

† General Maurice (*United Service Magazine*, September, 1890)
and Mr. Ropes ('Campaign of Waterloo,' 55, and elsewhere) have
very properly dwelt on the difficulties which beset Ney from the want
of a staff.   Ney, too, required some hours at least to make himself
master of the whole situation; and Napoleon was not just to him in

Grouchy received the orders of Napoleon and Soult, transmitted by the unfortunate Labédoyère, at between nine and ten in the morning. It is due to an ill-fated soldier—the chief cause of a tremendous disaster for France—to point out that in the first hours of June 16 he had acted very differently from Ney, and had shown the energy and the attention to be expected from him. He had, perhaps, received the command of the French right by word of mouth, like Ney, on the previous evening. Be that as it may, he sent a message to Vandamme to push forward and to draw near Sombreffe, and possibly another message to Gérard to second the movement; and he advanced with his cavalry to Fleurus soon after daybreak. He met at this place the outposts of Zieten, and he had reported to the Emperor by five in the morning that large Prussian columns were round St. Amand and Ligny—that is, we have seen, the corps of Zieten—a report confirmed by Girard from Wangenies on his left.[*] Grouchy, accordingly, made a halt at Fleurus, awaiting the orders of Napoleon. The Emperor appears to have attached little credence to the information obtained from the Marshal; he persisted in believing that Blucher could not be near in force, and certainly would be unable to make a stand against him, so he gave Grouchy the orders before referred to, and continued the movement on Sombreffe he had thus directed.[†]

---

withholding his command until the last moment. Nevertheless, this again is confusing lesser with greater causes, and giving too much weight to the first. Something may be said for Ney as regards the 15th, very little indeed as regards the 16th. The mistakes and worse that were committed were emphatically his own, and can only be ascribed to the agitation and disorder of his mind.

[*] These operations of Grouchy on the French right are much better described by H. Houssaye, 'Waterloo,' ii. 138, 139, than by any other historian. They deserve attention, and are in marked contrast with Ney's conduct.

[†] As for Napoleon's disbelief that Blucher could be at hand in force, see H. Houssaye, 'Waterloo,' 139, 140, and Charras, i. 117, 118.

With the single exception of the corps of Lobau, left in reserve just outside Charleroy, in order to assist either Ney or Napoleon, the whole right and centre of the French army was in motion between nine and ten in the forenoon, the point of assembly being Fleurus, rather more than four, or even five, miles from Sombreffe. Vandamme and his corps were at the head of the movement, preceded by Pajol's and Excelmans' squadrons. The Guard advanced from Charleroy and Gilly, followed by Milhaud and his heavy cavalry. Gérard, on the right, marched from before Châtelet, part of his troops, however, being still beyond the Sambre. Napoleon was at Fleurus soon after eleven ; he received at that place the latest report of Grouchy ; the whole corps of Zieten, its outposts falling back, lay in dark masses around St. Amand and Ligny, some two miles from Fleurus, and two or three from Sombreffe. The Emperor at first would hardly believe his eyes, but the situation was plainly before him ; he gradually drew from it the correct inference. The forward—nay, threatening—position of Zieten made Napoleon suspect, and rightly suspect, that Blucher must be at hand in great force. His previsions for the day were therefore, in fact, vain ; he could not easily dispose of the Prussian chief; he had to make preparations for a great, perhaps a decisive, battle. His army was not yet fully in line ; it was not assembled, indeed, until about one, the corps of Gérard having been much retarded by the passage of his soldiers in the rear across the Sambre. Napoleon, therefore, avoided a premature movement ; he called up the division of Girard from Wangenies, detaching it from the command of Ney, and he marshalled his whole army around Fleurus, waiting the development of his enemy's movements. Meanwhile he ascended a windmill near the town, and from its top carefully reconnoitred the scene. At first he only perceived the corps of Zieten, but by noon the corps of Pirch and Thielmann had gathered, on a long line, around Sombreffe, at a considerable distance, however, we have seen, from Fleurus.

Blucher was by this time arraying his army on the positions he had chosen some weeks before as the probable scene of a great battle. We must glance for a moment at the tract of land about to become the theatre of one of the most desperate conflicts of that age. The ground from Fleurus slopes, by a gentle incline, until it sinks into a rather broad valley; from this it rises again, forming a low range of hills spreading west and east from the village of Sombreffe, on a distance of from five to seven miles. The Ligny, an affluent of the Sambre, a stream of little width, but deep, and with high banks, runs in a tortuous course through the valley referred to, gathering into its waters several lesser feeders, and meeting or approaching from west to east the hamlets of Wagnelée, Le Hameau, La Haye, St. Amand, the town of Ligny, and the hamlets of Tongrinnes, Tongrinelles, Boignée, and Balâtre. Beyond the Ligny the range of hills extends from the village of Brye, perhaps the highest point, to Sombreffe, and thence southwards, above the Ligny, to Tongrinnes, Tongrinelles, Boignée, and Balâtre. But the range is nowhere of difficult ascent; it encloses in an amphitheatre of great extent the undulating lands of the valley beneath. The lateral road from Namur to Nivelles, the proper line of junction of the allied armies, runs through Sombreffe, near or along the hills, and thence runs onwards to Quatre Bras, where it meets the great main-road from Charleroy to Brussels; but before reaching Quatre Bras it traverses the ancient Roman road, and approaches the village of Marbais before mentioned. At Fleurus the main-road from Charleroy to Namur stretches through the valley until it joins the lateral road from Nivelles to Namur, at a little distance only from Sombreffe; it thus forms a broad avenue in that direction, available for the advance

8

of an army. The Roman road, practicable for all arms, extends about five or six miles to the west of Fleurus, and thence cuts the lateral road from Nivelles to Namur, at a point about four miles from Sombreffe. Good country roads, in addition to the main Chaussée, connect the points of Quatre Bras and Sombreffe about, we have said, seven miles from each other, and Quatre Bras is only some five miles from Brye and Marbais. The villages along the course of the Ligny are strongly constructed, and afford good positions of defence ; and this was especially the case with the town of Ligny, then a mass of narrow streets, and lofty and solid buildings, crowned by an old château, which has since disappeared. In June, 1815, the expanses of the open ground were covered with thick and high crops of rye where they were not broken by copses and woodland.

The summer sun was high in the heavens, lighting up a scene still of smiling peace, but soon to be ravaged by the devastation of war, when Blucher had placed his army on the ground. The main object of the veteran Marshal was twofold : at once to extend his army towards Quatre Bras, in order to attract support from his colleague, and also to shield his own communications with Namur, and especially to guard the road from Charleroy to Fleurus, and thence to near Sombreffe, a line open to the enemy's advance. Blucher believed that Napoleon's army was almost wholly before him ; he had no idea that Ney was only a few miles off, near Quatre Bras—that is, directly upon his flank and rear—with forces which ought by this time to have formed a united mass of nearly 46,000 men. But he was confident in himself and his troops ; 'they could conquer Algiers,' he had written, 'could they but cross the sea.' His one thought was of the coming battle. He marshalled his army upon a far-spreading front, extending from Wagnelée on his extreme right to Boignée and Balâtre on his extreme left, Ligny and

Sombreffe almost marking his centre. The distance formed a long line of not less than from six to seven miles and upwards. Zieten's corps, composed of the four divisions of Steinmetz, Pirch II., Jagow, and Henkel, and of a division of cavalry under Röder, and supported by near 100 guns, held the right and right centre of the Prussian position from Wagnelée to beyond Ligny. It occupied the villages of La Hameau, La Haye, and St. Amand, hastily fortified since the evening before. It was collected in Ligny in great force, the town, too, having been placed in a state of good defence, the bridges across the Ligny, however, not having been broken. Behind the corps of Zieten stood the corps of Pirch, its four divisions of Tippelskirchen, Krafft, Brause, and Langen, with the cavalry of Jurgäss and some eighty guns being assembled as a reserve of Zieten along the low range of eminences before noticed; it filled the ground nearly between Brye and Sombreffe, and looked down on the masses of troops in its front. To the eastwards was stationed the corps of Thielmann, forming the left centre and the left of Blucher. It was also made up of four divisions, those of Borcke, Kemphen, Lück, and Stulpnagel, with the horsemen of Prince William of Prussia and eighty-eight guns; it was extended upon a very wide tract from near Sombreffe to Tongrinnes and thence to Balâtre, a distance not far from three miles. It hardly occupied Sombreffe at all, and did not occupy the other villages to Balâtre in force; but it held strongly the road from Charleroy, by Fleurus, towards Sombreffe, in order to repel the enemy's attack. The whole Prussian army numbered about 87,000 men, including 8,000 cavalry and some 220 guns.*

The proximity of Ney to the flank and rear of Blucher, especially were Ney in force around Quatre Bras, as his

---

* We have adopted the estimate of Charras (i. 125, 126) as regards the strength of the two armies at Ligny.

master had every right to expect, obviously made this position utterly false ; it might expose the Prussian army to an immense disaster. Apart, however, from this circumstance, the position was in itself open to the gravest objections. The extreme right of Blucher was completely ' in the air ' ; his right and right centre, though well protected in front, were liable to be turned, and even pierced through ; his left centre and left, especially his extreme left, were employed in covering his communications with Namur, and were far too extended. The brunt of the battle at hand would fall on the corps of Zieten and Pirch ; but the troops of Pirch drawn up along the low hills in the rear presented an easy mark to the French artillery, and could be ravaged and half destroyed before they could fire a shot.

Wellington had joined Blucher a little after noon ; he had left Brussels at about six in the morning, had reached Quatre Bras within a few hours, had written the letter to Blucher referred to before, and, seeing that there was only a small French detachment at Frasnes—the few hundred men on the spot the evening before—he had hastened to consult his Prussian ally, having first, as was but just, highly praised Perponcher for having moved his division to Quatre Bras, though in contravention to his own orders, and having left the command at Quatre Bras to the Prince of Orange. What exactly passed between the Duke and Blucher is not fully known. German writers, who have asserted that the concentration of Blucher around Sombreffe was upon the condition that he would have the aid of Wellington—a statement, we have seen, clearly untrue—have also insisted that the old Marshal accepted battle on June 16 on the positive assurance of his colleague that he would come to his assistance in force on the spot ; but this is inconsistent with all the known evidence. It is likely enough that Wellington, misled by the errors of his staff before mentioned, and believing that he would have a much larger part of his army at Quatre Bras than was possible as affairs really stood, may have held out hopes to Blucher of support, but certainly nothing like a pledge was given.   There is no reason to doubt the statement of Muffling that the only expression in this sense that fell from the lips of the Duke was, ' Well, I will come provided I am not attacked myself ';* and it is perfectly plain that Blucher had his preparations made for a great battle before he even met his colleague.† It is more to the purpose, and it deserves notice, that Wellington, with his fine tactical judgment, disapproved of the arrangement of the Prussian army on the ground, and especially objected to the exposure of the corps of Pirch to the enemy's batteries.   But he remonstrated in vain with the aged and stubborn warrior.   He left Blucher's headquarters at Brye between one and two, and characteristically dropped these words to his staff, ' If they fight here they will be damnably mauled,' a prediction verified in every respect.‡

Napoleon's forecast for the day had, we have said, proved false ; Blucher was offering him battle with three-fourths of the Prussian army.   The situation was wholly different from what he thought it would be, but he saw in it the prospect of decisive success.   The faults of his adversary's dispositions were apparent ; the Emperor made ready to turn them to the best advantage.   The enormously extended line of Blucher, especially on his left, the accumulation of the troops of Pirch in positions where they were fatally exposed, and the weakness of the Prussian extreme right, did not escape the eye of the

* Muffling, ' Passages of my Life,' 237.   For the whole conversation between Wellington, Gneisenau and Muffling, see pp. 233, 238.

† This subject is very exhaustively and fairly treated by Mr. Ropes, ' Campaign of Waterloo,' 145-147.   The matter hardly admits of a doubt.

‡ Ropes, ' Campaign of Waterloo,' 152.   The Duke's *mot* was long remembered.

great master, supreme in the art of the higher tactics. Napoleon would paralyse the whole corps of Thielmann with a force comparatively small, but easily moved, by menacing Blucher's communications with Namur; he would fall on the Prussian right and right centre, drawing as large a force as possible to these points, and threatening at the same time the extreme Prussian right; and when *Zieten* and Pirch had become exhausted, and his guns had done their work on Pirch in the rear, he would launch his reserve against the Prussian centre, and force the hostile army to abandon the field. This would secure a victory, but not a decisive victory; the means of obtaining this consummation were not wanting.

Ney by this time would surely be master of Quatre Bras; he would have sent a division to Marbais as had been directed; he would have not far from 46,000 men in his hands; he would be on the flank and rear of the enemy, and at a short distance. The Emperor sent a despatch to the Marshal at two in the afternoon, ordering him to drive away any hostile force in his front, and then to attack and surround 'a body of troops, assembled between Sombreffe and Brye'—that is, to descend on Blucher's flank and rear, and so to complete the defeat of the Prussian army. Meanwhile Napoleon kept his army around Fleurus, masking as long as possible his projected movements, and giving time to Ney to carry out his orders; but he had his preparations made for the great intended attack.*

Grouchy, on the French right, was to keep Thielmann

---

* The terms of the despatch of 2 p.m., referring mainly to 'a body of troops,' are certainly perplexing. It has been inferred that Napoleon did not sufficiently reconnoitre the ground, and even at 2 p.m. had not descried the corps of Pirch and Thielmann. This, however, is incredible. It appears more probable that the ambiguous words were a mistake of the staff, badly directed throughout the campaign. The point is not very important, as we shall see a subsequent despatch written within an hour and a quarter, was quite plain.

on the spot, with the cavalry of Excelmans and Pajol, making demonstrations towards the road to Namur; he was to be supported by Hûlot's division of the corps of Gérard—Hûlot had replaced the deserter Bourmont—and by the cavalry of Maurin from the same corps, holding the road from Charleroy to Fleurus, and thence towards Sombreffe. Vandamme, with the divisions of Lefol, Berthezène, and Habert, Gérard with the divisions of Pêcheux and Vichery, were to attack the Prussian right and right centre, assailing Zieten and Pirch from Le Hameau, La Haye, and St. Amand to Ligny. Girard and Domon's horsemen were to second the movement, and to menace Blucher's extreme right at Wagnelée. The Imperial Guard and Milhaud's heavy cavalry were to be held in reserve to deal the final stroke when Zieten and Pirch had spent their strength, and, as was inevitable, had suffered much, and when Ney should appear on the flank and rear of the enemy. The French army, including the corps of Lobau, was in number rather more than 78,000 men, comprising some 13,000 horsemen and 240 guns, and Lobau was about to be summoned on the field. Napoleon believed, and rightly believed, that the Prussian army* was in his grasp, and could not escape destruction. He remarked to Gérard, his best and most trusted lieutenant: 'The issue of the campaign may be decided within three hours. If Ney executes his orders properly, not a gun of the Prussian army will escape; it is caught in a fatal position.'†

* 'Comment.,' v. 140, 141.

† Nearly all historians and commentators have agreed that Napoleon's plan of attack was perfect. The double movement of Napoleon in front, and of Ney on Blucher's flank and rear, was the best possible; and had Ney done his duty, Ligny would have been a second Jena, and very probably the campaign would have come to an end. It is scarcely necessary to notice the carping criticism of Davoût, Rogniat, and Charras, that Napoleon should have turned Blucher's right, and not made his principal attack on Blucher's centre, this being combined

The French army remained motionless, the purpose of its chief for the moment concealed, until a little after two o'clock. Within a short time, however, making a change of front by the right, it reached the positions it was to take. The fierce Battle of Ligny had begun at three in the afternoon. The division of Lefol, supported by that of Berthezène, advanced boldly against St. Amand, the soldiery ardent and eager for the fray; but the division of Steinmetz within the fortified village, turning its buildings and enclosures to account, held the enemy at bay for a time and repelled his efforts. At last the proverbial 'French fury' and numbers prevailed; St. Amand was stormed and occupied after a desperate struggle, but Vandamme was unable to advance further, kept back by the fire of Zieten's batteries. Meanwhile Girard,* after a similar onslaught and a like resistance, had made himself master of Le Hameau and La Haye, and was approaching Blucher's extreme right at Wagnelée. His position and that of Vandamme had become most threatening, for a bold movement might bring them to the heights of Brye. Blucher sent Pirch II. and a large part of the corps of Pirch, to endeavour to retake the captured villages and to dislodge the enemy from the vantage-ground he had won.

It was now considerably after four; while the French had been making progress in this direction, Ligny had been the scene of a murderous conflict, almost without a parallel in the annals of war. The town, the key of the Prussian right centre, was held by the divisions of Jagow and Henkel; the approaches on the southern bank of the

---

with the attack of Ney. Napoleon has triumphantly refuted such remarks ('Comment.,' vi. 146, 147). In fact, one attack would have led to a defeat of the Prussian army; the other should have annihilated it.

* Girard, the leader of this division, must not be confounded with Gérard, the chief of the 4th French corps. He was a distinguished veteran.

Ligny were attacked in force by Vichery and Pêcheux, Gérard from the rear directing the movement. As at St. Amand, the Prussians made a determined stand; houses, gardens, and buildings placed in a state of defence enabled them to offer a stern resistance; but at last the French, pressing forward with savage energy, drove them fiercely across the bridges of the stream, which had not, we have seen, been broken. Gérard's troops in exultation swarmed into the town; a terrible scene of carnage took place in the streets, each side fighting with desperate courage, ' no quarter being given or asked,' every man being animated, as it were, with mortal hatred, and half maddened by the consuming thirst for revenge. After a time Blucher reinforced his troops, sending another detachment from the corps of Pirch. Gérard was gradually compelled to recross the Ligny, but he held his ground firmly and continued the battle. Meantime on Napoleon's right, as he had expected, Grouchy had succeeded in keeping Thielmann in check. In this direction feeble demonstrations only were seen.

The Battle of Ligny had only just begun, when Napoleon, in observation before Fleurus, sent another and pressing message to Ney at a quarter past three.* Whatever may be thought of the previous despatch, this letter, sent through Soult, was in the plainest terms: Ney was informed that 'the engagement was already hot,' and was ordered to fall on the right of the Prussian army, and so to ' envelop' its flank and rear; ' the fate of France,' it was added, ' is in your hands.' A short time afterwards, probably about half-past three, Napoleon received a message from Lobau, to the effect that Ney was engaged with a part of Wellington's army, and that this was about 20,000 strong.† He reflected that Ney might not be

---

* This despatch, as well as the despatch of 2 p.m., will be found in Charras (i. 122, 134) and in La Tour d'Auvergne, ' Waterloo,' 113, 114.

† See the evidence on this important point furnished by H. Houssaye, ' Waterloo,' ii. 161, 162.

willing or able to descend on Blucher's rear in sufficient force; so he sent a despatch to D'Erlon, in command of the rearward corps of the Marshal, enjoining him to make the movement which Ney had been directed to make, but to attack Blucher's right flank rather than his rear, 'to strike the Prussian army at St. Amand, on the line of Ligny.' This letter, scribbled in pencil, and badly worded —here again we see the handiwork of Soult—was given to a staff officer of the name of Forbin-Janson, a duplicate being given to Colonel Baudus, an officer of Soult, with directions to carry this to Ney; and even if we may doubt that we have the real document—for the proof of it is very imperfect—it seems indisputable that an order in this sense was sent to D'Erlon, quite independently of the two letters to Ney.*

* We subjoin the text of this alleged order, transmitted to us from the memory of General de Selle, in command of the artillery of D'Erlon's corps, and, it would seem, copied into the papers of Baudus, which have been shown by his descendants to M. H. Houssaye :

'MONSIEUR LE COMTE D'ERLON,
   'L'ennemi tombe tête baissée dans la piége que je lui ai tendu. Portez-vous sur le champ avec toutes vos forces à la hauteur de Ligny et fondez sur Saint Amand. Monsieur le Comte d'Erlon, vous allez sauver la France, et vous couvrir de gloire.
                                        'NAPOLEON.'

We confess we are sceptical as to the genuineness of this alleged despatch. Napoleon never wrote to a subordinate in such language. But the present writer, alone among English writers, has never doubted that some such order was sent to D'Erlon besides the letters to Ney of 2 p.m. and 3.15 p.m. The evidence on this point, enormously strengthened by M. H. Houssaye, who has made it conclusive, has always seemed to him ample and sufficient, and the evidence to the contrary most unsatisfactory ('Great Commanders,' 329; 'Disputed Passages of the Campaign of 1815,' 68). It is idle to reject the positive testimony of Baudus, which partly appeared in 1841, and has now been fully brought to light ; besides, it is confirmed by evidence which seems to the present writer overwhelming. Baudus wrote thus (H. Houssaye, 'Waterloo,' ii. 162, 163): 'Le Colonel de Forbin-Janson avait reçu l'importante mission de porter l'ordre qui devait faire marcher le 1re corps en arrière de la droite de l'armée prussienne.

Meanwhile the battle had continued to rage, with little change in its general character, along the fronts of the contending armies. Blucher, anxious for his right, and drawing again from his reserves, sent the division of Tippelskirchen and the squadrons of Jurgäss from the corps of Pirch to assist Zieten; he conducted in person one furious charge; La Haye was retaken by the Prussians after repeated efforts; Girard, a warrior on many fields of fame, was slain. The French, however, clung to Le Hameau and St. Amand; and Vandamme before long had driven back the enemy, his fresh division of Habert and the horsemen of Domon having been skilfully directed against the Prussian flank. During all this time Gérard had manfully held his ground at Ligny, and had kept up the murderous fight; he had been reinforced by batteries of the Imperial Guard, which set part of the doomed town in flames; Blucher strengthened in vain the worn-out troops of Henkel and Jagow with part of the division of Krafft from the corps of Pirch, here again weakening to no effect his reserve. On the Prussian left Thielmann still remained inactive; Grouchy kept his divisions fast to the ground they held. It was not, indeed, until the even-

---

... Au moment où l'affaire était fortement engagée, sur toute la ligne, l'empereur demanda au Maréchal Soult un officier éprouvé pour porter au Maréchal Ney le duplicata de l'ordre concernant le Comte d'Erlon. Le major-général m'ayant fait appeler, l'empereur me dit, J'ai envoyé au Comte d'Erlon l'ordre de se diriger avec tout son corps d'armée en arrière de la droite de l'armée prussienne. Vous allez porter à Ney le duplicata de cet ordre, qui a dû lui être communiqué. Vous lui direz que, quelle que soit la situation où il se trouve, il faut absolument que cet ordre soit exécuté, que je n'attache pas une grande importance à ce que se passera aujourd'hui de son côté; que l'affaire est toute où je suis, car je veux en finir avec l'armée prussienne. Quant à lui, il doit s'il ne peut faire mieux, se borner à contenir l'armée anglaise.' Part of this most important statement, but not the whole, appeared in the ' Études sur Napoléon,' by Colonel Baudus, published, we have said, in 1841. We shall recur to this subject, one of the very greatest importance, when we consider the movements of D'Erlon on June 16.

ing advanced that Thielmann abandoned his timid attitude, solicitous for his chief line of retreat on Namur.
Meantime, as Wellington had foreseen, the French
artillery wrought frightful havoc among the divisions of
Pirch still in position on the heights in the rear; 'every
discharge,' Napoleon has informed us, 'told';* the ground
was strewn with masses of the dead who had perished
where they stood. The Prussian army, in a word, was
being wasted away, while the Emperor had husbanded
his great reserve, and had it in hand. Let Ney or D'Erlon
but appear, and the corps of Zieten and Pirch would be
cut to pieces or compelled to lay down their arms, and
the corps of Thielmann could hardly escape.

It was now about half-past five o'clock; Napoleon had
begun to marshal his reserve—the Guard and Milhaud to
fall on Zieten and Pirch in front; the time had come for
his lieutenants to deal the mortal stroke, to fall on the
flank or the rear of Blucher's army, and to make the
results of the fight decisive. At this moment a message
came from Vandamme to the effect that an enemy's
column 'more than 20,000 strong' was 'issuing from the
woodland in his rear, and was evidently moving upon
Fleurus.' Vandamme, not oblivious of his disaster in
1813, hastily informed his master that, if not strongly
reinforced, he would be compelled to abandon Le Hameau
and St. Amand, to lose the ground that had so hardly
been won, and to retreat, if he would avoid a fatal reverse.
Napoleon sent an aide-de-camp to reconnoitre the mysterious column.† This was, no doubt, not advancing in

---

* 'Comment.,' v. 144: 'Tous les boulets de l'armée française qui
manquaient les premières lignes frappaient dans les reserves; pas un
coup n'était perdu.' Wellington said afterwards, doubtless from a
report, 'The Prussians were dotted in this way—all their bodies
along the slope of the hill, so that no cannon-ball missed its effect
upon them' (Ropes, 'Campaign of Waterloo,' 155). Napoleon and
Wellington exactly concurred.

† According to Napoleon ('Comment.,' v. 142) the aide-de-camp
was Dejean, a general officer of great experience. We may say here,

the direction which Ney or D'Erlon should properly take, for it was not approaching Blucher's flank or rear, but apparently threatening the flank of the French army ; yet the Emperor, either convinced from what he had heard, or losing his wonted presence of mind, did not take the precaution, it may be affirmed, to order the aide-de-camp to summon this body of troops to the field, should it turn out to be a part of his own army.

After rather more than an hour had elapsed—that is, between six and seven o'clock—the aide-de-camp returned with the intelligence that the strange apparition was the corps of D'Erlon, which, as had been ordered, had drawn near the scene of the conflict, but had gone considerably out of its way. Napoleon again missed the occasion, whatever the reason, and did not call upon his subordinate to take part in the battle, though D'Erlon could still have done important service ; and in a short time the column which might have completely turned the scales of fortune was seen to disappear. While this misadventure was taking place Napoleon suspended the movement of his reserve. The divisions of Vandamme and Girard, already hard pressed, and hearing that a great hostile force was upon their flank, became stricken with panic, and in part gave way ; some battalions of Lefol fled in such terror and dismay that their chief actually turned his guns against them. Blucher caught at the opportunity presented to him. Rallying the soldiery of Tippelskirchen and Jurgäss, and supporting them with cavalry drawn from the corps of Thielmann, he made a desperate onslaught on the French left ; his heroic ardour inspired his troops ; Le

at once, that Napoleon's account of what may be called the D'Erlon incident, one of the greatest importance, is very unsatisfactory. A great mistake, the Emperor felt, was made, and he concealed the facts. See ' Great Commanders,' 329, and ' Disputed Passages of the Campaign of 1815,' 68. This, also, is the view of M. H. Houssaye (' Waterloo,' ii. 203).

Hameau was retaken after a terrible struggle; the whole line of Vandamme seemed about to yield. Napoleon had already sent Vandamme part of Grouchy's horsemen; he was reluctantly compelled to employ his reserve; the Young Guard, and even a part of the Old—the veterans of a hundred battles—were pushed forward to restore the fight; but the issue remained for a time uncertain.

Blucher still believed that he had in his front by far the greatest part of the French army, though the roar of cannon towards Quatre Bras, in his rear, announced that a battle was raging at a little distance. He had received a message from Wellington not to expect assistance; he must have beheld the great reserve of Napoleon, now moving from before Fleurus towards Ligny; he knew that Zieten and Pirch had suffered enormous losses, and that only Thielmann's corps remained intact. The contest, in a word, was going against him; but the heroic though very thoughtless chief saw only what was before his eyes, and, elated by his late partial success, he resolved to make a desperate effort to secure victory. He had ordered Thielmann some time before to take a more active part in the strife; Thielmann had attacked Grouchy, but had been repulsed; he was directed to send his divisions of Stulpnagel and Borcke towards Ligny, and so to cover the Prussian centre.

Meanwhile Blucher had collected every available man from the exhausted corps of Zieten and Pirch, employing, in addition to the divisions already engaged, parts of the divisions of Brause and Langen, and had launched them against the French left, which, reinforced by the Young Guard, had again taken Le Hameau and driven the enemy back. The old Marshal, conspicuous on a white charger, a gift of the Prince Regent of England, places himself at the head of the masses he leads. His purpose is, by an attack pressed home, to outflank and crush Vandamme and his supports, and to force·Napoleon from his line of

retreat by Fleurus to Charleroy, perhaps to precipitate
him into the defiles of the Sambre. His hoarse voice is
heard amidst the din and yell of the fight, telling 'his
children not to let the Grande nation lord it over them
again; to have at the enemy, in God's name, with the
cold steel.' The shout of ' Vorwarts !' echoes from rank
to rank; once more a tremendous conflict rages along
the whole line from Wagnelée to St. Amand. For a
moment it seems that the attack will succeed ; the Young
Guard is borne back by superior numbers; the troops of
Vandamme hesitate, even fall back ; sounds of victory are
heard among the exulting Prussians. But their efforts
fail against the warriors of the Old Guard ; these oppose
a barrier to the enemy that nothing can break ; the French
rally behind ' the column of granite '; once more the line
of fire extending beyond St. Amand marks the repulse of
Blucher and his baffled troops, while the superior French
artillery mows them down in hundreds.

While this terrible conflict was in progress, Thielmann
had again vigorously attacked Grouchy, but had failed,
for the second time, with the loss of some guns. He was
now so deeply engaged with the enemy that Stulpnagel
and Borcke could not reach Ligny. Meantime the flames
had consumed whole quarters of the town. Gérard had
recrossed the river and gained ground ; the soldiery of
the defence had shown signs of yielding. Napoleon, after
receiving the report of the aide-de-camp, had long before
made ready to deal a final stroke ; the combination that
should have annihilated Blucher had been frustrated, but
he could not the less reckon on more than a partial
triumph. The corps of Lobau was now at hand. Soon
after seven the greater part of the Imperial Guard and
Milhaud's cavalry were advancing on Ligny and the
enemy's centre. The Emperor understood perfectly the
state of the battle. ' They have no reserve,' he quietly
said, as his glass swept the field. At about eight the

great body of magnificent troops, which he had kept in hand to deal a decisive blow, had joined Gérard and his well-tried divisions.   Under the fire of their batteries, powerful and well placed, the Guard and Milhaud got over the stream.   Shouts of ' No quarter !' were heard among the fierce soldiery.   Vichery and Pêcheux forced their way through the streets of Ligny, reckless of blazing buildings and of the scene of carnage.   The victorious columns, bursting through the ranges of guns, which endeavoured in vain to check their advance, were seen approaching the low hills which, on the left, stretch to Brye and the adjoining heights.   The Prussian centre, in a word, denuded of support, and presenting only a few exhausted bodies of troops to the formidable reserve, carrying all before it, was broken through at once by the overwhelming shock ; the effect, Soult wrote, ' was a transformation scene at a theatre.'

Blucher, hurrying to the spot on hearing the fatal news, flung the squadrons of Roder and some battalions of foot-men against the exulting enemy ; but the horsemen re-coiled before the serried squares of the Guard ; Milhaud's mailed troopers completed the defeat.   In one of these encounters the aged chief was thrown from his charger, and only saved by the presence of mind of a devoted aide-de-camp.   What might have been the result of the campaign had he been slain by some unknown French soldier ?   The victors had soon mastered the heights ; along the extended line from west to east their foot and horse bore the still fighting and stubborn beaten army back.   The corps of Lobau had by this time reached the field, but it was half-past nine, and darkness gathered on the scene.   Napoleon rightly desisted from a pursuit by night, but the mere delay caused by the mischance of D'Erlon very probably saved the defeated host.   Its retreat was orderly and well conducted.   Zieten and Pirch steadily rallying their men, fell back only a few miles northwards ;

Thielmann held Sombreffe for a considerable time. The French bivouacked on the ground they had won, but they made no attempt to follow the enemy. Napoleon returned to Fleurus, now his headquarters. The losses of Blucher were about 18,000 men on the field, so frightful had been the effects of the French artillery; but from 8,000 to 12,000 flying men disbanded. The losses of the Emperor were about 11,000 men; few prisoners and only some thirty guns were taken.*

June 16 witnessed another passage of arms, well contested and bloody, but unlike Ligny. We left Ney at Frasnes, between ten and eleven o'clock, having just received the orders of Napoleon and Soult to assemble the mass of his forces around Quatre Bras, and to make the other dispositions set forth before. The Marshal, we have seen, had let the precious hours slip; he had done nothing to draw together the army, nearly 46,000 strong, placed under his command; he had made no attempt to occupy Quatre Bras, which he had been directed to seize on the afternoon of the 15th. Even now he did not thoroughly and loyally carry out the orders he ought to have instantly obeyed; his conduct still gave proof of irresolution—nay, of distrust of his master. He, indeed, directed Reille and D'Erlon to advance, but Reille alone was to hold Quatre Bras, and to proceed further; D'Erlon was to remain two miles in the rear, at Frasnes; one of his divisions was to occupy Marbais, a position which Reille, being before him, ought to have been told to seize, for this was of supreme importance; and while he ordered a single brigade of Kellermann to move on

---

* There are many excellent accounts of the Battle of Ligny. The reader may consult Alison, Siborne, Hooper, Thiers, the Commentaries of Napoleon, Charras, La Tour d'Auvergne, H. Houssaye, Damitz and Clausewitz. The résumé of Clausewitz, cited by Mr. Ropes ('Campaign of Waterloo,' 171), is in parts very able and comprehensive; but Clausewitz is far from candid in several most important passages of his narrative.

9

Frasnes, he placed the three remaining brigades at Liberchies—that is, at some distance from the old Roman road, where Napoleon had written that they should be placed.* This was neglect, delay, and even disobedience; yet Ney had received an order about noon, which ought to have fixed his purpose at once, and compelled him to act with prompt energy. At about nine Reille had been apprised by Girard—then in observation around Wangenies—that 'large Prussian masses' were seen in the direction of Quatre Bras. These were the divisions of Zieten at St. Amand and Ligny. Reille sent an officer of lancers to make a report to Napoleon. The Emperor, about to leave Charleroy, wrote sharply to Ney, whose indecision was being made manifest, commanding him 'to unite the corps of Reille and D'Erlon, and the corps of Kellermann,' adding that 'with these forces you should defeat and destroy any enemies in your front.' 'Blucher was yesterday still at Namur; it is most improbable that he could have troops near Quatre Bras; you have to deal only with those on the way from Brussels.'† This order was peremptory and distinct; yet Ney still would not fully comply with it; he remained in his hesitating, halting mood; he had no mind really to obey the Emperor.‡

Napoleon's aide-de-camp, when on his way to Frasnes, had communicated the orders sent to Ney, to Reille and D'Erlon, at Gosselies and Jumet, and had directed these

* This order will be found in La Tour d'Auvergne, 'Waterloo,' 146, 147. Ney clearly was not disposed to do what Napoleon had told him to do.

† This most important order will be found in La Tour d'Auvergne, 'Waterloo,' 105, and is No. 9 of ' Documents inédits.'

‡ Mr. Ropes has examined more thoroughly and impartially than any other commentator the conduct, or rather the misconduct, of Ney on the morning of June 16. See 'Campaign of Waterloo,' 116, 128. We have only space for a single sentence (p. 187): ' The whole management of Marshal Ney on this day shows distrust of the Emperor's judgment, unwillingness to take the most obvious steps, finally disobedience of orders.'

Generals to have their troops under arms. Ney transmitted, probably to Reille, the instructions he had received, but sent nothing, it would appear, to D'Erlon and Kellermann, except his own orders, referred to already. This was rather careless if excusable conduct; but at this conjuncture another delay took place, not to be laid, however, to the charge of the Marshal. Reille, after receiving Girard's report, became alarmed at the supposed approach of the enemy. He sent a despatch to Ney describing his fears; he told him that he would not advance towards Quatre Bras until he had obtained his superior's orders.* Ney, to do him justice, directed Reille to march at once; but Reille did not receive the message until after noon; nearly two hours were thus unfortunately lost. Reille set off from Gosselies without further delay; but no additional orders, it seems, were sent to D'Erlon and Kellermann in the rear; D'Erlon remained for some time motionless. It was after one when the chief part of Bachelu's division, joining the fraction detached the evening before, appeared at Frasnes, and drew near Quatre Bras. It was followed by the division of Foy at a little distance, and by that of Jerôme, still some three miles behind; but D'Erlon was even now considerably in the rear. The light cavalry of the Guard had remained around Frasnes; but Ney at this moment had not more than some 9,000 infantry and 1,800 horsemen, including the troops of Foy, but not taking into account the squadrons of Lefebvre-Desnoëttes and the brigade of Kellermann, this last only a short way from Frasnes, to oppose to the enemy immediately in his front.

Had the Marshal acted with insight and vigour—had he been, as Napoleon had written, the man he once was —he might have assembled before Quatre Bras by ten in the morning the whole corps of Reille at least, with the

* 'Documents inédits,' No. 11; La Tour d'Auvergne, 'Waterloo,' 149, 150.

single exception of Girard's men, in addition to the light
cavalry of the Guard—that is, about 22,000 sabres and
bayonets, with more than forty guns, and with D'Erlon
and Kellermann at a short distance. Had he effectually
carried out Soult's and Napoleon's orders, he might have
had almost his whole army in hand—in other words, nearly
46,000 men, with not far from 100 guns—even allowing
for the hesitations of Reille, at four in the afternoon at
latest. In either case he would have destroyed Perponcher's division, the only hostile force in his path, or
compelled it to make a disastrous retreat. He could
almost certainly have defeated and driven back the
reinforcements coming to Perponcher's aid ; he could
have easily made himself master of Quatre Bras, and,
above all, he would have had ample means to send to
Napoleon the body of troops, which, falling on the flank
and rear of Blucher, would have annihilated the Prussian
army at Ligny.*

Apart from the cavalry of the Guard and Kellermann,
Ney, we have said, disposed of nearly 9,000 foot and
1,800 horsemen at this moment, the two divisions of
Bachelu and Foy, the squadrons of Piré, and from twenty
to thirty guns. Perponcher had some 7,000 infantry,
soon to be reinforced by a single battalion, the brigades
of Saxe-Weimar and Bylandt, perhaps fifty sabres, and
not more than sixteen pieces.† The disproportion of
force was therefore great, and the Nassauers and Dutch
Belgians were young and raw troops, not to be compared
with the well-trained French, though they manfully stood
this day to their colours.‡ Nevertheless Reille, who had

---

* The reader may be referred again to the admirable comments of
Mr. Ropes. See especially pp. 177, 178, 186.

† For these figures compare Charras (i. 153, 154) and Siborne ('The
Waterloo Campaign,' 143, 1895 edition), both careful writers. Siborne,
however, is not correct in giving Ney 16,189 foot at 2 p.m. Jerôme's
division was still in the rear.

‡ A fruitless attempt was made by the French to appeal to these
troops as old comrades : Charras, i. 157, 158.

joined Ney, like Vandamme, full of evil memories of the
past, entreated the Marshal not to fall on; Wellington's
army, he insisted, might be at hand in the immediate
rear of Perponcher. Ney, however, rejected these counsels
of fear; he was the 'bravest of the brave' in the face of
an enemy; he fired his first shot at two in the afternoon.
The ground was favourable to the defensive; the great
main-road from Charleroy to Brussels, an avenue for an
army, ran, indeed, from Frasnes directly to Quatre Bras
—a collection of four or five buildings only, at the point
where the lateral road from Nivelles to Namur joins; but
the Bois de Bossu, a dense piece of woodland, covered
the battalions of Perponcher to his right; the large farm
of Gemioncourt and its walled enclosures were close to
the main-road in his front; on either side, and at no great
distance, were the farms and enclosures of Pierrepont
and Pireaumont; the adjoining lands were thick with
hedges and crops of rye; the whole formed a good position to hold—at least for a time.

Perponcher and the Prince of Orange, now in chief
command, had placed their troops with much skill on
the ground, concealing their weakness in numbers as far
as possible. They had occupied Gemioncourt and the
Bois de Bossu with eight battalions, had kept two in
reserve at Quatre Bras, and had placed their scanty
artillery, for the most part, on the great main-road. It
is unnecessary to dwell in detail on the combat that
followed, of which the result could be hardly doubtful.
Ney endeavoured to turn the position of the farm of
Pireaumont which Bachelu occupied after a brief struggle.
Foy drove the enemy out of the farm of Gemioncourt;
the approaches to Quatre Bras were nearly won; the
horsemen of Piré and the well-served French guns did
much execution on infantry having but little support.
Saxe-Weimar still clung to the Bois de Bossu, but a
charge led by the Prince of Orange, in person, to disable

the hostile artillery, failed; the Prince was very nearly made a prisoner. The defence, in a word, was unsuccessful; Quatre Bras was almost in Ney's grasp. But the French had been held in check for more than an hour, a service of the very greatest value; time was secured for reinforcements to appear on the scene.*

The battle was thus going against the allies, when Wellington, after his interview with Blucher, returned to Quatre Bras. Meanwhile the division of Jerôme, nearly 8,000 strong, had reached the field and reinforced the French. Ney now disposed of between 18,000 and 19,000 men, with from thirty to forty guns. The position of affairs had become very critical, but the British Commander, an eye-witness wrote, 'remained impassive and cold as ice, as though the French were a hundred miles off.' He congratulated Perponcher and the Prince of Orange, and curtly told them they had done very well. His coolness and presence of mind were rewarded. At about half-past three he received a large addition of strength; a brigade of Dutch-Belgian cavalry, under Van Merlen, from 1,000 to 1,100 sabres, and the 5th British division, led by Picton, with a brigade of Hanoverians, ere long followed by a part of the Brunswick contingent, with its Duke as chief, appeared on the scene at the very nick of time.† Picton and the Hanoverians might have been on the field much sooner, but Wellington, always apprehensive for his right, had

---

* Justice has not been done by English writers to the importance of Perponcher's defence. No doubt his troops were not very good; but they gained what was greatly wanted—time. See, for the conduct of the Dutch-Belgian contingent in the campaign, Van Loben Sels, 'Précis de la Campagne de 1815,' an excellent work.

† Siborne and other English writers make Picton's division and the Hanoverians reach Quatre Bras at about half-past two or a quarter to three ('The Waterloo Campaign,' 145, 1895 edition). But they were not up until half-past three at the earliest. See Chesney, 'Waterloo Lectures,' 113; Charras, i. 157; H. Houssaye, 'Waterloo,' ii. 193; and Van Loben Sels, 196, 197. There are other authorities to the same effect.

made them halt at Waterloo, near the road to Nivelles;
they had not begun their march thence until after noon.
The Duke had now a force about equal in numbers to
that of Ney, but this was largely composed of beaten
and inferior troops; he had fewer guns than the French,
and these not as effective; he was, therefore, not yet a
match for his enemy. He made ready, nevertheless, for
a stout resistance; he perceived that Ney was preparing
a grand attack; he placed Picton and the Hanoverians
on his left, beyond and near the lateral road from Nivelles
to Namur, with detachments towards Quatre Bras and
Pireaumont. The Brunswick contingent was arrayed
from the Bois de Bossu, and thence to Quatre Bras;
Perponcher and the Prince of Orange were drawn back in
second line.

It was now past four. Ney had received the message
from the Emperor despatched at two from Fleurus; he
addressed himself to carry out his master's orders—that is,
to seize Quatre Bras, and to send a detachment in force
to fall on the flank and rear of Blucher at Ligny. He
must have felt how ill he had seconded his great chief;
how Reille and himself had been gravely to blame; especially how unfortunate it had been not to have sent a
division long before to Marbais, where this would be on
the Prussian rear; but even now he did not summon
D'Erlon to the field and the cavalry of Kellermann left
behind; he would not engage the light cavalry of the
Guard. He resolved to make the decisive effort with
troops already contending against an enemy, weaker, no
doubt, but equal in numbers to himself. Bachelu was to
attack the left of Wellington; Foy was to advance on
Quatre Bras by the great main-road; Jerôme to carry
the Bois de Bossu; Piré and the artillery were to support
the movement.

A fierce conflict ensued with varying fortunes, and
continued about an hour and a half. Bachelu, under the

protection of powerful batteries, advanced boldly against
Picton; his soldiers had to make their way through close
hedges and crops of rye; but, as usual, the column failed
against the line, as the Carthaginian phalanx failed against
the Roman legion. At the word, it is said, of Wellington
on the spot, Picton's men fell on the French in disorder,
and forced them back to the position they had held.
The victors, however, pressed forward too far; they were
dexterously assailed in flank by a battalion kept in reserve, and were charged, when blown and exhausted, by
Piré's squadrons; they, too, in turn were compelled to
fall back. Bachelu, however, made no further attempt to
attack his formidable enemy in front; he made little
more than demonstrations for a time, and contented himself with menacing Wellington's extreme left.

Meanwhile the course of the battle had turned against
the Duke on other parts of the scene of events. Van
Merlen had bravely charged the infantry of Foy, but he
had been routed by Piré's troopers; the beaten squadrons
were driven beyond Quatre Bras, and suffered heavily
from the fire of an English battalion, which, deceived by
their uniform, mistook them for French. Ere long the
Brunswick contingent was engaged, and met a not
dissimilar fate. The Duke's infantry yielded to Foy and
Jerôme; his artillery was dismounted in part by the
guns of Ney, which kept up a destructive fire along the
whole line; his cavalry was completely defeated; he fell
when leading a fruitless charge. This marked success on
their centre and left inspired the French with enthusiastic
ardour; Foy advances along the great main-road; Jerôme
expels part of the enemy out of the Bois de Bossu; Saxe-
Weimar's men are compelled to leave the field; Piré's
cavalry, elated by its brilliant success, and conspicuous
for its daring and courage on this day, bore right down
on Picton and the Hanoverians of Best, now almost the
only unbroken troops of Wellington. A sanguinary and

well-sustained struggle followed ; the horsemen fell on the British 42nd and 44th before these were able to complete their squares ; but after a desperate contest they were just driven back. Every other effort of the brave troopers failed against Picton's steady and silent squares, whose murderous fire wrought great havoc. ' Remember Egypt !' the warrior shouted to the 28th. The British, in a word, showed on the 16th what, in a few hours, they were to do at Waterloo. One Hanoverian battalion, however, was, it is related, caught and cut to pieces ; and some of Piré's men rushed into Quatre Bras, and but for a chance might have laid hands on Wellington. Meanwhile Jerôme and Foy had advanced further ; a step more, and they would reach Quatre Bras.

The situation for Wellington had again become ' extremely critical,'* when, fortunately, he was again reinforced. This fresh support was composed of part of Alten's third British division, comprising a Hanoverian brigade, about 5,400 infantry and twelve guns. The Duke's army was now much superior in numbers to that of Ney—some 26,000 men against 18,000 or 19,000 ; but the Brunswickers and Dutch Belgians had been defeated ; it was certainly not superior in effective force.† It was now about half-past five o'clock. Delcambre, the chief of the staff of D'Erlon, reached the field and reported to the Marshal that the Emperor had summoned D'Erlon to Ligny. Nearly at the same moment the despatch of a quarter-past three arrived, informing Ney, for the second time, that he was to fall on Blucher's flank and rear, and

---

* Siborne, ' The Waterloo Campaign,' 173, 1895 edition.

† Charras (i. 161) seems to be in error in stating that a Nassau contingent under Kruse came to Wellington's assistance at this time. See Siborne, 'The Waterloo Campaign,' 173, 1895 edition. On the other hand, Siborne is certainly wrong in making Ney bring up the whole of Kellermann's cavalry on the arrival of Alten. Of four brigades, only one reached Quatre Bras. All the authorities are now agreed on this point.

telling him that the fortunes of France were in his hands. This despatch, addressed to Gosselies—another of Soult's mistakes—reached Quatre Bras at least an hour late; it ought to have been directed to Frasnes or Quatre Bras; the officer—there is much controversy as to who he was—had made a circuit of six or seven miles. Ney lost his temper and presence of mind on receiving this news; he forgot that his master had ordered D'Erlon to march to Ligny; he forgot, too, that D'Erlon was by this time, in all probability, at too great a distance to come to his aid in any event; he peremptorily told Delcambre to recall his chief to Quatre Bras, exclaiming, with an imprecation : 'Would that those English cannon-balls would make me a corpse!' an act of grave disobedience and of thoughtless haste, attended with the worst results for Napoleon and France. We must turn for a moment to follow the movements of D'Erlon, of the first importance among the incidents of June 16. That General, habitually, we have said, backward, had only received a single order from Ney. He did not reach Gosselies from Jumet until near two, and having made a long halt at Gosselies, he was not on the old Roman road until after four, still at a distance of some four miles from Quatre Bras, where he ought to have been several hours before.*

At this point D'Erlon met Forbin-Janson, the officer charged with Napoleon's message, we have said, to come directly to Ligny, without regard to Ney. Forbin-Janson had taken the straight road by Mellet, unlike the other officer, who had gone round by Gosselies, with the order of a quarter-past three to Ney. He gave the Emperor's orders probably at half-past four in the afternoon. D'Erlon at once turned his whole corps towards Ligny, marching rapidly, it would seem, for the country was open; but Forbin-Janson was a dull and puzzle-headed

---

* Compare on this point H. Houssaye, 'Waterloo,' ii. 200, and La Tour d'Auvergne, 'Waterloo,' 173-176.

man; he could not interpret an obscure despatch in pencil—here once more we find the shortcomings of Soult —and D'Erlon directed his men towards Fleurus—that is, we have seen, on the flank of Napoleon, not on St. Amand or Brye, on the flank or rear of Blucher. The Emperor, we have said, accepted the report of Vandamme, that D'Erlon's corps was an enemy's column,* and despatched an aide-de-camp to ascertain the fact; and he did not, as we have taken care to point out, direct his messenger to summon D'Erlon to the field either before or after he discovered that D'Erlon's troops were French.

At about half-past six Delcambre rejoined D'Erlon with Ney's imperative command to march on Quatre Bras. D'Erlon, improperly, and very unwisely, complied, to the intense indignation of his own soldiery, who rightly felt they ought to fall on the enemy at hand, and showed signs of unsteadiness and want of discipline.† D'Erlon, however, adopted a half-measure—a characteristic of inferior men—and returned to Ney with three of his divisions only; he detached a single division, under Durutte, with orders to act 'with extreme caution.' Durutte reached Wagnelée on the far right of Blucher, in time to see the closing scenes of the battle; but he had moved slowly in obedience to the orders of his chief; he only exchanged a few cannon-shot with the enemy in retreat. But had D'Erlon's corps, 20,000 strong, been launched, even as late as seven in the evening, or half-past seven, on the flank of Blucher at Wagnelée and St. Amand, it could practically have accomplished

---

* The staff officer who informed Vandamme that D'Erlon's corps was part of an enemy's army was, it is said, afraid to reconnoitre sufficiently clearly : H. Houssaye, 'Waterloo,' ii. 172. Here is another proof how bad the French staff service was in this campaign.

† In this account of the movements of D'Erlon we have followed H. Houssaye, 'Waterloo,' ii. 200-205. This learned and masterly narrative nearly corresponds with that of Thiers, and seems to the present writer conclusive as to the true facts.

Napoleon's purpose, and effected the destruction of the
Prussian army.* In any event, had it reached the scene
of action, the Emperor would have had a fresh corps in
his hands; very possibly, with the additional fresh corps
of Lobau, he would have ventured on a pursuit at night;
certainly he could have made the retreat of his enemy a
complete rout.†

* Clausewitz, cited by Mr. Ropes ('Campaign of Waterloo,' 167), is
here uncandid. He asks whether Blucher must have been 'completely overthrown' had 10,000 men been thrown on his rear.
D'Erlon's corps was 20,000 strong; and no impartial student of the
battle can doubt that, had 15,000 or 20,000 men been directed by Ney
or D'Erlon on Blucher's flank or rear, while the Emperor attacked
his centre in front, the Prussian army must have been destroyed.
Clausewitz, cited by H. Houssaye ('Waterloo,' ii. 177), is also
disingenuous on another important point. He says that D'Erlon
would have been too late had he been directed on Brye—that is, on
Blucher's rear—at half-past six or seven. That is true; but he might
have been directed on Wagnelée and St. Amand—that is, on Blucher's
flank—and had this happened he would have achieved decisive
success. Durutte, we must recollect, reached Wagnelée, and might
have struck the enemy hard had he chose. See H. Houssaye,
'Waterloo,' 215.

† H. Houssaye ('Waterloo,' ii. 202, 203) has brought together a
great amount of evidence to confirm the statement of Colonel Baudus,
and to prove that D'Erlon received a direct order from Napoleon to
march on Ligny. The present writer has long ago been satisfied with
the proof afforded by the well-known letter of Soult of June 17,
shamefully garbled by Charras: 'Si le Comte d'Erlon avait exécuté
le mouvement sur Saint Amand que l'empereur a prescrit, l'armée
prussienne était entièrement perdu'; and by the well-known letter of
Ney to Fouché of June 29 : 'J'allais faire avancer le 1er corps, quand
j'appris que l'empereur en avait disposé.' But this additional evidence
is very valuable, and is quite conclusive. The story told by D'Erlon
himself ('Documents inédits,' No. 22), and accepted by some French
and by most English writers, is, at best, unsatisfactory, and may now
be finally dismissed as untrue. That story is briefly this—that there
was no direct order to D'Erlon, but that Labédoyère was the bearer of
the note of 3.15 p.m. to Ney (so often referred to), or of a duplicate of
it ; and that, while D'Erlon had gone forward to Frasnes, Labédoyère
took on himself to turn aside the 1st corps to Ligny. But (1) Labédoyère was with the Emperor near Fleurus at this very time (Petit,
'Souvenirs Militaires,' 98), and (2) D'Erlon (in his 'Vie Militaire,' 95)
contradicts the whole story, and tells one altogether different. It is

While D'Erlon had thus been wandering between two
fields of battle, without making his presence felt on either,
Ney had made another determined attack on Wellington.
The Marshal had felt the effects of his master's appeal,
that the destinies of his country depended on him ; he
had nerved himself to attempt a supreme effort.   But, as
Napoleon has truly written, Ney, thinking only of the
forces within his immediate ken,* and distracted by vexa-
tion and passion, still would not avail himself of the
cavalry of the Guard, or of Kellermann's three brigades
in the rear; he engaged only the wearied troops he had
on his hands, with the addition of the single brigade of
Kellermann—800 or 900 cuirassiers of the first quality—
which had been near the scene, for some time, at Frasnes.
Had he employed the fresh troops he might have employed,
he could not have achieved decisive success ; he could not
now overwhelm Wellington ; the issue of the operations
of the day hung on the movements of D'Erlon and his
corps, and this had been recalled by Ney from the essential
point Ligny, in contravention of the Emperor's positive
orders !

The Marshal's attack nevertheless was vigorously
pressed home, and for a time seemed to be of brilliant
promise.   Wellington had distributed the reinforcements
he had lately received along his front from his left to his
right, from where Bachelu menaced him to Quatre Bras
and the Bois de Bossu ; he had placed his worn-out and

---

idle to accept such statements in face of the clear and consistent
statement of Baudus, confirmed as it is by irresistible evidence.   See
'Disputed Passages of the Campaign of 1815,' 68, 69.   Besides,
D'Erlon, in all that he has written on the subject, evidently is trying
to exculpate himself, in respect of the enormous mistake that was
committed on June 16.

   * 'Comment.,' v. 200 : 'Toujours le premier dans le feu, Ney oubliait
les troupes qui n'étaient pas sous ses yeux.   La bravoure que doit
montrer un général-en-chef, est differente de celle que doit avoir un
général de division.'

beaten troops in his rear; but Picton's division and his Hanoverian supports stood in squares; his chief calmly awaited the enemy's onset. The assault of Kellermann's horsemen, sustained by a heavy fire of guns, had for a moment a very marked effect. The 69th was caught before it could form square, lost a colour, and a great number of men; the 33rd was driven into the Bois de Bossu; the 30th was for a time in peril, but ere long had beaten the bold squadrons off. Meanwhile Piré's cavalry had renewed its brilliant efforts, sweeping along in the rear of the mailed troops before it. A combined attack was made by the French infantry from the Bois de Bossu, now in part mastered, towards Quatre Bras, and thence towards the road from Nivelles to Namur. The struggle raged terribly for more than an hour, but Kellermann's cuirassiers had ere long recoiled from before Picton's indomitable squares; they were assailed by the destructive fire of the British infantry, and of fresh batteries which had just reached Wellington. They were suddenly carried away by a panic; this became a signal for the whole French line to fall back by degrees, defeated indeed, but still threatening in defeat.*

Long before this Baudus, the bearer of the despatch of which Forbin-Janson had had the duplicate, had reached the field of Quatre Bras and held an interview with Ney. He found the Marshal vigorously directing the fight; he had lost two of his chargers, and had not spared himself; but he flamed out when he saw Napoleon's messenger, refused to countermand the recall of D'Erlon, and, ' with a face purple with passion,' turned furiously away. It was by this time more than seven o'clock; Cooke's first division of British Guards and two battalions of

---

* Siborne's account of this episode of the battle is very good : ' The Waterloo Campaign,' 174-188, 1875 edition. All the French writers make too much of the cavalry attacks ; they were very brilliant, but proved completely fruitless against the British foot in squares.

Brunswickers arrived on the scene, with two batteries
of sixteen guns; Wellington had now more than 31,000
men, with some seventy guns, against the 18,000 or 19,000
of Ney, the remains of Kellermann's brigade, and about
forty-five pieces.   The scales of fortune had been turned;
the contest was now altogether unequal.

The Duke took the offensive without delay ; the Guards
drove Jerôme out of the Bois de Bossu; Foy was compelled to retreat along the great main-road; Bachelu fell
back from the road from Nivelles to Namur, which at one
time he had nearly attained; Gemioncourt and the other
two points of vantage were captured.   Ney, regaining his
energy and presence of mind—the great qualities he had
exhibited splendidly in his career—by degrees drew his
army out of fire; he gave proof of the fine tactical skill of
which he had given proof when before Wellington, at
Redinha among the hills of Portugal; he retired upon
Frasnes with comparatively little loss.   In one respect
the Marshal had done good service : he had prevented
Wellington from sending a man to Blucher; to that
extent he had given his master support.   But so large a
force had been entrusted to him, that he really deserves
little credit for this; and his conduct in other respects
must be severely censured.   Had he acted with even
ordinary vigour and insight, he might, as we have pointed
out before, have had 22,000 men before Quatre Bras by
the early forenoon; he might have had 46,000 or so by
four in the afternoon; in either case he could have
defeated every enemy in his front, and he would have
been able to carry into effect Napoleon's grand combination, and to destroy Blucher.   Nay, had he not most
improperly recalled D'Erlon in defiance of the Emperor's
commands, he could have secured the same results;
Ligny would have been a disaster, fatal to Prussia.
From first to last, his conduct on June 16 showed indecision, neglect, delay, and disregard of his master's orders.

His losses at Quatre Bras were some 4,300 men; those of Wellington were 300 or 400 more. D'Erlon did not reach Quatre Bras until after the end of the contest, his whole corps having been, so to speak, paralysed.*

These briefly were the operations of June 16, marked by the battles of Ligny and Quatre Bras. The superiority of Napoleon on this day must be apparent to the real student of war; it was seldom more distinctly displayed. Passing by the charge of inaction in the morning, which seems to us far from well founded, unquestionably he misinterpreted at first the intentions of his foes, reasoning on assumptions false in themselves, but in accord with well-conceived strategy; he thought he could easily dispose of Blucher, and reach Brussels on the 17th. But his arrangements for the 16th were in the highest degree excellent; they not only fell in with his own ideas, but perfectly met the situation that actually occurred; this is what impartial history ought to dwell on. Had the commander of his left simply done his duty, had he conformed to positive and plain orders,† Blucher must have been annihilated on the field of Ligny; Wellington could hardly have escaped a disaster next day. The Emperor at St. Helena justly repeated the remark he had made to Gérard on the 16th: " Had my left done what it ought to have done, I would have crushed the enemy."‡ His plan of attack at Ligny was also perfect ; the movement against the centre of Blucher, combined with the intended movement against the flank and rear, must have secured for

* The reader may be referred to the authorities before mentioned as regards Ligny, for an account of Quatre Bras. Siborne, if not always accurate, has taken great pains with details.

† The reader must again be referred to Mr. Ropes' admirable commentary on Ney's conduct. Soult, years after Waterloo, remarked to Sir William Napier : ' Ney neglected his orders at Quatre Bras ' (' Life of Sir William Napier,' i. 505).

‡ Napoleon Correspondence, xxxii. 275: ' Je les écrasais a Ligny si ma gauche eût fait son devoir.'

the French an overwhelming triumph.   Soult wrote,
without exaggeration, on the 17th that "the Prussian
army would have been destroyed, and perhaps 30,000
prisoners made."* Napoleon, too, conducted the battle
with conspicuous skill; he made the most of his adversary's mistakes; he encouraged Blucher idly to waste his
strength, and then, husbanding a great reserve until the
moment came, he defeated the old Marshal and won a
battle, which but for the merest accidents must have
been decisive.†

Yet amidst these splendid illustrations of the art of war
Napoleon made, we believe, one signal mistake.   He
always expected a great deal from his lieutenants; he not
unreasonably gave credit to the report of Vandamme that
D'Erlon's corps was an enemy's column, and as it was
approaching his flank, near Fleurus, not moving against
the flank or the rear of Blucher, the inference was natural
and not strained.   But the Emperor ought to have
ordered the aide-de-camp sent to find out the facts to
summon D'Erlon to the field, if D'Erlon was at hand;
he omitted to do this, not once, but twice, and the result
was in the highest degree unfortunate, for D'Erlon could
have overwhelmed the Prussian army even at the eleventh
hour.   Napoleon, in a word, missed a great occasion; he
had not the nimbleness of mind he once had; this may
have been the cause of a real error; it is undoubtedly the
cause that, from first to last, his account of this memorable incident is obscure and untrue.

June 16, it must be said once more, ought to have
witnessed the ruin of the Prussian army, followed probably by a great defeat of Wellington.   The heroism

* 'Documents inédits,' No. 17 ; La Tour d'Auvergne, 'Waterloo,'
184.

† Mr. Ropes has described, better than any other commentator,
how admirably Napoleon conducted the Battle of Ligny ('Campaign
of Waterloo,' 171, 175).

shown by Ney in this campaign, and his tragical fate a few months afterwards, ought not to blind us to the evident fact that it was mainly due to his faults and misconduct that this consummation was not accomplished; on the 16th he was worse than a failure. Twice at least on that day, in Napoleon's words, the 'fortunes of France' were left in his hands; twice at least he most wrongly threw them away, through indecision, neglect, and positive disregard of his duty. Had he assembled his army early on the 16th, had he had it together even by four in the afternoon—nay, had he not recalled D'Erlon in contempt of his master—he would probably have crushed Perponcher, defeated Wellington, and made the movement which would have destroyed Blucher.

He did not achieve what he might have achieved; the excuses made for him are those of mere partisans, or of detractors of Napoleon scarcely worthy of notice. Reille, too, was gravely to blame for his delays; D'Erlon most improperly set at naught an order of the Emperor which he should have obeyed. The operations of the French left, in a word, were misconducted throughout the day; this, we believe, was for them perhaps the worst mischance of the campaign.* The irresolution, however, the want of daring, the timidity exhibited by the French commanders—nay, the disobedience and insubordination

* Napoleon has thus described, with very little exaggeration, what Ney might have accomplished on June 16 (' Comment.,' v. 199, 200) : ' Le maréchal se porta sur les Quatre Bras, mais seulement avec la moitié de son monde. Il laissa l'autre moitié pour appuyer sa retraite à deux lieux derrière ; il l'oublia jusqu'à six heures du soir, où il en sentit le besoin pour sa propre défense. Dans les autres campagnes ce général eût occupé à six heures du matin la position en avant des Quatre Bras eût défait et pris toute la division Belge, et eût on tourné l'armée prussienne, en faisant par la chaussée de Namur, un détachement qui fut tombé sur les derrières de la lignes de bataille, ou en se portant avec rapidité sur la chaussée de Genappe, il eût surpris en marche et détruit la division de Brunswick et la 5ᵐᵉ division Anglaise qui venaient de Bruxelles, et de la marché à la rencontre des 1ʳᵉ et 3ᵐᵉ divisions Anglaises, qui arrivaient par la chaussée de Nivelles.'

of Ney—point to a general cause operating to affect their conduct. These men had lost the confidence of the victorious past; they knew that Napoleon had a world in arms against him; they felt at least that his ultimate triumph was almost hopeless. Hence it was that Ney would not act with vigour, and make the forward movements he was bound to make; that Vandamme was ready to see an enemy at hand in D'Erlon; that Reille hesitated when he should have advanced; that D'Erlon avoided a responsibility he should have taken on himself, and returned to his immediate superior, probably to save himself from blame. Napoleon's lieutenants, in short, were more or less demoralised; a kind of paralysis had fallen on their arms.*

Turning from Napoleon to the allied chiefs, little is to be said for their strategy on June 16. Their original errors still had their effects; the excessive dissemination of their forces; the extreme apprehension of Wellington for his right; his distance at Brussels from his colleague at Namur, and the immobility of both at the outset of the campaign—all this had consequences that had not disappeared. Apart, however, from considerations of this kind, their operations on the 16th were marked by one great strategic mistake. Had Wellington strengthened

---

* Napoleon ('Comment.,' v. 198, 199) thus describes his subordinates in 1815: 'Le caractère de plusieurs généraux avait été détrempé par les évènements de 1814; ils avaient perdu quelque chose de cette audace, de cette résolution, et de cette confiance qui leur avaient valu tant de gloire et avaient tant contribué aux succés des campagnes passées.' Charras (i. 59) wrote in the same sense: ' Quelques uns avaient éprouvé de rudes défaites dans des commandements isolés et en gardaient la mémoire. D'autres, ébranlés par les cruels souvenirs de 1813 et 1814, désespéraient de l'issue de la guerre, à la vue des masses armées de la coalition et de la faiblesse des moyens de défense. Tous étaient restés braves intrépides; mais tous n'avaient pas gardé l'activité, la résolution, l'audace des premiers jours. Il en était dont le moral n'était plus à l'épreuve d'un revers.' The author of this striking passage, we must recollect, was one of Napoleon's most determined libellers.

his left as he ought to have done, he might have been
at Quatre Bras in sufficient force to give his colleague
powerful support at Sombreffe; in these circumstances
both might have given battle to Napoleon with a good
prospect of success. When Blucher had rashly marched
on Sombreffe, leaving Bulow behind, Wellington evidently
felt that he was bound to assist the veteran warrior as
well as he could; but his orders to collect his army at
Quatre Bras were many hours too late. Under these
conditions the allied leaders ought not to have risked all
in a conflict at Sombreffe and Quatre Bras; they might
have guessed that Napoleon probably would be superior
in force; they escaped a disaster, Blucher especially, by
the merest freak of fortune. In fact, they set at naught a
principle of the first importance, seldom violated, it has
truly been said, with impunity. They tried to concentrate in the face of a foe concentrated already for some
time, and Blucher at least ought to have been destroyed.
Napoleon has pointed out with convincing truth that,
being as they were 'under the guns of their enemy,'
Blucher ought to have fallen back at least to Wavre,
and Wellington to have fallen back at least to Waterloo;
in that case they would have avoided extreme peril; they
might have been able to draw together their superior
forces. Their mistake is now recognised even by fair
English critics.* The measure, indeed, of Napoleon's
strategy and that of the allies on the 16th may be fairly

* For the admirable and unanswerable remarks of Napoleon on
this point, see 'Comment.,' v. 205-207. General Shaw Kennedy
('The Battle of Waterloo,' 172) candidly says: 'The determination
of Blucher and Wellington to meet Napoleon's advance at Fleurus
and Quatre Bras was totally inconsistent with the widely-scattered
positions in which they had placed their armies. Their determination
in this respect amounted, in the fullest extent, to that error which has
so often been committed in war by even great commanders—of endeavouring to assemble on a point which could only be reached by a
portion of the troops intended to occupy it, while the enemy had the
power of concentrating upon it his whole force.'

taken by a simple comparison of the armies on the scene
of events. But for the misconduct of Ney the Emperor
would have had his whole forces together at Quatre Bras
and Ligny. Blucher had only three-fourths of his own,
Wellington not a third, and that brought up piecemeal.
Enormously superior as they were in numbers, they were
distinctly inferior on the decisive points, or, rather, would
have been but for a mere mischance; and Blucher, to
say nothing of the Duke, ought to have met his ruin.

A few remarks must, likewise, be made on the tactics
of the allies in these battles. Blucher exhibited in the
highest degree his best and most characteristic qualities—
daring, perseverance, and the heroic spirit; he nerved his
soldiers to make the most desperate efforts. But his
arrangements at Ligny, we have seen, were faulty; he
aimed at too much in endeavouring to draw near Wellington, and at the same time to guard his communications
with Namur; his front was extended on too broad a
space; his reserve was frightfully exposed to his enemy's
guns. In the battle, too, he wasted his strength with
little reflection; he left Thielmann out of action until it
was too late; he made fruitless attempts to overwhelm
Napoleon's left; his centre, when the crisis came, was
not nearly enough occupied, though this was not wholly
his own fault. He was, in short, in his adversary's
language, 'always the old hussar'; strategically and
tactically he was bold but imprudent.

As for Wellington, his conduct at Quatre Bras was
marked by his wonted constancy, coolness, and tactical
skill. He fought admirably a losing battle for hours;
arranged his troops with habitual insight and judgment
on the ground; made the most of auxiliaries not of the
best quality; turned his British infantry to the fullest
advantage. His tenacity was, as always, conspicuous;
he held his army together by his own endurance and
courage; he assumed the offensive at the right moment.

He made, however, two evident mistakes, though these were mistakes of strategy, hardly of tactics. He made Picton's division and the Hanoverians halt at Waterloo until it was all but too late; he might have had at least 10,000 more troops at Quatre Bras than he had, had he not continued to fear for his right, a misconception retained to the last.* A word, too, should be said on the fine conduct of Perponcher on June 16. He did admirable service, we have seen, on the 15th; had he not marched his division to Quatre Bras, Ney would have seized this important point unopposed; the result of the day might have been very different. Perponcher, too, and his chief did excellently on the 16th; they disposed their forces very skilfully on the ground; though their soldiers were little more than a forlorn hope, they were a forlorn hope that accomplished a great deal.

Passing from the chiefs to the belligerent armies, these, too, require a brief notice. The French gave full proof of the martial virtues of the race; they were daring, devoted, terrible in success; Piré's horsemen are entitled to high praise; the Imperial Guard was worthy of its great renown; Napoleon's and Ney's artillery were effective in the extreme. Nevertheless, the army exhibited the defects to be expected in an instrument of war hastily put together, and abounding in dangerous, and even weak, elements. Want of discipline was more than once apparent; Lefol turned his guns against his own infantry, smitten with terror when they beheld the approach of what was said to be a hostile column; Kellermann's noble cuirassiers gave way to panic; D'Erlon's men broke out into murmurs when turned away from Ligny. Worse than all, profound distrust largely existed between officers and men; an old soldier stepped out of the ranks and bade Napoleon beware of Soult; more than one General was charged by his troops

* See Charras, i. 168, a remarkable passage.

with treachery; several officers followed the shameful example of Bourmont.

As for the Prussian army, it was badly directed, exposed to trials it ought not to have endured, thrown away on parts of the scene of the conflict, and it had no corps equal to the Imperial Guard. It gave proof, however, of heroic qualities—ardour, energy, constancy, fierce and stubborn courage, and especially devotion to Blucher and all its chiefs; it was soon to show that it could disregard a most severe defeat, and baffle the calculations of the great master of war, who indisputably rated it below its real worth. The forces commanded by Wellington at Quatre Bras were a specimen of his motley army of many nations and tongues. His Dutch-Belgian levies and Brunswickers were for the most part raw troops, and, though not wanting in boldness and true courage, were no match for the French infantry and the brilliant French horsemen. But the British foot and the Hanoverians, in a somewhat less degree, proved themselves to be all but indomitable in the field. Once or twice, indeed, they were successfully attacked before they resumed the formation required to repel cavalry; but the furious charges of Piré's and Kellermann's troopers 'foamed themselves away' against squares as solid as rocks.*

June 16, like the day before, was 'incomplete' as regards Napoleon's objects. He had not shattered Blucher's army to atoms; Wellington had, if with difficulty, held his own against Ney. But the Emperor's prospects were still full of promise, so superior had been his masterly strategy. The allied chiefs could no longer hope to unite on the lateral road from Nivelles to Namur, the line on which they would naturally join; they had lost Sombreffe, which involved the loss of Quatre Bras; they would be compelled to fall back into an intricate

---

* See Siborne, 'The Waterloo Campaign,' 170, 1895 edition, and 'Waterloo Letters.'

country of marsh, woodland, and hill, with inferior roads,
forming the upper part of the valley of the Dyle. It
would be difficult in the extreme to bring their armies
together, on any field of battle, in front of Brussels; it
was in their adversary's power to make this impossible;
in fact, they were nearly in the position of Beaulieu and
Colli when these Generals fell back on Acqui and Ceva
after Montenotte.

Napoleon had thus gained an immense strategic advantage, though his success had fallen short of what it ought
to have been; nor was this the measure of the advantages
he could secure. Blucher's army had been scotched if
not slain; it could not, great as was the energy of its
chief—and he was for the moment disabled—be made
ready to fight again for at least a whole day, even if Bulow
should come to its aid. Wellington's forces at Quatre
Bras were most perilously exposed should Napoleon and
Ney fall suddenly on them; and Wellington could not
assemble 60,000 troops round or near Quatre Bras on
June 17. The situation was one of the many of those
in which the General of 1796 had shown what he could
do in the presence of enemies thus placed, and in which
he effected marvels of war. A large part of his army had
not been engaged at all; would he, leaving Blucher for
the present alone, attack Wellington with the great mass
of his forces, and endeavour to overwhelm him before he
could escape? Would he, acting more in conformity
with true strategy, follow Blucher with a detachment
comparatively small, taking care that this should observe
him, and hold him in check, and then turn against
Wellington in still largely preponderating strength?
Would he renew the glories of Castiglione and Rivoli, or
the still recent glories of Montmirail and Montereau? Or
would malignant influences intercept the rays of the sun
of Austerlitz that seemed about to rise, and cause it to set
in a night of disaster?

CHAPTER VI

THE OPERATIONS OF JUNE 17

Retrospect of the operations since the beginning of the campaign—Advantages obtained by Napoleon — Great opportunities presented to him on the morning of June 17—The two alternative movements he might have made, of which either should have secured him decisive success—Authorities cited on the subject—Napoleon at Fleurus the night of the 16th—Exultation of the French army after the victory of Ligny—Overconfidence and negligence—The retreat of the Prussians not followed or observed — Conduct of Ney and of Soult — No communication between them—Letter of Soult to Ney on the morning of the 17th—Intention that the French army was to halt for that day—The state of his health the real cause of the inaction of Napoleon—He proceeds to Ligny—Review of his army—He resolves to pursue Blucher with Grouchy, and to attack Wellington—This combination correct, but very late—Orders to Grouchy—The Bertrand despatch—Its great importance—Retreat of the Prussian army to Wavre—Napoleon reaches Quatre Bras and follows Wellington—Character of the pursuit—Napoleon halts before Waterloo—Movements of Grouchy—He reaches Gembloux— His letter of 10 p.m. to Napoleon—His faulty dispositions—Napoleon on the night of the 17th—His dispositions and confidence—Dispositions of Blucher and Wellington—The prospect for June 18.

WE may now glance back at the memorable events attending Napoleon's invasion of Belgium. The operations of the great master had not had the decisive success he had reason to expect; but they had, nevertheless, been very successful. His previsions had been, in the main, realised; he had found the allied centre at its inner flanks weak, had broken through it, and held it in force. Blucher had rushed to battle inconsiderately, as had been foreseen ; Wellington, in this instance certainly behind the time, and hesitating until it ought to have been too late, had failed to give his colleague adequate support. As the result, the Emperor had been able, with an army in numbers very inferior, to encounter adversaries numerically almost twice as strong, in a position of vantage before they could unite ; he had only just missed a victory that might well have been final—as regards the contest, at least—in Belgium. But if he had not destroyed the Prussian army at Ligny, and if Ney had done no more, so grave were his faults, than hold Wellington at Quatre Bras in check, the complete success which had eluded him, so to speak, hitherto appeared to await him on June 17.

To understand this thoroughly, we must recur to the situation at the close of the preceding day, though we have given it already a passing notice. The defeat of Ligny having forced Blucher away from Sombreffe, Wellington would be compelled to retreat from Quatre Bras. The allied chiefs, therefore, had virtually lost their natural and proper line of junction—the lateral road from Nivelles to Namur ; if they did not fall back on their respective bases, they would be obliged to retire into a most intricate country, where in any case it would be difficult in the extreme to bring their divided armies together, and where Napoleon had it in his power all but certainly to prevent this movement. Their separation, therefore, might be considered assured—a capital object of their antagonist. In all human probability it would become wider, and this, were the campaign prolonged, would necessarily be of the greatest advantage to him— would multiply largely his chances of reaching his enemies when apart, and of defeating them in detail.

More than this, however, was attainable on June 17 ;

the decisive success which Napoleon had not yet won was now, it may be affirmed, within his grasp. Blucher's army had been severely worsted; it had lost not far from 30,000 men, including stragglers and fugitives beyond recall; it was short of munitions and supplies of all kinds; its heroic chief was for the moment broken down. If, taken as a whole, it had not lost its energy, and though Bulow was at hand with his corps, it could not give battle on the 17th to an enemy in anything like powerful force. Wellington, on the other hand, after the results of Ligny, was at Quatre Bras—so to speak, 'in the air'; he could not, we have said, assemble 60,000 men on that point. As we shall see, he had assembled 45,000 only, part of these being inferior troops; he was confronted by Ney, who, having been joined by D'Erlon, was at the head of a force nearly equal in numbers—allowing for the losses he had sustained—and to a considerable extent of superior quality; and he had Napoleon on his flank, seven or eight miles distant, with an army still at least 65,000 strong, and flushed with a splendid if a dearly-bought victory. It should be observed, too, that a very considerable part of the forces of Ney and his master had not been engaged; the corps of D'Erlon had hardly fired a shot; Lobau had not taken part in the struggle at Ligny; the Imperial Guard had not suffered much; the light cavalry of the Guard and three-fourths of the corps of Kellermann literally done nothing at Quatre Bras; the mailed squadrons of Milhaud were almost intact; in short, Napoleon had nearly 60,000 fresh troops, who could be directed at once against the enemy without subjecting them to any excessive effort.

In these circumstances the Emperor had the choice of two great alternative movements at least, of which either, as affairs stood, ought now to secure him a complete triumph. Should he ascertain by daybreak, as was to be assumed, what the real position of his enemies was, he

might detach an insignificant force only to observe Blucher,
and hang on his retreat; and then, drawing together the
great mass of his forces, he might, in conjunction with
Ney, fall upon Wellington, and launch 100,000 men at least
against a General who had only 45,000 in hand, and that
in a position in which it was almost impossible to escape.*
This movement would probably overwhelm the Duke—
certainly force him to make a disastrous retreat; yet a
better and more judicious movement could be made,
and would have, perhaps, even more important results.
Blucher's army, though beaten, was still numerous;

---

* Apologists of Napoleon and of the allies have concurred in concealing, as much as possible, the enormous advantages which the
Emperor could have secured on June 17. The truth, however, has
come out by degrees. As regards the first alternative, above mentioned, General Shaw Kennedy ('Battle of Waterloo,' 153) says :
'Napoleon's operations, up to the evening of the 16th, had, in their
general result, been successful by Blucher's being defeated and separated from Wellington ; but, to reap the fruits of his combinations and
success over Blucher, it became necessary to strike against Wellington with the utmost rapidity and vigour ; and it was impossible that
circumstances could have been more favourable for his doing so than
those which actually existed on the morning of the 17th. The Prussian
army was in full retreat. Wellington's army, not yet fully collected,
stood only seven or eight miles from Napoleon's, and Ney was in
contact with Wellington's front. Wellington's left was completely
exposed, and stood on the great chaussée, by which chaussée Napoleon
had the immense advantage of being able to advance perpendicularly
to the line of the Anglo-allied army, and thus to attack it to the
greatest advantage before it was by any means fully in junction, and
on its left flank at right angles to its line of battle ; while simultaneously with Napoleon's attack on the left Ney would have assailed
Wellington's front. . . . Napoleon should have led his last man and
horse against the Anglo-allied army, even had the risk been great in
the highest degree, which, as has been seen, it clearly was not. Had
Napoleon attacked the Anglo-allied army with his whole force, and
succeeded in defeating it, there could be little question of his being
able to defeat afterwards the Prussian army when separated from
Wellington.' See also Ropes, 'Campaign of Waterloo,' 197, 198.
This alternative seemed the best to Soult, who knew better than
Napoleon what British soldiers were : H. Houssaye, 'Waterloo,'
ii. 240.

Bulow could reach it with 30,000 men. Napoleon was therefore bound to be on his guard against it, while he turned against his British antagonist. Following the precedents he had so often and so grandly made, he might pursue Blucher, and keep him in check with a restraining wing of considerable strength—from 30,000 to 40,000 men. This would at once prevent Blucher from drawing near his colleague, would possibly still further shatter the Prussian army, and would secure the communications of the Emperor from attack; and, having taken this precaution, Napoleon might still assail Wellington with from 70,000 to 80,000 men—that is, in immensely superior numbers—and equally gain a victory that should be decisive.* There was no reason that Napoleon should

---

* This was the second alternative; the history of war from the days of Turenne to those of Napoleon proves that it was by many degrees the best. See 'Comment.,' v. 201, 202. It was that which Napoleon adopted, but it was adopted many hours too late; it was miserably executed by a most incompetent lieutenant. Charras (i. 203 and ii. 128) sums up what Napoleon could have accomplished on the 17th; it will be observed he suggests a third alternative—falling on Blucher instead of Wellington. This is also suggested by Clausewitz; but obviously, as Jomini has pointed out, it was the least judicious course: 'Si Napoléon eût galopé jusqu'au plateau de Ligny, il aurait su immédiatement, vu, pour ainsi dire, de ses propres yeux, où était l'armée prussienne, et reconnu qu'il avait deux partis à prendre, à prendre sur le champ; ou, se mettre avec toutes ses forces à la poursuite des Prussiens, ou lancer sur eux sa cavalerie légère appuyée de deux ou trois divisions d'infanterie, et avec le gros de ses troupes, se porter aux Quatre Bras. Dans le premier cas, surpris au moment où son armée était encore assez mal en ordre, avec caissons et gibernes vides, Blucher n'aurait pas échappe à la destruction; dans le second il aurait subi des pertes, sensibles; et Wellington, privé de son appui, aurait été accablé sous les efforts réunis de Ney et de Napoléon. . . . Le 17, dès l'aube du jour, il aurait du se précipiter à la poursuite de Blucher avec tous les combattants de Ligny, ou lancer une quinzaine de mille hommes seulement sur les traces du vaincu, et avec le reste de ses forces, courrir aux Quatre Bras s'y réunir à Ney, y attaquer Wellington et, dans un cas comme dans l'autre, il aurait anéanti l'une des armées alliées, et mis en suite l'autre hors d'état de rien entreprendre de sérieux avant longtemps.'

not give directions for either operation by four in the morning; in either case part of his forces, whether small or large, could be on the track of the Prussians by five or six, following the lines of their retreat, which the simplest diligence ought to have discovered several hours before; and the great body of his forces and those of Ney could be in front of Wellington and on his flank by eight or nine. In one event or the other the Emperor must have triumphed, and it deserves notice that nothing more was required than the insight, the energy, and the decision he had exhibited over and over again, and that in not an extraordinary degree.

Napoleon could have obtained these results; it is not difficult, after the event, to see what he might have achieved at this conjuncture. Had he been seconded as he ought to have been—above all, had he been the Napoleon of 1796 to 1809—it is probable in the extreme that he would have secured them. We proceed to consider how the immense success that was within his reach on June 17 was all but lost to him, and Fortune became adverse. Napoleon, we have said, had returned to Fleurus, his headquarters, after Ligny; he reached that place at about eleven at night; he gave orders to Grouchy, in command of the French right, to pursue in a general way the Prussian army, with the cavalry of Excelmans and Pajol. It is said, indeed, that he indicated the probable lines of retreat — that is, northwards by the villages of Tilly and Gentinnes, the direction being taken by the corps of Zieten and Pirch, and eastwards along the roads from Sombreffe to Namur—that is, towards the communications which Thielmann had so jealously guarded.*

---

* Jomini ('Précis de la Campagne de 1815,' 188) says that Napoleon ordered General Monthyon, an officer in the highest place on the staff of Soult, to follow the Prussians in the direction of Tilly and Gentinnes; but he gives no authority. The order, if given, was not carried into effect.

The Emperor then retired to rest, utterly exhausted, as he had been on the night of the 15th; it appears certain that he saw no one, and had no conversation on the position of affairs until between six and seven in the morning. Meanwhile exultation ran riot in the camp of the French, round Ligny; the most ordinary outpost duty was hardly performed. The Prussians, who had left rearguards, even at Brye and Sombreffe, on the very ground held, it may be said, by the enemy, were not followed, or even observed; there was a general feeling that Blucher had been disposed of, and that no more would be heard of him for several days at soonest. The same sentiment, unfortunately, pervaded the chiefs; they were like the princely noblesse of France before the day of Agincourt, described by the magical hand of Shakespeare; they were convinced the defeated army was routed, and were in disorderly retreat upon Namur, even Liége. Not a squadron was sent to reconnoitre the tract around Tilly and Gentinnes; Pajol and Excelmans did no more than advance along the roads leading from Ligny to Namur. This was bad enough, but it was not the worst; Ney, furious at what he deemed his ill-treatment as regards the diversion of D'Erlon and his corps, sent no report of what had occurred at Quatre Bras; Soult, characteristically indolent and remiss, disliking the Marshal, and disliked by him, wrote nothing to Ney about the results of Ligny; the French army was thus, so to speak, left in the dark, and in a position of false confidence, at the very moment when vigilance and activity were needed to reap the fruits of success—nay, even to avert danger, always possible in war.*

* For the operations of the belligerent armies on June 17, of supreme importance, and still not thoroughly ascertained, the original and contemporaneous documents, as far as they are forthcoming, should, of course, be studied in the first instance. The narrative of H. Houssaye ('Waterloo,' ii. 218-280) is thoroughly well informed

It was, we have seen, between six and seven in the morning when Napoleon received, for the first time, any intelligence respecting his own army. This was brought by General Flahault, the aide-de-camp despatched with the first orders to Ney, on June 16; that officer described the engagement at Quatre Bras and the results, and, it is said, severely condemned the Marshal for his procrastination, indecision, and delays. A short time afterwards a report came in from Pajol to the effect that the Prussians were in full retreat along the roads to Namur and Liége—that is, towards their communications with the Rhine; Pajol added that he had already made many prisoners. The Emperor did not think fit to act on these statements; it was not until an hour at least had elapsed that he sent a detachment of some force to ascertain what was going on at Quatre Bras, and that he despatched the division of Teste, of the corps of Lobau, to support Pajol in his pursuit of the enemy. He appears to have made no other inquiries, especially as to the lines of the Prussian retreat; he certainly for the present assumed, in common with Soult and all his lieutenants on the spot, that Blucher had been routed, and was recoiling on his base. Meanwhile, at between seven and eight, and probably near the later hour, Napoleon dictated a letter, through Soult to Ney, setting forth his views as to the existing state of affairs, and as to the operations to be undertaken on June 17.*

In this despatch, every letter of which should be studied, Soult, with very little candour, pretends that he had made Ney aware of what had taken place at Ligny; and he

---

and masterly. The commentary of Mr. Ropes ('The Campaign of Waterloo,' 197-244) is excellent. Siborne ('The Waterloo Campaign,' 259, 323, 1895 edition) contains useful details. For the Prussian side reference may be made to Clausewitz, Damitz and Ollech.

* This most important despatch is No. 7 in the 'Documents inédits,' and will be found in La Tour d'Auvergne, 'Waterloo,' 211-213.

proceeds to point out to the Marshal how serious had been his mistakes and shortcomings on the previous day. Ney had not assembled his divisions as he ought to have done; they had acted separately, and he had, therefore, suffered loss. Had the corps of Reille and D'Erlon been together at Quatre Bras, not a man of the English corps would have escaped; had D'Erlon executed the movement upon St. Amand to be made by the Emperor's positive orders, there would have been an end of the Prussian army; 30,000 prisoners would probably have been taken.* Soult then informs Ney, who, it would appear, was thought to be apprehensive about his own position, that the British army could not possibly act against him, that if it made the attempt the Emperor would strike it in flank, in force, and that in that event it would be 'destroyed in a moment'; and the Marshal was finally directed to keep his army together, to take a position at Quatre Bras, and to attack Wellington should there be only a rearguard at that place. Turning to the Prussians, the Chief of the French Staff shows next what the situation seemed to be in his own eyes and those of his master, and what was to be done on the present day. He asserts twice that Blucher was in complete rout, and was being pursued by Pajol on the way to Namur and Liége; he adds that a prisoner of distinction had dropped the words that 'Blucher had destroyed the Prussian monarchy for the second time.' Most important of all, he closes the despatch by announcing that the French

---

* We transcribe the following passages from this despatch; they tell the simple truth, and, in our judgment, are conclusive as regards the D'Erlon incident : ' L'empereur a vu avec peine que vous n'avez pas réuni hier les divisions ; elles ont agi isolément ; ainsi vous avez éprouvé des pertes. Si les corps des Comtes Reille et d'Erlon avaient été ensemble, il ne réchappait pas un Anglais du corps qui venait vous attaquer. Si le Comte D'Erlon avait exécuté le mouvement sur Saint Amand qui l'empereur a ordonné, l'armée prussienne était totalement détruit, et nous aurions fait peut être trente mille prisonniers.'

army was to make a halt for the day; this was 'necessary to obtain munitions, to rally scattered men, and to call in detachments.' Not a word is said about a general pursuit, or even about following the line of Blucher's retreat.

Napoleon's lieutenants had served him ill. At Ligny they had neglected their obvious duty; they had not ascertained where the Prussians had gone; they had assumed too lightly that Blucher was out of the case for a time, and that he was falling back upon his base towards Germany. No communication, too—an unpardonable fault—had taken place between Ney and Soult; the French army had been, so to speak, brought to a stand; undoubtedly it had suffered a great deal. The Emperor had been culpably left in the dark; he believed that Blucher was in retreat on Namur and Liége with a discomfited and demoralised army. Yet these considerations will not explain the apparent remissness and want of energy of which he gave such proof at this critical juncture. We almost wholly reject the charge of in-activity made against him for the morning of the 16th; we fully acknowledge it as regards the morning of the 17th, and no candid inquirer has sought to deny it.* It

* Jomini ('Précis de la Campagne de 1815,' 185) significantly says : 'Pour ceux qui se rappellent l'étonnante activité qui présida aux évènements de Ratisbonne en 1809, de Dresde 1813, de Champ Aubert et de Montmirail en 1814, ce nouveau temps perdu sera toujours une chose inexplicable de la part de Napoléon.' This inactivity produced murmurs in the French camp. Charras (i. 186) tells us that Vandamme exclaimed on the morning of the 17th : ' " Le Napoléon que nous avons connu n'existe plus ; notre succès d'hier restera sans résultat." Vandamme était devenu frondeur. Mais Gérard, tout devoué au chef, exprimait la même pensée en d'autres termes. "Il déplorait d'incomprehensible, irrémédiable lenteurs." ' Clausewitz, seeing the facts, but ignorant of the real cause, has written that 'Napoleon was affected by a kind of lethargy.' See also Ropes, 'Campaign of Waterloo,' 200. Siborne ('The Waterloo Campaign,' 268, 1895 edition) adds his testimony in these words : ' A glorious opportunity had presented itself for the attainment of his

is idle to throw the blame on French Generals alone; there must have been some more potent if less manifest cause for the strange immobility of the French army, and for the state of ignorance and disunion in which its chiefs were left. If we bear in mind that Napoleon has never had an equal in following up a defeated enemy—that, in Napier's words, 'his battle was the wave that effaces the landscape'—we can judge what, but for some disturbing influence, he would have done on the night of the 16th and during the next few hours. He would not have gone to sleep without finding out the real direction of the retreat of the Prussian army, and that without the possibility of a doubt; he would have taken care to have reports from Ney and Soult, and seen that his orders were carried out by both; he would have had his restraining wing ready soon after daybreak to hang on the Prussians, perhaps to bring them to bay; he would have had everything prepared to attack Wellington, in front and flank, three or four hours at least before noon.

The real if the unsuspected cause of this inactivity and delay was, we believe, the state of Napoleon's health. This, we have seen, had been long declining; he was affected by two local disorders occasionally giving him the acutest pain; he was subject to a malady which, though compatible with bodily strength and the force of his splendid intellect, when the fit, so to speak, was not on him, made him drowsy, lethargic, good for nothing, when the fit came. Two distinguished officers have recorded that he was extremely ill throughout the night of the 16th, so ill that he could not issue a single order.*

original design of defeating both armies in detail, but which was completely lost by a most extraordinary and fatal want of energy and vigour in seizing upon the advantages which the victory of Ligny had placed within Napoleon's reach.' Charras (i. 186) truly remarks: ' La victoire était suivie des long rétards. . . . Et avec les rétards revenaient les étonnements, les murmures de tous.'

* H. Houssaye, 'Waterloo,' ii. 482 ; Dorsey Gardner, ' Quatre Bras, Ligny and Waterloo,' 35-37, a very valuable note.

We have no doubt this was the true cause of the kind of
paralysis that fell on the French army and its chief, and
that produced the strange inaction which has appeared so
unaccountable to a host of critics.*

* There was nothing 'mysterious,' as has been alleged, about the
state of Napoleon's health in 1815. He was suffering from a disease
of the lower bowel and of the bladder, which made riding exercise
very painful, and also from strangury. The malady, however, which
caused most mischief was an occasional suspension of the proper
functions of the skin, which stopped perspiration, reacted on the
brain and nervous system, and produced lethargy for the time. When
relieved from this affection, his energy and the powers of his intellect
were quickly restored. This accounts for the intermitting vigour and
slackness we see in his conduct in the campaign of 1815. The pre-
scriptions of Corvisart for the Emperor are, we believe, still in existence.

    M. H. Houssaye (' 1815,' i. 613) has accurately and minutely de-
scribed the physical, and, indeed, the mental and moral, condition
of Napoleon as he was leaving Paris for Waterloo : ' L'empereur ne
supporta pas trois mois ce supplice sans en être affaibli moralement et
physiquement. À la fin de mai, il n'était plus l'homme du 20 mars.
Il avait gardé intactes les qualités maîtresses de son vaste génie, mais
les qualités complémentaires, la volonté, la décision, la confiance
avaient décliné en lui. La nature éminemment nerveuse de Napoléon
était soumise aux influences morales. Les contrariétés très vives, les
grandes inquiétudes, tous les tourments d'esprit, comme aussi parfois
l'excès des fatigues et l'état atmosphérique lui donnaient simultané-
ment de douloureuses crises d'ischurie, et même de strangurie, des
contractions de l'estomac et une toux spasmodique, épuisante. Ces
accidents, qu'il avait déjà éprouvés en Russie, se reproduisirent
plusieurs fois durant les Cent Jours, à la suite de son rude voyage à
travers les Alpes, dans la neige et dans la rafale, et sous l'action
désépreuves et des amertumes qui l'accablèrent à Paris. L'esprit
influait sur le corps qui réagissait alors sur l'esprit. Pendant ces
crises, d'une durée assez longue, l'empereur tombait dans un profond
abattement. Il perdait tout espoir et toute energie. Il avait des
heures d'angoisse ou d'horrible visions lui montraient la France
vaincue et démembrée. En plein jour, il cherchait dans le sommeil
l'oubli momentané de ses souffrances et de ses pensées. Lorsqu'il
était seul, il lui arrivait de pleurer ; Carnot le surprit en larmes devant
un portrait de son fils. L'empereur n'avait plus en lui le sentiment du
succès il ne croyait plus à son étoile. Il dit à Mollien, "Le destin est
changé pour moi. J'ai perdu là un auxiliaire qui rien ne remplace."
Il hochait la tête quand on le félicitait sur le résultat d'une election ou

The Emperor left Fleurus at about nine o'clock, accompanied by Grouchy, who for some time had been awaiting his orders in vain. Grouchy has remarked that his master was 'extremely fatigued.' Napoleon, unable to bear the jolting of his carriage, mounted a horse, and drove at rather a slow pace to Ligny. He was in an irritable and unsettled mood; he sharply told Grouchy he would give him his commands as soon as the fitting moment had come. The field of battle presented an

---

sur quelque manifestation populaire. " C'est le temps," répondait il, " qui nous apprendra, si la France veut me conserver mieux qu'elle n'a conservé les Bourbons." '

Thiébault (' Mémoires,' v. 341) has left this striking description of the appearance of the Emperor at this time: ' Je ne cessai de le considérer, et mes regards s'attachèrent sur lui avec d'autant plus d'avidité, je pouvais ajouter de souffrance, que plus je l'examinais, moins je parvenais à le retrouver tel qu'au temps de sa force et de sa grandeur. Jamais l'impression que sa vue me fit éprouver, à ce moment où le destin allait prononcer entre le monde et lui, jamais cette impression n'a cessé de m'être présente. Son regard, jadis si formidable à force d'être scrutateur, avait perdu la puissance et même la fixité ; sa figure, que si souvent j'avais vue comme rayonnante de grâce ou modelée dans l'airain, avait perdu toute expression et tout caractère de force ; sa bouche contractée ne gardait rien de son ancienne magie ; sa tête elle même n'avait plus ce port qui caractérisait le dominateur du monde, et sa démarche était aussi embarrassée que sa contenance et ses gestes étaient incertains. Tout semblait dénaturé, décomposé en lui ; la pâleur ordinaire de sa peau était remplacée par un teint verdâtre fortement prononcé qui me frappa.' This vivid and suggestive portrait may be overcharged ; but the physical decline of Napoleon was accompanied, as is so often the case, with a decline in moral force and strength of character, as we have said ; and it is not surprising, considering his position, that he had begun to lose his old self-confidence long before Waterloo.

Charras (i. 79, 80) gives us, not unfairly, this account of Napoleon at this conjuncture : ' Napoléon était vieux avant l'âge. Le long exercice du pouvoir absolu, les efforts prolongés d'une ambition sans limites, le travail excessif du cabinet et de la guerre, les émotions, les angoisses de trois années de désastres inouïs, la chute soudaine de cet empire qu'il avait cru fondé à jamais, l'odieuse oisiveté de l'exil, une double maladie, dont les crises se multipliaient en s'aggravant, avaient profondément altéré sa vigoureuse organisation. Son œil brillait du même éclat ; son regard avait la même puissance ; mais son corps alourdi,

appalling spectacle; the villages in which the conflict had raged were choked with the dead and untended wounded; Ligny was a heap of ruins, and of mutilated and charred corpses. The French army, however, was in the joyous mood of the Gaul; the sounds of the multitudinous cheers which greeted its chief were heard three or four miles off by a Prussian rearguard, covering cautiously the retreat of Pirch and Zieten. The Emperor passed his victorious troops in review, thanking officers and men

---

presque obèse, ses joues gonflées et pendantes indiquaient la venue de cette époque de la vie ou la décadence physique de l'homme a commencé. Il subissait maintenant les exigences du sommeil, que naguère il maîtrisait à son gré. Les fatigues des longues journées à cheval, des courses rapides lui étaient devenues insupportables. Il avait gardé la même facilité, la même abondance, la même force de conception; mais il avait perdu la persévérance de l'élaboration de la pensée et, ce qui était pis, la promptitude, la fixité de la résolution. Comme certains hommes au déclin de l'âge, il aimait à parler, à discourir, et perdait de longues heures en stériles paroles. À prendre un parti, il hésitait longtemps; l'ayant pris, il hésitait à agir, et dans l'action même il hésitait encore. De sa précédente ténacité, il ne lui restait que cette obstination fréquente, et déjà bien funeste, à voir les faits non tels qu'ils étaient, mais comme il aurait convenu à son intérêt qu'ils fussent. Sous les coups répétés de la défaite, son caractère s'était brisé. Il n'avait plus cette confiance en soi, élément presque indispensable à la réussite des grandes entreprises; il doutait maintenant de la fortune qui pendant quinze années avait prodigué de si prodigieuses preuves au général, au consul, à l'empereur. Il sentait même, c'est lui qui l'avoue, un abattement d'esprit, il avait "l'instinct d'une issue malheureuse."' This mass of testimony may be, and we think is, exaggerated; but it is sufficient to confute the statement of Thiers—itself contradictory ('Histoire du Consulat et de l'Empire,' vi. 440)—that Napoleon's activity had not diminished in 1815. At all events, it fully explains, and, we believe, can alone explain, Napoleon's conduct in the early morning of June 17, and, indeed, in a few other passages of the campaign. It is curious to read in Chesney's 'Waterloo Lectures' (72) that there was no falling off in the powers of the Emperor in 1815; but disregard of plain fact is a characteristic of this petty detractor of supreme genius. Lord Wolseley ('Decline and Fall of Napoleon') is the only English commentator who gives due, perhaps more than due, weight to the condition of Napoleon's health as an important factor in the campaign.

and distributing rewards; he properly gave orders for the relief of the wounded, attending especially to the Prussians, ill treated by the Belgian peasants, in return for many acts of oppression; he spent some time in talking about the state of France, and the Jacobinism and folly of Parisian politics.

It was now between ten and eleven o'clock; the detachment sent to observe Quatre Bras came back with the news that a considerable part of Wellington's army was still around that place. About the same time messages arrived from Excelmans and Pajol, despatched, we have seen, some hours before, on the track of the Prussians, but only on the roads to Namur and Liége. Pajol reported that he had seized a battery and some trains, and had picked up stragglers near Mazy on the way to Namur. Excelmans announced that he was marching on Gembloux, 'where the enemy was massed in great force.' On receiving this intelligence Napoleon made up his mind at once; his energies appear to have returned to him; he would, conforming to the true principles of his art, send a strong restraining wing to pursue Blucher, and to make it impossible for him to assist his colleague, or to threaten the line of the operations of the French; he would attack Wellington, with the mass of his forces, joining hands with Ney in the neighbourhood of Quatre Bras. Beyond question this was the true course to adopt; strategy of this very kind had repeatedly given Napoleon splendid and decisive success, but it was a course that ought to have been adopted five or six hours before. Might not a grand opportunity have passed away? might not the promise of the morning have become doubtful ?*

* It has been rightly said that the campaign of 1815 should be studied, watch in hand, hours—nay, half-hours—are of such importance. This is especially true as regards the operations of June 17, and notably as regards those of Grouchy. M. H. Houssaye has traced them out with admirable accuracy and precision, and has

The lame and impotent conclusion that the victorious French should make a halt for the day was thus abandoned ; but it was abandoned, we repeat, extremely late. The army was now divided into two groups, the first more than 33,000 strong with 96 guns, the second more than 72,000 with 240 guns,* the division of Girard, which had greatly suffered, having been left at Ligny to care for the wounded, and 'to form in any event a reserve.' The first group was composed of the corps of Vandamme, without Domon's horsemen ; of the corps of Gérard and the division of Teste ; and of the cavalry of Excelmans, and part of that of Pajol, his division of Subervie having been detached at Ligny ; it was placed under the command of Grouchy ; its mission was to act against Blucher. The second group was to be in the Emperor's hands ; it comprised the corps of Lobau, without Teste ; the Imperial Guard and Milhaud's cuirassiers ; the cavalry of Subervie and Domon, and the army of Ney, at and around Frasnes—that is, the two corps of Reille and D'Erlon, the light cavalry of the Guard and Kellermann's squadrons ; this combined force was to assail Wellington. It was now about eleven in the forenoon.† Napoleon gave Grouchy his long-expected orders ; he still believed that Blucher was retreating towards his base, still probably unable to take the field, though Excelmans' report had turned his attention to Gembloux, a place north of the roads to Namur and Liége. There have been many discussions as to the exact terms of these orders, but their plain and general

---

brought fully out the truth. Grouchy, it may be said at once, is not a faithworthy witness ; he has shamefully misrepresented time and garbled documents.

  * We again adopt the figures of Charras (i. 189, 190). Charras has taken infinite pains to be correct.

  † M. H. Houssaye has fixed this time, and, indeed, the time of all the operations of the 17th, as we have said, conclusively.

import is not doubtful. According to the version given
by Grouchy, the Marshal was to pursue the Prussians, to
attack them and to complete their defeat, and not to lose
sight of them in any event. The Emperor added that he
was about to join Ney, to attack the English army should
it make a stand on the southern verge of the Forest of
Soignies—a great wood between Quatre Bras and Brussels.
He closed his remarks by directing Grouchy to correspond with him by the lateral road from Nivelles to
Namur, running at Quatre Bras, we have seen, into the
great main-road from Charleroy to Brussels often referred
to.* So far all the different accounts coincide, but
Napoleon has subjoined an important statement : Grouchy
was always to hold a position between the Prussian army
and the great main-road on which the Emperor was to
advance ; he was thus to be in constant communication
with his chief, and to be able to come into line with him.
Gérard has positively said that this last order was given ;
that Napoleon pointedly remarked to Grouchy : ' Press
the enemy hardly, and, above all, be always in contact
with me by your left.'†

It is possible to argue about the Emperor's words ; but
Grouchy's force was a restraining wing ; his duty, there-

---

* It is fair to give the *ipsissima verba* of Grouchy's version
('Observations sur la Relation de la Campagne de 1815 '), cited by
Charras (i. 190, 191) and by H. Houssaye ('Waterloo,' ii. 225) :
' Mettez-vous à la poursuite des Prussiens. Complétez leur défaite en
les attaquant des que vous les aurez joints, et ne les perdez jamais de
vue. Je vais me réunir au Maréchal Ney pour attaquer les Anglais,
s'ils tiennent de ce côté-ci de la forêt de Soignes. Vous corre-
spondrez avec moi par la route pavée (route de Namur aux Quatre-
Bras).'

† Thiers, ' Histoire du Consulat et de l'Empire,' vi. 470. Thiers
says he had the very words from the lips of Gérard—no friend of
Grouchy, but an honourable man. Napoleon's version of this order
will be found in ' Comment,' v. 149 : ' Grouchy avait l'ordre positif de
se tenir toujours entre la chaussée de Charleroi à Bruxelles et Blücher ;
afin d'être constamment en communication, et en mesure de se réunir
sur l'armée.'

fore, was not only to attack the Prussians, to defeat them
if he could, to hold Blucher in check, but also to interpose between the allied chiefs; and this is exactly what
the passage in dispute implies.* There is a presumption,
accordingly, all but equal to proof, that Napoleon gave
the order in question. Grouchy accepted it, we shall see,
in this very sense, though he has dishonestly endeavoured
to conceal the truth. The responsibility of a weighty
charge alarmed Grouchy; nor was his anxiety without
sufficient cause. He may have remembered how, years
before, he had failed to seize Cork, in the absence of
Hoche, this being certainly within his power, and how
completely he had miscarried at Bantry; he had never
had a great independent command; he was a good
cavalry officer, but unfit to be a General-in-Chief. Besides, he had already quarrelled with Vandamme, a
malevolent and wrong-headed man; and he was well
aware that Vandamme and Gérard considered themselves,
as they were, very superior to him, and chafed at being
placed under the Marshal's command. Grouchy, he tells
us,† remonstrated with his master; pointed out that the
Prussians were far off in retreat; that they had gained
'fourteen hours' upon their pursuers; that the French
troops at Ligny had not expected to march that day, and
that they would be unable to march for a considerable
time. The Marshal added that he feared he could not
hold Blucher in check; that he had not sufficient force
with 33,000 men to restrain an army still 90,000 strong;

---

* Jomini ('Précis de la Campagne de 1815,' 188, 189) has no real
doubt but that Napoleon's version of his orders to Grouchy is substantially correct. 'Il est de mon devoir d'observer que l'ordre
mentionné dans la relation de Ste. Hélène, était tellement conforme
au système des lignes intérieurs au quel Napoléon avait dû le plus
grand nombre de ses victoires, qu'en ne saurait révoquer en doute qu'il
l'ait effectivement donné.'

† Grouchy, 'Observations sur la Campagne de 1815,' 12, 13, quoted
at length by La Tour d'Auvergne, 'Waterloo,' 217, 218.

that the Prussians appeared to be falling back on Namur ; and that, if this were the case, he would be at a great distance from the main army and widely divided from it, Napoleon, Grouchy has alleged, was not pleased with these remarks; asked him angrily, it has been said, ' was he to give him lessons ?' and repeated, as was the fact, ' that it was Grouchy's business to ascertain the line of the enemy's retreat.'*

A short time after this interview, such as it was—that is, at about half-past eleven o'clock—Napoleon sent another order to Grouchy, expressed in positive and unambiguous terms.† Soult had lingered at Fleurus and had not yet reached Ligny; the Emperor dictated the letter to Bertrand, the most trusted, perhaps, of his surviving officers; Grouchy certainly received it before noon. This order is one of the highest importance; it was most discreditably suppressed by Grouchy, who even denied that it had an existence ; it was not unearthed until 1842. It has been slurred over by the worshippers of success, by apologists for the allies, by Napoleon's detractors; to this hour it has hardly received the close attention it deserves, but it sets forth clearly the ideas of the Emperor at the time, and throws a flood of light on the subsequent conduct of Grouchy.‡

* M. H. Houssaye ('Waterloo,' 227) has given us good reasons for suspecting that this alleged conversation between Grouchy and Napoleon was either imaginary or has been misrepresented. Grouchy is, we repeat, not to be trusted in his statements. He hardly could have told the Emperor that the Prussians had gained 'fourteen hours' on him, when the time was not more than ten or twelve, and when Excelmans was in touch with them at Gembloux. He hardly could have said that the retreat of the Prussians was on Namur, when it was known that Gembloux was largely occupied by them. There are many other inconsistencies.

† It is questionable whether the new order was made upon the information already given by Excelmans, or upon fresh information supplied by General Berton : H. Houssaye, 'Waterloo,' ii. 229 ; Charras, i. 192.

‡ This despatch was first published in a work called ' Notice

In this remarkable paper the Emperor orders Grouchy to march on Gembloux with the mass of his forces—that is, to turn away from the roads towards Namur and Liége, supposed hitherto to be the only line of Blucher's retreat, and to occupy a place leading northwards on the roads to Brussels — that is, in a direction completely different. Napoleon then desires his lieutenant to reconnoitre the 'roads to Namur and Maastricht,' to 'pursue the enemy,' and to correspond with headquarters by the lateral road from Nivelles to Namur, joining the great main-road from Charleroy to Brussels, observing again that he was going in person to Quatre Bras. The despatch nearly ends with these most significant words : ' It is important to ascertain what are the enemy's designs ; he is either separating from the English, or both are seeking to unite in order to cover Brussels or Liége, and to try the chances of another battle ;' and it concludes with an injunction to Grouchy to keep all his troops well in hand.

From this pregnant testimony we can fully gather what was passing in Napoleon's mind at this moment. He probably still suspects that Blucher is falling back on his base—at least, with the chief part of his forces; he therefore directs Grouchy to observe the roads to Namur and Maastricht, and to dog the enemy's movements in that direction. But evidently he is greatly struck by the reports he has just received, that the Prussians are in large numbers at Gembloux, so he commands Grouchy to repair to that place, where he would at once all but certainly come in touch with the enemy, and where, too,

Biographique sur le Maréchal Grouchy,' Paris, 1842. It will be found at length in La Tour d'Auvergne, ' Waterloo,' 220, 221. Grouchy repeatedly denied that it existed ('Observations sur la Campagne de 1815,' 13, 30 ; cited by M. Houssaye, ' Waterloo,' ii. 231), and, when confronted by the fact, changed the hour of its reception from the forenoon to three o'clock, a scandalous misrepresentation : H. Houssaye, *ante*.

he would be on the way to Brussels ; and he then plainly
points out that it was quite possible that Wellington and
Blucher would endeavour to join hands in order to defend Brussels, and to run the risk of a battle.   The order
accordingly proves that Napoleon, if perhaps still sceptical,
was nevertheless alive to the contingency that the allies
would try to unite ; and it indicates distinctly that it was
Grouchy's mission to keep Wellington and Blucher
apart.*

While Napoleon, suspecting the truth, but still un-
convinced, and ignorant of the operations of Blucher's
army, was thus maturing his arrangements, many hours
late, the Prussians were safely effecting their retreat.   As
we have seen, they fell back after Ligny, only a short

* Mr. Ropes ('Campaign of Waterloo,' 210, 211) is one of the very
few commentators who have seen the full significance of this despatch.
We quote these just and discriminating observations : ' There is in
this letter no trace of that certainty as to the position of affairs so
plainly exhibited in the verbal orders.   The news that a Prussian
corps has been seen at Gembloux has evidently made a strong impression on the Emperor.   It may very possibly indicate that Blucher
is not falling back to Namur.   The statement is twice made in the
letter that the Emperor is in doubt as to the intentions of the
Prussians, and the chief task now imposed upon Grouchy is to
ascertain those intentions.   The precise danger to be anticipated is
stated explicitly.   Grouchy is warned in so many words that the
Prussians may be intending to unite with the English, to try the fate
of another battle for the defence of Brussels, which was exactly what
they were intending to do, and what they succeeded in doing.
Whether they are or are not intending to do this is the principal
thing for Grouchy to find out.'   Mr. Ropes (219-223) is also properly
severe on those commentators, for the most part English, who either
ignore or give no weight to a documeut of supreme importance.   But
the object of these writers is obvious : they seek (1) to show that
Napoleon never had any inkling of the designs of Blucher and
Wellington to unite after Ligny and Quatre Bras ; (2) to justify the
essentially faulty, in point of strategy, operations of the allies on
the 17th, which, indeed, gained Waterloo, but ought to have lost it ;
and (3) to exculpate or excuse Grouchy, and to throw on Napoleon
the whole blame of the disaster of June 18.   It is the duty of history
to overthrow the superstructure of misrepresentation and sophistry
which has been raised in consequence.

way; Thielmann held Sombreffe during the night of the
16th; Brye was even occupied by a Prussian rearguard.
Blucher had been borne to Mellery, a village a few miles
from the field; the veteran had been cruelly shaken, and
was still almost unconscious; his lieutenants for a time
did not know what to do. His command, however, de-
volved on Gneisenau, the Chief of his Staff; and Gneisenau,
apparently about midnight, directed that the whole army
should make for Wavre, a small town on the Dyle, nearly
twenty miles from Sombreffe, about ten miles from the
great main-road to the west, and some seventeen or
eighteen from Brussels.

Pirch and Zieten decamped towards break of day, a
part of their forces having already moved. As we have
said, the French outposts gave no sign; the retreat was
not molested, or even observed. This, the right column
of the defeated army, marched steadily along the country
roads leading by Tilly, Gentinnes, and Mont St. Guibert
to Wavre. It left a detachment not far from Tilly to
watch the enemy; it was around Wavre about noon, having
not seen even a trace of the French; it was encamped
at Bierges, St. Anne, and Aisemont on either bank of the
Dyle, many hours before the evening had closed. Thielmann was in command of the left column; he also, soon
after sunrise, broke up from Sombreffe; but he was in
charge of the artillery parks of Ligny; he made for
Gembloux, but his march was slow; he halted at Gembloux until near two, a delay that enabled Excelmans, we
have seen, to come up with his troops, and that might
have been in the highest degree disastrous. He was not,
however, attacked or pursued. He reached Wavre
between ten and twelve at night, and took a position at
La Bavette, near Wavre, on the western bank of the
Dyle. As for Bulow, he had been informed of the defeat
of Ligny by midnight; he had advanced from Hannut
along the old Roman road to Basse Baudeset on the 17th,

nearly reaching Thielmann; he then diverged to his right, moving by Walhain and Corry and the adjoining country. He established his bivouacs at Dion le Mont, not far from Wavre, on the eastern bank of the Dyle, but very late. He had left a detachment behind at Mont St. Guibert, relieving the detachment placed near Tilly, to observe the enemy should he appear. The march of the Prussians had been made difficult by torrents of rain and bad roads; but the troops had not been cowed by defeat; they moved to Wavre with remarkable speed and energy, burning to have the revenge for which they thirsted. An army still of 90,000 men, of whom 30,000 were quite fresh, with from 270 to 280 guns, had thus been assembled around Wavre by the end of the night of June 17; it had received supplies and munitions in part from Maastricht; it was ready to march and to fight on the morrow. A beaten enemy had, perhaps, never escaped so easily; and yet the retreat was made in the face of the warrior who had chased Wurmser through the defiles of the Brenta, and after Jena had annihilated his foes.*

The march of the Prussian army to Wavre had immense results in the events that happened; it has been ascribed to an implied design to co-operate with Wellington on the field of Waterloo. The object, no doubt, of the allied leaders had been to join hands from the outset of the campaign; and probably Gneisenau was aware that Wellington had many months before chosen Waterloo as a good defensive position,† and had a general idea that a

---

* No wonder that Siborne ('Waterloo Campaign,' 294), in ignorance of the state of Napoleon's health, and of the real cause of his inaction on the morning of June 17, has exclaimed: 'Whither had fled the mighty spirit which had shone forth with such dazzling brilliancy in former wars?'

† Wellington Despatches, xii. 129; letter to Lord Bathurst, cited by Charras, i. 201. The position of Waterloo had been surveyed by engineers of the Duke a short time before the campaign began: Ropes, 'The Campaign of Waterloo,' 290.

retreat on Wavre, about ten or eleven miles from Waterloo, would be in accord with the Duke's projects. But it is wholly untrue that, in falling back on Wavre, Gneisenau contemplated a movement on Waterloo to join Wellington; he could not know when he gave his orders what the plans of Wellington were at the time, or even the position of the British army; his correspondence proves that he had no such idea;* he had a grudge against the Duke for the delays of the 15th and the 16th; and, as we shall see, he was unwilling at the decisive moment to break up from Wavre and to risk a march on Waterloo.

It is equally untrue that the retreat on Wavre, if there was an intention to approach Wellington, was the inspiration of genius it has appeared to be in the eyes of the mere idolaters of success. As Napoleon has pointed out with conclusive logic, Wavre is at a much greater distance from Waterloo than Sombreffe is from Quatre Bras, and, what is much more important, is only connected with Waterloo by bad country roads, running through a tract of defiles and woodland, not by any main-road like that between Quatre Bras and Sombreffe; if Gneisenau, therefore, wished to draw near Wellington, he ought not to have retired on Wavre: he should have endeavoured to reach his ally by a more direct march from Ligny. The means were not wanting; the operation, as a whole, would have been as easy, as affairs stood, and as safe, as the retreat to Wavre.† The Prussian army might have

* H. Houssaye, 'Waterloo,' ii. 234.

† We quote these admirable remarks of Napoleon, 'Comment.,' v. 205; English and German writers avoid them, for they cannot be answered: 'Apres avoir perdu la bataille de Ligny, le général prussien au lieu de faire sa rétraite sur Wavre, eût du l'opérer sur l'armée du Duc de Wellington, soit sur les Quatre Bras, puisque celui-ci s'y était maintenu, soit sur Waterloo. Toute la rétraite du Maréchal Blücher dans la matinée du 17, fut à contresens, puisque les deux armées, qui n'étaient qu'a 3,000 toises l'une de l'autre, pendant la soirée du 16, ayant pour communication une belle chaussée, ce qui les pouvait faire

been directed north-westwards, and not northwards; it might have reached the Dyle, not lower down at Wavre, but higher up the stream at Moustier and Ottignies; the roads either way were of much the same character; and having crossed the Dyle at Moustier and Ottignies, it could without difficulty have come into line with Wellington. Thielmann and Bulow could have made the movement securely in the rear of Zieten and Pirch, and in the events that took place they would not have been molested. The allies, therefore, might have united on the night of June 17; and if so, history would rightly assert that they had outmanœuvred their great antagonist, for they would be in his front in overwhelming force, not separated from each other by a wide and dangerous interval of space. It is true that neither the movement on Wavre nor the suggested movement could have been successful had the French army been properly directed, and in sufficient time; but the second was as feasible as the first, and infinitely better, in the position of affairs at this conjuncture. The retreat to Wavre, in fact, was a bad half-measure; for the allies it ought to have been the harbinger, not of victory, but of disastrous defeat.

Meanwhile Napoleon had begun to make the great offensive movement against Wellington, rightly conceived, we have said, but much too late. The corps of Lobau, the Imperial Guard, and other supports, had been directed to Marbais, at between ten and eleven o'clock,* on their way to join Ney, still before Quatre Bras. The two armies, we have seen, were to fall on the Duke, and to attack him in front and flank, should he try to make a stand. At about noon Soult, who had now joined

considérer comme réunies, se trouvèrent, le soir du 17, éloignées de plus 10,000 toises et séparées par des défilés et des chemins impraticables.'

* For the time, see H. Houssaye, ' Waterloo,' ii. 225.

Napoleon, wrote to Ney, commanding him to attack.* This despatch, it will be observed, was more peremptory than the despatch of a few hours before, which referred to an attack in the event only of the enemy having a rear-guard at Quatre Bras. Ney did not receive the earlier despatch—the first intelligence he had obtained of Ligny —until about nine in the morning, or even later. He could not have received the second despatch until one o'clock, but neither had the slightest effect on him; he made no movement, and did not even assemble his troops, acts of gross misconduct and contempt of orders, even though probably, as affairs now were, the Marshal could not have attacked in sufficient time; a most precious opportunity had been almost lost.

We turn to the operations of Wellington on the morn-ing of the 17th, big with important results in the future. By the night of the 16th nearly the whole of the Duke's cavalry and part of the rest of his reserve had joined the troops which had fought at Quatre Bras; he had assembled some 45,000 men at that place, the other parts of his army being at Nivelles, at Braine le Comte, Enghien, and even more westwards; 45,000 men, it is unnecessary to say, would have been unable to resist Napoleon and Ney united, and Wellington must have been in extreme peril, had his enemy fallen upon him, as was possible, in the early forenoon. His position, too, was made all the more critical because he had heard nothing about the events of Ligny, an officer who had carried a report having been severely wounded. In fact, Wellington, we have said, was 'in the air'; his position might have been made fatal.

The Duke slept at Genappe on the night of the 16th, but he was in the saddle at two in the morning, a con-trast to his great adversary in this respect. His first act

* 'Documents inédits,' No. 16; La Tour d'Auvergne, 'Waterloo,' 214, 215.

was to send an aide-de-camp with a small escort to ascertain what had become of the Prussian army. The aide-de-camp fortunately met Zieten, conducting the retreat not far from Tilly. He returned with a message that, though defeated, the Prussians were falling back on Wavre. Soon afterwards—that is, at about eight o'clock —this news was confirmed by an officer despatched by Gneisenau. The Duke, who had had an account of the defeat of Blucher,* and must have known how critical his position had become, replied, with characteristic presence of mind and decision, that his purpose now was to retreat on Waterloo ;† he would accept battle at that place could he be assured of the support of two, or even of one,‡ Prussian corps d'armée. The retreat began about ten in the forenoon ; it was conducted, all military critics have said, with no ordinary precision and skill; the cavalry of Uxbridge masked the movement; the infantry marched on well-chosen lines in excellent order. By one in the afternoon the great mass of the army was far from Quatre Bras; Uxbridge and the cavalry alone remained ; Wellington and his lieutenant continued to be on the spot.§

The retreat was wellnigh over before Napoleon had passed Marbais on his way to Quatre Bras. He had expected to hear the guns of Ney, but all was silent in

* For a very characteristic description of Wellington's reception of the news of Ligny, see Lord Malmesbury's Letters, ii. 447.

† Muffling ('Passages from my Life,' 240) hints that he suggested the retreat on Waterloo, but this is most improbable.

‡ Muffling ('Passages from my Life,' 241) says one corps, other writers two.

§ It has been argued that Wellington was not in real danger at Quatre Bras, on the morning of the 17th ; he would have retreated at once had Ney and Napoleon attacked even at a very early hour. But the Duke would hardly have retreated before he had heard about the movements of the Prussians—that is, until eight a.m. He did not begin his retreat until ten ; he might have been attacked in overwhelming force at eight or nine.

the direction of Frasnes; the Emperor arrayed his army in order of battle and advanced. Uxbridge had placed some light squadrons on the road from Nivelles to Namur, in order to watch the enemy's movements; these fell back when Napoleon's forces were seen to be at hand; the general retreat of the British cavalry began. Napoleon reached Quatre Bras at about two o'clock. Indignant at the conduct of Ney, he had ordered D'Erlon to press forward with his corps; the uniting armies met at Quatre Bras, evacuated by the allies for several hours. Ney had hitherto given no sign of life; he had simply let his troops move forward from Frasnes; the Marshal and D'Erlon were both rebuked for the failure and disobedience of the preceding day. Napoleon said, with emphasis, 'The cause of France has been lost.'

Complaining, however, was worse than useless.* Napoleon, without the delay of a moment, addressed himself to pursue the retreating army. By this time his powers seem to have been revived; Richard, in a word, was himself again; but he must have bitterly felt how, whatever the reason, he had let a great opportunity slip, and how long before he might have brought an army to bay, which now he could only expect to annoy.† He placed himself at the head of his troops, followed by D'Erlon, Lobau, the Guard, and Reille, his masses of cavalry being for the most part in front. He urged vehemently, it is said, the pursuit in person.‡ Little,

* For the remarks made by Napoleon to Ney and D'Erlon see H. Houssaye, 'Waterloo,' ii. 259.

† M. H. Houssaye ('Waterloo,' ii. 260) has very fairly stated what Napoleon might have accomplished on the morning of the 17th: 'Il avait laissé échapper l'occasion d'exterminer l'armée anglaise. Wellington, presque toutes ses troupes encore en position, sa ligne de retraite sur Genappe compromise, sa gauche débordée par Napoléon, son front attaqué par Ney, eut été forcé d'accepter une bataille virtuellement perdue.'

‡ The evidence on this point is very conflicting. Compare 'Waterloo Letters,' 6-96, 133, with H. Houssaye, 'Waterloo,' ii. 261-263.

however, really was accomplished. The squadrons of Uxbridge retired in perfect order, crossing the Dyle on their way at points selected before; a body of French lancers defeated a body of British hussars in a sharp skirmish in the streets of Genappe, but in turn was ridden down and routed by the British Life Guards; thenceforward the enemy became very cautious. The losses on either side were, in fact, trifling—only from 200 to 300 men—a sure sign of the inefficiency of the pursuit; indeed, the storm of rain which had broken on the country for leagues had made even the great main-road not easy for a march, had flooded all the adjoining tract, and had made military operations wellnigh impossible. At about half-past six o'clock the Emperor reached the heights of La Belle Alliance, in front of Waterloo, but at some distance; he perceived bodies of foot and horse in the mist; and he ordered Milhaud to open fire and to pretend to charge. The thunder of many batteries answered the challenge; a large army, with Wellington, was on the spot. 'What would I have given,' Napoleon exclaimed, 'to have the power of Joshua, and to arrest the march of the sun!'* But the march of the sun in the morning had not been turned to account.

We pass on to the movements of Grouchy, of supreme importance for the results of the contest, but misrepresented or ill-explained for years, and even now not completely explained. The Marshal lost no time in assembling his army when he had received the despatch of his master written by Bertrand; he was one of those men who blindly depend on superior orders, but who, without initiative and clear insight, are often unable to comprehend their full import, and, catching at a shadow, drop the real substance. At about noon his 33,000 men were under arms,† and ready to begin the march to Gembloux,

* 'Comment.,' v. 200.

† The time is fixed by M. H. Houssaye ('Waterloo,' ii. 292) by absolutely conclusive evidence.

the direction their chief had been enjoined to take. We must bear in mind what his position was at this moment. Pajol, we have seen, had come up with the enemy on the way to Namur; but he soon discovered that he was in contact with stragglers only, and that the Prussians were not, on that line, in force; he returned to Mazy and halted there for some hours, having heard from peasants that a large part of the hostile army was in retreat by St. Denis and Leuze towards Louvain, that it was moving away from its communications with Namur and Liége, was marching northwards, and drawing towards Brussels.   It would appear that Pajol did not send this report to Grouchy for a considerable time, but Grouchy, like Napoleon, had been made aware that the Prussians were around Gembloux 'in great force,' and that Excelmans was on his way to reach them, and Gembloux was the point Grouchy was himself to attain.

This intelligence ought to have made the Marshal reflect that, in all probability, the Prussian army was abandoning the direction of Namur and Liége, and was not falling back on its base at all; it certainly ought to have induced him to advance on Gembloux and to find out the enemy without the loss of an instant; and it is fair to remark that Grouchy seems at first to have had the latter object distinctly in view.   He had assembled his forces with praiseworthy haste, but the march to Gembloux was made extraordinarily slow, and was retarded by a series of delays, largely to be ascribed to Grouchy himself.   The corps of Gérard around Ligny was the nearest to Gembloux, and should have been the first to move; but Grouchy, afraid to annoy Vandamme, whose corps was at St. Amand, some distance to the left, placed Vandamme and his troops at the head of the columns on their march; nearly two hours were thus unnecessarily lost.   In addition Gembloux might have been reached by at least two roads; but Grouchy crowded his army into one column on a single road, and this again greatly retarded his march. The result was that Vandamme did not reach Gembloux until seven o'clock, and Gérard not until nine in the evening; and yet Gembloux is only eight miles from Ligny, and not more than ten from St. Amand. Unquestionably the storm and bad roads had impeded the march; but these obstacles had been overcome by the Prussians, who had moved at a very different rate of speed; and Napoleon had made a march of twenty miles at least, and that in the presence of an enemy in his front, even if he had the advantage of the great main-road from Charleroy to Brussels. Meanwhile Thielmann, whose corps had been reached by Excelmans, and who, we have seen, had halted at Gembloux a great deal too long, had been allowed to escape almost unobserved; and Excelmans, who on this eventful day seems to have been as over-confident and careless as most of his fellows, had advanced only to Sauvenière, a village two or three miles beyond Gembloux, and did not hang with his horsemen on the retreat of the enemy.

This was an inauspicious beginning of a pursuit which ought to have been pressed with all the more celerity because it had been undertaken very late. By the night of the 17th the whole Prussian army was being gathered together around Wavre—that is, ten or eleven miles from Waterloo—while Grouchy's army, scarcely more than a third in numbers, was at or near Gembloux—that is, at least sixteen miles from Napoleon's camp. These distances were already not of happy omen. Nevertheless, whatever has been said, there was still no reason that Grouchy should not be able successfully to perform his task, should not be able to reach and to attack the enemy —above all, should not hold Blucher fast, and keep him away from Wellington, fulfilling the true part of a restraining wing, if he had the capacity of anything like a real chief.

In the course of the night Grouchy received numerous reports, all indicating that the Prussians were in retreat northwards; had abandoned their communications with Namur and Liége; and were either making for Wavre, as the fact was, or for Perwez, in the direction of Louvain, the evidence preponderating that Wavre was the object of their march. Excelmans pushed forward some squadrons to Nil St. Vincent and Sart les Walhain, villages only seven or eight miles from Wavre, and heard that the enemy was on his way to that place; a detachment sent to Perwez gave the same intelligence. The inhabitants of Gembloux and the peasantry of the adjoining tract—in sympathy with the French, and hating the Prussians—spoke of Prussian movements on Perwez or Wavre; there was even a rumour that Blucher was trying to join Wellington—that is, was near Wavre—with the intention of reaching Waterloo.* Upon this information, surely significant enough, Grouchy wrote to Napoleon at ten at night. This despatch should also be studied with care. In this communication the Marshal tells his master that he is at Gembloux and his cavalry at Sauvenière; that the enemy, ' 35,000 strong,' is retreating; that the Prussians were divided into two main columns, one moving on Wavre, the other on Perwez; that a third column was falling back on Namur; that a part of these forces, ' it might be inferred,' was ' on the way ' to join hands with Wellington, and that another part was perhaps making ultimately for Liége. The Marshal adds that he was sending his cavalry forward, and that, according to the intelligence it should bring in, he would march either on Wavre or Perwez. The despatch ends with these most important words, showing plainly that Grouchy understood his mission : ' If the great body of the Prussians is retiring upon Wavre, I will follow them in that

* H. Houssaye, ' Waterloo,' ii. 247.

direction, so that they shall not be able to reach Brussels, and that I may separate them from Wellington.'*

The information Grouchy had already obtained should have led him to conclude that the Prussian army was, for the most part, at least, assembling at Wavre. But considering it even from his own point of view, the course he ought to adopt should have been plain to his mind. He might disregard any hostile force on its way to Perwez— that is, to Louvain—for this was in far eccentric retreat, and could neither molest Napoleon nor assist Wellington. But he was bound to follow without delay, and carefully to attack and hold in check, any hostile force making for Wavre; for this obviously was drawing near Wellington —nay, might be seeking to come to his aid; and this was the more necessary because the Emperor had told Grouchy that it was his intention to attack the English in front of the Forest of Soignies, distant only ten or eleven miles from Wavre.

The means of securing the Marshal's object and of enabling him to fulfil his duty were not difficult, and ought to have been apparent. He ought to advance on Wavre as quickly as possibly, and so to direct his march as to have the power to strike Blucher in flank were he trying to join Wellington; and this operation was possible—nay, quite feasible. Gembloux is some fifteen miles from Wavre, and from the roads on which the Prussians would march in case they were on their way to Waterloo; it is about ten miles from the Dyle at Moustier and Ottignies, whence there were roads to Wavre, to the line of the enemy's possible movement, and to the positions now held by Napoleon. The course for Grouchy to take was,

* This despatch will be found in La Tour d'Auvergne, 'Waterloo' 230, 231. Grouchy shamefully garbled it afterwards, feeling the full significance, regard being had to his subsequent conduct, of the expression that he would 'separate' the Prussians from Wellington: Ropes, 'The Campaign of Waterloo,' 360, 361.

therefore, as it were, marked out; he should make for Wavre by daybreak on June 18; but he should direct his movement to the Dyle at Moustier and Ottignies, crossing the river at these points by the bridges, which, like those on the Sambre, remained intact; it would be then within his power either to advance on Wavre, should the Prussians be remaining at that place, or to attack Blucher, to hold him in check for a space of time, sufficiently long, at least, to prevent him giving support to his colleague—and the attack, we must bear in mind, would be on Blucher's flank, and about as perilous as could be conceived—and especially to co-operate with the main French army should the Emperor be in need of his aid. Had Grouchy formed this resolution on the night of June 17, and carried it out intelligently on the following morning, he would have atoned for the faults even now to be laid to his charge; Blucher, humanly speaking, could never have joined Wellington; Waterloo could never have been a victory for the allies.

The lines taken by the Prussians in their retreat from Ligny ought to have been ascertained by the dawn of June 17. For this Soult was responsible, in the first instance; but Napoleon, too, must be held responsible—they would have been discovered had he been the Napoleon of old. Grouchy was sent to find them out, but many hours too late; and his march on Gembloux had been so retarded, and Excelmans had given proof of so little zeal and skill, that the direction taken by the enemy remained uncertain. But the evidence obtained by Grouchy on the night of the 17th pointed in the main to a retreat on Wavre. It did not really point to a retreat on Perwez; the movement on Wavre was the one most probable, and the only one that could endanger Napoleon; Grouchy, therefore, we repeat, ought to have provided against it by adopting the measures before referred to; had he done this he would have redressed the many shortcomings and mistakes of the day; he would have stopped Blucher on his way to Waterloo; he would have averted from France a frightful disaster. No remarkable insight or energy were required; besides, independently of the reports before him, he ought to have acted in the spirit of his orders—and these he understood—and to have so conducted his operations as in any event to interpose between the allied commanders. He ought, in a word, to have borne in mind that in war, should a doubt exist, a General should assume that his enemy would do what is best for his interests, and that the military art is one of a fine calculation of chances, and of making the most of the opportunities these may present.*

Unfortunately Grouchy was one of those chiefs who cling to the letter and miss the real import, and are incapable of bold and original movements. He never even thought of directing his army on Moustier and Ottignies; he did not move a division on the night of the 17th towards these points; he did not contemplate an early or rapid march on Wavre—nay, even a march on Wavre at all—though he had indicated Wavre as the place on which he would move should he learn that the enemy was there in force. On the contrary, his orders show that he was chiefly thinking of making his way towards Perwez —that is, to his right, far away from Napoleon, and not toward Wavre, where the Prussian army was; Vandamme and Excelmans were to advance to Sart les Walhain; Gérard was to follow the movement, and to send his horse to Grand Leez, 'for the enemy was falling back on

---

* This is well put by Charras (ii. 110): 'Grouchy devait tirer sa résolution des circonstances. En pareil cas, l'hésitation n'est pas permis : il faut baser ses opérations sur la supposition qui son adversaire a agit et agira pour atteindre le résultat le plus favorable à ses interêts et conformement au caractère qu'on lui connait. Il n'y a pas d'autre règle de conduite rationnelle. L'art du général serait bien vulgaire, si on n'avait jamais à opérer que sur des ordres parfaits, sur des données certaines.'

Perwez'; Pajol was to march to Grand Leez from Mazy.
The truth seems to be that he had taken it into his head
that the Prussians were retreating on Perwez—that is, in
the last event, on Louvain—and that his only duty was to
follow and attack Blucher; he did not reflect that his
paramount duty—and yet he was fully aware of this—was
to play the part of a commander of a restraining wing,
and to interpose between Blucher and Wellington.

Leaving Grouchy blindly following a fatal course, we
turn to Napoleon, now before Waterloo. There was no
sign in him on the night of the 17th of the sluggish
lethargy clearly seen in the morning. He superintended
in person the positions occupied by his troops, placed
D'Erlon, Milhaud, Domon, Subervie, Lefebvre - Desnoëttes—in fact, the parts of his army at present on
the spot—in a line extending from Plancenoit to Mon-
plaisir, and sent pressing orders that Lobau, the Imperial
Guard and Reille should come into line from the rear as
quickly as possible. A farmhouse called Caillou was made
his headquarters, but he took little rest on this memorable
night. Wellington and his army were now in his front,
but Napoleon feared that his adversary would not offer
him battle; he believed that the Duke and Blucher, conforming to judicious strategy, would retire behind Brussels,
combine their forces, and then make ready to meet him
in overwhelming numbers; he would not be given again,
he supposed, the opportunities given at Ligny and Quatre
Bras. His leading idea—and this almost engrossed his
mind—was to bring the British commander to bay before
he could decamp and join his colleague; he did not
seriously think that Blucher, wherever he might be,
would venture to make a flank march of the most
perilous kind on the chance of being able to reach
Wellington; in his heart of hearts he was convinced, with
all his lieutenants, that the Prussian army was not yet in
a condition to fight. Above all, had he not despatched

Grouchy many hours before to pursue it, to attack it, to make it impossible that it should come to the assistance of the Duke's army, should it even have the power of giving battle?

A report from Milhaud that an enemy's column was making for Wavre—this was the detachment called in from Tilly—did not affect the Emperor's fixed belief; he refused to suppose that Blucher could march from Wavre on Waterloo; besides, this might be only a stray column endeavouring to approach Brussels, whither we had seen Blucher, he thought, might march. It appears to be probable, nevertheless, that on receiving this news Napoleon sent a message to Grouchy;* but if this was the case, it never reached the Marshal; and certainly Blucher and the Prussian army were not uppermost at this moment in the Emperor's mind. Napoleon left his headquarters after midnight to observe the positions of the hostile army; he contemplated, he has informed us, a night attack should the Duke be showing signs of retreat; his orders prove this statement to be correct. But all was silence in the enemy's camps; 'the Forest of Soignies looked like a conflagration; the horizon shone with bivouac fires';† the only sounds were the faint rumble of guns, and the dash of the torrents of rain that had not ceased to fall. Napoleon returned to his farmhouse, hopeful, but not satisfied; his adversary was evidently making a stand; but would the state of the weather permit an attack to be made?

At about two in the morning the message arrived, sent by Grouchy at ten on the night of the 17th. This despatch, it should be borne in mind, was calculated to inspire Napoleon with complete confidence as to the possible operations of Blucher on June 18. The Prussian army was represented as not being in great force, and as divided into two, or even three, columns, falling back on

* H. Houssaye, 'Waterloo,' ii. 270.   † *Ibid.*, 279.

Wavre, Perwez, and Namur; and the Marshal had pledged himself that were it moving on Wavre, in considerable strength, he would take care 'to separate Blucher from Wellington.' The Emperor felt that he need have no fears as to his veteran enemy; his lieutenant understood his duty, and would hold him in check; he had only to direct his whole forces against Wellington, the opinion he had already held for some time.

It is probable, however, that, before he had heard from Gembloux, he had formed a design of attracting part of the forces of Grouchy, and in certain circumstances the principal part, to the scene of the great battle obviously now at hand, and that he adhered to the design after Grouchy's message. We have reached one of the most perplexing episodes of the campaign, which has not received sufficient attention, and on which just enough light has been thrown to make the darkness, so to speak, more visible. Napoleon has positively asserted that he sent two messages on the night of the 17th, directing Grouchy to send a detachment of 7,000 men and sixteen guns to St. Lambert, a little village near the Lasne, about four miles from the French lines, and to fall at an early hour on the left flank of Wellington; the Marshal was to support the movement, with the mass of his army, when he had ascertained the whereabouts of Blucher.* This statement has been summarily rejected by most critics, but their arguments seem to us of no great weight; the reasons to the contrary are so cogent and so increasing in force. There is literally nothing in the circumstance that no such orders can be found on the records of the Chief

---

* 'Comment.,' v. 154, 155. An attentive student of war will observe how these alleged orders conformed to Napoleon's statement that when he detached Grouchy, on the morning of the 17th, he directed the Marshal to keep between Blucher and the great main-road from Charleroy to Brussels.

of the French Staff; the same remark applies to the all-important order written by Bertrand in the absence of Soult. Nor is there much in the circumstance that the orders in question seem to be inconsistent with a well-known despatch of Soult, written in the forenoon of June 18, to which we shall advert afterwards. Napoleon may not have consulted Soult, with whom he was by no means satisfied; he may have thought it advisable to keep his counsel to himself. There are solid grounds, on the other hand, for accepting the Emperor's distinct assertion. The movement on St. Lambert was exactly in Napoleon's manner; it was the counterpart of the movement on Marbais, which Ney was ordered to make on the 16th; it was in accord with the plan of attack at Waterloo. Again there is clear evidence from independent sources that Napoleon expected Grouchy to be in line with him at an early hour on June 18; this most pregnant fact has only been lately disclosed, but it is of extreme significance, and we shall recur to it. Finally, it is not to be assumed that, in a matter of this kind, the Emperor deliberately wrote a downright falsehood; this is very different from the inaccurate and partial statements to be found in his narratives of the campaign, and recent investigation, it should be added, has tended to confirm, in the main, these writings. On the whole, we incline to think these orders were given; this would account for much that is now obscure; but unquestionably they never reached Grouchy; he would have been too eager, if they had, to comply with them. The bearers of the despatches may have been killed or made prisoners; and unhappily there were traitors and deserters in the French army.*

Meanwhile Wellington had been preparing himself to encounter Napoleon in front of Waterloo. In addition to the forces which had fallen back from Quatre Bras, he had drawn to the scene of action at hand from 23,000 to

* See Thiers, ' Histoire du Consulat et de l'Empire,' vi. 475, 476.

26,000 men, comprising a part of the 2nd corps of Hill. These moved from Nivelles and other points; he was at the head of an army about 70,000 strong. He might have assembled many more troops; but he still persisted in fearing for his right, an extraordinary conviction in the existing state of things. He placed from 17,000 to 18,000 men, including a part of Colville's British division, at Hal and Tubize, far away on his extreme right, in the belief that ' the enemy might turn him in that direction.'* This admittedly was a grave strategic error; the excuses made for it may be dismissed; it exposed him to immense danger in the great strife that ensued, danger that he might wellnigh have averted.†

Meantime the aged but heroic Blucher, superior to defeat and illness and pain, had resolved to lead his army to the aid of his colleague—a magnificent instance of energetic daring; on the return of the messenger sent to Quatre Bras in the morning, he had made answer to the Duke, on the evening of the 17th: ' I shall not come with two corps only, but with my whole army—upon the understanding, however, that, should the French not attack us on the 18th, we shall attack them on the 19th.'‡ This, however, seems to have been only a verbal message expressing the determination of the old warrior; it was

---

* Wellington to the Duc de Berry: Despatches, xii. 476.

† It is scarcely necessary to refer to Napoleon ('Comment.,' vi. 179): ' Il faut tenir l'armée réunie, concentrer le plus de forces possibles sur le champ de bataille, profiter de toutes les occasions ; car la fortune est femme ; si vous la manquez aujourdhui, ne vous attendez pas à la retrouver demain.'

‡ General Maurice (*United Service Magazine*, September, 1890) has contended that these emphatic words were not uttered on the evening of the 17th, but are contained in a letter written to Muffling on the morning of the 18th. But Muffling ('History of the Campaign of 1815') fixes the time as the evening of the 17th; and it is improbable, in the highest degree, that Wellington would have made a stand at Waterloo, if he had not had some assurance of the kind, before the night of the 17th.

not, we have seen, until late on the night of the 17th that the whole Prussian army was around Wavre; up to that time it was impossible to know whether it would be able to march on Waterloo; munitions, and supplies, too, had to be delivered to the troops. It appears to be certain that the official statement, that the march was to be positively made, was not written until near midnight on the 17th, and did not reach Wellington until about two in the morning.* The credit of the project, too, belongs wholly to Blucher;† he insisted on the movement being made with persevering ardour. Gneisenau hesitated and made strategic objections, undoubtedly not without the greatest weight; this is sufficient proof that, in ordering the retreat on Wavre, he had had no immediate purpose of joining Wellington.

The plan of the allied commanders, therefore, was this: Wellington, with an army of about 70,000 men, of whom scarcely 40,000 were really good troops, was to resist the attack of Napoleon in immensely superior force, regard being had to the quality of his army. Blucher was to march from Wavre to the aid of his colleague, each being divided from the other by ten or eleven miles of a very impracticable and intricate country. It should be remarked, too, and this is important, that Wellington and Blucher both thought that all Napoleon's army was before Waterloo, with the single exception of the corps of

---

* We altogether dismiss a story—first heard of many years after Waterloo—that Wellington rode to Wavre and had an interview with Blucher on the night of the 17th. (1) The story is almost incredible; no Commander-in-Chief ever did a thing of the kind. (2) There was never a whisper about it in the Prussian or the British army. (3) There is abundant evidence that Wellington flatly contradicted it when he heard of it. (4) The story is really inconsistent with the only known documents in existence. Mr. Ropes has properly rejected it, as a myth, in the last edition of his work.

† Some writers have referred these discussions to June 16, but the evidence greatly preponderates that they took place at Wavre on the night of the 17th.

13

Vandamme ; they had no conception that Grouchy was approaching Wavre with an army fully 33,000 strong.*

These dispositions secured a great and decisive triumph ; they have been extolled by the courtiers of fortune ; but they cannot mislead an impartial student of war ; they were essentially ill-designed, and hazardous in the extreme. They implied, from the allied point of view, that Wellington was to withstand Napoleon at the head of nearly 100,000 men, with an army really not half as strong, for a space of certainly five or six hours, in all probability of many more. Was this combination likely to succeed ? was it not rather big with the promise of a French victory ?† They implied, too, in the actual situation of affairs, that Blucher would surely be able to reach Waterloo, though Grouchy, with a powerful restraining wing, was gathering on his flank. The history of many a campaign has shown that the chances were that this movement would be arrested, and that Wellington would be left without support from his colleague. This strategy, therefore, was in principle bad ; it ought to have proved in the highest degree disastrous ; but it was the natural result of the faulty arrangement, which directed the Prussian army to Wavre, divided from Waterloo by practically a great interval of space, and which prompted the resolve to march from Wavre on Wellington. But it was the great object of the allies, it may be urged, to unite ; how otherwise were they to effect their junction ? Napoleon was shown how this was to be done, without incurring immense unnecessary risk, and in conformity to the true rules of the military art. As Blucher ought not to have rushed to Sombreffe, and have dragged Welling-

* Wellington Despatches, xii. 478 *et seq.*

† Napoleon (' Comment.,' v. 208, 209) has put this view of the case forward with admirable clearness and force. Clausewitz, cited by Mr. Ropes (' The Waterloo Campaign,' 243), has in vain attempted a reply. Mr. Ropes easily disposes of his very disingenuous and untrue remarks in a few sentences.

ton, as it were, to Quatre Bras; as, in the position of affairs existing on June 15, they ought to have fallen back on Wavre and Waterloo; so, in the position of affairs on the night of the 17th, they ought to have fallen back behind Brussels; in that event they would be perfectly safe; and they would be able to oppose nearly 200,000 men to an adversary who could assemble hardly 110,000.* In that case certainly they would not have gained Waterloo; but they would really have out-generalled their mighty foe; and instead of exposing themselves, and even their cause, to peril, they would have assured the ultimate success of the allies.

Napoleon and Wellington had now met, for the first time; each drew his lot from the urn with a steady hand;

* Napoleon has proved this with characteristic force of logic ('Comment.,' v. 210, 211). This is another of the passages German and English commentators avoid, because it is unanswerable. 'On demandera: Que devait donc faire le général anglais après la bataille de Ligny, et le combat de Quatre Bras? La postérité n'aura pas deux opinions. Il devait traverser, la nuit du 17 au 18, la forêt de Soigne sur la chaussée de Charleroi; l'armée prussienne la devait également traverser sur la chaussée de Wavre: les deux armées devaient se réunir, à la pointe du jour, sur Bruxelles, laisser des arrières gardes pour défendre la forêt, gagner quelques jours pour donner le temps aux Prussiens dispersés par la bataille de Ligny de rejoindre leur armée, se renforcer de quatorze régiments anglais qui étaient en garnison dans les places fortes de la Bélgique, ou venaient de débarquer à Ostende de retour d'Amérique et laisser manœuvrer l'empereur des Français comme il aurait voulu. Aurait-il avec une armée de 100,000 hommes traversé la forêt de Soigne, pour attaquer, au débouché les deux armées réunies, fortes de plus de 200,000 hommes, et en position? C'était certainement tout ce qui pouvait arriver de plus avantageux aux alliés.' Mr. Ropes ('The Campaign of Waterloo,' 235, 243, 244) has also made some very judicious observations on the subject in the same sense as Napoleon. Perhaps the best commentary on the retreat from Ligny to Wavre, and on the project of a march from Wavre to Waterloo, with the results that ought to have followed, will be found in Prince La Tour d'Auvergne, 'Waterloo,' 204, 205. It is remarkable that almost every eulogist of the allied operations has admitted that they involved the greatest danger. As for Blucher's march on Waterloo, it occupied more than the time we have allowed.

each was confident as to the issue of the impending struggle. Yet there was much in the situation as it existed, and as it appeared to both, that might have caused apprehension as to coming events. For aught the Emperor knew, his adversary had his whole army assembled; if so, it would largely exceed the French army in numbers. He had had no experience of the qualities of British troops; but Salamanca, Vittoria, and many other fields were ominous signs of what they could do in battle; he had a General before him who had never known defeat; had baffled and beaten his best lieutenants; had overthrown his gigantic power in Spain. And Blucher, wherever he was, could not be far off; and Blucher had, over and over again, confounded his calculations by his heroic energy. Could Napoleon rely on Grouchy with complete trust? might not the old warrior, threefold Grouchy in strength, appear at Waterloo and turn decisively the scales of fortune? And Napoleon must have felt that this was his last chance; were he to fail in this hazard, Europe in arms—nay, an exasperated France —would make him their victim. Nevertheless these thoughts had no fears for that soaring spirit, exulting within its proper sphere—war; the sun about to rise would see the ruin of the British army; and were the British army out of the way, ' of what use would be the other armies about to cross the Rhine, the Alps, and the Pyrenees?'*

Wellington, on the other hand, as things appeared to him, might well have felt the gravest misgivings. He believed that Napoleon was before him with 100,000 men, all French troops of excellent quality. Could he resist these with an army of many races and tongues, not to be

* ' Comment.,' v. 208 : ' Si l'armée anglo-hollandaise eût été détruite à Waterloo, à quoi eût servi aux alliés ce grand nombre d'armées qui se disposient à franchir le Rhin, les Alps, et les Pyrénées ?' No prouder testimony could be given to the value of a British army, and to the power of England.

compared in strength to that of his enemy, during the
long hours that must pass before Blucher could join him ?
What if his adversary should attack in the early morning
—and this, we shall see, was Napoleon's purpose—could
Blucher, separated by miles of forest, bad roads, and
intricate defiles, be on the field in time to avert a disaster ?
And Napoleon, Wellington knew well, was very different
from Masséna, Marmont, and Soult—mere satellites of
that mighty sun. His presence in the field, the Duke
has written, was equal to 40,000 men ; he had never been
defeated except at immense odds against him. Nevertheless, the British commander was in high heart ; his
calm constancy was not disturbed ; he said simply and
curtly, ' All will go well.'*

Sciolists and partisans have asserted that at this juncture Napoleon had been ' outgeneralled ' by the allies,
and that their success on June 18 had been rendered
certain. Nothing can be more untrue—nay, absurd ;
strategically the advantage was still on the Emperor's
side ; if only his lieutenants would be worthy of him,
the chances were still that he would gain Waterloo.
The junction of Blucher and Wellington would in any
event be difficult in the extreme, and could only take
place late ; even now, had Grouchy been a capable
chief—nay, had Gérard been at the head of his army—that
junction could have been made impossible. And what
Napoleon were to fall on Wellington at nine in the
morning, as would have happened but for the state of
the weather, and perhaps a grave mistake ; and what if
Grouchy should appear at St. Lambert in obedience to
orders he might have received ? Under all these conditions the probabilities were that Wellington would be
defeated, and Blucher would fail.† Napoleon, therefore,

* Letter to the Duc de Berry, 3 a.m., June 18 : Wellington Despatches, xii. 476.

† See Charras, ii. 77, 78, and Lord Wolseley, ' Decline and Fall of
Napoleon,' 188, 189.

was not 'outgeneralled'; his efforts against the British commander, especially if they were made at an early hour, would, it is likely, be attended with success. But we venture to think—and we hope we set prejudice aside —that in no event could Napoleon's success on June 18 have been complete and decisive. He would have over- whelmed Blucher on the 16th at Ligny had Ney and D'Erlon been equal to their tasks; in that case the campaign might have closed in Belgium. He had it in his power to inflict a crushing defeat on the allies upon the following day, but owing, we believe, to a kind of suspension of his great faculties by disease, he missed the occasion as he had never missed it before; Achilles had been in a state of lethargy in his tent. If still favourable, the chances for the battle of the 18th were much less favourable than they had previously been; and many chances were becoming adverse. We cannot accept his statement, true as to June 16 and 17, that 'but for the faults of his lieutenant he would have made an end of his foes at Waterloo.'*

* Napoleon Correspondence, xxxii. 275 : 'Je les écrasais encore à Waterloo, si ma droite ne m'eût pas manqué.'

CHAPTER VII

THE OPERATIONS OF JUNE 18—THE PRELUDE TO WATERLOO

The night of June 17—The condition of the two armies—Confidence
of the French—Ominous symptoms—Feelings that prevailed in
the allied army—Wellington prepares for battle at an early hour
—Overconfidence of Napoleon—He postpones the attack—This
unfortunate for him—The position of Waterloo—Its great natural
strength—Disposition of Wellington's forces to resist Napoleon's
attack—Blucher at Wavre—Hesitation of Gneisenau—The Prussian army begins its march on Waterloo—It is dangerously and
unnecessarily delayed—Blucher sets off to join Wellington—
Grouchy—He misdirects his army—He marches towards Wavre,
very late, and slowly—Magnificent appearance of Napoleon's
army before the attack—The Emperor—Soult—Grouchy.

THE tempestuous night of June 17 severely tried the
endurance of the two armies, brought at last face to face
for a tremendous conflict. The rain continued to fall in
torrents for hours; the roll of thunder sounded in the
far distance; lightning flashed, in tongues of flame, from
between the clouds; superstition had its tales, for many
years afterwards, of dread forms of death and terror
appearing in the skies. Scarcely more than half of the
French army had as yet reached the field; the soldiery,
in their hastily formed encampments, stretched themselves
on the sodden and miry ground, amidst crops of rye
trodden under foot, and drenched with wet; the bivouac
fires, dense with smoke, and yielding little warmth, only

illuminated faintly the darkness around. Many divisions, we have seen, were still in the rear; the corps of Lobau and Reille, and Kellermann's horsemen, spread around Genappe four miles from headquarters. The men of the Imperial Guard toiled painfully through the storm, and reached the front in the morning only, in an angry mood and a sorry plight. Hunger and privation, too, made the ordeal worse; the store of food for four days, which, as their wont was, the legions of Napoleon carried with them, had been by this time wellnigh exhausted; it was long after daybreak before a fresh distribution was made.

Nevertheless, amidst passing murmurs and discontent, there was no sign of despondency or weakness in the slowly gathering host; the French had the conqueror of many years at their head; they were elated by their triumph over the detested Prussians; they looked forward with eager hope to the morrow, and to the victory they would wrest from the English in retreat before them. Still, apart from material distress and hardship, many things concurred to impair the moral power and essential strength of that high-hearted army. The country, for miles around, was covered with stragglers, irregularly hastening to join their colours; hamlets, villages, and farms had been ravaged by widespread pillage; the bonds of discipline had been dangerously relaxed. The worst symptom, however, was the deep distrust of many officers and chiefs prevailing among the troops. Ney, it was rumoured, had been sharply rebuked; Soult and his staff were angrily censured; the Old Guard mingled its complaints with talk of treason; the crime of Bourmont and others was laid to the charge of leaders in high and inferior place. Napoleon, in fact, and Napoleon alone, held that formidable but ill-compacted array together; should his eagles fail in their swoop, what would be the result? would they ever soar to the sun again?

Some provision had been made in the opposite camp to mitigate the sufferings the dreary night brought with it. The greater part of Wellington's army had reached its positions before the storm had burst; the men had accumulated the masses of wood which had fed the fires seen from afar by Napoleon; these had diminished the discomfort caused by rain and cold. The troops, too, had been well supplied with food, regularly paid for, as was the rule of their service; and they were all assembled within a space comparatively small, straggling and in-discipline being unknown among them. The night, how-ever, was difficult to bear; the bivouacs, like those of the enemy, were on the rain-drenched ground, and amidst rye 'dripping on you, as if from a bath'; the soldiery, of whom thousands had marched twenty, thirty, and even forty, miles, from the valleys of the Senne, the Dender and the Scheldt, sank wearily to sleep, overcome by fatigue. This was especially the case of the cavalry, which had covered the retreat from Quatre Bras; and some of the divisions, which had arrived late, were almost as severely tried as the French.

The feelings that pervaded that armed assemblage of many peoples and tongues, as might have been expected, were very different. Perponcher had suffered heavy loss at Quatre Bras; thousands of the Dutch-Belgians had been brothers in arms of the French; Napoleon for these men was a very God of War, the Duke a commander almost unknown; no wonder that the courage of part of these troops was shaken. The Brunswickers, too, had been beaten on the 16th; but they were eager to avenge the fall of their Duke; they were animated by the stern Teutonic spirit; many were ere long to show they could fight to the death. As for the Hanoverian and other German levies, these were young troops to a very great extent; but they were in-spired by the patriotism of 1813; they were longing to measure themselves with the enemy. The men of the

German Legion and the British soldiery were, it is unnecessary to say, the backbone of the army, the power on
which Wellington must chiefly rely; they were in the
mood that had made them terrible on many a hard-
fought field. Even the young and raw battalions had
acquired the steadiness and strong sense of duty characteristic of troops under the Duke's command; they were
to do great things in a fierce and protracted trial. As
for the veterans of the Peninsular War—and many regiments of these were happily present—they looked forward
to the coming struggle with the most complete confidence,
and quietly laughed at the fears and misgivings of weaker
comrades. They had met and beaten the French before;
they were about to meet and beat them again; they knew
nothing of Napoleon, they knew Wellington; they had
absolute trust in their chiefs and their officers; Busaco,
Salamanca, Vittoria, and a march of victory from the
Tagus, across the Pyrenees to the Garonne, were the
signs in which they had been taught to conquer.

During the night the sounds, in places, were heard of
the tools of the sappers employed in strengthening the
outworks in advance of the allied line, which were being
made formidable points of defence. Wellington seems to
have thought that his adversary would attack at an early
hour; he was on horseback soon after five in the morning;
he rode to the field unaccompanied, it has been said, by
his staff, many of these gallant but ill-trained youths.*
At about six the assembly rang along the army's front;
the men rose, 'cold and blue, dirty and unshaven,' from
the dying watchfires; but they had soon addressed themselves to their manifold tasks, the 'note of preparation,'
an eye-witness wrote, 'reminding me forcibly of the
distant murmur of the sea beating against an iron-bound
coast.' The leaguers, held by the armed masses, seemed
stirring with life; here the guns, 'their deep voices still

* A survivor of Waterloo told this to the present writer.

silent,' were being moved in batteries to selected points; there horsemen were tending their battle-steeds for the fight; here, again, footmen were despatching their morning meal—the last many a brave man was ever to taste; squadrons and regiments were taking the positions they were to defend. The echoes of martial music spread far and wide; the Highland pibroch, with its shrill notes, blending with the thunder of the drum and the blare of trumpets; staff officers were descried pointing out everywhere the stations the different corps were to occupy. The most curious feature of the marshalling of the host was, perhaps, the rapid crackling of musketry along the whole line; the soldiery discharged their pieces in the air, in order to load them again for the conflict at hand. The French army, though in the near distance, as yet remained motionless and made no sign; the outposts only watched the enemy's doings; mist and rain half enshrouded the imperial arrays. In truth, large parts of the army were still far off, and Napoleon had no notion of an attack made piecemeal by day, though he had certainly contemplated a night attack, should his antagonist have tried to retreat in the darkness.

The Emperor had been engaged during part of the night in reading and dictating despatches referring to the state of opinion in Paris, and to the questionable attitude of the Houses he had lately convened. Sinister rumours reached him, too, of missives disseminated far and wide, presaging his fall and his army's ruin; the Belgian plains would witness an immense disaster; they would be the sepulchre of the last host of the Empire. His confidence, nevertheless, was absolute—nay, overweening—when at eight in the morning he called his lieutenants together to partake in the last meal they were to share with him. Napoleon estimated the Duke's army at its full normal strength,* 90,000 men, for he was

---

* Allowing for the losses at Quatre Bras and in the retreat.

not aware that a large body of troops had been left round Hal; he was undertaking an operation which, he has told us himself, should be avoided if possible, and must be hazardous, attacking a great master of defence in a position chosen by himself; yet he felt convinced that, with a force he calculated as 69,000 Frenchmen, he could certainly defeat—nay, destroy—a force largely superior, he thought, in number. 'The chances,' he said, 'are nine to one in our favour'; in this we see his too sanguine and sometimes presumptuous temper.

He gave little attention to the remarks or the warnings of the companions in arms seated at his board, many of these in a mood wholly different from his own. His brother Jerôme informed him that he had heard a report at Genappe that Blucher was about to march from Wavre to join Wellington. Napoleon rejected the idea as almost extravagant; should the enemies unite, it would be behind Brussels; in any case Grouchy would dispose of Blucher. Ney declared that Wellington was about to retreat, and that his columns were making for the Forest of Soignies; the Emperor replied, and in 'part truly: 'It is now too late; Wellington would expose himself to certain destruction; he has thrown the dice; they have turned up for us.' Napoleon even seems not to have taken much heed of the advice of lieutenants well acquainted with the British army, and taught by bitter experience in Portugal and Spain. Reille told him that British troops in position were formidable in the very highest degree, and that he ought to try to manœuvre them out of the ground they held. D'Erlon, it is believed, said much the same; but neither seem to have deeply impressed their master. Of all Napoleon's subordinates, Soult was the least hopeful; even now his mind was not without forebodings. The Chief of the Staff knew, as the Emperor did not, what the qualities of a British army were; he had wished, we have seen, that Grouchy's restraining wing should be

composed of a smaller force, so that the force to attack
Wellington should be more powerful. 'There are men
on that hill,' he observed, 'will die where they stand
sooner than retreat.' Napoleon's angry retort, it is said,
was: 'You think Wellington a great General because he
beat you ; I tell you he is a bad General, and the English
are bad troops; we will make a mouthful of them.'* Alas
for genius when foredoomed by Providence ! it was with
Napoleon before Waterloo as it was before Moscow.

Napoleon had given positive orders that the attack
should begin at nine in the morning; he had seen his
opportunity, and had resolved to seize it.† His army,
however, was not nearly assembled on the field where it
was to give battle at that early hour; some regiments
were not in line until ten and afterwards. It is probable,
however, that, without making much effort, it might have
been collected on the ground by about ten ; had a determined and general attack been then made, it is not easy
to deny, as we review the incidents of the day, that it must
have gained a real if not a decisive victory; the chances,
at least, in its favour would have been very great. But
unpropitious Fate interfered at this juncture; Napoleon
formed a purpose, perhaps to be justified in a military
sense as he thought the situation was, and supported by
the highest authority on the spot, but most unfortunate
for him in events that followed. The position to be
assailed was obviously strong; the approaches to it were
beset by obstacles; the ground, broken in hollows in
places, and thick with crops of rye, had been rendered
difficult in the extreme by the torrents of rain, which had
made fields, enclosures, woods, sodden, heavy, and hard
to traverse. The wind was now brisk ; the sun was begin-

* These and other interesting details, many collected for the first
time, will be found in H. Houssaye, 'Waterloo,' ii. 309, 315.

† This order will be found in La Tour d'Auvergne, 'Waterloo,' 251.
Charras has most discreditably suppressed it.

ning to shine; it certainly would be of no small importance that Napoleon's cavalry and artillery, his best arms,
should have the means of manœuvring with some kind of
freedom. At the instance of Drouot,* one of his most
skilful officers, the commander of the artillery of the
Guard, the Emperor consented to postpone the attack,
in order that the ground should dry and harden.

It has been surmised that in coming to this resolve
Napoleon had it in contemplation to gain time for
Grouchy, as he expected, to reach the field in compliance with orders probably sent; † it has been surmised,
too, that he had an intention of displaying leisurely his
army in complete array before the Dutch-Belgian troops
of Wellington, and so to impress them with a sense of its
power; and, of course, delay made his preparations more
mature, and secured time for his soldiers to rest, and to
make more ready for battle. His paramount object, however, it is all but certain, was to obtain two or three hours
to make the ground easier for his movements in attack.
Opinions from then to now have differed as to whether this
was a supremely important—nay, an attainable—object; ‡

* In the *Moniteur*, July 24, 1815, Drouot said in the Chamber of
Peers : 'Au jour il faisait un temps si effroyable qu'il était impossible
de manœuvrer avec l'artillerie. Vers 9 heures le temps si leva, le vent
sécha un peu la campagne.'

† Writers differing so widely as Thiers and Siborne agree in thinking that Napoleon was waiting for Grouchy to come up, but there is
no trace of this in Napoleon's writings.

‡ Jomini ('Précis de la Campagne de 1815,' 199) says : 'Quatre
heures n'auraient pas suffi pour sécher un terrain comme celui la. . . .
Dans la situation des affaires, ce rétard de quatre heures fut une faute.'
Charras (ii. 76, 77) is of the same opinion, and severely condemns
Napoleon for the delay. On the other hand, M. Houssaye ('Waterloo,'
309) cites authorities of weight in a contrary sense. From the point
of view held by Napoleon, that Blucher would not venture to march
from Wavre on Waterloo, or that if he made the attempt Grouchy
would stop him, or that Grouchy would appear on the field himself, it
was evidently important to let the ground become consolidated, in
order to facilitate the movements of guns and horsemen. Drouot,

all that can be affirmed positively is that on June 18 the sun in its courses fought against Napoleon. Had the battlefield been in its ordinary state, he would have fallen on his enemies much sooner than he did; and in that event, despite Blucher's energy, and the remissness and shortcomings of Grouchy, Waterloo, humanly speaking, would have been a victory for France.

Wellington's army had taken its order of battle before Napoleon put off the attack. We must briefly describe the famous position, known to history by the name of Waterloo, and fiercely assailed and defended on this memorable day. The hilly ridge of La Belle Alliance, with a ridge towards the north-east, and the adjoining tract, extending in a semicircular sweep from near Frischermont, by Plancenoit and Rossomme, to Mon Plaisir, marked generally the ground held by the French army; the allied army spread along the ridge of Mont St. Jean, and thence to a considerable distance westwards, occupying different points of vantage in its front, and the reverse slope of the ridge to the village of Mont St. Jean. The interval of space between the two ridges is less than a mile.

It is composed of two valleys stretching east and west, which form the watershed of feeders of the Dyle and the Senne, and sink into flats, or rise into eminences of little height. The great main-road from Charleroy to Brussels traverses the valleys where they part at their topmost levels, and runs across the ridge into the village of Mont St. Jean; it meets at this point the road from Nivelles to Brussels, uniting with the great main-road, the two making a long acute angle. The eastern valley narrows

eminently a conscientious man, was inconsolable at having given advice which proved so unfortunate in the event. See a most interesting conversation set forth in Thiers, 'Histoire du Consulat et de l'Empire,' vi. 513, 514. The remarks of Drouot, that but for the delay a decisive victory would have been assured, are exaggerated, but contain a great deal of truth.

into a ravine from which the Ohain, a streamlet, descends hard by the hamlet of the same name; the western trends into a wider space, separating the villages of Merbe-Braine and Braine l'Alleud from the ridge of Mont St. Jean. This ridge rises from the valleys by a gentle ascent; before it spreads a series of advanced posts, so to speak, the château of Hougoumont, with its wooded and walled enclosures; the large and solid farm of La Haye Sainte, with its buildings, gardens, and a gravel-pit at hand; and east-wards the petty hamlets of Papelotte, La Haye, and Smohain, little more than mere clusters of peasant dwellings.

Along the crest of the ridge, extending from Ohain and thence far away to Wavre, ran a cross-road connecting Ohain with Braine l'Alleud; this formed in itself a strong obstacle, for it was bounded in parts by thick double hedges, and in parts sank into hollows between high banks; it nearly marked the front of Wellington's chief line of battle. The slope behind the ridge, up to the village of Mont St. Jean, formed, as it were, a great place of arms very favourable to the assemblage of reserves out of the sight of an enemy, and sheltered from his fire; it proved to be of immense importance in the coming battle. The tract formed by the two valleys in front of the ridge was in places intersected by country roads, and it was largely covered by thick masses of rye, rising from enclosures here and there, not easy of access. To the north of the ridge, at a distance of about two miles, rose the Forest of Soignies, with its dark verdure; the village of Waterloo was half hidden within its southern verge; and to the east, especially, spread a succession of woods around the ravines and defiles through which the stream of the Lasne flows, and stretching from St. Lambert almost to Plancenoit.*

* This description, of course, applies to the position as it existed in 1815. The whole ground has been much changed since that time.

The allied position has been compared to a vast natural fortress, protected in front by a well-defined glacis, and by outworks admirably fashioned for defence; with a parapet and a way behind the curtain to screen the garrison, and to give it freedom of action, and with huge courts in the rear in which the supports of the garrison could collect unobserved and in safety. It had also this immense and special advantage: The ground was favourable not only for defence, but for counter-attack; the three arms— artillery, cavalry, and infantry—could manœuvre upon it, and easily assume the offensive should the occasion arise.

Wellington arrayed his army—70,000 strong as a whole, including 13,500 horsemen and 159 guns*—upon a front about three and a half miles in extent, from Smohain towards his extreme left, to Braine l'Alleud on his extreme right, but scarcely half that distance for his main battle. He expected the Prussians from Wavre in the forenoon; this, probably, was the chief reason that his line in that direction was comparatively weak—very much weaker than his centre and right. His extreme left was formed of the light cavalry of Vivian and Vandeleur, and of the Hanoverians of Wincke; these troops had no reinforcements from the rear. His left centre was composed of Picton's division, and of the Hanoverians of Best, all tried at Quatre Bras; in front was Bylandt's brigade of Perponcher's division; in the rear was Ponsonby's heavy British cavalry, the Dutch-Belgian horse of Ghigny, and Lambert's brigade of British infantry, which had reached the field by forced marches from Ghent. This part of the army filled the space between the extreme left and the great main-road; at this last point it joined the right centre and right of Wellington. All these parts, taken

---

* As usual, we have adopted the figures of Charras (ii. 11), who has taken infinite pains. Siborne ('The Waterloo Campaign') makes the numbers 67,661, and 156 guns; but this probably does not include British commissioned and non-commissioned officers.

14

together, formed what we have called the main battle of
the British commander. The Duke's right centre was
composed of Alten's third division—this also, for the most
part, proved at Quatre Bras ; the right, extending to the
road from Nivelles to Brussels, comprised the British
Guards of Cooke—the martial flower of the infantry—its
brigades directed by Byng and Maitland. Behind these
two divisions a powerful reserve was assembled — the
Household Cavalry of Somerset and a regiment of British
dragoons in line with that of Ponsonby, but with the great
main-road between ; the Dutch-Belgian horsemen of Van
Merlen and Trip ; the fine squadrons of Arentschild, of
the German Legion ; the Nassauers of Kruse, a large body
of Brunswickers, and the British and German Legionary
cavalry of Grant and Dornberg. This large reserve, carefully arrayed behind the line in its front, almost filled the
angle between the great main-road and that from Nivelles
and Brussels, of which the apex reached Mont St. Jean.

Apart from the troops forming his extreme left, the main
battle of Wellington, Bylandt's brigade excepted, was
arrayed on a front, rather more than a mile and a half in
breadth, just behind the cross-road from Wavre, by Ohain,
to Braine l'Alleud, the powerful reserves behind in the
rear on the reverse slope of the ridge. This disposition
of the British General's forces concealed even his first line
from the enemy to some extent, and kept its reinforcements almost wholly out of sight ; the very opposite of
Blucher's arrangements at Ligny, it sheltered the defenders
of the position from fire, presented many difficulties to
the attack, and masked the real strength of the Duke's
army. The events of the day proved that it deceived
Napoleon more than once.

The main battle of Wellington, nevertheless, did not
comprise the whole of the troops he commanded. West
of the ridge of Mont St. Jean, where the village on that
side extends, the extreme right of the allied army was

placed. It was divided into two distinct parts; one of these was at a considerable distance from its supports. The first part contained Mitchell's brigade of Colville's division, the chief part of which had been left at Hal and Tubize, and the main body of Clinton's second British division—the brigades of Adam, Duplat, and W. Halkett —English, German Legionary, and Hanoverian soldiers; it held the village of Merbe-Braine, and thence extended to the right centre of the Duke's army, just west of the road from Nivelles to Brussels. The second part, almost isolated, was stationed around the village of Braine l'Alleud, about a mile from Merbe-Braine; it was formed of the Dutch-Belgian division of Chassé, an able soldier trained in the school of Napoleon; it was greatly to distinguish itself in a most fiery trial.

It remains to notice the troops who were placed to defend the approaches to the main position—the outworks of the great natural fortress. On Wellington's left and extreme left, Saxe-Weimar's brigade held the little hamlets of Papelotte and La Haye, and had detachments as far as the hamlet of Smohain. La Haye Sainte, in advance of the Duke's left centre, was occupied by some 400 men of the German Legion; the adjoining gravel-pit by part of the British 95th Rifles, a regiment celebrated in the Peninsular War. To the right Hougoumont, with its buildings and large enclosures, was held by a detachment of the British Guards, by one battalion of Perponcher's men, and by a few Hanoverian troops—in all, from 1,200 to 1,400 strong; and Hougoumont, like the other advanced posts, had been hastily prepared for defence. As for the artillery of the army, it was distributed, in rather even proportions of guns, along the front; not many batteries were in reserve. Under Wellington, the real soul of the defence, Picton commanded the left, the Prince of Orange the centre, and Hill the right of the army as a whole.

This, briefly, was the position on which the British chief,

14—2

with an army far inferior in essential force, made ready to
resist the attack of Napoleon at the head of an army much
more powerful; and the ground had been occupied in the
manner referred to.   The position itself, we have seen,
was of great natural strength; its approaches formed excellent points of vantage; its front, for the most part, gave
facilities for a plunging and very destructive fire.   It was
partly protected along its crest by an obstacle; it supplied
ample room for assembling large reserves out of the
enemy's sight, and screened from his guns; it afforded
good opportunities for counter-attacks.   The Duke had
generally turned to the best advantage the favourable
situation he had chosen for a great defensive battle.   He
is not to be blamed because his extreme left was weak, for
he expected the Prussians many hours before they reached
the field; and, as it was, this part of his line was never
forced or turned.   He occupied admirably the ridge of
Mont St. Jean, placing his troops with perfect judgment
on the ground, whether for the defence or for offensive
movements; he availed himself most skilfully of the feature
of the position most, perhaps, in his favour, and so arrayed
even his first line and nearly all his reserves that they
should be exposed as little as possible, and should present
a comparatively small mark to the enemy—should, especially the reserves, be largely beyond his reach.   Wellington, too, as a rule, occupied his advanced posts ably; that
of Hougoumont made a most stubborn and successful
resistance; this greatly impeded and weakened the attack.

The British commander, nevertheless, made two mistakes in these fine defensive arrangements.   La Haye
Sainte was much the most important of the allied outposts; it was on the great main-road from Charleroy to
Brussels, and though this and the road from Brussels to
Nivelles had been obstructed by strong stockades, this
point was the key of Wellington's left centre, and covered
a vulnerable part of his whole position.   La Haye Sainte,

too, was commanded by the French ridge to the north-east; it was made an object of incessant and very formidable attacks. Its loss, we shall see, proved most unfortunate; for these reasons it ought to have been held by a force much more powerful than that which held it.* It is difficult, besides, altogether to justify the detachment of Chassé so far as Braine l'Alleud, or even the immense accumulation of troops on Wellington's right—these, too, for the most part, the best of his army. We see here the apprehension for his right which beset him from the beginning of the campaign, and which had caused him to make the great strategic error of leaving a large force far off around Hal and Tubize.†

While Napoleon's attack was being retarded, Blucher was on the march to Waterloo from Wavre. To understand this operation and all that it involved, we must look back at the state of the Prussian army and at the positions it held. It had been all assembled, we have seen, around Wavre towards midnight on June 17; it still numbered about 90,000 men, and nearly 300 guns. Of its four corps, that of Bulow lay around Dion le Mont, having sent a detachment to Mont St. Guibert, about six or seven miles from Wavre, in order to observe the enemy's movements; that of Pirch was encamped at St. Anne and Aisemont, both corps on the eastern bank of the Dyle, that of Pirch being the most forward; the corps of Thielmann was at La Bavette, and that of Zieten at Bierges, each on the western bank of the river. Faithful to the pledge he had given a few hours before, Blucher had ordered Bulow and Pirch to break up at the peep of day on the 18th, and to advance as quickly as they could to St. Lambert, four

---

* See on this point the judicious remarks of General Shaw Kennedy, 'Battle of Waterloo,' 174-176.

† Napoleon is unjust in his comments on Wellington's conduct at Waterloo, but there is truth in the following ('Comment.,' v. 210): 'Le général anglais ne jugea pas qu'il devait être et serait attaqué par sa gauche; il crut qu'il le serait par sa droite.'

miles, we have said, from Napoleon's camp; they were to
conceal from the enemy, as much as possible, their troops;
they were not to attack the French right until it was fully
engaged.* But Zieten and Thielmann were to remain
where they were for the present; they were to watch the
operations of a French corps supposed to be on the march
from Gembloux, and believed to be that of Vandamme—
14,000 or 15,000 strong. Blucher, like Wellington, was
under the false impression that nearly all the French army
was before Waterloo; he had not the slightest idea that
Grouchy was on his way to Wavre with at least 33,000
men.†

The veteran wrote to his colleague early on the 18th
that, suffering as he was, he would be at the head of his
men, would join Wellington, and fall on Napoleon's right.
'I would rather,' the heroic warrior exclaimed, 'be tied to
my horse than fail to take part in the fight.' Blucher set
off from Wavre at about eleven o'clock, Bulow and Pirch
having been for many hours in movement. He thought
of nothing but of the struggle at hand. He urged on the
troops he met with characteristic energy. With Gneisenau,
however, it was quite otherwise; he had hesitated before,
and now hesitated again. He felt all that was risked in a
very hazardous march. His distrust of Wellington had
become intense. 'Wellington was as false as an Indian
Nabob.' He saw that should the British commander
retreat, the Prussian army would be in the lion's mouth,
and in all probability would be destroyed. He directed
the aide-de-camp who had saved Blucher at Ligny to
inform Muffling that he must ascertain—this was a few
hours only before Waterloo—whether Wellington had
determined on giving battle.‡ He saw Bulow and Pirch
on their way not without grave misgivings. Had he
known the real strength of Grouchy's army, Gneisenau

---

* Ollech, 188-191.   † *Ibid.*, 188.
‡ *Ibid.*, 189.

would not improbably have found means to prevent a movement being made from Wavre at all.

The troops of Bulow and Pirch, in accordance with Blucher's orders, were under arms at five in the morning, those of Zieten and Thielmann staying in their camps. Here, however, a capital mistake was made,* which greatly retarded the Prussian army, and might have led to the most disastrous results. Zieten and Thielmann were on the western bank of the Dyle ; they were at least two or three miles nearer St. Lambert than Pirch and Bulow, and, besides, had not a river and a town to pass ; they ought, therefore, to have been the first to advance towards Waterloo. But Zieten's men had suffered greatly at Ligny ; Thielmann had hitherto been rather slow and remiss ; they were detained at Wavre, this causing the loss of some hours. Another grave error was also made in the disposition of the corps of Pirch and Bulow. Both were on the eastern bank of the Dyle, in the rear, there-fore, of Zieten and Thielmann ; but Pirch was nearly two miles in advance of Bulow, and, of course, ought to have moved before him. The losses of Pirch at Ligny had, however, been heavy ; the troops of Bulow were intact and fresh. It was arranged, accordingly, that Bulow should begin the march, and should be the first to show himself to the enemy.

As the inevitable result, the columns of Bulow had to defile more or less past those of Pirch. Confusion and intermingling followed. It was seven in the morning before Bulow's first troops appeared in the narrow streets of Wavre. Some time was required to get through the town. A fire, too, which broke out caused much delay, and the crossing of the Dyle was, besides, tedious. The

---

* M. H. Houssaye ('Waterloo,' ii. 280, 282) has explained this most important passage of the campaign, and has accounted for the extreme slowness of the Prussian operations better than any other historian. His research and insight are admirable.

march from Wavre to St. Lambert, moreover, was impeded by all kinds of obstacles, and it was not until after ten in the forenoon that the advanced guard of Bulow reached St. Lambert, the mass of his forces being hours in the rear. The march of Pirch was even more retarded; his troops were not in full movement until noon. Half were not over the Dyle until one; the remainder were still on the eastern bank.* Half of the whole Prussian army was thus extended in disunited and straggling columns, far from each other, on a perilous flank march. Had the commander of Napoleon's restraining wing, charged to interpose between Blucher and Wellington, taken on this morning the course he ought to have taken —and this was indicated by the true principles of war— he would not only—as we shall point out—have been able completely to stop the enemy, but very possibly would have wrought Bulow's ruin.

We turn to Grouchy, the evil genius of France and of Napoleon, on the great day of Waterloo. The Marshal, we have seen, had followed the Prussians with extreme slowness on June 17; had only reached Gembloux in the evening, part of his cavalry being beyond at Sauvenière; and was thus fully fourteen miles from Blucher. This delay was certainly to be deplored; but had Grouchy fulfilled his mission, and done what his master had a right to expect, subsequent events proved that there was as yet no danger. At ten at night, we have said, he had informed the Emperor that the Prussians were in retreat not in great force either towards Wavre or towards Perwez—that is, Louvain. He had promised that, were they for the most part falling back on Wavre, he would pursue them in that direction, in order to keep Blucher apart from Wellington. The intelligence he had already received ought, we have pointed out, to have induced him to move at daybreak on the 18th to Moustier and Ottignies, and

* Ollech, 193.

to get over the Dyle at these places ; for a march towards
Perwez would be a false movement, but a march on
Moustier and Ottignies would be in the true direction.
It would bring him to Wavre should Blucher be halting
there, would enable him to stop Blucher if on the way to
Waterloo, and would draw him within easy reach of the
main French army, should the Emperor be in need of his
support.

Grouchy, however, had formed no such resolve, and had
lingered at Gembloux ; but, as the night advanced, reports
came in to him which ought irrevocably to have fixed his
purpose had he had a ray of the inspiration of a true
soldier. He learned that the enemy was assembled around
Wavre, and that without the possibility of a doubt ; and
at three in the morning of the 18th he wrote to the
Emperor that Blucher was falling back towards Brussels
in order to effect his junction with Wellington ; that he
was in retreat by Corbaix and Chaumont—the first a
village on a line with Moustier and Ottignies, the second
a village between Wavre and Perwez, and both being on
the roads to Wavre—so that the Marshal's army would
march at once, by Sart les Walhain, on Corbaix and
Wavre.* The information that the Prussians were at
Wavre ought now, we repeat, to have caused Grouchy to
make for Moustier and Ottignies without the delay of a
moment, for the reasons we have before referred to ; but
the Marshal remained blind to his true mission, and
turned aside from the path of success and safety, in an
evil hour for his country and himself. He thought only
of reaching his enemy, not of standing between him and
his allies. The false news that Blucher had fallen back in

---

* The genuineness of this despatch has been questioned, but it
seems to us to have been certainly genuine. Soult clearly refers to it
in a despatch we shall notice afterwards. M. H. Houssaye contends
that Grouchy wrote, not at 3 a.m., but at 6 a.m. ('Waterloo,' ii. 287),
but the text seems to be 3 a.m. Soult refers to it as written at 2 a.m.
The despatch is in La Tour d'Auvergne, 'Waterloo,' 318.

part, by Chaumont, made Grouchy still cast his eyes towards Perwez. Instead of directing his army towards Moustier and Ottignies at break of day, he directed it towards Wavre by a rather shorter road—that is, by Sart les Walhain and the adjoining country. This was an enormous, if not a fatal, mistake. In addition, his orders were that the march was to be at a late hour; Vandamme was not to leave his camps until six in the morning, Gérard not until eight o'clock. Pajol, supported, we have said, by the division of Teste, was to march early, but by the eccentric road of Grand Leez.*

Grouchy did not leave Gembloux even at the time, late as this was, he had originally designed. Vandamme and Gérard were not on the march until between eight and nine in the morning; as on the 17th, the troops followed each other in one huge column. The movement towards Wavre was made at the rate of little more than a mile and a half an hour. Even worse, Grouchy sent no reconnoitring-parties towards Moustier and Ottignies to bring him news of the position of the imperial army; had he taken this obvious and simple precaution, the conse-sequences, we shall see, might have been momentous.†

We pass on to the tent of Napoleon contemplating, we have seen, a decisive attack on Wellington; he had re-solved to make his principal effort at about one; the delay, therefore, was one of three hours at least; he gave his final orders at about nine;‡ he then retired to take a short rest. The evidence respecting the state of his health at Waterloo is extremely conflicting.§ He gave

* These orders will all be found in La Tour d'Auvergne, 'Waterloo,' 313, 317.

† Mr. Ropes' narrative in treating this part of Grouchy's conduct, or, rather, misconduct, is specially good ('The Campaign of Waterloo,' 254, 255).

‡ M. H. Houssaye ('Waterloo,' ii. 501, 502) has examined the evidence with great care and research. See 313.

§ This order will be found in La Tour d'Auvergne, 'Waterloo,' 258.

proof of occasional vigour and energy, but he seems to have suffered from his peculiar illness at times, though not to the same extent as during the night of the 17th. One incident was not of auspicious omen. He had directed his chief engineer, Haxo, to reconnoitre the enemy's left, and to find out if there were any field works. Soult, years afterwards, remarked that the Napoleon of Jena and Austerlitz would have performed this important task himself.

The insight and capacity of the great master fully appear, however, in the plan he had formed for the attack; this was at once comprehensive, simple, and grand. The Emperor had quickly perceived that his adversary's left was, by many degrees, the weakest part of his line. He had perceived, too, that one of the ridges he held commanded La Haye Sainte and Wellington's left centre; so he resolved to turn his enemy's left, and at the same time to make a determined effort against his left centre; and with this last object he collected a great battery of nearly eighty guns along the ridge.* This grand attack was to be carried out by the corps of D'Erlon, sustained by Lobau and the Imperial Guard, and by masses of cavalry in support; should it prove successful, it would cut Wellington off from Brussels, and from his immediate line of retreat; and it would force him into a difficult country where he could hardly escape defeat—nay, perhaps destruction. This attack was to be combined with a feint made by Reille against the enemy's right, at an earlier moment, in order to distract him and to make him detach troops from the positions really assailed in force.†

---

* We cannot agree with M. H. Houssaye ('Waterloo,' ii. 324), that Napoleon contemplated a real attack on Wellington's left centre and centre only.

† All commentators agree that the plan of Napoleon's attack was admirable. See Jomini, Charras, Siborne, Thiers, *in loco*.

The legions of Napoleon had, meanwhile, been proudly taking their ground upon their last field. The spectacle was remembered for years as the most imposing that had ever been seen in that age of incessant war; it was the flicker shooting up before all was darkness. The valleys in front of the ridge of Mont St. Jean seemed alive with the magnificently stern array of battle descending from the adjoining heights; the eye rested far and near on masses of footmen, on long lines of cannon, on thousands of horsemen being gathered together for the great impending conflict. Admirable order pervaded that seeming chaos of war; eleven columns unwound themselves from the multitudinous host, and moved, with perfect regularity, to their appointed stations. On Napoleon's right, from near Frischermont to the great main-road, spread in foremost line the corps of D'Erlon which had missed its mark at Ligny; the light cavalry of Jacquinot was on its right flank; this body of men, eager to retrieve their late mischance, were to make the first effort against the hostile left and left centre. Behind D'Erlon were ranged the mailed squadrons of Milhaud and Lefebvre—Desnoëtte's light cavalry of the Guard. These horsemen were to support the infantry in their front, and to second the grand attack when the opportunity arose. On Napoleon's left was the corps of Reille, extending from the great main-road to that from Nivelles to Brussels; it was to make the feint against Wellington's right; on its left flank were the horsemen of Piré, with the heavy cavalry of Kellermann, and the heavy cavalry of the Guard in its rear. In the centre, on either side of the great main-road, stood the corps of Lobau and the cavalry of Subervie and Domon. Behind, at a short distance, appeared, in the silence of strength, the deep and massive columns of the Imperial Guard—the Triarii of the Emperor's battles; these bodies of troops were to join at the fitting time in the attack of D'Erlon, and to deal, as their chief hoped, the final and the mortal stroke. The artillery was for the most part in front of the line; but, as was Napoleon's wont, there were ample reserves of guns to be employed at the master's bidding; a great battery, we have said, had been formed on the ridge opposite La Haye Sainte. The army numbered about 72,000 men, including 15,000 cavalry and 240 guns.* It had been so arrayed on the field that all parts of the hostile position seemed equally threatened. But its vast masses, unlike those of Wellington, were completely in view to the last man; this doubtless impressed many of the Duke's auxiliaries, but it had no effect on the British and German Legionary troops. 'We will show Boney to-day how to defend a position,' was a remark made, it has been said, by Wellington himself.

While the French army was being thus assembled, Napoleon turned his attention again towards Grouchy, the lieutenant entrusted with a powerful restraining wing, and charged to see that Blucher and Wellington should not effect their junction. We have come to another of the difficult passages of the campaign, with respect to which our knowledge remains imperfect, and the evidence we possess is hard to interpret. Marbot, the author of the well-known and delightful 'Memoirs,' was one of the Emperor's trusted officers; he had been made a General of Brigade after the skirmish at Genappe; he was in command on June 18 of a regiment of Jacquinot's cavalry on the extreme French right. At about eleven o'clock he received a message from Napoleon, sent through La Bédoyère, and ordering him to detach reconnoitring-parties to the bridges of Moustier and Ottignies, upon the Dyle. 'Grouchy was certainly marching towards the main army from that direction.' Marbot did what he was told to do, but found no French troops at Moustier and Ottignies; he reported the fact to the Emperor without loss of time;

* Charras, ii. 15.

he was then ordered to make search for Grouchy again.
'The Marshal must be coming by the bridges of Limale
and Limelette,' lower down the Dyle, and three or four
miles from Wavre.*

This most important evidence proves that Napoleon
believed that his lieutenant was approaching his camp;
it is significant, in the very highest degree, that Marbot's
official report on the subject was discreditably suppressed
by the Bourbon Government, eager to throw the blame
for Waterloo on its great fallen enemy.† Marbot's statement, however, unequivocal as it is, is not the only proof
which distinctly points to the conclusion we have just
referred to. A Polish officer, of the name of *Zenowicz*,
made a deposition, soon after the battle, that the Emperor
at about ten in the morning took him aside, and, walking
up a low eminence, said, indicating the horizon to his
right: 'I am awaiting Grouchy, I am awaiting him with
impatience; go and join him, and do not quit his side
until he debouches upon the line of my battle.'‡ It is
also significant in the extreme that *Zenowicz* was the
bearer of the despatch from Soult to Grouchy, on which
we shall briefly comment at once.

This remarkable and, be it observed, independent
evidence shows, as the fact was, that Napoleon had as yet
no notion that Blucher was drawing near him at this
conjuncture. But it shows also, what is more important,
that the Emperor was convinced that Grouchy was
approaching the imperial army from the Dyle; and it
corroborates, with almost conclusive force, Napoleon's
statement, that on the night of the 17th he twice ordered

---

* Marbot, 'Memoirs,' iii. 405, 406.

† This report should, if possible, be discovered. The present
writer received some time ago a courteous intimation from an authori-
tative source that it was not forthcoming.

‡ M. H. Houssaye ('Waterloo,' ii. 447), and especially Thiers
('Histoire du Consulat et de l'Empire,' vi. 483), who has transcribed
the very words of Zenowicz.

Grouchy to come to his support, with a detachment, or with the mass of his forces.

The proof could hardly admit of question, were it not confronted with the despatch written by Soult to Grouchy, to which we have just above referred. This despatch was written by Soult at ten in the morning of the 18th; it apparently is at odds with the statements of Marbot and Zenowicz; assuredly it requires to be closely studied. It was a reply to Grouchy's letter of ten on the night of the 17th, in which Grouchy, it is to be borne in mind, let his master know, among many other things, that he had not as yet made up his mind whether he would follow the Prussians by marching on Wavre or Perwez. Soult, doubtless with this letter before his eyes, informed Grouchy that the Emperor had received this report from Gembloux, but informed him further, that whereas he had referred only to two Prussian columns, marching by Sauvenière and Sart les Walhain—that is, in the direction of Wavre and Perwez—intelligence had been received— and this we know was the case—that a third column was moving on Wavre by Géry and Gentinnes—that is, on a line between Gembloux and the main French army. Soult then tells Grouchy that Napoleon was about to attack the English army at Waterloo, near the Forest of Soignies, and proceeds to direct Grouchy to march on Wavre—he was to reach that place as quickly as possible—and to drive away any part of the Prussian army which might be coming in that direction. The despatch next emphatically desires the Marshal ' to come near us, to connect his operations with our own, and to be in close communication with us.' This last phrase is repeated twice.*

Napoleon probably never saw this despatch; but, as a matter of course, he is responsible for it. It is idle, too,

* This despatch has been noticed by all historians and commentators. It is set forth at length in Prince La Tour d'Auvergne's ' Waterloo,' 260, 261.

to contend that it does not contain an order to Grouchy
to advance on Wavre, or that it is consistent, in its seeming purport, with the allegations made by Zenowicz and
Marbot. But in this, as in all instances of the kind, we
should endeavour to reconcile the evidence as a whole,
and, gathering it together, to arrive at the real truth.
This is not impossible, even not difficult, if we carefully
examine and peruse the despatch, though assuredly this
is most obscure—nay, misleading. Soult urges Grouchy
to march on Wavre, because Grouchy was doubting
whether his movement ought not to be on Perwez rather
than Wavre; and Wavre, as contra-distinguished from
Perwez, indisputedly was the right direction to take.
But Soult's despatch does not end at this point; it warns
Grouchy that an enemy's column is moving on Wavre by
Géry and Gentinnes—that is, between the restraining wing
and the main army; it intimates that he is to attack or to
intercept this; and it orders the Marshal, with marked
stress of language, to come into communication with the
Emperor, about to fight a decisive battle in front of
Waterloo.

Now, how, in addition to a march on Wavre, was
Grouchy to accomplish the two last objects, in themselves infinitely the most important, and plainly, according to the despatch, held to be the most important? The
one and the only means was to take the course which he
ought to have taken of his own purpose—that is, to cross
the Dyle at Moustier and Ottignies, or even lower down
at Limale and Limelette, and to reach Wavre by this
line of march, for by this operation he would at once
get to Wavre, would fall on any hostile force near or
around that place, and would be coming into closer
relations with the imperial army. The despatch, therefore, if intelligently read, falls in with what Marbot and
Zenowicz relate—and Zenowicz, we must not forget, was
the bearer; it is in accord with Napoleon's belief, and

probably direct orders; by implication, though not expressly, it orders Grouchy to cross the Dyle in his advance on Wavre, and on his way to draw near Napoleon, striking at the same time any enemy found in his path.* The despatch, however, is ill-worded, vague, and perplexing. It ought to have stated in precise language that Grouchy should pass the Dyle before he moved on Wavre, and should send reconnoitring parties, at least, at once towards Waterloo. But Soult in this, as in other instances, proved himself to be a sorry Chief of a Staff. For the rest, writers whose object it is to charge Napoleon with an immense disaster, and to exonerate Grouchy from all blame, have found in this despatch and in another from Soult, to which we shall ere long refer, a kind of godsend in behalf of their views; but their arguments, we shall see, are mere sophistry.

It was now after eleven in the forenoon. The French army was in its positions on the field. It bore the appearance of a gigantic fan spreading out from its end in the master's hand. It was resplendent with the pomp and circumstance of war. From Frischermont to Plancenoit, to La Belle Alliance, and thence to Mon Plaisir, the lowlands were dense with an armed multitude of men, of battle steeds, and of grim tiers of cannon. The sun shone on cuirass and pennon, on eagles gathering for their deadly flight, on uniforms radiant with many brilliant colours—the garb of a proud and exulting host. The Emperor, accompanied by a gorgeous staff, had ridden slowly before the long-drawn lines, bowing to the standards inscribed with a noble roll of glory. The air

---

* For this or nearly this view of the real meaning of Soult's despatch, see Gérard, 'Dernières Observations,' 19 *et seq.;* Ropes, 'The Campaign of Waterloo,' 266-269 ; Thiers, 'Histoire du Consulat et de l'Empire,' vi. 508, 509; and Prince La Tour d'Auvergne, 'Waterloo,' 373, 374.

15

rang with the acclaim of the proud and confident legions, and with the swell of the sonorous music of war; the echoes were borne, a mighty rush of sound, to the ridge of Mont St. Jean. But all was silence in the positions of the hostile arrays ;* a great part of Wellington's troops was not even visible; but they sternly awaited the enemy's onslaught, though he appeared to be an irresistible force. Before he had dictated his final orders, Napoleon had reconnoitred the ground from the low eminence of La Belle Alliance. He found a point from which he could survey the whole scene of action, on a little hillock not far from Rossomme. He took his seat before a table on which his maps had been laid. At half-past eleven o'clock he gave the signal for attack. The fire of three guns from the batteries of the Imperial Guard rang through the summer air; the troops of Reille formed into columns and moved; the tremendous drama of Waterloo had begun.

---

* So Homer ('Iliad,' iii. 2 *et seq.*) described, thousands of years ago, the bearing before battle of two great different races :

'Τρῶες μὲν κλαγγῇ τ' ἐνοπῇ τ' ἴσαν, ὄρνιθες ὥς,
Οἱ δ' ἀρ' ἴσαν σιγῇ μένεα πνείοντες 'Αχαιοί.'

CHAPTER VIII

THE BATTLE OF WATERLOO TO THE DEFEAT OF D'ERLON'S CORPS

Napoleon's reliance on his lieutenants—This very marked on the day of Waterloo—Description of Hougoumont and its enclosures—The feint converted into a real attack—Advance of the division of Jerôme—Bold and persistent attacks—Stubborn and successful defence—Waste of the strength of the French—The apparition of the advanced guard of Bulow—Soult's letter of 1 p.m.—His postscript—Grouchy directed to march to the field of Waterloo—His movement on Walhain—His despatch of 11 a.m.—With other officers he hears the cannon of Waterloo—Admirable advice of Gérard to march and join the main army—This rejected by Grouchy, who continues to march directly on Wavre—Napoleon's first grand attack—Advance of D'Erlon's corps—Vicious formation of its columns—Attack on La Haye Sainte—Stubborn defence—The charge of Somerset and Ponsonby—Defeat of cuirassiers—Complete defeat of D'Erlon—State of the battle at 3 p.m.

IT was an inevitable result of the far-spreading operations in war, conducted by him for a series of years, that Napoleon should place much reliance on his lieutenants; we have seen this already in the campaign of 1815; it was to be made very manifest on the day of Waterloo, owing largely, perhaps, to the state of the Emperor's health, which had deprived him of the energy of his prime, and had greatly lessened his old activity in the field. The attack on Hougoumont was a notable instance how his trust in subordinates proved vain, with most untoward results. Napoleon, we have seen, had intended that this effort was to be a mere feint against Wellington's right, in the hope that it would cause him to weaken his left and embarrass his dispositions on the field; this diversion is not even referred to in Napoleon's first orders for the fight. But, from whatever reason—Reille, of course, the commander of the 2nd corps, must bear the blame*—the feint was converted into a real attack, in great force, and was, besides, very ill directed. This was the first error in the tactics of the French on this day.

Hougoumont was the very part of the Duke's position which ought not to have been selected for an onslaught pressed home. It was in front of the allied right and right centre, much the strongest division of the allied line; it was commanded, at a distance of a few hundred yards, by the artillery of the defence, along the ridge, and had it been taken, it could not have been held by the enemy; it was in itself a position of formidable strength. Hougoumont may be briefly described as a large Flemish château, surrounded by its chapel and solid farm buildings, and rising from an enclosure of difficult access, forming a quadrangle of some 600 yards on each side, and encompassed by a thick hedge and a ditch. The southern end of this little park, that next to the French, was composed of a wood of copse and grown trees, of two open fields, and of a small orchard on its western bounds; beyond, separated by another thick hedge and its ditch, and running up to the northern end, extended a little and a greater orchard; in nearly the midst of these a large garden stood, walled on two of its sides, and on the other two parted off by a dividing ditch and fence; and west of the garden, near the main enclosure, its avenue leading to the road from Nivelles to Brussels, was the château with its appurtenances, a natural fortress in themselves. The whole position presented a series of strong obstacles, exceedingly

* Reille, Arch. Guerre ; cited by H. Houssaye, 'Waterloo,' 327, 328.

hard to assail and master; and it had, we have said, been hastily fortified in the night. The walls of the château and its buildings had been pierced with loopholes, and platforms had been raised along the walls of the garden to give musketry its deadly play; the hedges had been thickened in some places; and the entrances to the château had been closed by barricades, save where the northern entrance led to the allied line, and enabled supports to be sent to the defence. The garrison, we have said, was made up of from 1,200 to 1,400 men, British Guards, Dutch-Belgian and Hanoverian troops.*

At half-past eleven o'clock, we have seen, Reille's soldiery began the attack on Hougoumont. A brigade of Jerôme's division, sustained by the fire of its own corps, and of batteries of Piré and Kellermann, and throwing out swarms of skirmishers along its front, advanced boldly down the low ridge to the east of Mon Plaisir, and made rapidly across the plain for the allied position. The columns suffered heavily from the fire of hostile guns, which opened at orders given by Wellington—he had ridden to the spot with part of his staff, and, very different from his great antagonist, showed extraordinary activity on this, as on the day before—they were even checked for a few moments; but they pressed forward with headlong dash, and had soon reached the southern edge of the main enclosure. They were driven by shells—this was also by the Duke's direction—out of the open fields which they first entered; then they broke into the adjoining wood, forcing the passage of the hedge and ditch after a sharp struggle.

A fierce conflict now raged for rather less than an hour, the assailants endeavouring to make their way through the copse and the higher trees above it, the defenders, very inferior in numbers, stubbornly contesting every inch

* An excellent and elaborate description of Hougoumont and its defences will be found in Shaw Kennedy, 'Battle of Waterloo,' 89-92. The accounts of Siborne and Charras are also good.

of the ground, and making repeated charges, broken as
these were by the obstacles in their path. Wellington,
who had carefully watched the progress of the fight, had
sent a battalion of Brunswickers to support the defence ;
but this reinforcement came rather late ; the soldiery of
Jerôme, after protracted efforts, at last made themselves
masters of the wood, and compelled the opposing troops
to fall back. The French, exulting at this first success,
and bravely led by devoted officers, rushed with loud
shouts across the ditch and hedge dividing the wood from
the two orchards ; another effort, and they fondly hoped
the position would be stormed and won. In a short time,
however, they were cruelly undeceived ; the murderous
fire of the British Guards, one of the best characteristics
of the British Infantry—the sons of the bowmen of Crecy
and Agincourt—burst out from the platforms along the
walls of the garden, and from the crenellated apertures
made in the château ; it was sustained by the fire of the
auxiliaries ; the onset of the assailants came to a stand.
The French, however, refused to give way ; they retaliated
by a dropping fire from the wood ; but this was desultory
and feeble compared to that made from sheltered defences
with deadly aim. Three of their men probably fell for one
of their enemy.

The wood in front of Hougoumont had been won ;
Napoleon's object had been in part attained ; the Duke
had not, indeed, detached from his left ; but his attention
had been directed to his right and right centre, and turned
aside from the grand attack being prepared against him.
Guilleminot, the chief of Jerôme's staff, a very skilful and
experienced soldier, urged his chief to desist from further
efforts, involving certain loss and probable defeat ;* but
the Prince, carried away by the impetuous ardour which

---

* 'Waterloo Letters,' 262—General Sir Alexander Woodford: ' I
had much conversation with General Guilleminot. The first attack
he advised ; the others, he said, he did not agree in.'

marked the conduct of many French officers on this day, engaged, with little reflection, his second brigade.* These troops also spent their strength in vain against enemies who had them at an immense advantage; they tried, with fruitless daring, to climb the walls of the garden, and to force their way into the thickly-hedged orchard; they fell in scores, stricken down by destructive missiles.

Meanwhile the survivors of the first brigade made a determined effort to carry the château itself; they pushed forward along its western front, and tried to penetrate into the northern entrance, not barricaded like the southern gate. A few succeeded in forcing a door open, but instantly met the death they had recklessly courted. The château, in fact, was not to be thus taken; artillery ought to have been brought nearer in order to shatter the walls and buildings; but Reille and his subordinates never thought of this; not a petard, not even a few bags of gunpowder, were employed to break down the defences of the place. Wellington, meantime, had reinforced the garrison with some 300 men of the British Guards. These fresh and choice troops, assisted by their supports, drove Jerôme's second brigade far back into the wood. Foy's division was then moved to sustain the attack, by this time a regular and fiercely-contested combat; this powerful reserve occupied the wood again, and even took possession of the double orchard; but the château and the garden continued to resist; the defenders were never dislodged from these points by the enemy. The efforts of the assailants by degrees slackened; the scene presented a confused spectacle of partial attacks baffled by a persistent defence, the French being continuously smitten by an overmastering fire. The advantage already remained on the side of ˌthe allies; they successfully opposed about

---

* Napoleon recalled Jerôme from Hougoumont, perhaps to show his disapprobation of his brother's recklessness.

3,000 men to nearly 10,000,* and these were mowed down in heaps, and foredoomed to failure.

It was now nearly an hour after mid-day. Ney had been entrusted with the conduct of the grand attack to be made by D'Erlon's corps against Wellington's left and left centre. The Marshal sent a message to the Emperor that all was ready. Napoleon had listlessly watched the progress of the fight round Hougoumont; he had, it has been said, fallen asleep before his maps and his table.† He mounted a charger, and now took a survey with his field-glass of the whole scene of action before masses of smoke should screen the prospect from his view. After a few moments a kind of cloud seemed gathering not far from the heights of St. Lambert at a distance; the Emperor thought he perceived a body of troops. In reply to a question, Soult remarked this was ' probably a detachment from Grouchy, from 5,000 to 6,000 strong'‡—most significant words that have been little noticed, but that clearly show that Soult, as well as his master, believed that Grouchy was marching on Waterloo from across the Dyle. The opinions of the imperial staff were divided. Some officers thought the apparition a wreath of mist; but Soult persisted he could descry soldiers piling their arms;§ and Napoleon adhered to the conclusion he had already formed.

The Emperor sent at once a reconnoitring party to discover what the assemblage of armed men was; he detached the light cavalry of Subervie and Domon, with orders to march in the direction of St. Lambert, and either to join Grouchy or to keep back the enemy, accord-

---

* See the figures, Charras, ii. 35.

† Dorsey Gardner, 36 ; Baudus, cited by H. Houssaye, 'Waterloo,' ii. 501.

‡ 'Comment.,' v. 169. Careful attention should be given to these words.

§ Baudus, cited by H. Houssaye, 'Waterloo,' ii. 332.

ing as the facts should be ascertained. In a short time he obtained intelligence which dissipated any doubts he may have had on the subject. The cavalry scouts of Marbot, already despatched for some time towards Moustier and Ottignies, had taken an inferior Prussian officer prisoner; he carried a letter from Bulow to Wellington announcing the arrival of Bulow's corps at St. Lambert. He was brought before Napoleon, and freely answered his questions. The troops in the distance were the advanced guard of Bulow; the rest of his corps was on the march to join him. The three other corps of the Prussian army had been in bivouac around Wavre the night before, and had not had a glimpse of an enemy. The force under Grouchy, it was supposed, was on its way to Plancenoit, to come into line with the main enemy.*

These tidings were obviously extremely grave, but they did not greatly disconcert Napoleon. His army before Waterloo, he believed, was not yet in danger. He had received, but at a very late hour, the despatch written by Grouchy at three in the morning, and this, though less reassuring than the despatch of five hours before, was nevertheless still calculated to inspire confidence. In this letter the Marshal had informed his master that Blucher was in retreat on Brussels, in the expectation of joining Wellington; that he was falling back by Corbaix and Chaumont; and that Grouchy was on the point of moving on Sart les Walhain, whence he would proceed to Corbaix and Wavre. This indicated that Grouchy was on the track of the enemy; that whether he should march on Wavre by Moustier and Ottignies—indisputably, we have seen, his proper course—or whether he should march by Sart les Walhain and Corbaix — that is, beyond the eastern bank of the Dyle—he could not fail to hear of and to reach Blucher—Corbaix is only about six miles from

* 'Comment.,' v. 169, 170. Napoleon's account is much the best, and there is no reason to question its accuracy.

Wavre—and if Blucher should be at Wavre, or making an attempt to move on Waterloo, the commander of the restraining wing, whose letters prove he understood his task, would be able to prevent Blucher from joining his ally. The main French army, therefore, if menaced was not imperilled. Besides, the whole corps of Bulow was still distant; its advanced guard only was at St. Lambert; the remaining Prussian corps were probably far off. The battle might be won, and Wellington beaten, before Blucher could reach the field in force, should he even venture to make a most hazardous march.

Napoleon at this moment was most impressed by the fact that Grouchy's advance from Gembloux must be very slow, or otherwise he must have heard long before from the Marshal; and he was apprehensive that the detachment of 7,000 men, which he had most probably directed Grouchy to make, might be caught and destroyed by Bulow as it was approaching Waterloo. To ward off the danger as far as possible, he now ordered Lobau to follow Subervie and Domon; to choose a strong position towards St. Lambert; and to fall on the Prussians when he should hear Grouchy's guns. Bulow would then be placed between two fires; his corps, about 29,000 strong—a detachment, we have seen, had been left at Mont St. Guibert—would be in grave straits should it be assailed in front and rear by the 17,000 or 18,000 men of Lobau and by part of the troops of Grouchy. The Emperor therefore remained confident that Grouchy was at hand with a detachment of the mass of his forces, and probably by the way of Moustier and Ottignies. If this were the case, Lobau and Grouchy would destroy Bulow, and Waterloo would be a more complete triumph for France.*

* Napoleon's narrative of these incidents ('Comment.,' v. 170-172) has not been sufficiently studied. It bears all the marks of truth, and proves (1) that Napoleon expected Grouchy to reach the field with the detachment at least of 7,000 men, which he had most probably ordered

A short time before Bulow's troops were seen, Soult had written another despatch to Grouchy. This bears the date of one o'clock on June 18. Unquestionably it was a reply to Grouchy's message sent at three in the morning of the same day, but it alludes to Grouchy as having written an hour before.* This letter is as vaguely and badly worded as the previous letter of ten in the morning, but, if rightly interpreted, it bears nearly the same meaning. Soult informs Grouchy that his master generally approves of the advance on Sart les Walhain, and thence on Corbaix and Wavre. 'This conforms to the dispositions made by His Majesty.' But while Soult sanctions the march on Wavre, he repeats the injunction to Grouchy he had made before: 'The Marshal was to manœuvre in our direction, to come into close contact with us'; and he positively orders Grouchy to march on Waterloo, where the battle was being waged, and to 'come into line without delay with our right.' This, again, indicates a march on Wavre, no doubt by Corbaix; but this village is on a line with Moustier and Ottignies. The despatch summons Grouchy to the field of Waterloo, and the way to accomplish this was to approach Wavre indeed, but by Moustier and Ottignies and the western bank of the Dyle. Soult then added a postscript, probably under Napoleon's eye; Grouchy was apprised that Bulow was threatening the right flank of the main army; he was emphatically commanded to 'approach and join us,' and

---

him to make; (2) that he did not think the main French army in danger through the apparition of Bulow; (3) that Lobau was sent towards St. Lambert, not merely to keep Bulow back, but to co-operate with Grouchy in attacking Bulow; (4) that the Emperor thought, and rightly thought, that he had little or nothing to fear from the mass of the Prussian army.

* This letter will be found in La Tour d'Auvergne, 'Waterloo,' 270, 271. It was written in pencil, and almost illegible, like much of Soult's work. The date 2 a.m., instead of 3 a.m., is palpably a mistake.

to crush Bulow, ' who would be caught in a fatal position.'
This is a strong corroboration of proof, already nearly
conclusive, that the Emperor had directed Grouchy on
the night of the 17th to draw near him with a detachment
or the mass of his army, and that he believed Grouchy to
be at a short distance, and able with Lobau to deal Bulow
a mortal stroke.*

We pass on to the operations of Grouchy, destined
fatally to deceive his master, while on his way from
Gembloux to Sart les Walhain.   His march, we have
seen, had been very late and very slow, faults for which
he must bear the whole blame.   And he had not reconnoitred in the direction of Moustier and Ottignies—that is,
of the imperial army—unpardonable remissness attended
with disastrous results : for had he taken this obvious step
he would have ascertained how affairs stood, and soon
after noon would have been in communication with
Marbot's horsemen, despatched by the Emperor to bring
him to the field of Waterloo.   A little before eleven o'clock
the Marshal had reached Walhain, a village about a mile
west of Sart les Walhain, and therefore a mile nearer
Napoleon's lines.   He wrote another despatch at this
place to his master, which gives proof of great want of
intelligence, and shows how little he had done to ascertain
the facts.†

In this letter Grouchy informs the Emperor that Blucher
was still in retreat on Brussels, but that a considerable

---

* If any candid inquirer will put together the positive statements of
Napoleon, as regards the detachment from Grouchy, the evidence of
Marbot and Zenowicz, the two letters of Soult on the 18th at 10 a.m.
and 1 p.m., and this postscript, the inference to be drawn seems to us
almost irresistible.   The evidence, it will be observed, is independent
and cumulative.

† Mr. Ropes ('The Campaign of Waterloo,' 286-288) is the first
historian who has proved that it was not at Sart les Walhain, but
Walhain, that Grouchy halted.   M. H. Houssaye ('Waterloo,' ii. 289)
has added a good deal to the evidence on the subject.

part of the Prussian army was being assembled in the plains of the Chyse, a stream flowing towards Louvain from the north-east of Wavre. The mass of the army was probably taking this direction, perhaps in order to join Wellington at or near Brussels. The restraining wing and its chief would on the present evening be round Wavre, and so would interpose between Blucher and Wellington, the last presumed to be falling back upon Brussels.* It is unnecessary to point out how false this information was. So far from being in retreat on Brussels, still less from diverging into the plains of the Chyse and towards Louvain, Blucher was on the march from Wavre to Waterloo—that is, against Napoleon, not away from him. So far from Wellington being on his way to Brussels, he was awaiting his antagonist's attack at Mont St. Jean. And from this, of course, it follows that Grouchy's purpose to advance on Wavre by the evening of the 18th, in order to be in a position between the two hostile armies, was utterly vain, being in contradiction to the facts, and was leading him most disastrously astray. It had also this further evil effect: it induced Grouchy to imagine that there was no need that he should turn his attention towards the main French army, or that he should accelerate his tardy march on Wavre. On this very evening he would stand between Blucher and Wellington.† He was not called upon to move with increased celerity.

At this time—that is, not long after eleven o'clock—the positions held by Grouchy's army were these : The cavalry of Excelmans had pushed forward, and had reached La Baraque and the Bois d'Huzelles, points between three

* This despatch will be found in La Tour d'Auvergne, ' Waterloo,' 324.

† It deserves notice how in this, as in other despatches, Grouchy shows that he understood the real purport of the letter he received from Napoleon through Bertrand. This he discreditably suppressed. The fact speaks for itself, and should silence his apologists.

and four miles from Wavre; the heads of Vandamme's columns had passed Nil St. Vincent, a village some seven miles from Wavre and near Corbaix; the corps of Gérard was around Walhain and Sart les Walhain; the horsemen of Pajol and the infantry of Teste were on the march from Grand Leez to Tourinnes, and were perhaps two or three miles from Nil St. Vincent. It should be observed, too—and this is very important—the movements of Grouchy had completely escaped the notice of the Prussian detachment at Mont St. Guibert, commanded by an officer of the name of Ledebur; in fact, Excelmans and Vandamme were at this moment almost between Ledebur and the Prussian corps at Wavre.

This was the situation when Grouchy, with Gérard and other officers, who had met at Walhain—the dwelling has at last been ascertained—heard a rumbling sound towards the west at a distance. This rapidly swelled into a continuous roar. It was the thunder of the cannon of Waterloo, loud, Grouchy exclaimed, as that of Wagram. Gérard, a soldier of real insight and resource, urged his chief at once to march towards the scene of the battle, in which the Emperor was evidently engaged. Gérard's reasoning did not admit of an answer. By moving in the direction of Wellington, the restraining wing would exactly perform its task. Grouchy would stop Blucher were he halting at Wavre, or would intercept him were he on his way to Waterloo, or would come into line with the imperial army, should the hostile commanders have joined hands. This was palpably the true—nay, the obvious—course. Nor could Grouchy conceal from himself that Blucher had gained nearly a march on him, and that Blucher's movements were not distinctly and completely known. The means, too, to make the proposed movement were easy and at hand. The cavalry in advance should seize the bridges of Moustier and Ottignies, and cross the Dyle, a march from La Baraque

of about three miles; the corps of Vandamme and Gérard
should follow as quickly as possible; the horsemen of
Pajol and the division of Teste should push on towards
Wavre, in order to mask the operations to the left, and
to make demonstrations against the enemy. Within two
or three hours the position of affairs would be made plain;
within five or six Grouchy would have been within reach
of the Prussian or of the main French army.

The attempts made by Grouchy to answer Gérard show
how disastrous it may be in war, as in other spheres of
the conduct of man, to stick at the letter and to miss the
essential spirit. The Marshal said that his orders were to
follow the Prussians, and that this object could be best
attained by marching on Wavre by the line he was taking;
that the Emperor had told him that he would attack
Wellington should that General make a stand before the
Forest of Soignies, but that he, that is, Grouchy—and this
we believe to be true—had received no command to draw
near the main army; and that even were he to advance
towards Waterloo, the distance was so great he could not
be on the field in time. The unfortunate chief could not,
or would not, understand that Wavre could be reached
by the western bank of the Dyle and by the bridges of
Moustier and Ottignies almost as quickly as by any other
way, if it was necessary to proceed to Wavre at all; that
his paramount duty—and this he knew—was to interpose
between Blucher and Wellington; that he could not
possibly accomplish this should Blucher endeavour to
march from Wavre on Waterloo, unless he should cross
the Dyle by Moustier and Ottignies, or conceivably by
Limale and Limelette; that were he to move towards
the Emperor without delay, he would effectually make
his presence felt hours before he should even approach
Waterloo; and that in any event, in his perplexing
position — due to his own remissness, inactivity, and
mistakes—his only course was to press forward towards
the sound of the cannon.

Grouchy, however, it is believed, would have yielded, had not Gérard's language been peremptory and his bearing stiff. The jealousy of each other, so characteristic of the warriors of France from the day of Roncesvalles to the day of Spicheren may have closed his ears to the counsel of manifest wisdom.* The Marshal insisted on making for Wavre along the eastern bank of the Dyle —that is, keeping completely away from Waterloo. He angrily rejected the prayer of Gérard to allow him to march with his single corps towards Napoleon. Disregarding the advice of almost all his officers—a General of Artillery was the only exception, and he did not urge his objections long—and despite the angry murmurs of his own soldiery, more intelligent than their purblind leader, Grouchy directed his army to march on Wavre by the roads he had marked out for himself in the morning. Had he listened to his colleague and taken the true course, he might perhaps have gained a triumph for his own arms, certainly have saved France from an immense catastrophe.

While Grouchy was proceeding on his ill-starred march, Napoleon had been making the grand attack on Wellington's left and left centre. The intention of the Emperor had at first been to sustain this effort with twenty-four guns only; but perceiving the advantage the ground gave him, he had resolved to support it with nearly eighty. Soon after one o'clock, while Jerôme and Foy were squandering their forces around Hougoumont, a tremendous fire opened from this great battery, and was continued to its right by batteries of inferior force. From La Haye Sainte to Papelotte and La Haye, the valley and the ridge of Mont St. Jean were shrouded in volumes of dense smoke broken by the quick flashes of the red artillery. The guns of the assailants searched the allied position at distances of from 500 to 800 yards, carrying

* See La Tour d'Auvergne, 'Waterloo,' 328.

devastation and death in their tempest of missiles.* The allies replied, but with much fewer pieces ; their batteries, in fact, were rather dispersed. The position of the great French battery enabled it to throw a concentrated, and even a raking, fire on a considerable part of the enemy's forces.† The troops of Bylandt, who, from whatever cause, stood, we have said, in front of Wellington's line, and, accordingly, were very much exposed, suffered terribly from the destructive storm of shot ; and though the soldiery of Picton and Wincke, the main stay of the defence in this direction, were ordered to lie down, and to withdraw behind the crest of the ridge to seek shelter, they also lost a large number of men, and even the reserves in the rear were not unscathed. After about half an hour of this weighty cannonade, Ney gave D'Erlon the signal to begin the attack. This was to be conducted by the whole infantry of the 1st corps, from 17,000 to 18,000 men, seconded by Bachelu's division of the 2nd corps, the only one not engaged at Hougoumont, this advancing to the western edge of the great main-road, and sustaining D'Erlon in that direction.

The 1st corps was composed of four divisions, those of Allix,‡ Donzelot, Marcognet and Durutte. It was to storm the enemy's position, from La Haye Sainte to Papelotte and La Haye. The French columns presented an aspect of most imposing force, as, preceded by a multitudinous swarm of skirmishers, and supported by

* Charras describes the great artillery attack as beginning at noon. He relies on this hour, because it was then Grouchy heard the intensity of the cannonade. But Charras is contradicted by all other authorities.

† This was because part of the French ridge, on which the great battery was placed, curved towards the allied line. The effect of the fire is noticed by most writers.

‡ Nearly all the English accounts transpose the positions of Allix and Donzelot, and are in this respect misleading. Allix was not present on the field.

16

the artillery thundering over their heads, they advanced through the low and broken ground which divided them from La Haye Sainte and the ridge of Mont St. Jean. The war cry of 'Vive l'Empereur!' rose over the din of the fight; brave officers, detaching themselves from the ranks, urged on their men with impassioned gestures; the soldiery, though making their way slowly through thick masses of rye and miry ground, were eager to close with the foe in their front. These great waves of onset seemed of irresistible might; but there was no cavalry on the flanks of the columns to the left,* and the columns of Allix, Donzelot and Marcognet were arrayed in formations so vicious and ill-conceived that they were infinitely less formidable than they appeared to be. Unlike what had usually been the tactics of the French, they were not composed of battalions in separate columns, or of battalions deployed with columns on their flanks: they were made up of a succession of deployed battalions, each following the other, at short distances between. They were thus literally phalanxes of great but varying depth, and with comparatively narrow fronts, heavy masses difficult to handle, and terribly exposed to horsemen and to infantry in line.†

The three divisions were each about 400 yards from the other, three wide intervals of space before; they advanced in echelon, the leading echelon on the left. This, formed

* Napoleon ('Comment.,' vi. 150) notices this mistake.

† Mr. Ropes ('The Campaign of Waterloo,' 305) and Charras (ii. 25, 26) have described clearly and well the nature of the vicious formation of these columns, and have pointed out the resulting dangers and mischiefs. Charras says, 'Ces étranges colonnes presentaient donc ici douze, là vingt-quatre et vingt-sept rangs d'épaisseur, et un front variant de cent cinquante à deux cent hommes, suivant la force des bataillons . . . sur un terrain favourable, cette formation, complètement, et a juste titre inusitée, aurait été bien dangereuse; sur le sol accidenté, bourbeux, qu'il fallait parcourir, c'était une folie. On se mettait à la merci d'une charge de cavalerie.' Napoleon at St. Helena laid the blame to the charge of D'Erlon.

of the brigade of Quiot, of the troops of Allix, reached La Haye Sainte at about two o'clock, and swarmed round the place in furious attack. La Haye Sainte was a solid Belgian farmhouse, with an orchard towards the south, and a kitchen-garden northwards, and with the ordinary farm buildings on two of its sides; and, as we have seen, it was only defended by some 400 men of the German Legion, commanded by a fine English soldier, Baring. Though greatly exposed to the enemy's guns, it had not been destroyed by their fire, or even much injured. It deserves notice that it had not been ravaged by shells, and that the assailants, as had been the case at Hougoumont, were not provided with the means of breaking down the enclosures and the walls. Quiot's men, surrounding the place in overwhelming numbers, had ere long mastered the orchard and the kitchen-garden; but their efforts failed against buildings they could not escalade or enter. They suffered heavily from the fire of the little garrison, and of the enemy's guns that commanded the place. As had happened at Hougoumont, their valour remained for the time fruitless.

Meanwhile, the brigade of Bourgeois, the second of Allix, with the divisions of Donzelot and Marcognet on its right, had reached the ground at the foot of the ridge of Mont St. Jean, and, though smitten severely by a heavy fire, advanced resolutely against the allied line. The troops of Bourgeois, greatly superior in force, dislodged the 95th from the gravel-pit they held, but the riflemen fell back a few hundred yards only, and kept plying the assailants with the fire of their deadly weapons. Donzelot, supported by Bourgeois on his left, now pressed forward up the slope of the ridge. The Dutch-Belgians of Bylandt, already shattered by the cannonade to which they had been exposed, and attacked by Marcognet's men in flank, began to waver, and almost at once gave way; they fled in precipitate rout upon the reserves, pursued by

16—2

the execrations of Picton's troops, who were prevented with difficulty from firing on them.* Loud shouts of victory burst from the French columns; they swept through the hedges on the cross-road from Ohain to Braine l'Alleud, which formed an obstacle to attack in this part of the line; they reached at several points the crest of the ridge.† It seemed as if they would master the position by another effort. Wellington's left centre was for a moment in grave danger. Napoleon and his staff, watching the scene from a distance, believed that the battle was even now half won.

But here the assailants met foemen worthy of their steel. They were suddenly brought to a stand amidst their seeming triumph. The troops of Picton had lain down and were behind the ridge. At the voice of their commander they rose, formed line, fired a murderous volley, and charged with the bayonet. The battalions of Kempt and the battalions of Pack, although outnumbered nearly three to one, fell on their enemies, entangled and intermingled as these were by the very confusion caused by their partial success. The superiority was then, as always, seen of the British line over the French column, especially over columns such as D'Erlon's were. The fire from the contracted fronts was feeble, the dense masses were unable to deploy; they were soon weltering in increasing disorder, smitten by a destructive fire, and

---

* Siborne ('The Waterloo Campaign,' 396) is just to the troops of Bylandt, contemptuously called 'les braves Belges' by more than one English writer. He points out that they had suffered greatly on the 16th at Quatre Bras, and had not unnaturally been demoralised in their forward position by the crushing fire of the French artillery on June 18.

† It has been denied that the columns of Donzelot and Marcognet reached the crest of the ridge, but they certainly did. See ' Waterloo Letters ' in many places. One sentence must suffice (72) : ' The French columns forced their way through our line ; the heads of the columns were on the Brussels side of the double hedge.'

assailed in front and flank. Nevertheless, they were kept together by their very weight; they made a stubborn resistance and struggled hard; Picton and many of his best officers and soldiers fell.*

At this crisis of the fight an avalanche of war fell suddenly on the French columns, already disorganised, staggering, giving way. The horsemen of Ponsonby, we have said, were behind Picton's line; they were drawn up along the reverse slope of the ridge, concealed from the enemy, and comparatively out of fire. Uxbridge seized the occasion with skill and resource, and gave the signal for a charge pressed home. The squadrons, known afterwards as the Union Brigade, and composed of the 1st Royal and Enniskillen Dragoons, and of the Scots Greys, famous since the day of Blenheim, swept over the ridge, and through openings in the hedges on the cross-road, and, making their way through the intervals between the hostile columns, Picton's infantry cheering them as they rushed on like a torrent, burst in terrific force on the astounded enemy, as little expecting them as an apparition springing out of the earth.

The effects of this magnificent charge were instantaneous, complete, and decisive. While the soldiery of Kempt and Pack continued their attack, the horsemen fell on the flanks of the dissolving masses, broke into them as they began to yield, made immense havoc among men who could hardly use their weapons—in a word, turned defeat into a frightful rout. Within less than twenty minutes two or three thousand prisoners had fallen into the hands of the victors, the eagles of two regiments had been captured, the troops of Bourgeois, of Donzelot, and of Marcognet, huddled together, paralysed, and, in their closely packed bodies, unable to make a prolonged re-

---

* Picton was well known as a warrior of the Peninsula in the French army. On the morning of Waterloo Napoleon had asked, 'Où est la division Picton?'

sistance, were hurled in confusion down the slopes of the ridge which they had but just ascended in the confidence of a coming triumph. From 10,000 to 12,000 excellent troops—and no one will deny their fine qualities—had, in short, been utterly beaten and scattered by about 3,000 or 4,000 British infantry and 1,200 horsemen; cavalry has never achieved more splendid success; this was certainly in a great measure due to the strange and bad formation of D'Erlon's columns—the second great fault in the tactics of the French at Waterloo.

It would have been well had Ponsonby's great charge been checked and stopped when he had gained his object. His horsemen, however, carried away and getting out of hand—too common a characteristic of British cavalry—rushed impetuously up the opposite ridge, drew actually near the great French battery, and overturned a small battery in the valley below, cutting down the gunners, who bravely fell by their pieces. Here, however, their headlong onset was stayed; they were attacked, when disordered and in confusion, by bodies of lancers and cuirassiers in front and flank; they paid dearly for their bold temerity. They were, in fact, nearly cut to pieces; not half their number returned to their posts; their gallant leader, Ponsonby, was slain.*

* It is idle to disparage the French army at Waterloo; it gave proof of heroic courage, too often made fruitless by the inconsiderate conduct of its chiefs. But it is well to point out the peculiar effects and characteristics of Ponsonby's charge, seconded as it was by Picton's men; it took the enemy by surprise, and they could offer a feeble resistance only. 'Waterloo Letters,' 72: 'I came in contact with the head of the column . . . no preparation had been made to resist cavalry; nor do I think there could have been, as there was not above a hundred yards to go over after we saw each other. . . .' 61: 'The enemy's column (near which I was), on arriving at the crest of the position, seemed very helpless, had very little fire to give from its front or flanks, was incapable of deploying, must have already lost many of its officers in coming up, was fired into close with impunity by stragglers of our infantry who remained behind. As we approached,

Another disaster befell the French arms not far from this scene, and at the same time. Wellington had hastened from near Hougoumont when his left centre was attacked; he had taken his stand by an elm-tree, not far from the point where the great main-road meets the cross-road from Ohain to Braine l'Alleud; here, surrounded by his staff and distinguished foreign officers, he watched the vicissitudes of the battle, ever active, ever ready to sustain the defence. The partial success of the enemy at La Haye Sainte, and the danger that threatened this part of his line, should this advanced post be stormed and held, made him resolve to reinforce the garrison of the farm; he sent a Hanoverian battalion, detached from Alten's division, to join the hard-pressed and worn-out troops of Baring. Meanwhile, Napoleon, who from the first had shown that he had perceived the immense importance of La Haye Sainte on the verge of the Duke's centre, and who had been vexed that D'Erlon's attack had not been supported by cavalry on its left, had despatched a brigade of Milhaud's cuirassiers to second Quiot's men should an opportunity arise; this was placed in a fold of the ground just south of La Haye Sainte. As the Hanoverians advanced, the mailed squadrons, bursting out on their enemies, took them by surprise and drove them back, routed, upon Alten's line; they boldly pressed forward, and seemed about to charge.

Turning to account the occasion again, Uxbridge directed Somerset's heavy cavalry against the cuirassiers just at the time when he launched Ponsonby's horsemen. Putting himself at the head of the 1st and 2nd Life Guards, of the Blues, and of the 1st Dragoon Guards, he gallantly led the charge in person. Milhaud's men, the

---

the front and flanks began to turn their backs inwards; the rear of the columns had already begun to run away.' Napoleon ('Comment., vi. 150) especially praises Ponsonby's charge. The mêlée is admirably and fairly described by M. H. Houssaye, 'Waterloo,' 346-348.

veterans of many a day of renown, met their adversaries
boldly and with confident hearts; the hostile squadrons
'came to the shock like two walls in perfect lines'; the
struggle for some moments was fierce and terrific.* The
cuirassiers were better armed and better swordsmen than
their foes, but the superior strength and weight of the British
trooper and of his horse prevailed, and after a fiery trial of
force the French horsemen recoiled, were ridden down in
scores, and were driven back beaten. It is but just, however,
to remark that they apparently were inferior in numbers,
and several squadrons were caught in the hollows between
the banks on the cross-roads from Ohain to Braine
l'Alleud, and were borne down into the gravel-pit near
La Haye Sainte, where some of these unfortunate horsemen perished.† The cavalry of Somerset, like that of
Ponsonby, was also carried away, and urged the pursuit
much too far; its squadrons suffered besides from the fire
of Bachelu's footmen before it regained the positions it
had held.‡

The defeat of the cuirassiers and of the greatest part of
the corps of D'Erlon compelled Quiot to abandon his hold
on La Haye Sainte. The fortune of D'Erlon's fourth
division had been less disastrous than that of its fellows,
but this had likewise been forced to retreat. Durutte had
taken on himself not to form his columns in the strange
and ruinous fashion that had been ordered; he had
judiciously kept two battalions in reserve. He came in
conflict with the Hanoverians of Best and Wincke, and

---

* A spirited description of this cavalry mêlée, one of the hardest
fought of the day, will be found in Siborne, 'The Waterloo Campaign,'
408, 409.

† This incident is the subject of one of Victor Hugo's finest pieces
of narrative. But he has enormously exaggerated the facts.

‡ Uxbridge, afterwards Lord Anglesey ('Waterloo Letters,' 9), says
that the French were completely surprised and taken aback by the
charges of Ponsonby and Somerset, whose troops had been kept in
reserve behind the ridge.

reached the crest of the position on the allied extreme left; but he was more or less involved in the defeat of the rest of his corps. He was charged by Vivian's and Vandeleur's horsemen as he fell back, but he was disengaged by the light cavalry on D'Erlon's right. He effected his retreat without much loss. Meanwhile Napoleon's attention had at last been turned to the waste of his forces around Hougoumont. He directed a battery of howitzers against the place; large parts of the buildings were set on fire and destroyed by shells. Many wounded men perished, and many brave men fell; but the garrison clung to the orchard, the garden, and the remains of the château. The position was surrounded, but not taken.

It was now three in the afternoon. The grand attack of the Emperor had completely failed; the feint on Hougoumont, changed into a real attack, had only led to disastrous results. The losses of the French had been already very great; from Hougoumont to La Haye the ground was strewn with the carnage and the wrecks of a desperately contested battle. But Wellington also had cruelly suffered: hundreds of his best troops had fallen at Hougoumont; his finest cavalry had been almost destroyed; Picton's infantry had been severely stricken; the Dutch-Belgians of Bylandt had fled; the weak points of the position had been discovered; the Duke's left and left centre had been in grave peril. Had Napoleon at this conjuncture been able to attack with the corps of Lobau and the Imperial Guard, and with his superb and almost intact cavalry, he would probably have turned and forced this part of the allied line, if a decisive victory was already beyond his reach. But Bulow was beginning to make his presence felt. Lobau had been detached to throw him back and hold him in check. Grouchy was on what might be called a fool's errand, were this not to lead to an appalling catastrophe for France, and was simply marching away from his master. The battle was soon to enter upon a new phase; its character was, in a great measure, to change; it was still to rage for hours with varying fortunes. But Napoleon felt himself constrained to abandon his original plan of attack; thenceforward the efforts his army made against its enemies were to be often disconnected, ill-combined, wanting in judgment and insight.

The Emperor in the next phase of the contest was to have greatly to complain of Ney, who gave proof of the faults he had committed at Quatre Bras. He was himself placed in most difficult straits. It is almost impossible to pronounce a decided judgment; but signs were not to be wanting that the overconfidence shown by Napoleon in the early morning was being replaced by very different feelings, and that more than once, perhaps, he was deficient in the perfect self-reliance, in the readiness, in the daring of old, which he said himself he no longer possessed in 1815.

CHAPTER IX

THE BATTLE OF WATERLOO TO THE REPULSE OF
BULOW AND HIS CORPS

Napoleon receives the news of Grouchy's tardy and false movement,
and of Bulow's advance from St. Lambert towards the Bois de
Paris—The Emperor's plan of attack profoundly modified—His
orders to Ney—Intense cannonade—Ney masters La Haye Sainte
probably about 4 p.m. — Disregarding Napoleon's orders, he
projects a grand cavalry attack against the allied right centre—
Extreme imprudence of this conduct—The attacks of Milhaud
and Lefebvre-Desnoëttes—The French cavalry fail—Napoleon
not aware of the attacks until it was too late—Renewal of the
cavalry attacks by Milhaud, Lefebvre-Desnoëttes, Kellermann,
and Guyot—Why the Emperor gave his sanction to them—Attack
of Bulow on the French right—It becomes very dangerous —
Napoleon compelled to strengthen Lobau by the Young Guard
—Magnificent resistance made to the cavalry attacks—They
ultimately fail—Ney and Wellington—Part of the Old Guard
sent to retake Plancenoit—Bulow repulsed—Fresh attacks made
on the allied line—The position of Wellington still critical—State
of the battle ; this is still undecided.

WHILE Ney and D'Erlon had been making the grand
attack, ending, we have seen, in a complete reverse,
disastrous intelligence had reached Napoleon. He had
received the letter written by Grouchy from Walhain at
eleven in the morning, which informed his master that
Blucher was falling back on Brussels; that the mass of
the Prussian army was being probably concentrated in
the plains of the Chyse, to the north-east of Wavre and

towards Louvain; and that the restraining wing would attack Wavre, but not until late in the afternoon, and would stand at that place between Blucher and Wellington, supposed to be in retreat on Brussels. This despatch, utterly opposed to the facts, proved that Grouchy had marched with extraordinary slowness from Gembloux, and was not nearly in contact with the enemy, now known to be in part at Wavre, in part at St. Lambert;* that Blucher had gained several miles on Grouchy; and that the chances were faint that, even if Grouchy should draw near the main army by Moustier and Ottignies, he could be in a position to fall on Bulow's flank and rear, as both Napoleon and Soult thought would be the case when the postscript to the letter of one in the afternoon was written. It seemed probable, on the contrary, from Grouchy's language, that the Marshal would march to Wavre as slowly as he had marched to Walhain; that he would not be at Wavre until the evening of the day; and that he might even diverge towards the plains of the Chyse, hoping still to interpose between the allied commanders, who in his view were making for Brussels.

It had become evident, therefore, to Napoleon that his lieutenant was on a wrong, possibly a fatal, course; that he must now expect that Bulow would be free to march against the right flank of the main French army, while this was attacking Wellington in front; that this diversion must be grave, and might become most perilous, and that it must be resisted, and if possible baffled. Simultaneously the Emperor was made aware by Marbot's

---

* 'Comment.,' v. 174 : 'L'Empereur reçut de Gembloux des nouvelles bien fâcheuses. Le Maréchal Grouchy, au lieu d'être parti de Gembloux à la pointe du jour, comme il l'avait annoncé par sa dépêche de deux heures après minuit, n'avait pas encore quitté ce camp à dix heures du matin. L'officier l'attribuait à l'horrible temps qu'il faisait ; motif ridicule.' Gembloux is a mistake for Sart les Walhain, and two in the morning should be three; but Napoleon's disappointment appears plainly.

horsemen and those of Domon that Bulow was moving from St. Lambert, and was making his way towards the Bois de Paris, a piece of woodland about a mile from the extreme French right, and about two from Plancenoit, near the French rear, and that an attack from this direction might be ere long expected.

Napoleon has told us that, when he first heard that Bulow's advanced guard was at St. Lambert, he had considered whether he should not change the course of the battle, and direct his main attacks against Wellington's right, and not against the allied left and left centre. On reflection, however, he gave up this idea, for reasons weighty, and indeed conclusive. It was now after three in the afternoon, and he did not recur to the project, though he knew that Bulow was free to march against his right flank. He resolved to continue the attack on Wellington, and at the same time to keep Bulow away. In his present situation he could do nothing better, unless, indeed, he were to retreat, a movement, Clausewitz has remarked, which Turenne would have made, but which for Napoleon was out of the question : for, apart from his characteristic aversion to tactics of this kind, in the existing condition of affairs in France he could not temporise ; victory was his only chance of safety. The Emperor, however, profoundly modified the plan of attack he had formed in the morning, and adopted a plan in many respects different. He felt that while Bulow was menacing his right he would be gravely endangering this part of his line should he endeavour to turn Wellington's extreme left. This might bring disaster on the whole French right. He therefore abandoned the effort against that part of the Duke's position, which was certainly the weakest and the most easy to master.* The corps of D'Erlon, besides, had

---

* Charras (ii. 80) blames Napoleon for this modification of his original plan ; but Charras is a partisan, and most commentators are against him. The immense importance of the approach of Bulow at this juncture should be carefully noted.

suffered immense loss. Napoleon had made himself aware of this, for, soon after it had been driven back to its lines, he had ridden in person to see how affairs stood, had addressed encouraging words to the defeated soldiery, and had spoken to the officers in command ; he had doubtless learned that, for some time at least, this part of his army was not equal to another grand attack.

The Emperor therefore resolved to make his next great effort against Wellington's centre and left centre. The means to be employed were admirably designed, and had his orders been duly carried out, the result would certainly have been different from what it was to be. He had long perceived the importance of La Haye Sainte, an outwork in front of Wellington's centre ; were this seized and occupied, the French would possess an avenue into the midst of the allied position. Napoleon accordingly directed Ney to make himself master of this point of vantage, to establish himself firmly within the buildings, and to wait until the opportunity had come to make an attack in force on Wellington's centre—this also to be conducted under Ney's command.* This great attack was to be sustained by a large part of the Imperial Guard, and by the mass of the still intact cavalry ; and it was to be seconded on the left and the right by Reille and D'Erlon, who, likewise, were for the present only to threaten the enemy, and not to make a decisive movement. Meantime Lobau was to hold Bulow in check ; the grand attack was to be deferred until Bulow had been encountered and his corps repulsed.

To sustain, and at the same time to mask, the on-

* The import of Napoleon's orders to Ney has never been questioned. Jerôme, who had been wounded at Hougoumont, and had returned to his brother, emphatically wrote to his wife ('Mémoires,' vii. 22): 'L'Empereur avait ordonné au Maréchal Ney de se maintenir dans La Haye Sainte en la crénélant, et en y établissant plusieurs bataillons, mais de ne faire aucun mouvement.' See also Gourgaud, 'Campagne de 1815.'

slaught to be made on Wellington's centre, several batteries were withdrawn from Napoleon's right; their fire was directed on La Haye Sainte, and on other parts of the enemy's line, while renewed demonstrations were made against Hougoumont, and against Papelotte, La Haye and Smohain, for the present, however, mere attacks of skirmishers. The cannonade became most intense and destructive; the French guns, very superior in numbers, and placed for the most part in positions of vantage, carried havoc and death into the allied ranks; these were, certainly, to some extent shaken. Had Wellington's army been as exposed as that of Blucher had been at Ligny, its losses by this time might have been fatal to it; but the troops even in front, and especially the reserves, were kept as much as possible behind the ridge of Mont St. Jean, and though they suffered greatly they were able to bear the ordeal.

Under the protection of this terrific fire the soldiers of Quiot advanced against La Haye Sainte again; they were reinforced by two of Donzelot's battalions; the place was once more encompassed by a swarm of furious assailants. The little garrison had been to some extent strengthened, but the defenders were never in sufficient numbers; they were now very inferior in force. A desperate struggle, however, raged for a while, the French endeavouring in vain to master the buildings—these, as before, had not been attacked by shells, and appliances for breaking in had, as before, been wanting—Baring and his brave men stubbornly maintaining their hold. The result was for a time uncertain. At last, probably at about four o'clock, reiterated attempts to set the farm offices on fire, spite of determined efforts to quench the flames, proved to a considerable extent successful; and the ammunition of the defence began to fail: the supply, for some unknown reason, had been inadequate from the first. The French burst in by the entrance of a large

barn on the west side of the house ; a bloody fight of a
few minutes ensued ; but Baring and his followers were
compelled to abandon the place ; few of the garrison and
its supporters lived to tell the tale.   Two battalions were
sent from Alten's division to make an effort to regain a
position of vantage, the importance of which the allies
had perceived too late—the Duke nobly took the blame
on himself—but one of these was suddenly attacked and
almost destroyed by a body of cuirassiers who skilfully
seized the occasion, and the other was with difficulty
disengaged by Somerset's horsemen.*

The fall of La Haye Sainte was welcomed by the
French soldiery, impressionable, but intelligent, with
enthusiastic acclaim.   The left centre and centre of
Wellington were now greatly exposed ; his enemy had a
path opened into the midst of his line, along the great

---

* The importance of the capture of La Haye Sainte is obvious ;
the left centre and centre of Wellington became very much exposed.
For some valuable remarks on the imperfect preparations made for
the defence of the post, see Shaw Kennedy, 'Battle of Waterloo,'
122, 123, 174.   It would be most desirable to ascertain the time when
La Haye Sainte fell, especially in order to form a just estimate of the
subsequent tactics of the French ; but the accounts are conflicting,
and cannot be reconciled.   Wellington (Despatches, xii. 619) says
2 p.m. ; but this is clearly a mistake.   From Napoleon's narrative
('Comment.,' v. 174), it may be inferred that the time was about 4 p.m.
This agrees with Jomini, who wrote soon after the event (' Précis de
la Campagne de 1815 ').   Charras (ii. 36, 37) fixes the time at a little
before 4 p.m. from the testimony of an eye-witness.   On the other
hand, Shaw Kennedy, who was on the spot ('Battle of Waterloo,' 122),
positively states that the hour was about 6 p.m. ; and Siborne (' The
Waterloo Campaign,' 476, 478) concurs.   The probabilities indicate
that the time was about 4 p.m. : for otherwise (1) the great cavalry
attacks, ill-conceived as they were, could hardly have been attempted
if La Haye Sainte were still in the hands of the enemy ; and
(2) Bachelu's division would hardly have been withdrawn from La
Haye Sainte, as it was, at about 4 p.m. had not the place been in the
power of the French.   On the whole, the evidence preponderates that
La Haye Sainte was stormed and occupied at about 4 p.m. ; but this
is not certain.   Mr. Ropes ('The Campaign of 1815') makes the time
near four ; M. H. Houssaye (' Waterloo,' ii. 378) makes it about six.

main-road from Charleroy to Brussels; the allies must
have been placed in grave peril had a grand and determined attack been pressed home. But Bulow was already
striking Napoleon's right flank. The Emperor, we have
said, had resolved to repel this effort before falling in full
force on Wellington. It was the plain duty of Ney to
obey his orders, to occupy La Haye Sainte in adequate
strength, and to bide his time, until he should receive a
signal from his master to make the decisive onslaught,
which, it should be recollected, he was himself to lead.
But the unfortunate Marshal had been stung to the quick
by the reproaches addressed to him for his delays on
June 16. In his case, too, as in that of warriors of his
type, the hot fit often succeeded the cold; he believed
that victory, won by his own exertions, was within his
grasp. Wellington had, we have seen, withdrawn a considerable part of his army behind the ridge to escape the
effects of the tremendous cannonade; there were movements of the impedimenta in his rear; some of his
auxiliaries were already flying from the field. Ney
thought he saw the signs of retreat at hand. On the
spur of the moment, without reflection, and in contravention of Napoleon's commands, he resolved to attack the
enemy with a mass of cavalry, and to change a retrograde
movement into defeat—nay, rout.

A more inconsiderate and reckless purpose has seldom
been formed in the annals of war; it was, we repeat, a
violation of positive orders; it was the third great error
of the tactics of the French at Waterloo. The attack, as
it was to be conducted, was to be made by horsemen,
exposed on a considerable space to the destructive fire of
the allied guns; it was to be made without the support of
infantry in force. It was to be made, too, against Wellington's right centre, exactly where his line was strong, and
could be easily reinforced; for at this point the cross-
road from Ohain to Braine l'Alleud did not present the

17

obstacles which had proved so fatal to the luckless cuirassiers a few hours before; and it was to be made against masses of infantry still unbroken, capable of being greatly increased in numbers, and in a large part, at least, composed of men of proved constancy and worth. No wonder that experienced British officers, as they saw the preparations being made for this waste of military strength, felt that the effort was premature, and was doomed to failure. 'We had no idea that the attack would be made upon our line standing in its regular order of battle, and that line as yet unshaken by any previous attack of infantry. . . . Our surprise at being so soon attacked by this great and magnificent force of cavalry was accompanied by the opinion that the attack was premature, and that we were perfectly prepared and secure against its effects, so far as any military operation can be depended upon.'*

* Shaw Kennedy, 'Battle of Waterloo,' 115, 116. That the first great attack of the French cavalry was made in opposition to Napoleon's express orders, and was due to Ney alone, has been established by incontrovertible evidence, and has been only questioned by partisan writers like Charras. Napoleon ('Comment.,' v. 203) says, and with evident truth : 'Le mouvement de la cavalerie sur le plateau, pendant que l'attaque du Général Bulow n'était pas répoussée, fut un accident fâcheux ; l'intention du chef était d'ordonner ce mouvement, mais une heure plus tard, et de le faire soutenir par les seize bataillons d'infanterie de la Garde et cent pièces de canon.' Gourgaud ('Campagne de 1815,' 96) pointedly remarked: 'Le Maréchal Ney, emporté par trop d'ardeur, et oubliant l'ordre qu'il avait reçu (de se maintenir dans La Haye Sainte sans faire aucun mouvement) déboucha sur le plateau avec les cuirassiers de Milhaud et la cavalerie légère de la Garde.' Jérôme is not less explicit ; the attack by cavalry alone was never contemplated by Napoleon, and was distinctly premature. 'Mémoires,' vii. 23 : 'L'Empereur ordonna au Maréchal Ney de se porter avec une grande partie de la cavalerie, deux corps d'infanterie et la Garde, sur le centre de l'ennemi pour donner le coup de massue et certes c'en était fait de l'armée anglaise si le Maréchal eut exécuté les ordres de l'Empereur, mais, emporté par son ardeur, il attaqua trois quarts d'heure trop tot.' Rogniat, a detractor of Napoleon, declared ('Considerations sur l'Art de la Guerre,' 235) : 'Lorsque la cavalerie s'engagea sur les lignes anglaises Napoléon parut surpris et douta un moment que les masses de cavalerie qu'il voyait au milieu des anglais, lui appartinssent, et

Ney had told Drouot in the morning that the French cavalry, under his leading, could do great things; he hurried to Delort, one of Milhaud's lieutenants, and demanded that a body of cuirassiers should be placed in his hands. Delort referred the Marshal to his superior officer; Milhaud protested against an attack to be made in difficult ground, under the worst conditions; Ney angrily replied that the whole cavalry had been entrusted to him, but did not add that he was not to stir until Napoleon bade him. Milhaud reluctantly obeyed what seemed an imperative command; his splendid division of mailed horsemen was given to Ney to be at his disposal; it was followed, as it began its movement, by the light cavalry of the Guard, perhaps because, chafing at its inaction at Quatre Bras, it broke away from its experienced chief, perhaps because Milhaud called on Lefebvre-Desnoëttes to support him.

This mass of superb horsemen, about 5,000 sabres, had, as it advanced, to cross the great main-road. It was compelled to defile for fully 1,200 yards, exposing its flank to the fire of the allied guns; but though hundreds of saddles were emptied, it kept together, and boldly pressed forward, protected by a storm of shot from the French batteries, and by Bachelu's division in skirmishing order, this having been sent from La Haye Sainte to Hougoumont. The squadrons ere long had reached the low ground between these two places, from whence they were to ascend the ridge. This formed a front of only a few hundred yards, far too contracted for such a body of men; the assailants were frightfully ravaged by grape and

---

lorsque qu'il en eu la certitude il sembla mécontent de cette charge prématurée. . . . Si donc l'Empereur avait vu partir la cavalerie, il eut vraisemblement donné des ordres pour l'arrêter.' To the last hour of his life Napoleon charged Ney with this capital mistake, and insisted it was a main cause of the disaster of Waterloo. It is important to bear in mind the truth on this subject in considering the conduct of Ney and of Napoleon during this passage of Waterloo.

17—2

round shot, as they struggled up the miry and rain-drenched slope. But they retained their formations, and exulted in proud confidence; the 'bravest of the brave' was at their head, accompanied by many a brilliant officer; the cuirassiers were the men of Borodino and Eylau, whose weighty and dauntless onset had achieved wonders; the troopers of Lefebvre-Desnoëttes were choice soldiers, selected from the flower of the cavalry of France. The multitudinous shouts of 'Vive l'Empereur!' swelled in tumultuous roar towards the enemy's line; sabres flashed out in thousands in the summer air; the sun shone on a still ordered array rushing up the low eminence it had all but mastered, in the pomp of war, and in strength that appeared invincible. Its rays lit up the glittering armour and the dark helmets of a serried succession of mailed squadrons; they fell on the gay pennons of a forest of lances, and on the martial forms of masses of light horsemen clad in brilliant and many-coloured garb, like the 'cohorts gleaming in purple and gold' of the great Assyrian ruler. The spectacle 'was magnificent, but was not war,' words spoken of a grand effort of British cavalry by a gallant Frenchman, before Sebastopol, in another age.

The allied artillerymen had plied their deadly work until the enemy had reached the edge of the ascent; they suddenly disappeared at Wellington's command. The rushing tempest of horsemen swept over the ridge, finding little to arrest its course for a moment; the abandoned guns were seized by the elated troopers, who saw in the feat a presage of quickly-coming victory. But Wellington, as always, full of resource in the field, had his preparations made to resist the storm; he had already moved part of Chassé's division at Braine l'Alleud from his extreme right; he had directed Mitchell and Clinton to the scene of action, and considerable bodies of these fresh troops had marched from Merbe-Braine to reinforce the main order of battle; behind was collected a great array of cavalry; his menaced front, in a word, was extremely strong. The allied infantry was drawn up in squares, forming a double line of defence; the squares were arrayed checkerwise, so that the intervals between the first line were covered by the second at a short distance in the rear. The two lines gave each other powerful support; a most formidable front of fire was presented.

The French cavalry did not flinch; they charged boldly down the reverse slope of the ridge, where the British masses were assembled. Their onslaught fell first on the Guards of Maitland, and on the right of Alten's division, commanded by an excellent chief, Halkett. The horsemen dashed furiously against the first line of squares, striking at the angles, the most vulnerable points, endeavouring to break them up by the impulse of the assault, attacking the defenders with sword and lance, here and there annoying them with the fire of musketoons and pistols. They did not, however, attempt to crush any square by bearing down in concentrated force against it, as unfortunate Murat said afterwards they might have done. Their attacks were desultory and ill-connected, imposing as they were; and as they recoiled from the faces of the first line of squares—living citadels, so to speak, of fire edged with bayonets—they vainly wasted their efforts against the second. Meanwhile the murderous volleys of the infantry of the defence had told with frightful effect upon the assailants; the British and German soldiery stood firm—'rooted, as it were, in the earth.' Though some of the auxiliaries wavered and showed signs of yielding, no part of the allied front gave way; all withstood a shock, terrible for its moral effect, but, if steadfastly resisted, wanting in real material power.

By degrees the French squadrons became commingled, their order confused, their ranks broken; a mass of fresh cavalry was then launched against them—the horsemen of Arentschild, Van Merlen, Trip, and Dornberg—supported by the survivors of Somerset's troopers. Baffled, but indignant, and still fighting hard, the assailants were unable to resist this attack; they were forced back over the crest of the ridge, which they had just won in the sure hope of a triumph at hand. As they fell back, the artillerymen, who had taken refuge in the squares, returned to the guns they had lost for a moment. No precaution had been taken to provide means to spike them—another proof of the reckless want of forethought characteristic of nearly all the attacks at Waterloo; they had not even been overturned, as they might have been. Their destructive discharges at a short distance wrought havoc among the retiring squadrons.

Ney was a dauntless hero in the stress of battle. This reverse might well have made him pause; it only nerved him to make redoubled efforts. The French cavalry, too, greatly as they had suffered, had not lost heart, and were eager to come to blows again; they were re-formed in the low ground beneath the ridge, sheltered in some measure from the artillery of the defence. Ere long the proud squadrons began the attack anew; but this was conducted with more caution than before; Lefebvre-Desnoëttes kept his men in reserve, while Milhaud and his cuirassiers advanced towards the ascent. The narrow space where the onset was made presented once more the same splendid sight; the waves of horsemen rolled grandly forward; they had broken against impenetrable masses of rock; they flowed on again in the majesty and force of the storm.

Meanwhile Napoleon had reached the scene. It has been said that, from his station near La Belle Alliance, he was unable to descry the first advance of Ney; but it is more probable that he had been some time on horseback, and that he had failed to notice the Marshal's movement, because he was far away to the right engaged in making preparation to resist Bulow, whose attack was rapidly becoming more and more threatening.* When the Emperor and his staff arrived before Wellington's front, the second great cavalry attack had just begun. As the still well-ordered squadrons drew near the ridge, and the eye rested on those formidable masses of war, the hopes of the troops at hand and of their officers rose high; nothing, it was thought, could stop that overwhelming onset. It was otherwise, however, with the experienced leaders on the spot. Soult exclaimed: 'That man is endangering us as he did at Jena.' Napoleon, indignant that his orders had been set at nought, remarked: 'The madman! he is ruining France for the second time. This is a premature movement, of which the results may be fatal.'† But half of the great reserve of cavalry had been engaged; it was now impossible to recur to his late plan. Napoleon said: 'All this is an hour too soon; but it has become necessary to support what has already been done.'‡ He directed Kellermann to go to the aid of Ney with his horsemen; it is doubtful whether he did not give a similar order to Guyot, the chief of the heavy cavalry of the Guard, though he denied this to the latest hour of his life.§ The Emperor's purpose was largely determined by two facts—Bulow was thundering in force on his flank, and it was essential to avoid a retrograde movement; and the French infantry between La Haye Sainte and Hougoumont had been greatly thinned, and were becoming exposed should Wellington venture on a counter-attack. Napoleon entrusted once more the conduct of the battle

---

* Compare H. Houssaye, 'Waterloo,' 358, and Ropes, 'The Campaign of Waterloo,' 308, 309.

† 'Comment.,' v. 177, vi. 150, and authorities cited by H. Houssaye, 'Waterloo,' ii. 349.

‡ 'Comment.,' v. 177, vi. 150, and H. Houssaye, 'Waterloo,' ii. 364.

§ Compare 'Comment.,' v. 178, and vi. 150, 151, with the evidence to the contrary in H. Houssaye, 'Waterloo,' 365.

to Ney; he seems to have ridden off again to make head against Bulow. It appears to be certain that, as was his wont, he gave Ney no precise orders as to the methods by which he was to direct the attacks.

It was now between five and six o'clock; the attack of Bulow had become formidable in the extreme. Half of that General's corps had not come into line at St. Lambert until near one; the other half not until after three. It was well that Grouchy was far distant. Blucher had joined his lieutenant long before this time. The veteran, impatient as he was to take part in the great fight raging, with many vicissitudes, within his view, had sent reconnoitring parties to ascertain that his flank and rear were safe; he did not advance until they had returned. He pushed forward, but with two of his four divisions only. The way from St. Lambert through the narrow valley of the Lasne, a mere ravine closed by defiles and woodlands, was wellnigh impassable for troops in order; it has been said that had it been occupied by the French the Prussians could never have reached the scene of action. Lobau, however, remained behind the Bois de Paris; Bulow's men, though not opposed in their march, toiled with the greatest difficulty through a maze of obstacles; but Blucher followed the edge of the columns, breathing his heroic spirit into his devoted soldiery. 'Drag the guns through the mire, my lads!' he exclaimed. 'Have at the enemy! You would not see me break my word.' They emerged at last from the intricate valley, burning to avenge the defeat of Ligny.

The old Marshal had at first resolved not to engage this part of his troops until his two rearward divisions had come up; but urgent messages had arrived from Wellington, entreating him to attack without a moment's delay. The sight of the cavalry charging up the ridge of the Mont St. Jean, and of the serried masses of the Imperial Guard—ready, apparently, to deal a decisive stroke—made the aged warrior, so to speak, throw away the scabbard. At about half-past four his leading divisions, under Losthin and Hiller, issued from the Bois de Paris; they announced their presence by a rolling fire from all their guns. It was this that perhaps chiefly caused Napoleon to support Ney, lest the French army should lose its attitude of offence.* Lobau, Subervie, and Domon had only some 10,000 men—Lobau had, we have said, been deprived of the division of Teste—to oppose to an enemy already superior in numbers; but they held Losthin and Hiller successfully in check until the divisions of Ryssel and Hacke had reached the field. Lobau, unable to resist an enemy nearly threefold in force, fell back fighting in good order, and gradually approaching the main army. The Prussian line now extended from near Frischermont, close to Wellington's extreme left, towards Plancenoit on Napoleon's right rear; it was at Plancenoit not many hundred yards from the French army's flank. Bulow's troops, fully 29,000 strong, were now masters of a part of the field; his divisions on the left made a determined effort to storm Plancenoit, and to hold the village as a preliminary to a more decisive attack. The Prussian guns already swept the Emperor's line of retreat; the pressure on the French became so great that he was compelled to detach the Young Guard, about 4,000 strong, to defend Plancenoit, and to throw the assailants back. A desperate conflict raged for a time, but Bulow's columns were for the present repulsed.

---

* Bulow wrote that 'he attacked to let the British army get breath.' Blucher thus describes the position of affairs at this crisis of the battle (Prussian official report; see La Tour d'Auvergne, 'Waterloo,' 407): 'La superiorité de l'ennemi était trop grande; Napoléon envoyait continuellement en avant des masses énormes, et quelque fermeté que les troupes anglaises missent pour se maintenir dans leur position, il était impossible que de si héroiques efforts n'eussent enfin des bornés.' The great majority of English commentators altogether underrate the capital importance of Bulow's diversion.

Meanwhile a struggle, perhaps the most fiercely contested, certainly the most extraordinary in its tragic but grand incidents, that was witnessed during the long period of the wars of the French Revolution and the French Empire, had been going on for more than an hour between Hougoumont and La Haye Sainte, in front of Wellington's right centre. The second cavalry attack of Ney had failed like the first, though conducted with rather more judgment and skill; but when the squadrons of Kellermann, and perhaps of Guyot, had been placed by Napoleon in the Marshal's hands, his confidence rose to the highest point of daring, and he made preparations for another decisive onslaught. It was in vain that Kellermann, of Marengo renown, who, like all the French cavalry chiefs on this day, disapproved of the course on which Ney was bent, entreated him to pause in his headlong movement—at least, to keep a reserve of troopers out of the reach of the enemy; Ney insisted on employing the whole of the great array of horsemen entrusted to him. Provision, however, was made, though this was far from adequate, for seconding the great efforts about to be made by the masses of squadrons soon to be launched on their course. Piré, on the left, was ordered to menace the enemy's right, and to endeavour to search the squares of the defence by an enfilading fire from batteries on the road from Nivelles to Brussels; clouds of skirmishers were directed to support the attack where this was practicable by a dropping but continuous discharge of musketry; horse artillery was moved to points towards the bottom of the ridge, to take part in the conflict should an occasion offer itself.

But the Duke had his arrangements likewise made; they were perfectly conceived, and admirably carried out. The whole of Chassé's division, at first too distant, was now drawn from Braine l'Alleud, and placed in reserve, in order to strengthen the main front of battle; the

allied extreme right was thus ranged behind the right
centre. This was a reinforcement of fully 6,000 men. At
the same time, Mitchell's brigade and Clinton's division,
the brigades of Adam, Duplat, and W. Halkett, were
moved forward to defend the space between the western
verge of Hougoumont and the Guards of Maitland, and
to strengthen the line, greatly weakened at these points;
and cavalry was detached to hold Piré in check, and, if
possible, to drive him away, a large body of cavalry, as
before, being kept in reserve. On his left, where D'Erlon
maintained an incessant fire of skirmishers, the Duke
withdrew the hard-pressed troops of Wincke, and brought
Lambert's brigade into line, Picton's infantry still making
good their positions, and Vivian and Vandeleur's squadrons
still covering the extreme left. The allied front was thus
greatly contracted, and presented a formidable line of
resistance; it nearly held the ground originally held by
what we have called Wellington's main order of battle.

Seventy-seven squadrons, from 10,000 to 11,000 horsemen, all splendid troops of the best quality, had ere long
begun the third great cavalry attack. These imposing
masses were once more assembled within the narrow space
in the low land between La Haye Sainte and Hougoumont; they were literally packed together in their dense
ranks. Once more, and in a greater degree than before,
they presented an easy mark to the allied batteries, which
played on them with destructive effect. Men and horses
were quickly struck down in hundreds; but the shouts of
'Vive l'Empereur!' rent the troubled air; and once more,
covered by a tremendous fire from their own guns, the
surging torrent of horsemen struggled up the ridge, and
became masters of the enemy's cannon in their front.
Once more they rushed down on the squares before them,
assailing them fruitlessly indeed, but with dauntless
courage; once more they recoiled from the volleys they
could not reply to; once more they were driven back by

the allied cavalry, and were compelled to re-form, baffled, but still ardent, in the valley below.

These furious charges were repeated over and over again. Wellington said to Jomini afterwards that 'nothing finer was ever seen in war'; but the results obtained were very far from commensurate with the enormous havoc wrought among these noble but doomed horsemen.* It was in vain that the twofold line of squares was penetrated and attacked on every side; that, in the Duke's language, 'the French cavalry rode around our squares as if they had been their own.' It was in vain that Piré plied his guns from a distance; that little bodies of infantry crept up to the ridge, and endeavoured to search the enemy with their fire; that light artillery, moved up the slope, made deadly discharges; that, when the assailants were forced back, the French batteries far away opened with fatal results upon the infantry of the defence. In these reiterated, and even heroic, charges, not a single square was borne down by an attack pressed home; and if perhaps two or three auxiliary squares gave way—and even this is extremely doubtful—not a British or German Legionary square was broken.† No doubt the losses of the allies were great, especially from the fire directed against them; no doubt the moral effect of the attacks was immense in the case, we shall see, of Wellington's inferior troops. But the meteor flag of England still continued to wave on that death-strewn ground; like the 'deep Scottish circle' at Flodden, the invincible squares— it appears these were sixteen in number—withstood the

* 'Précis de la Campagne de 1815,' 210: 'Le Duc de Wellington m'a assuré lui-même qu'il n'avait jamais rien vu de plus admirable, à la guerre, que les dix ou douze charges réitérées des cuirassiers Français sur les troupes de toutes armes.'

† Most French writers insist that several British squares were broken and several British colours taken. The contrary is certainly the fact; there is no real evidence that even an auxiliary square was broken.

desperate efforts made to break them up, and by degrees every charge became weaker and weaker; the French horsemen, their battle steeds exhausted, their officers having fallen in scores, slowly losing heart, brave men as they were, began to feel they could not overcome their enemy.* It deserves notice that, though some of the allied guns, when in the hands of the French for a moment, were overturned and made useless, not one was spiked.

The allied right and right centre had thus withstood the succession of attacks directed against it, as the left and left centre had defeated the attack of D'Erlon. At one point only, in Wellington's front, had anything like a real impression been made; the capture and occupation of La Haye Sainte by the French had made a dangerous gap in the Duke's centre, which might have given a great opportunity to Ney, had the Marshal known how to turn it to account; but Ney, disobeying his master's orders, had neglected, we have seen, to hold this post, and to make it a base for future attacks, which possibly might have given France a victory, and he had recklessly 'massacred my cavalry,' in Napoleon's bitter phrase, in repeated efforts inevitably without decisive results.

* It would be most unjust to question the splendid courage of the French cavalry at Waterloo; but these charges were badly conducted even as cavalry charges. Uxbridge, an impartial judge and a noble-hearted soldier, wrote afterwards ('Waterloo Letters,' 10) : 'The French very frequently attacked our squares, but never in overwhelming masses, and with that vigour and speed which would have given them some chance of penetrating. No heavy mass, having a well-formed front, actually came collectively against our bayonets. Constantly a few devoted fellows did clash with them, and some pierced between the squares, and when I had not cavalry at hand I frequently entered the squares for protection. In the afternoon a very heavy attack was made upon the whole of our line on the right of the road, and connecting itself with the troops attacking Hougoumont. It was chiefly made and frequently repeated by masses of cuirassiers, but never in one connected line, and after the first grand attack of the morning they never came on with the degree of vigour which could give them a hope of penetrating into our immovable squares of infantry.'

But though the great cavalry attacks had comparatively failed, it is not to be supposed they had been fruitless. Many guns of the allies had been dismounted; the sabre, the lance, the musketoon, the pistol, in the hands of determined and trained soldiers had not been useless. The French squadrons trampled down in their repeated charges hundreds of men caught in the act of forming square. The enfilading fire of Piré, too, had done much mischief, though not so great as it ought to have done; the skirmishing footmen had wrought a great deal of havoc; above all, the concentrated fire of the distant French batteries had laid thousands of brave men in the dust. Nearly all the squares had been fearfully straitened; some were mere skeletons of fine bodies that had been wasted away; the men in all were weary, exhausted, well-nigh worn out. The principal effect, however, of the cavalry onslaughts had, as always, been of a moral kind; this had been in no ordinary degree disastrous. The very best troops in the squares felt it difficult to endure 'the frightful sameness,' as it had been called, of a defence against charges made ten, or even twelve, times; they became impatient, angry, eager for their revenge. 'When shall we get at them?' was a cry often bursting from the ranks, and yet such a movement might have been fatal. The inferior troops were sometimes too terrified or too ill-disciplined to fall into the formations that alone could give safety; in this situation they were either cut to pieces or swelled an ever-increasing crowd of fugitives making away from the field by the great main-road to Brussels.*

* Major Mercer ('Waterloo Letters,' 218) thus describes an attempt made by a raw body of Brunswickers to form a square: 'Their ranks, loose and disjointed, presented gaps of several files in breadth, which the officers and sergeants were busily employed filling up by pushing, and even thumping, their men together; while these, standing like so many logs, with their arms at the recover, were apparently completely

The worst effects, however, were seen in the auxiliary cavalry; the squadrons of Van Merlen and Trip were unable to withstand the shock of the mailed horsemen of Milhaud and Kellermann. One Hanoverian regiment of hussars, damned to everlasting fame, rode away with its commander by the Duke's orders; the poltroon had refused to cross swords with cuirassiers. The cavalry of Arentschild and Dornberg, and the remains of Somerset's and Ponsonby's brigades, had to do the work of these men; the two brigades had dwindled down to a mere handful of troopers. Wellington, in fact, had been nearly left without cavalry, if we except the brigades of Vivian and Vandeleur on his left.

In these great attacks Ney had justified his proud title; he had been the 'bravest of the brave' in a brave army. Repeatedly he led the charges in person, harangued his men with impassioned words and gestures; more than once stood boldly by a captured gun, defying the enemy with the sword he boldly waved. But this was the conduct of a soldier, not of a General-in-Chief;* he directed recklessly and badly this part of the battle. Apart from his disobedience of his master's orders, and from his turning away from La Haye Sainte, and not waiting until a decisive movement had been made from that point against the Duke's centre—a movement that might have had immense results—Ney had neglected to employ the only means that might have gained for his noble cavalry real success.

The enfilading fire of Piré on the French left was much less effective than it might have been, and it ought to have been supported by an enfilading fire from La Haye

stupefied and bewildered. I should add that they were all perfect children. None of the privates, perhaps, were above eighteen years of age.'

* So Livy says of one of Hannibal's opponents, a mere fighting man (xxv. 19): 'Tanquam eadem militares et imperatoriæ artes essent.'

Sainte on the right, which must have told severely upon the infantry of the defence. Had this twofold artillery attack been made, the squares would have been raked, and must have frightfully suffered; some probably could not have stood their ground; this would have perhaps trebled the power of the cavalry of the attack. But where Ney was most wanting, and was even very remiss—his mind, as on the 16th, had not its true balance—was seen in his neglect to make any effective use of the masses of infantry on the ground. The whole of Bachelu's division and part of that of Foy might have been safely withdrawn from the fruitless assaults on Hougoumont.* This post, which had cost such a vain waste of life, might even have been masked for a time;† they might have been moved to the crest of the ridge to support the horsemen; the squares would have been compelled to deploy to resist the footmen. This would certainly have greatly added to the power of the attack, even if the result had remained uncertain, when we recollect how the Duke's right centre had been reinforced. Ney, in short, as had been the case at Quatre Bras, did not employ the force which he might have employed; he did not make, or even attempt to make, a proper use of the three arms, which if possible ought always to act in concert; without artillery and infantry in sufficient force on the spot, he almost threw away the superb cavalry.‡

* See H. Houssaye, 'Waterloo,' ii. 376, where this is well pointed out. See also Foy, cited by H. Houssaye *in loco*, and 'Waterloo Letters,' 256, 305.

† Marbot ('Mémoires,' ii. 476) significantly says: 'Nous nous obstinâmes a attaquer les fermes de La Haye Sainte et de Hougoumont, au lieu de les masquer par une division et de marcher sur les lignes anglaises déjà fortement ébranlées. Nous arrivons en le temps de les détruire avant l'arrivée des Prussiens ce qui nous aurait assuré la victoire.'

‡ Mr. Ropes ('The Campaign of Waterloo,' 309, 310) has made excellent comments on the faulty tactics of Ney in this part of the battle: 'Marshal Ney determined to carry the allied centre by charges

It is difficult, too, to acquit Napoleon altogether from blame in this most important matter. No doubt, as was his wont, he had entrusted the direction of the attack to a well-tried lieutenant; no doubt he was engaged at this very time with Bulow, and really was fighting two battles; and he was endeavouring to resist a most dangerous offensive movement. But the Emperor appears to have given no orders to the Marshal, during this phase of the conflict, to turn to account the infantry at hand; assuredly such orders might have been given. And for a short time Napoleon had an opportunity, it would seem, to employ a part at least of the Imperial Guard. Bulow had been repulsed by the Young Guard; his attack was for the present suspended. Had even* 6,000 or 7,000 men of the Old Guard, supported by artillery, been directed, at this crisis of the battle, along the great main-road beyond

---

of cavalry. He seems to have made no effort to support this attack by the infantry of the 2nd corps, although it would certainly have been quite possible to have withdrawn at least Bachelu's division from the wood of Hougoumont, and to have used it with good effect. . . . No use whatever was made of the very great advantage afforded by the position of La Haye Sainte for the posting of batteries which should sweep the whole line of the allies, dismount their guns, riddle their squares, and render their infantry unable to resist the shock of cavalry.'

* Charras is a systematic libeller of Napoleon; his gross injustice mars the value of a very able work, and his criticisms of Napoleon are always to be received with suspicion. But we believe there is truth in the following passage (ii. 84), though the danger of Bulow's attack must be borne in mind, and it is easy to be wise after the event: 'Du moment où, abandonnant bien à tort son projet de forcer l'aile gauche des Anglo-Hollandais, Napoléon s'était décidé à diriger l'effort principal contre leur centre, il fallait qu'il l'y portât rapidement. Sans hésiter, il devait alors faire appuyer les escadrons de Ney par toute l'infanterie de la Vieille Garde, par cinquante bouches à feu, et laisser à Lobau, et à la division de la Jeune Garde, le soin de contenir les Prussiens de Bulow le plus long temps possible. C'eût été, sans doute, une détermination bien grave, bien périlleuse; mais c'était la seule qui présentât quelque chances de succès; et plus elle était différée, plus ces chances déjà bien faibles, diminuaient.'

18

La Haye Sainte against Wellington's centre, the consequence might have been momentous in the extreme.
Napoleon did not employ this splendid reserve; perhaps—
for he did not know what British infantry was—he
believed that Ney would succeed with cavalry alone, as
had often happened in the case of the weaker Austrian
footmen; perhaps he judged that it was impossible to
move a man of the Guard until Bulow had been driven
back completely—and the Prussian attack on his flank
was of the most formidable kind; perhaps he thought
Wellington's forces almost exhausted.   But he did not
take a decisive step at this moment—we may probably
see in this conduct the want of readiness, of sudden inspiration, of perfect self-confidence, we sometimes see in
the Napoleon of the campaign of 1815.

The conduct of Wellington during this phase of
Waterloo stands in striking contrast with that of Ney.
Unquestionably he had overlooked the importance of La
Haye Sainte.   It may have been well for him that this
important post was not attacked as Napoleon had intended.   But his tactics were admirable in every other
respect.   He reinforced his right centre at the proper
moment; he distributed his forces with great skill at most
points on the field; he husbanded his resources with remarkable judgment.   Years after Waterloo he said that
Napoleon had won most of his victories by the power of
artillery; he did not add that the Emperor failed at
Waterloo partly because the Duke had taken care that his
army should be exposed as little as possible to its fire.
His calm constancy, too, in this desperate conflict compared well with the impetuous recklessness of the French
Marshal.

Very probably, as he looked at his fast-diminishing line,
he felt that he had done wrong in leaving a great detachment at Hal and Tubize: assuredly he had expected
Blucher to be on the field in force many hours before.

But his stern confidence never gave way for an instant; as, vigilant, active, watching every turn in the fight, he rode from point to point along his imperilled front, he never lost his self-reliance and steadfast presence of mind. 'Hard pounding this, gentlemen,' he said to his staff; 'but let us see who can pound hardest.' 'Stand firm, men,' he exclaimed, as he threw himself more than once into a square. 'What would they say of us in England if we were beaten?' He, in short, multiplied himself like Richmond over the field, and was the master spirit of a magnificent defence. He no doubt felt he was in grave danger; the words 'Night or Blucher' fell from his lips; but he never flinched or thought of retreat. To anxious lieutenants seeking his orders he held the same laconic but noble language: 'Hold out to the last man; go on with the fight. If there is nothing else to be done, stand and die at your posts.'

Had the Archduke Charles been in Wellington's place, he would probably have fallen back at this juncture, as he did at Wagram; but Wellington was made of sterner stuff. Napoleon more than once believed he was drawing off the field, but the strong-hearted Englishman had no such idea in his mind; and this tenacity and determination were at last rewarded. The diversion made by Bulow gave him immense relief. He had learned by this time that other Prussian supports were not distant, and at about six, or some time after, Ney's attack had altogether slackened; the Marshal, in fact, had sent word to his master that he must have fresh infantry to continue the struggle.

'Infantry! Where am I to find them? Do you wish me to make them?' was Napoleon's angry reply to Ney's aide-de-camp, Heymès. At this moment the attack of Bulow had become formidable in the highest degree, and almost successful.* The Prussians, as usual, inspired by

* The reader should again notice the immense importance of Bulow's attack. Justice has not been done to it by most English

their old chief, had returned in force, and furiously assailed Plancenoit. The Young Guard had recoiled after a murderous struggle; the village had been seized and at last occupied; the Prussian guns were again directed against the Emperor's right flank; their projectiles occasionally reached the great main-road, the only line of retreat of the French army. Napoleon had no choice but to ward off this most dangerous attack. We do not agree with those critics who contend that at this grave conjuncture he could have weakened the Guard and detached a part of it to fall on Wellington's centre; the occasion, if it existed, had by this time been lost. He had already three or four battalions of this noble array guarding his rear from between Rossomme and Caillou; eight battalions, the Young Guard, had been engaged; he had only twelve or thirteen remaining in hand.

He now sent off two battalions of the Old Guard to reinforce the troops driven out of Plancenoit, and held the others in reserve to await events. He really had nothing he could safely despatch to Ney, and he was indignant with his lieutenant when made aware how his magnificent cavalry had been wasted. He told the aide-de-camp that the Marshal must bide his time, must renew the attack with infantry and horsemen combined, but must be less reckless and incautious than he had been. He added that if the Prussians were repulsed he would support Ney with the Imperial Guard, and fall on Wellington with all that he could spare of that mighty force. The effect of the attack of the handful of the Old Guard was extraordinary, and for a time decisive. They marched against the enemy in their disciplined strength, sustained by the other French troops on the spot. Nothing withstood that terrible and weighty effort.

---

writers, though the legend that the Prussians only reached Waterloo to complete a victory has been long exploded even in England.

After a struggle not lasting half an hour, Plancenoit was retaken, and the defeated men of Bulow were driven backward nearly into the defiles of the Lasne. Bulow seemed to be completely—nay, irretrievably—repulsed; Napoleon's flank was for the present secure; Lobau, Subervie, and Domon distinctly gained ground, and even approached the Bois de Paris.

Ney angrily chafed at his master's message, but set himself at last to conform to his orders. A pause took place after the great cavalry attacks; the main French batteries continued their work of destruction. Ere long masses of infantry and cavalry issued from around Hougoumont, and made several efforts against the allied right centre. These attacks were made too late, and proved vain.* The French squadrons had become a wreck; the French footmen had cruelly suffered; the battalions of Duplat and W. Halkett, comparatively fresh and admirably placed along the front assailed, were able to drive the enemy back in defeat. At two important points, however, of Wellington's line distinct advantages were gained by the French, which show how much might have, perhaps, been achieved, had well-combined attacks been made three hours before, with cavalry still unbroken, and with infantry not exhausted.

On Napoleon's extreme right Papelotte was mastered by Durutte. The attack was made by the Emperor's positive orders. The occupation of this post cut the Duke off from Bulow, and greatly strengthened the menaced French wing; and D'Erlon's troops by this time, re-formed and rested, made formidable onsets on the allied left and left centre. The most important success, however, was attained at La Haye Sainte, comparatively neglected for some time, since Ney had turned away to begin the great cavalry attacks. Guns were brought up to this point,

* See authorities collected in H. Houssaye ('Waterloo,' ii. 377), especially the notes of Foy and the 'Waterloo Letters.'

which, though soon silenced, wrought havoc in Alten's dwindling division. French infantry advanced beyond it, and kept up a destructive fire from the great main-road on the Duke's weakened and now imperilled centre. The consequences were grave in the highest degree. They have been faithfully described by an impartial and able eye-witness, who beheld them from the ground held by Alten's men with dismay. 'La Haye Sainte was in the hands of the enemy, also the knoll on the opposite side of the road, also the garden and ground on the Anglo-allied side of it. Ompteda's brigade was nearly annihilated, and Kilmansegge's so thinned that these two brigades could not hold their position. That part of the field of battle, therefore, which was between Halkett's* left and Kempt's right was unprotected, and, being the very centre of the Duke's line of battle, was consequently that point above all others which the enemy wished to gain. The danger was imminent, and at no other period of the action was the result so precarious as at this moment.'†

It was now near seven o'clock in the evening; the battle was in no sense decided. Fortune cast on Napoleon a cruel smile. The attack of Bulow seemed completely spent; his columns had almost disappeared from the scene; the cannon of Grouchy at a distance was distinctly heard; the Marshal would surely hold the rest of the Prussian army in check. Blucher, as the Emperor continued to believe, with the obstinate conviction that sometimes possessed his mind, would not dare to advance from Wavre in force. In front Wellington's line had been greatly thinned and weakened; the reserves of the Duke could be hardly descried; the great main-road to Brussels was choked with terror-stricken fugitives.

Napoleon resolved to make a decisive attack on the

---

* C. Halkett, not to be confounded with W. Halkett, of Clinton's division.

† Shaw Kennedy, 'Battle of Waterloo,' 124.

allied centre, combined with an attack on the whole line.
The Imperial Guard was to make the principal attack;
but the Emperor had not the great and intact force with
which he had easily broken the Prussian centre at Ligny.
To outward seeming he retained the look of serene confidence he usually wore in the shock of battle. He still
believed that victory was within his power; but it is
difficult to suppose that he had not some misgivings in
offering this last challenge to Fate. The aspect and
feelings of his lieutenants were very different. Soult had
had gloomy forebodings from the first; Ney, still ready
to fight, was in a savage mood; Reille and D'Erlon had
wellnigh lost heart; the chiefs of the cavalry did not
conceal their anger. The soldiery, too, were not in a
trustworthy state; several officers had deserted in the
face of the enemy; signs of indiscipline and demoralisation abounded; loud murmurs were heard that the Guard
had been spared; distrust, suspicion, discontent prevailed.
In the opposite camp Wellington had also cause for doubt
and anxiety. His army, it has been said, was reduced by
20,000 men, so many auxiliaries had left the ranks; his
centre had been opened by the fall of La Haye Sainte.
But he had still a considerable and good reserve, of which
his adversary knew little or nothing; he could still rely
on his British and German soldiery; above all, he had
learned that a great Prussian force was near. As confident as Napoleon, and with better reason, he girded up
his loins for the final struggle, made preparations to
resist the impending attack, and sternly awaited the issue
of events.

CHAPTER X

THE ATTACK AND DEFEAT OF THE IMPERIAL GUARD—
IRRUPTION OF ZIETEN AND PIRCH — ROUT AND
FLIGHT OF THE FRENCH ARMY — GROUCHY AT
WAVRE

State of the battle before the final attack — Views of Napoleon
and Wellington — Pirch approaches to support Bulow, and
Zieten to assist Wellington's left—Dangerous position of the
allied army at about 7 p.m.—Advance of part of the Imperial
Guard—Brilliant efforts made by D'Erlon—Reille and the cavalry
backward—Ney conducts the attack—He again makes mistakes—
Struggle between the Imperial Guard and the troops defending
the allied right centre—Defeat of the Imperial Guard—Advance
of Wellington's army—Irruption of Zieten on Napoleon's extreme
right—Irruption of Pirch and Bulow on Napoleon's right flank
and rear—Flight and rout of the French army—Pursuit by part
of the Prussian army—Hideous scenes of terror and despair—The
operations of Grouchy on June 18, after he had rejected the
counsels of Gérard.

WE may glance for a moment at the state of the battle
while Napoleon was preparing his final attack. The
carnage in both armies had been immense. Except at
Borodino, and perhaps at Eylau, nothing like it had
been seen on any stricken field in the wars that grew
out of the French Revolution; and the conflict had
extended over a comparatively narrow space. The
French had lost the greater number of killed and
wounded; but the allies had been even more weakened

by the flight of thousands of bad auxiliary troops and desertion. From Napoleon's point of view there was still a prospect of a victory that might have a real moral effect, though he must have felt for hours that this could not be decisive. His right flank and rear, lately so gravely imperilled, appeared for the present secure from the enemy; Bulow's attack had been completely repulsed; a large part of the Guard held Plancenoit in force; Lobau, Subervie, and Domon had advanced towards the Bois de Paris; Durutte had captured and occupied Papelotte. On his left the assailants of Hougoumont had reached the enemy's main front. The château was a mass of burning ruins. Though the garden and the enclosures had not been taken, the defence had for some time slackened, and hundreds of Wellington's best troops had perished on the spot. Before his centre La Haye Sainte had fallen. His troops had access nearly to the midst of the allied position. In the attacks they had made on this vital point they had achieved success that was full of promise. The Duke's line was in grave danger along a considerable space. No doubt thousands of brave men had been sacrificed, with little result, in the wasteful attacks on Hougoumont; no doubt Ney had thrown away the noble French cavalry, and this was now unequal to any great efforts. But the corps of D'Erlon had recovered from its defeat; the soldiery had become active and daring again; and the Emperor had still nearly half of the Guard, fresh and full of heart, to make the decisive onslaught. And, we repeat, Napoleon at this crisis believed that Bulow had not the means to attack again. The cannon of Grouchy seemed approaching with increasing roar. Napoleon was convinced that his lieutenant would assuredly prevent the rest of the Prussian army from reaching the field. And, we repeat, he thought that Wellington had exhausted the reserves, which the Duke had husbanded and kept out of sight; and he saw that flying masses were crowding the great main-road to Brussels. Napoleon, therefore, had still hopes of victory, if his calculations were opposed to the facts ; and, besides, as he had shown throughout his career, he would never hear of a retreat on a field of battle ; a daring offensive, even in difficult straits, was always in his judgment the true course to follow.*   It is utterly unjust, as partisans have done, to represent his last attack at Waterloo as the desperate venture of a merely reckless gambler.

Wellington, on the other hand, had, from his point of view, good hopes of victory at this conjuncture ; and as he knew much better than his antagonist could know what the real position of affairs on the scene was, his point of view was more complete and accurate.   Unquestionably his whole line—especially at La Haye Sainte, where his centre had been weakened almost to breaking-point—was in more than one place in very grave danger.   Unquestionably his losses had been enormous : the flower of his cavalry, even of his choicest footmen, had perished ; his auxiliaries had largely disappeared from the field ; his army had been reduced, we have seen, to an appalling

* So, after severely blaming the Grand Condé's strategy and tactics at Nordlingen, Napoleon praises Condé for having risked everything on a final attack ('Comment.,' vi. 203). The Emperor was probably thinking of Waterloo : 'Condé a mérité la victoire par cette opiniâtreté, cette rare intrépidité, qui le distinguait, car, si elle ne lui a servi de rien dans l'attaque d'Allerheim, c'est elle qui lui a conseillé, après avoir perdu son centre et sa droite, de recommencer le combat avec sa gauche, la seule troupe qui lui restât. . . .   Des observateurs d'un esprit ordinaire diront qu'il eut dû se servir de l'aile, qui était encore intacte, pour opérer sa retraite, et ne pas hasarder son reste ; mais avec de tels principes, un général est certain de manquer toutes les occasions de succès, et d'être constamment battu. . . .   La gloire et l'honneur des armes est le premier devoir qu'un général qui livre bataille doit considérer ; la salut et la conservation des hommes n'est que secondaire.   Mais c'est aussi dans cette audace, dans cette opiniâtreté, que se trouvent le salut et la conservation des hommes ; car quand bien même le Prince de Condé se fut mis en retraite . . . il eût presque tout perdu.'

extent. But, partly owing to mistakes made by Ney and others, partly to his own admirable skill and energy, and to the heroic constancy of his British and German soldiery, he had successfully resisted every attack ; and he had just strengthened, for the moment, the defence of La Haye Sainte by sending a detachment of Brunswickers to the spot. In Chassé's division, too, he had a reserve still intact ; though the brigades of Adam, of Duplat, and of W. Halkett had suffered heavily, and had been engaged for hours, and all these troops, with Mitchell's brigade, now formed part of the front of the allied right centre, they were still able to make a formidable stand ; while on the allied left Picton's division and the troops of Lambert and Best, though harassed by the efforts of D'Erlon's swarms of skirmishers, were still manfully holding their ground, and the horsemen of Vivian and Vandeleur were wellnigh fresh.

The Duke, besides, had for fully two hours received most important support from Bulow ; indeed, but for this powerful and opportune diversion, which exposed the right, and even the rear, of Napoleon, to attacks that might have become fatal, and arrested the movement of the Imperial Guard, the allies, despite the errors and the shortcomings of the French, would most probably have been driven off the field. At this moment Bulow had been repulsed ; but Wellington had for some time been in communication with his loyal and aged colleague, and he had been informed that the attack would be soon renewed by the reinforcements already at hand. These reinforcements were part of the corps of Pirch. This body of men, we have seen, had been greatly delayed, having been entangled as they advanced with the corps of Bulow ; half, we have said, had not crossed the Dyle until two in the afternoon ; the other half had, in some degree, been held in check by a detachment of Grouchy's army ; and the march to St. Lambert and the Lasne had been very slow and difficult. But two of its divisions and its cavalry were now close to Bulow, and these, with the whole of Bulow's remaining forces, were about to make once more the attack on Napoleon's flank and rear, which had not only paralysed the French army, but had placed it for a time in no doubtful peril. An armed host, concealed from the Emperor's sight, was soon to issue from the woods and defiles of the Lasne to give assistance to Wellington that might prove decisive, and that must be of extreme importance.

This was not, however, the only, or even the most necessary, support which Wellington at this critical moment knew was to be afforded him by the Prussian army. Zieten, we have seen, had been encamped around Biérges—that is, on the western bank of the Dyle ; he had been kept, with Thielmann, near Wavre, to defend the place, and to observe the movements of Grouchy ; he had been sent off to take part in the great fight at Waterloo, Grouchy not having appeared on the scene by mid-day ; he had advanced by roads north of those followed by Bulow and Pirch, but in a parallel line, by Rixensart and Genval. His troops, however, had been confused with those of Pirch, as those of Pirch had been confused with those of Bulow ; his march, accordingly, had been greatly delayed. It was not far from six o'clock when his advanced guard reached Ohain, nearly two miles from Wellington's lines, and divided from them by a far from easy country.*

The Duke had despatched an aide-de-camp to urge Zieten to come to his aid, 'were it only with some 3,000 men ';† but Zieten hesitated, and even refused, for a time : 'he would not advance until he had all his troops in hand.' In truth, with the one exception of Blucher, every Prussian General was very cautious—nay, timid—on this memorable day. Zieten sent a staff officer to

* Ollech, 193, 194 ; H. Houssaye, 'Waterloo,' ii. 389.
† Letter of Major-General Freemantle, 'Waterloo Letters,' 21, 22.

observe the course of the battle ; his messenger was on the scene just at the moment when the attacks around La Haye Sainte had become most dangerous. He reported to his superior that Wellington's centre was giving way, and that the allied army was about to retreat in a disastrous flight, preceded by a horde of terrified fugitives. The Prussian commander, afraid of being involved in a rout that might be fatal, turned his men towards Frischermont and the Bois de Paris, in order to get into line with Bulow. The movement would have drawn him away from Wellington, and might have left the Duke and his hard-pressed army in the gravest straits. Most fortunately, however, for the allied cause, Muffling, the Prussian Commissioner, was on the spot. He told Zieten that Wellington was still holding his ground, but adjured him to march at once to support the Duke's left. The battle was in a most critical state ; a moment's delay, and it might be lost. Zieten, persuaded by this wise and most timely counsel, pushed forward with one division and a part of his cavalry from Ohain towards Papelotte and Smohain. Not long after seven his foremost horsemen had just attained this part of the field. Muffling, too, as he had hastened to join the Duke, had informed Vivian and Vandeleur, on the allied left, that Zieten was at hand, and that they were free to march to the assistance of their chief.* They made ready to give him support now most surely needed. Wellington, therefore, grave as his danger was, felt that certain and speedy relief was at hand.

It was now not far from half-past seven o'clock. All had been made ready for the decisive attack on Welling-

---

* For this important episode of Waterloo, see Muffling, ' Passages of my Life,' 246, 249. Muffling is rather given to boasting, but his statements, no doubt, are essentially correct. See also Ollech, 243, 244 ; H. Houssaye, ' Waterloo,' ii. 388. The reader will observe that the diversion made by Zieten was as important as that wrought by Bulow, if not more so.

ton's line, along his whole front. As before, the conduct
of this was entrusted to Ney, supported by D'Erlon and
Reille, on the French right and left, and by the surviving
cavalry chiefs; not a few of these had been slain or
disabled. The Marshal, as before, was given the fullest
freedom of action, and received no directions from his
master. But Napoleon kept the Imperial Guard in his
own hands, and formed it in person, to sustain and complete the great final movement. As usual, the attack was
heralded by a fierce, continuous cannonade. The French
batteries—their fire had never ceased—redoubled their
deadly discharges with fatal effect along the points of
vantage on which they were placed. Under their protection, as usual, the French columns advanced. But the
onset of Reille's troops was feeble and slow; they had
been wasted in the vain attacks on Hougoumont. They
still gathered around the fatal spot; they did not press
forward boldly against the enemy on the ridge.* The
ruined French cavalry, too, could not do much. It had
been partly re-formed in the low ground, from which it
had swept onward confident of assured victory; it was
now only able to menace and to hold in check the infantry
in its front, and to occupy the space it filled to prevent a
counter-attack.

It seems probable, however, that a large part of Reille's
corps could have been detached—as it might have been
detached before in the case of the great cavalry charges—
to second the supreme effort now being made; and Piré's
horsemen, who had been but slightly engaged, could have
been moved from the road from Nivelles to Brussels, and
been employed in supporting the attack on the left.†
Here again we see the want of forethought and judgment

* See H. Houssaye, 'Waterloo,' ii. 393, and the authorities *in loco*
carefully collected.

† This is well pointed out by Mr. Ropes, 'Campaign of Waterloo,'
337; and see pp. 317, 318.

so conspicuous in Ney at Quatre Bras and Waterloo;
this, and another false movement we shall soon notice,
was the fourth great error in the tactics of the French on
June 18. On Napoleon's right, however, and on his right
centre, the attack was vigorously and very ably directed;
for a short time it was all but successful. While Durutte
and Marcognet assailed and held fast the infantry of
Lambert, of Picton, of Best, and even attained the summit
of the ridge, D'Erlon moved the divisions of Allix and
Donzelot close to the great main-road, on either side of it.
A most determined attack was made from La Haye Sainte
on this already shattered and weakened part of the allied
line. Once more a wide and yawning gap was made in
Wellington's centre; the Brunswickers, who had filled it,
suddenly gave way. A large part of Alten's division,
which had already suffered enormous loss, was wellnigh
destroyed.* Indeed, the Duke's centre would probably
have been stormed and forced at this poiut—with what
results it is impossible to say—had not Vivian, followed
ere long by Vandeleur, and set free by the approach of
Zieten, most opportunely come up to support the defence.
Vivian's horsemen were exposed for a time to a destructive
fire, to which they had little or nothing to oppose. The
scales of Fortune hung for a moment in suspense.†

Meanwhile Napoleon had been arraying the Imperial
Guard for the great effort which, he believed, would bring
victory with it. Of the twenty-four battalions‡ comprising this superb force, eight, the Young Guard, we
have seen, had been detached to Plancenoit, to make
head against the first attacks of Bulow; two, followed

---

* The best and most circumstantial account of this remarkable
attack will be found in Siborne, 'The Waterloo Campaign,' 511-516.

† See 'Waterloo Letters,' under the head of 'Vivian's Cavalry
Brigade'; and see especially pp. 158, 159, 178, 179.

‡ Thiers ('Histoire du Consulat et de l'Empire,' vi. 499) says that
after Ligny the twenty-four battalions of the Guard were reduced to
twenty-three; but he gives no authority for the statement.

by a third, had repulsed the subsequent attacks; three guarded the line of the army's retreat at Rossomme, Caillou, and, further to the right, at Chantelet. Even if there had been no necessity still to observe the Prussians, all these troops were distant from the immediate scene of action; the Emperor had therefore only ten battalions in hand,* to be engaged in any event in the final attack.

Napoleon, who, at this crisis of his fate, showed himself to be equal to his former self, and gave proof of great energy and presence of mind, harangued this splendid soldiery as they defiled before him between La Belle Alliance and La Haye Sainte; he cheerfully told them they 'were to sup at Brussels;' 'they had but to deal a last blow on an exhausted enemy.' It was certainly his purpose that the whole of this force, from 5,000 to 6,000 veterans of proved renown, should be launched in one great attack against Wellington's line; but an interval of a few hundred yards divided six battalions at the front from four battalions following in the rear; an untoward incident, sudden and unforeseen, caused him to change the dispositions he had made. On his extreme right the troops of Durutte appeared to be in confusion, even giving way; a movement of disorder was seen in his re-formed squadrons, some of which were approaching the slopes of the ridge; sinister rumours reached him that fresh Prussian columns were on the march, and drawing near Smohain.

The Emperor saw the peril impending, and did not hesitate; it was of supreme importance that at this

---

* From Napoleon's narrative ('Comment,' v. 182, 183), it may be inferred that the Emperor had twelve battalions of the Guard at his disposal, but this seems to be an error. Charras, who has taken great pains to ascertain the truth, has proved (ii. 51) that the number was ten, and M. H. Houssaye substantially agrees. Of these ten battalions, six were given to Ney, and the remaining four kept in hand by Napoleon. English writers are quite wrong in maintaining that ten or twelve battalions of the Guard joined in the final attack.

moment discouragement should not fall on his army, and that the attack should be pressed at once; he addressed a few confident words to his officers at hand, sent aide-de-camp after aide-de-camp to reassure the troops of Durutte, and caused the intelligence to be spread far and wide, that Grouchy and his whole army were close to the field, and that a last effort of endurance would secure victory.* At the same time, for not a minute was to be lost, he placed the six foremost battalions at the disposal of Ney, who was to conduct the attack of the Guard; he again gave the Marshal no express order, but he added that he would support Ney with the four rear-ward battalions, which it was his purpose to lead in person against the enemy, as in the days of Arcola, Castiglione, and other scenes of his youth. Napoleon, of course, believed that the second attack would be made in immediate succession to the first; but this expectation was to prove vain. The second attack was never to take place; the result, as we follow the course of events, could hardly have affected the final issue; but the incident certainly was unfortunate.†

The six battalions were part of the Middle Guard, not such veterans as the renowned Old Guard, but soldiers of equally high quality; they were rather more than 3,000 men in number. They seem to have been arrayed in columns of battalions, probably by Napoleon's orders; for the mistake of the morning in the case of the corps of D'Erlon had taught a terrible lesson, and was not made again; the four battalions in the rear were formed by the Emperor himself, on a front of two battalions deployed, with one on

* Napoleon has been severely condemned for having circulated this false information. Exactly the same thing was done by Gneisenau at Ligny, and not a word of censure has been uttered. See H. Houssaye, 'Waterloo,' ii. 174.

† We have adopted in substance Napoleon's account of these incidents ('Comment.,' v. 183, 184). It records his own personal experience, and bears all the marks of truth.

either flank.* The six battalions composed four distinct
masses†—in all probability, close columns; they advanced
in echelons, divided by rather wide intervals of space;
they extended over a front of more than a thousand
yards in width; they were supported by artillery in the
distances between the columns. But on the left they
were not sustained by the troops of Reille, and there was
no cavalry to cover their flanks; as the great cavalry
attacks had not had the help of infantry, this and the
other infantry attacks were now without the help of
cavalry; the three arms in both instances did not act in
concert; the result in both instances was, of course,
disastrous.

The Guard, nevertheless, presented a most imposing
aspect as, amidst the din and roar and confusion of the
strife, this noble soldiery steadily made their way onward.
It was in vain that the enemy's guns rent gaps in their
masses; the ranks were quickly re-formed, and retained
their order; the display of dauntless courage and discipline
was above all praise. But here a grave, perhaps a capital,
mistake was made : the Guard ought to have been moved
along the great main-road, and launched from beyond La
Haye Sainte against Wellington's almost broken centre ;‡
it would have been in comparative shelter had this been

* 'Comment.,' v. 184.

† The French accounts of the attack of the Guard at Waterloo
represent it as having been made in one large column ; the English,
in two. M. H. Houssaye ('Waterloo,' ii. 392, 393) has studied the
subject with great care and research, and has, we think, proved that
both accounts are incorrect, and that the attack was made in four
distinct columns, or perhaps squares, advancing in four echelons, the
right the foremost. There has always been a difficulty, as the point
assailed was more than a thousand yards in extent, to understand
how one, or even two columns, could have spread over this space.
We have followed M. Houssaye's narrative as by far the most trustworthy.

‡ This is well pointed out by General Shaw Kennedy: 'Battle of
Waterloo,' 130.

done, and, with the troops of D'Erlon, it might have gained important success. From some unknown cause, however —perhaps because the ridge was most accessible at this point—Ney directed the Guard against that part of the allied front which had repelled the great cavalry attacks— that is, against the allied right centre; and this was at present, as it had always been, the strongest division of Wellington's line. At this moment, indeed, Vandeleur had come up to support the reserve of Chassé; and this, we have seen, was a large body of men. This false direction given to the Guard, and the absence of Reille's men, with the want of the aid of cavalry, was, we repeat, the fourth great tactical error of the French at Waterloo.

In spite of the tempest of shot directed against it, which made 'its ranks move at times like corn in a wind,' the Guard gradually approached the edge of the ridge in the space between La Haye Sainte and Hougoumont. The masses of bearskins overtopping the tall martial figures presented an easy mark to the enemy's guns; but there was still no sign of disorder or thought of retreat, and the artillery of the Guard wrought no little havoc on the allied line arrayed to resist the attack. The first echelon on the right assailed a body of Brünswickers, and put it to flight; it took possession of a British battery; it then turned fiercely against the left of Halkett's brigade, supported by a biting fire from the troops of Allix on its right, com- manded, as in the forenoon, by Quiot. This part of Halkett's men was composed of the British 30th and 73rd, which had been greatly exposed and had suffered heavy loss; whether from a mere accident, as some of its officers have declared, or from the effect of the onset of fresh troops, it recoiled, and for a moment was in more or less confusion.* The Guard, passing the summit of the

* French writers naturally attribute this incident to the efforts of the Guard, and possibly may be correct. On the other hand, British officers have represented it as due to the sudden interference of

ridge, seemed about to pierce through the enemy's line; Friant, a veteran chief of great distinction, who had been at its head, and had just been wounded, returned to the Emperor, and reported that there was not a doubt of victory.

But at this critical moment relief was at hand from the reserve, so carefully husbanded and placed by Wellington on the spot. Chassé, a very able and determined soldier —he had made his mark under Napoleon in 1814, and especially on the bloody day of Arcis-sur-Aube—turned a battery against the French as they advanced, and charged home with half his division at once. Three thousand men easily overthrew little more than 600; the Guard was driven down the slope of the ridge defeated, but still fighting with desperate valour to the last.* Meantime the second echelon of the Guard had fallen upon the right of Halkett's brigade—the 33rd and 69th British, already sorely tried at Quatre Bras, and stricken severely on the 18th for hours; for a moment the assailants had a slight advantage. The Guard, however, was left without support; a fierce struggle, hand-to-hand, followed. But the fire of the British musket and the formidable power of the British bayonet ere long prevailed; the second echelon yielded by degrees, and was, like the first, beaten off and com-

---

another regiment. But that the 30th and 73rd were in trouble for a few minutes is clear from the following ('Waterloo Letters,' 330) : 'That there was great giving way near this point, about this period, is certain enough.'

* The honour of being the first to repel the Imperial Guard certainly belongs to Chassé and his troops. He claimed it in a letter addressed to Lord Hill, and it was substantially acknowledged. See 'Rélation Belge de la Bataille de Waterloo,' 9-11. English writers have, not very creditably, omitted all reference to this most important incident. Siborne ('The Waterloo Campaign,' 525) notices the attack of Chassé's battery, but not the charge of his troops. Charras (ii. 55) is quite accurate in this matter. Sir H. Maxwell, in his 'Biography of Wellington,' published after this note was written (ii. 81), has done justice to Chassé.

pelled to fall back. The men endeavoured to rally in the hollows at the foot of the ridge, but they did not attempt to renew the attack.

The third echelon was composed of two battalions; it formed the principal unit in the attack; it was probably about 1,200 strong.* It advanced in imposing order up the slope of the ridge, throwing out skirmishers along its front like the other columns; Ney and many distinguished officers were at its head. It had apparently suffered less than the two beaten echelons—its artillery had ravaged the hostile line it attacked; it reached the summit of the ridge well-nigh unopposed. Suddenly a wall of scarlet seemed to rise before it: Maitland's Guards, who had been ordered to lie down to avoid the effect of the enemy's fire, leaped up at a word from Wellington's lips; one of those murderous volleys characteristic of British infantry burst on the astounded Guard, which stopped as if paralysed. Three hundred men were stricken down in a moment;† the fifth charger Ney rode on this day fell. The Guard, however, would not confess defeat; but in this, as in all instances, the British line was superior to the French column. The mass, comparatively unwieldy, was unable to deploy, and in the attempt masked its own guns, its only support; the rearward ranks wavered; all became confused. At an opportune moment Maitland's men charged home, and, assisted by part of Halkett's

---

* This was the principal attack of the Guard. This may be the reason that it has been represented as the only one, and made in one column.

† As to the effects of the fire of British infantry, see Jomini, 'Précis de la Campagne de 1815,' 229. See, too, Marbot, ii. 291. Bugeaud also has written strongly in the same sense. The destruction wrought by Maitland's Guards is thus described ('Waterloo Letters,' 257): 'The effect of our volley was evidently most deadly. The French column appeared staggered and, if I may use the expression, convulsed. . . . In less than a minute above 300 went down. . . .' P. 255: 'Part seemed inclined to advance, part halted and fired, others seemed to be turning round.'

troops, drove the shattered column, still resisting, down the fatal slope, their fire and their bayonets completing the defeat.

The fortunes of the fourth echelon were somewhat different. This was not at a great distance from the third.* It advanced to the ridge a little to the east of Hougoumont, unprotected, as it might have been, by Reille's men, and by cavalry, if we except one feeble effort ; it found itself exposed on its left flank to Adam's brigade, which smote it as it marched forward with a destructive fire. The Guard tried to form a front to oppose to the enemy. A bloody conflict of a few minutes followed ; but Colborne, the chief of the British 52nd, renowned in the Peninsular War, an officer of remarkable powers, fell suddenly on the flank of the column, and, supported by the fire of Adam's troops, drove it headlong to the bottom of the slope. 'Well done, Colborne !' Wellington exclaimed ; the Duke had hastened to the spot just in time to see this splendid effort.

The Guard had done all that brave men could do ; but it had made the attack under the worst conditions, un-protected, except by D'Erlon, on both its flanks. It had been directed exactly to the wrong point ; it had to en-counter an enemy, in position, in largely superior numbers, owing to the admirable arrangements made by Wellington ; it had been completely and finally beaten. Very probably the result would have been the same had the four battalions in the rear given the first six their support. The defeat of the Guard—that 'Medusa's head' which had stricken enemies with terror on many a field—sent a thrill of panic through the whole French army. The cry went forth from

* The fourth echelon was so near the third that British writers have described the attack of the Imperial Guard as made in two columns. For the conduct of Maitland's Guards, and of the 52nd, see 'Waterloo Letters,' 241-257, and 271-307. These writings are, of course, not quite accurate, but their object is to tell the truth, and they are very valuable.

Hougoumont to Papelotte, ' The Guard recoils !' The French soldiery felt that all had been staked and lost.

Napoleon's line of battle suddenly gave way; a movement of retreat, becoming more and more disordered, set in from every point on the scene of action; Reille and Piré, to the left, fell back with the defeated Guard, and the mass of the cavalry; Donzelot and Allix abandoned La Haye Sainte ; Marcognet, on the right, drew off with his men from the field. It was now a little after eight o'clock. Wellington seized the occasion with characteristic skill; he directed his army, worn out as it was, against an enemy he knew it need no longer fear; he let the horsemen of Vivian and Vandeleur loose; their squadrons swept the field as they hastened in pursuit, and carried dismay and terror in their almost unresisted progress.*

The beaten host was already beginning to break up, when its dissolution was precipitated by the apparition of a new enemy on the field. Zieten, with the infantry of Steinmetz and the horsemen of Roder, followed by other divisions in the rear—from 10,000 to 12,000 bayonets and sabres—burst on the weak and exhausted body of Durutte's troops. The Prussians had at first been mistaken for the army of Grouchy; but when the appalling truth became known, the French soldiery, deceived by false intelligence, and frantically exclaiming they had been betrayed, fled from Papelotte, and became a mere scattered horde, spreading consternation and despair far and wide. The victorious men of Zieten now passed through the wide gap made in Napoleon's extreme right ; they found nothing in their way to arrest their onset ; their artillery opened on the fugitives with terrible effect; their cavalry ravaged and swept away any enemies they met ; they had soon joined their allies, and both advanced in the flush of triumph against the

* Napoleon especially dwells on the results produced by the cavalry of Vivian and Vandeleur ('Comment.,' v. 184).

main French positions. Within less than half an hour the army, which had all but broken Wellington's centre, and had made such formidable attacks on his line, was hastening from the field in rapidly increasing rout.

Napoleon, like his army, felt that all was over when his Guard had been driven down the slope of the ridge. ' They are all mingled together !' he hurriedly exclaimed. In defeat, however, as in victory, he retained his composure ; he showed remarkable activity and resource in this his last struggle with Fate in war. He formed the four battalions of the Guard into as many squares, and ordered them slowly to fall back ; he hoped to rally his army upon these living citadels ; he charged the squadrons of Vivian and Vandeleur with the squadrons of his escort in vain. The squares of the Guard, islanded in a tumultuous flood of enemies around, and of waves of fugitives, made steadily their way towards La Belle Alliance ; they repulsed more than one fierce attack of cavalry. Rapidly dwindling, as they were, under a fire converging on every side, they sternly maintained their ground against overwhelming numbers.

They might possibly, in some measure, have covered the retreat ; but at this moment another tempest of war broke suddenly on the doomed French host. Pirch had come into line with Bulow, with the horsemen of Jurgass and with the divisions of Tippelskirchen and Krafft ; the attack on Plancenoit and its defenders was renewed ; from 40,000 to 45,000 men fell on an enemy now about 17,000 strong, and, striking at the right flank and rear of Napoleon, endeavoured to seize his only line of retreat and to annihilate his whole army on the spot. A terrible conflict raged for a time ; the French, conscious that everything depended on the stand they could make, fought with an energy and determination worthy of all honour ; the veterans of the Old Guard perished, but sold their lives dearly ; the Young Guard repulsed several furious assaults; Lobau and his troops made an heroic resistance. At last, after a savage hand-to-hand fight, amidst houses in flames, and a street choked with the dead, in which quarter was not sought or given, Plance-noit was stormed, and the remains of the gallant troops which had held it were pressed back, fighting, on the great main-road and confused with the wrecks of the rest of the army. Their noble efforts, however, had not been fruitless; they had kept the avenue of escape open; they had gained time for the ruined host to fly from the fatal field.

It was now nine o'clock; the shadows of night were closing over the scene of the late tremendous conflict. The French army had broken up in multitudinous rout; the four squares of the Guard, alone, maintained at a distance a hopeless struggle; like fierce beasts of prey, hemmed in by the forest hunters, they stood savagely at bay against a host of enemies. It was in vain that more than one British officer called on them to yield and to save their lives; they refused to surrender in words that have gone down to history; they were charged over and over again, but made many of their assailants bite the dust. At last, attacked on all sides, and completely overpowered, they were destroyed, and perished almost to a man.

Meanwhile Napoleon, still hoping against hope, and challenging adverse Fortune to the last, had ridden off to Rossomme and Caillou, and tried to rally the feeble reserve on the spot to make head against the triumphant enemy; but the remains of his army were in headlong flight; he left the scene with three battalions of the Old Guard still in perfect order, and steady as on a parade-ground amidst terrible sights of widespread confusion and despair. The French soldier, formidable, like his fore-father, the Gaul, in success,* has seldom been great and

* Polybius noticed this 2,000 years ago ('Hist.,' ii. 33).

stubborn in defeat; and few beaten armies have been placed in such terrible straits as that of Napoleon was when darkness fell on Waterloo. But the inherent vices in the French army of 1815 can alone explain the frightful spectacle of demoralisation and panic presented in that appalling rout. The want of coherence in an organisation new and untried; the distrust prevailing among officers and men; the shameless desertions that had taken place; the widespread belief that the catastrophe had been caused by treason—all this told with terrible effect on the perishing host and paralysed soldiers who a few hours before had given proof of heroic courage. Not an effort was made to form a rearguard, to make a show of resistance, and to keep back the enemy; broken battalions and squadrons trampled down each other without a thought save of precipitate flight; the great main-road was strewn with abandoned guns and trains, with weapons and armour thrown recklessly away; the fugitives took no heed of the commands of their chiefs, and often broke out against them in angry curses; the chiefs themselves had lost heart and had given up hope. Such scenes of terror, consternation, and despair had not been witnessed even in the retreat from Moscow.

Wellington and Blucher met at La Belle Alliance; each congratulated the other on an immense victory, the most decisive of that age, if we except Trafalgar. The stern nature of the Englishman melted, it is said, into tears at the thought of the many companions in arms he had lost; Blucher's whole soul was bent on revenge for Ligny. Parts of their two armies had been for some time in contact; English and Prussian bands broke out in exulting music; the deafening cheers of the victors rent the air far and near. It was now about half-past nine at night; the exhausted allied army was 'dying of fatigue,' and took its bivouacs on the death-strewn ground; Gneisenau was given the charge of pursuing the enemy in his rout.

By this time the troops of D'Erlon and Lobau, and of the Guard at Plancenoit, caught, as it were, in a vice between two armies, had fallen in great numbers, and had largely been made prisoners; the right wing of the French army had been all but destroyed. But a consider-able part of the centre had escaped, and the corps of Reille and the remains of the beaten cavalry had made their way from the field with comparatively little loss. No attempt, however, was made to rally these men; the armed multitude rolled, like an affrighted herd, onwards, the Prussian sabre and bayonet making havoc among many victims. The pursuit of Gneisenau, however, was not fierce or rapid; the troops of Pirch and Zieten, com-pletely worn out, halted only one or two miles from the field; those of Bulow advanced only four or five; the fugitive host was literally hunted down by a few thousand horsemen, a significant proof of the completeness of the rout. A stand might have been easily made at Genappe; but a few barricades that had been hastily thrown up were abandoned when the enemy's trumpets were heard; the terror-stricken masses crowded into the narrow streets of the town, forgetting the fords of the Dyle hard by; pent up and huddled together, they fought savagely to get through, and time was lost before they continued their flight. Many were captured, and many wounded or slain; but though the Prussians showed little mercy, the tales of butchery and massacre laid to their charge are probably the exaggerations of hatred and fear. The legend that Duhesme, the commander of the Young Guard, a veteran, with the scars of more than twenty years, was immolated in cold blood is happily untrue; he died of his wounds tended by Blucher's own physician. Larrey, too, the well-known Surgeon-General of Napoleon's armies, was saved by the intercession of a brother surgeon; he had been mistaken for his master, and was about being shot by a Prussian officer furious that he had missed the great prize.*

These sights of humiliation and dismay were, however, relieved, and made more conspicuous, by noble instances of constancy and real military worth. The three battalions of the Guard never lost their order; they steadily made their way through the flying masses; the Prussian cavalry attacked them in vain; they had the presence of mind to cross the Dyle near Genappe, and leisurely effected their retreat in safety. The squadrons of the light cavalry of the Guard, and one regiment of the heavy cavalry—this had not suffered so much as the others—appear to have joined this noble body of men; the remains of the defeated six battalions of the Guard, and some of the survivors of the horsemen of Milhaud, Kellermann, and Guyot, made at least attempts to re-form their ranks and to restore discipline. No eagles, too, were taken in the flight—a sure sign that the pursuit was really feeble; a faithful few guarded these honoured emblems; in fact, the only two eagles lost at Waterloo were captured by the British cavalry in their great charge against the troops of D'Erlon.

Individual examples of heroism were also not wanting; after the failure of the last attack of the Guard, Ney rode across the field, braving a thousand deaths, and tried to rally the soldiers of Durutte; he fought desperately in their ranks to the last—he was, indeed, always a soldier rather than a leader in war—and hundreds of the officers of the routed army endeavoured to do their duty in vain. Nevertheless, even after the pursuit had ceased—Gneisenau recalled his infantry at Genappe, and his horsemen at Frasnes—the aspect of the flight was not changed; the French army, now all but completely dissolved, sped onwards to the Sambre, which it had crossed but three days before in all the magnificence of war, and in the sure

* H. Houssaye, 'Waterloo,' ii. 421-423.

hope of victory. The hideous appearance of the field at Quatre Bras, thick strewn with naked corpses, ghastly white in the moon, quickened the terrors of the unnerved soldiery; they fled, it was said, as if they had had a glimpse of hell. The fugitives, scattered in little knots and bands, reached the Sambre, only to desert in hundreds, and to carry the news of the disaster through the northern provinces of France. A considerable mass assembled at Charleroy; the scenes of demoralisation became even worse than before. The famished soldiery, as they rushed into the town, seized the provisions, which had been in store for the army, and pillaged the treasure-chest, in their reckless passion; all signs of discipline and order disappeared; many even perished, squeezed to death or thrown over the bridge on the river, by the pressure of the mob of their frantic comrades. 'It was the horrors of Vilna,' it has been said, 'at the very gates of France.'

Napoleon, accompanied by a few of his chief officers, left the field finally with three battalions of the Guard. His attempts to rally his flying army had failed; but his stoical demeanour amidst the ruin around him remained unchanged. It is a tradition that he dropped the words, 'It has been ever thus since Crécy'; it is certain that in remarks on the battle, made long afterwards, he attributed his defeat to the conduct of the British soldiery, the troops he had slighted almost with contempt in the morning.* At Genappe he quitted the Guard and entered his carriage, having, it would seem, endeavoured to no purpose to form a kind of rearguard; he narrowly escaped falling into the hands of the Prussians, as he made his way through the town amidst the crowds of fugitives. At

---

* Napoleon Correspondence, xxxi. 240: 'Les Français, quoique si inférieurs en nombre, auraient remporté la victoire, et ce ne fut que la bravoure obstinée et indomptable des troupes anglaises qui les en à empêché.' A prouder testimonial has never been made to the qualities of the British army.

Quatre Bras he made a short halt, expecting to meet the
division of Girard left behind at Ligny, and ordered by
Soult to Quatre Bras before; but its commander had
apparently lost his head, and had marched to Charleroy,
involved in the universal rout. The Emperor then sent
two bearers of the fatal news to Grouchy, announcing
that the battle had been fought and lost, and directing
the Marshal to retreat towards Philippeville or Givet;
and several officers carried messages to the commandants
of the fortresses upon the northern frontier to effect a
general rallying of the defeated army, and as far as was
possible to provide for its wants, to restore its artillery,
and to supply it with other requirements of war.

Napoleon having given these orders—all that could be
given at the present conjuncture—set off for Charleroy,
and, passing the Sambre, reached Philippeville in the
forenoon of June 19. From that place he wrote to his
brother Joseph, informing him of the disaster of the day
before, and expressing a hope that he would receive the
support of the nation; in a short time he had set off for
Paris. He has been blamed severely for this conduct;
detractors have said that 'he was a deserter, as he had
been in Egypt and in 1812.' But the Emperor had, for
the moment, nothing to do on the frontier; he literally
was without an army; he had to think of the Chambers
of Paris, of a terrified France, too willing, perhaps, to
make him a victim. During the agony of the hours he
had just gone through, his self-contained composure had
once given way. It has been recorded by an eye-witness,
that at Quatre Bras Napoleon turned his eyes towards
Waterloo; silent tears trickled down cheeks almost life-
less, and pallid as if with the look of death.

We pass on to the operations of Grouchy, the paramount cause of this immense disaster for France. We
left the ill-fated Marshal at Walhain, having set at nought
the admirable counsels of Gérard, to cross the Dyle as

quickly as possible by Moustier and Ottignies, and to march to the sound of the great fight at Waterloo. He had resolved to continue the movement on Wavre by the direct roads on the eastern bank of the river—that is, many miles away from his master. By this time, Excelmans, we have seen, had been for some time at La Baraque; Vandamme and most of his corps had reached Nil St. Vincent; they were, therefore, at a short distance from Wavre; the corps of Gérard was round Walhain and Sart les Walhain; Pajol and Teste were between Grand Leez and Tourinnes—that is, a few miles eastward. The march of the army remained slow; and Grouchy, fixed as his purpose was, was affected by the thunder of the distant battle, and by the evident disapprobation of his own soldiery. He approached the Dyle more than once in person; but he still persisted in his fatal course; he actually withdrew squadrons of Excelmans from a place called La Plaquerie, only a few hundred yards from the bridge on the Dyle at Ottignies, Excelmans having assumed that Grouchy was about to cross the river and to push on to Waterloo and join his master.

By this time Ledebur, charged to observe Grouchy at Mont St. Guibert, and who, we have said, had not perceived the advance of the French, was almost surrounded by the Marshal's army; but he succeeded in effecting his escape to Wavre, after a short skirmish with the troops of Excelmans and Vandamme; he had received some assistance from part of the corps of Pirch, which soon afterwards resumed its march towards Waterloo, but was too late to take part in the battle. Between three and four, Grouchy, now near Wavre, received the despatch written by Soult at ten in the forenoon, which directed the Marshal, indeed, to march on Wavre, but emphatically told him he was to draw near the Emperor, about to engage in a great battle—that is, impliedly, if very obscurely, intimated that he ought to get over the Dyle, to move towards Wavre by the western bank, and, above all, to come in contact with the main army.   Shallow, obstinate, and not discerning the real import of the words, Grouchy exclaimed with glee that he had done perfectly right in disregarding the advice of Gérard, and took credit to himself for his skilful strategy.   But Gérard, if we are to believe Zenowicz, the bearer of the despatch, with true insight, caught Soult's meaning, and, breaking out into passion, vehemently said to Grouchy : ' If we are lost, the guilt will lie at your door !'*

Grouchy, satisfied with himself, and blind in his conceit, now ordered Vandamme to press on to Wavre, and to make a vigorous attack on the town ; the corps of Gérard was to second the movement.   His fixed idea was to fall on the enemy at hand.   He did not wholly neglect the injunctions of Soult—to approach the Emperor and the main French army ; but he committed this charge to Pajol and Teste—that is, to the very body of men which was farthest from the Dyle—and could not be over the river for a considerable time.

Vandamme and Excelmans, with Gérard not far in the rear, were around Wavre at about half-past four.   By this time Bulow was thundering on Napoleon's right flank ; Pirch, with half of his corps, was on his way to join him, between Wavre and St. Lambert ; Zieten was at a short distance from Ohain, making for Waterloo.   Grouchy had let the mass of the Prussian army elude his grasp ; it was in full march to join hands with Wellington.   The restraining wing had failed to fulfil its task.   Grouchy was merely striking at the tail, so to speak, of the enemy, not falling on his side, not assailing his head, not even standing between the hostile armies.   Thielmann had for some hours been left at Wavre with not more than 21,000 men.†

---

* See Thiers, ' Histoire du Consulat et de l'Empire,' vi. 508, 509. Thiers knew Gérard well, and probably had this from Gérard himself.

† Thielmann's corps, after Ligny, was about 18,000 strong ; but he had the support at Wavre of some troops of Zieten, and perhaps of Pirch, left behind.

He had been informed, probably between one and two, that Grouchy was marching towards him in largely superior force, and had sent to St. Lambert to seek orders; he was curtly told by Gneisenau, or perhaps by Blucher, that everything depended on what was being done at Waterloo, and that he must shift for himself as well as he could. He gave up all idea of moving towards his chief, and hastily placed Wavre in a state of defence, barricading the bridges of the town on the Dyle, throwing obstacles of all kinds across the streets, crenellating houses and other buildings to secure points of vantage. In this position, one of considerable strength, he steadily awaited his enemy's attack.

Vandamme was not slow in falling on. He assailed Wavre from the eastern bank of the Dyle, and mastered the suburbs on that side; but the single division he engaged was unable to cross the stream, and was decimated by a heavy fire from the town. Meanwhile, a little after five o'clock, Grouchy had received the message from Soult, written at one, directing him once more to move towards the main army, and also the postscript ordering him to attack Bulow, as Soult and Napoleon believed he could do.* What must have been the thoughts of the conscience-stricken chief when the bandage had fallen at last from his eyes?

Yet Grouchy, even at this supreme moment—not that any effort of his could now have had real effect—conducted his operations with remarkable want of judgment. He, indeed, sent Pajol and Teste, by this time at hand, to seize the bridge on the Dyle at Limale, and to hasten to the western bank of the river; but he permitted Vandamme still to waste his forces in attacks on Wavre that could have no object; he did not order Vandamme to support Teste or Pajol. At the same time, he directed a single

* This momentous despatch, like much of Soult's work, was scribbled in pencil, and could hardly be deciphered.

20

division of Gérard to assail Wavre near Biérges higher up
the Dyle, and so to support the efforts of Vandamme, as
if Wavre was still his main object.   Gérard fell severely
wounded in a fruitless attack, and it was not until Pajol
and Teste had got over the Dyle that Grouchy ordered
the two other divisions of Gérard to follow, and to pass
over to the western bank.   The Marshal now made towards
Napoleon's army; but it was past nine, and the attempt
could have come to nothing—Napoleon and his army had
succumbed.   Thielmann, too, held Grouchy in check for
a time; and though he was compelled to retreat some
distance, the French were detained in positions almost
around Wavre.   It was eleven at night before all fighting
ceased.   The attacks of Vandamme had meanwhile failed;
the Prussians continued masters of the town; Grouchy
and Thielmann had their bivouacs between Wavre and
Rixensart.

The cannon of Waterloo had long been voiceless.   The
unfortunate Marshal clung to a hope that his master—the
rumour had so run—was a victor; but Gérard, wounded,
it was feared, to death, was convinced that the result had
been very different.   Ten miles away the truth was revealed
in an appalling spectacle of wide-spread carnage, on which
night spread a funereal pall.   Wellington had lost more
than 15,000 men, Blucher very nearly 7,000.   Each had
dearly paid for their great triumph.   But the French army
had been virtually blotted out: from 30,000 to 40,000 men
had been killed, wounded, or made prisoners; from 8,000
to 10,000 were deserting; more than 200 guns had been
abandoned in the rout; in all probability 30,000 men of
the ruined host were never under arms again.*

* For the losses of the belligerent armies at Waterloo, see Charras,
ii. 67, 68; H. Houssaye, 'Waterloo,' ii. 415, 440.   The figures as
regards the French army are, of course, mere conjecture; enough to
say it was destroyed.

CHAPTER XI

REFLECTIONS ON WATERLOO, AND ON THE CAMPAIGN OF
1815

Faulty tactics of the French at Waterloo—Four distinct mistakes were
made—How far Napoleon is to be held responsible—Excellence
of Wellington's tactics — His strength of character was conspicuously seen—The result of Waterloo was due to the junction
of Blucher and Wellington—Consideration of the question whether
Grouchy could have prevented this — Position of the Prussian
army on the morning of June 18—Position of Grouchy and his
army—Grouchy could have arrested the march of the Prussians,
and interposed between the allied armies, had he marched to the
Dyle and crossed at Moustier and Ottignies by the early forenoon
—He could have attained the same end had he followed the
advice of Gérard and marched towards Napoleon at noon—Examination of reasoning to the contrary—Grouchy the main cause
of the defeat of Waterloo—Napoleon not wholly free from blame
—The strategy of the allied Generals on June 17 and 18 essentially
faulty—They ought, having regard to the chances, to have lost the
Battle of Waterloo—Review of the campaign of 1815 generally—
Napoleon and his lieutenants — Wellington and Blucher—The
belligerent armies.

THE original plan of attack at Waterloo, in the opinion
of all competent judges, was the best possible that could
have been designed.*   When, owing to the apparition of

---

* Jomini (' Précis de la Campagne de 1815,' 198) says : ' Napoléon
peut laisser ce plan sans crainte à l'éxamen des maîtres de l'art.   Il
ne pouvait rien faire de mieux.'   Even the partisan detractor, Charras,
admits (ii. 88) : 'La plan de la bataille est très beau, très solide.   Il révèle
le chef habitué à combiner les plus grandes actions de guerre ; il défie
la critique.'

Bulow on his right, and in some degree to the defeat of D'Erlon, Napoleon was compelled to abandon this, his second plan was also admirably conceived. But in this, as in other passages of the campaign, fine projects were marred by execution, not only faulty in itself, but sometimes directly opposed to the Emperor's purpose. In the conduct of the French chiefs at Waterloo, the timidity and indecision we see before Quatre Bras were succeeded by impatient daring and hasty want of caution. Ney, especially, was rash and injudicious in the extreme, and, as on June 16, he disobeyed his orders. Four distinct mistakes in tactics, we have said, were made; these had marked effects during the course of the battle, and were not without influence on the ultimate issue. The attack on Hougoumont, intended to be a mere feint, was turned into a real and a determined attack; it was conducted also without skill or prudence. The consequences were in many respects disastrous; hundreds of brave men were sacrificed in making efforts soon proved to be fruitless. The corps of Reille was paralysed by an enemy very inferior in force; its leaders were unable, perhaps unwilling, to furnish the support to the great cavalry attacks, and to the last attack of the Imperial Guard, which their infantry assuredly might have furnished had it not been wasted to very little purpose. The vicious formation of D'Erlon's columns was fatal to the success of the great first attack; this, too, was not sufficiently sustained by cavalry. The result was a complete defeat, which deprived the French army of fully 5,000 men, and reduced D'Erlon's troops for a time to impotence.

The third error was even much worse. Ney, disregarding his master's commands, was too impatient to remain at La Haye Sainte when that most important post had been won, and to wait until he could obtain the support of the Guard engaged in resisting Bulow; he prematurely directed the splendid French cavalry, and that without

the necessary aid of infantry, against the right centre of
the allied line exactly where this was in greatest strength,
and where the infantry of the defence were not in the least
shaken.   A terrible conflict raged for a considerable time.
The efforts of the devoted horsemen were brilliant in the
extreme; but, being inadequately sustained in every respect,
they failed against the British and German squares, and
this magnificent force, the greatest part of which the
Marshal was certainly allowed to engage, was so beaten,
so weakened, so worn out, that it was rendered useless, or
nearly so, during the rest of the day.   Finally, the fourth,
and this a capital, mistake : the part of the Imperial
Guard that made the last attack was moved, not against
Wellington's centre at La Haye Sainte, at this moment
in grave peril, but against his right centre, still comparatively strong ; and the attack, made with a very insufficient
force, was left without the support of horse and foot,
which to some extent at least might still have been given.
In addition to these palpable mistakes, it is doubtful if
Napoleon did not miss an opportunity to sustain the great
cavalry attacks by a part at least of the Imperial Guard
when Bulow had been repulsed by the Young Guard ; had
this effort been made, it might have had great results.
Good judges have thought it might have been made, and
the Emperor certainly did not prevent Ney from throwing
away five-sixths of the noble French cavalry.   On the
whole, the attacks made at Waterloo were often ill-combined, ill-directed, desultory, and especially faulty, owing
to the want of concert in the use of the three arms.
Napoleon himself has acknowledged this ; the day, he has
said with emphasis, was a day of ' most false manœuvres.'
And these errors of tactics were independent of what
possibly was the greatest error of all—that Napoleon
delayed the attack for three or four hours, for reasons that
have been largely disapproved, and so gave time to the
Prussians to reach the field.   It is difficult, however, to

pronounce a decided opinion on this. The delay in the events that followed was, doubtless, in the highest degree disastrous; but the authority of Drouot is of great weight, and the delay brought advantages with it that cannot be denied.

Napoleon is, of course, partly responsible for all these mistakes; he was in supreme command of the French army; yet considerations must be taken into account which in a great degree relieve him from blame. It may be said at once that he did not give proof at Waterloo, until it had become too late, of the activity and the presence of mind of Wellington; here he was inferior to his antagonist and to his former self. But in the earlier hours of June 18 he seems to have suffered from the lethargy of the preceding day; he was dozing, we are told, long after Hougoumont was attacked; he gave no attention to what was going on, until he ordered the château to be fired with shells.* Throughout the later period of the day he was in a position of extreme difficulty; he had to maintain a fierce and still doubtful struggle with Wellington, and to make head against the onslaught of Bulow; he was fighting two battles, in truth, under very bad conditions. He could not, therefore, superintend the whole scene of action, or control and direct events as the occasion required. This, probably, is the principal reason that he permitted Ney to do almost as he pleased, even though Ney had set his orders at nought, and was plainly committing the gravest mistakes; the Emperor had not the situation fully before him, and felt that, as things stood, he had better not cross the Marshal. But the chief excuse that is to be made for Napoleon is that at Waterloo, as in all his battles, he looked to his subordinates to do almost everything; he reserved to himself only the general direction of affairs. This was a distinctive feature of his military system, caused by the great extent of his opera-

* Dorsey Gardner, *ante*, 36 ; H. Houssaye, ' Waterloo,' ii. 501.

tions in war. From this point of view, much is to be said for him : he committed to Reille the attack on Hougoumont; he committed to D'Erlon the attack on Wellington's left and left centre ; he gave Ney generally the conduct of the fight. He could not suppose that Reille, D'Erlon, and Ney would make the faulty dispositions they did; in this sense he is infinitely less responsible than his lieutenants. We have indicated, indeed, the chief faults which alone, perhaps, should be laid to the charge of Napoleon ; he should not have sanctioned in any way the reckless use Ney made of his cavalry;* he may have lost a favourable chance of attacking with the Guard. For the rest, in the last scenes of Waterloo, he rose to the level of the Napoleon of old.

In spite, however, of this series of mistakes, the attacks at Waterloo would have proved successful before the Prussians made their presence felt, had not Wellington been at the head of the allied army, and but for the heroic conduct of his British and German Legionary troops. The formidable advance of D'Erlon would have hardly failed against a Continental army of 1800 - 1812 ; the great cavalry attacks would almost certainly have broken Austrian squares, and given Ney a triumph ; the Archduke Charles, we believe, in Wellington's place, would have retreated when La Haye Sainte was captured; the allied centre would have been probably pierced but for the energy and resource of the British General. Unquestionably, as we have endeavoured to prove, Wellington ought not to have offered battle at all ; unquestionably he made a grave strategic mistake in leaving a large part of his army at Hal and Tubize; unquestionably he did not fully perceive the importance of La Haye Sainte, and did not occupy that post in sufficient strength; probably

---

* Napoleon, we have seen, certainly allowed Ney to employ the cavalry of Kellermann when Milhaud and Lefebvre-Desnoëttes had been repulsed. He always denied that he gave the same permission as regards the cavalry of Guyot, his last cavalry reserve.

he placed at first too large a force on his extreme right. But when this has been said, his conduct on the field of Waterloo is a grand specimen of skill, energy, resource, and firmness of purpose. Let it not be forgotten that he expected the Prussians to reach him at least three or four hours before they appeared, and that from half-past eleven to half-past four he was exposed to all the efforts of an army greatly superior in real strength, his army being largely composed of very inferior troops. Yet he succeeded, during this fiery trial, in repelling every attack directed against him; and this was largely because he conducted the defence with conspicuous skill, turning the advantages of his position to the best account, keeping his men as much as possible out of a tremendous fire, making admirably judicious use of his reserves, so finely calculating his resources that he was nearly always able to confront his enemy with an adequate force. Wellington, in a word, proved himself to be at Waterloo, what he always was, a great master of tactics, especially in defence; this is his real title to renown in the campaign of 1815— it is a legitimate set-off against no doubtful strategic errors. His activity and vigour were also above praise; but what was most conspicuous in him was his best quality, tenacity, and grand strength of character. In this respect he was really a great chief; no other General of the coalition was here his equal—not even Blucher, hero as he was. Napoleon certainly underrated this stern power of endurance. Still, Wellington could not have held out at Waterloo but for the steadfastness of his British and German Legionary troops; they maintained their ground against furious attacks, while auxiliaries in thousands fled from the field; they were worthy of their illustrious leader.

The issue of Waterloo, however, was not determined by differences of tactics, or by the conduct of the armies engaged in the first part of the battle; it is to be ascribed to a deeper cause. No impartial student of war can deny that, many as were the mistakes made in the attack, and admirable as was Wellington's defence, the victory would have remained with Napoleon had he been able, even after three in the afternoon, to direct his whole forces against his enemy. The attack on Hougoumont had been ill-conducted; that of D'Erlon had completely failed. But the allied army had been greatly weakened; it could not have resisted a combined effort made by Lobau, the French cavalry, and the Imperial Guard. In this event Wellington's left would probably have been turned and his centre forced, according to the Emperor's design; in a word, the Duke would have suffered a real defeat, but not, as we think, the overwhelming reverse which might have happened at Ligny or on June 17.* This peril was averted by the intervention of Bulow; his onset on Napoleon's right flank prevented the decisive movement, and in a great measure paralysed the French army. The course of the battle was completely changed, and the apparition of Zieten and Pirch on the field made Waterloo an immense victory and an immense disaster. The result of the conflict was therefore determined by the junction of Wellington's and Blucher's forces on the same point. Wellington fought the battle on an assurance that this would take place; Blucher had pledged himself to support his ally. The

* On this subject we agree, in substance, with Mr. Ropes, 'The Campaign of Waterloo,' 327 : ' Let us suppose, then, that Napoleon could have combined his whole force against the army of Wellington during the whole afternoon ; that he could have given his personal direction to the conduct of the action ; that he could have followed up the repulse of the 1st corps with a new attack, in which Lobau should support D'Erlon, and in which the cavalry should take its proper part; that he had been on the spot when La Haye Sainte fell, and had improved that advantage as he well knew how to do ; that he had had the whole of the Imperial Guard—infantry, cavalry, and artillery—at his disposal for the carrying of Wellington's position : it seems to us there can be no reasonable question as to the result ; the Duke would have been badly beaten, and the action would, in all probability, have been over, or substantially so, by six o'clock. This question is not asked to gratify the imagination.'

principal reason, accordingly, of the event at Waterloo was the union of the two armies in furtherance of a pre-concerted plan, which crushed Napoleon by their overwhelming strength. But Napoleon had employed Grouchy to prevent this junction; he had given the Marshal a powerful restraining wing to keep Blucher away from Wellington. The question therefore arises, in considering what occurred at Waterloo: Could Grouchy, who, we know, miserably failed, have been reasonably expected to fulfil his master's purpose? Was it the more likely, having regard to the situation and the probabilities of war, that Blucher would be able to come into line with Wellington, or that Grouchy would be able to stop the veteran warrior, or even to come to Napoleon's assistance? The subject has been placed in a false light, or has been slurred over by many writers; the facts should be presented in their true aspect, and proper conclusions be drawn from them.

Undoubtedly, in the position of affairs that was witnessed on June 18, the conduct of Grouchy having been what it was, the main part of the Prussian army might have reached Waterloo at a comparatively early hour, as Wellington was convinced would be the case. Zieten and Thielmann, on the western bank of the Dyle, were considerably nearer the allied lines than Pirch and Bulow on the eastern bank. Had they been unmolested, and marched soon after daybreak, they might have been at St. Lambert, with about 25,000 men, in all probability at about ten or eleven, and have fallen on Napoleon's right flank at about twelve or one. Under similar conditions, had Pirch moved before Bulow, as his advanced position made the natural course, he could have been at St. Lambert, with perhaps 20,000 men, an hour or two probably after his colleagues; and Bulow need not have been greatly behind, assuming that he had not been kept back at Wavre with a large part of his corps, at least, to guard Blucher's communications and rear.

But in examining this question, we must consider, with reference to the matter in hand, not what the Prussian operations might have been, but what they actually were in the events that happened. Zieten and Thielmann were detained many hours at Wavre; Zieten was directed to Waterloo by the northern road through Ohain; Thielmann was kept back ultimately at Wavre the whole day in order to resist the attack of Grouchy; Bulow was moved forward before Pirch; Pirch was retarded a considerable time by the intermingling of his columns with those of Bulow. As the general result, great and unnecessary delay, apart from the obstacles that stood in its path, occurred in the movements of the Prussian army. Zieten did not break up from Wavre until about noon; he was not at Ohain until near six; he did not reach the field of battle in anything like force, and then with some 10,000 men only, until after the defeat of the Imperial Guard—that is, a short time after eight o'clock. As for Bulow, his advanced guard was not at St. Lambert until after ten in the forenoon; his whole corps, about 29,000 strong,* had not reached that place until after three; he did not begin his attack until half-past four, and then with only a part of his forces. The march of Pirch was even more delayed; he did not leave Wavre until noon; two of his divisions waited for a time to observe Grouchy; he was not at Plancenoit until after eight, and then with only 12,000 or 15,000 men; his forces and those of Bulow at Waterloo were not more than from 40,000 to 45,000 men; and in the march from Wavre they were divided by long distances, and spread out into disunited columns, on a flank march of the most hazardous kind should they come within the reach of an enemy. It should be observed, too, that, if we except Blucher, every Prussian commander gave proof of caution—nay, of timidity—in these movements. Gneisenau hesitated at the critical moment;

* Excluding the detachment of Ledebur.

Zieten was most reluctant to march to Papelotte, though informed that Wellington was in great danger; Bulow waited for hours before he made his attack; nay, even Blucher would not commit himself to a real effort against Napoleon until he had ascertained that his flank and rear were not threatened. The Prussian march, in a word, from Wavre to Waterloo, let the courtiers of Fortune say what they please, was ill-directed, irresolute, and dangerously delayed.

These being the uncontested facts, and the elements from which we must form our judgment, let us see whether Grouchy, giving him credit for ordinary capacity, insight, and skill, ought to have prevented the junction of Blucher and Wellington. We have indicated the operations which, beyond question, he ought to have resolved to carry out when, on the night of the 17th, he was at Gembloux with his army of 33,000 men. He had been placed at the head of a strong restraining wing; his companions in arms, and he himself likewise, must have been aware that his duty was to hold Blucher in check, while the Emperor should fall in full force on Wellington. Napoleon, when giving him his command, had all but certainly told him not only to pursue Blucher and to keep him in sight, but also to be in constant communication with the main French army; he undoubtedly added that he meant to attack Wellington, should Wellington make a stand before the Forest of Soignies. A short time afterwards the Marshal received positive orders, through the important message despatched by Bertrand, to march on Gembloux, to follow the enemy, and to correspond with his master at headquarters; and he was distinctly warned that the allied Generals might be seeking to effect their junction, and even to fight another battle. Grouchy reached Gembloux, though very late, on the evening of the 17th. At that place he learned, in the course of a few hours, that the Prussian army was assembled around Wavre; he wrote twice to the Emperor that he would march to that place—probably in the first letter; in the second, certainly—adding that he would try to keep the Prussians away from Wellington, a proof that he understood his mission. In the existing situation, what Grouchy ought to do was plain—he should break up from Gembloux at the earliest dawn; should march rapidly by the two available roads; should cross the Dyle by the bridges of Moustier and Ottignies, a distance of some ten miles from Gembloux; and should place his army on the western bank of the river: for by this movement, and by this alone, could he adequately perform his allotted task. Were Blucher halting at Wavre, he could attack him— perhaps most readily from the position he would have gained; were Blucher, as might be expected and feared, attempting to march from Wavre to join Wellington, Grouchy would be able to reach the Prussian army's flank, to attack it when placed in the worst conditions, and all but certainly to bring it to a stand—to defeat it in detail; above all, he would draw near Napoleon, and be soon in contact with the imperial army.*

Instead of making the movement the occasion required, Grouchy, we know, left Gembloux at a very late hour; marched extremely slowly to Walhain and Sart les Walhain; advanced along the eastern bank of the Dyle; persisted in this, spite of the entreaties of Gérard to cross the stream and to make for Waterloo; allowed Blucher to give him the slip, and to join Wellington with more than half his army; and, keeping many miles away from Napoleon, merely reached at Wavre the corps of Thielmann. But had he operated as he ought to have done, and as any true soldier would have done in his place, what he might have accomplished is hardly doubtful. On

---

* All commentators, Jomini, Charras, Thiers, La Tour d'Auvergne, Clausewitz, H. Houssaye, Ropes, and many others, agree that this was what Grouchy should have done. See authorities collected by Mr. Ropes, ' The Campaign of Waterloo,' 252-254.

the night of the 17th Excelmans and his horsemen were between Sauvenière and Nil St. Vincent; Vandamme was a little beyond Gembloux, Gérard a little behind the town; Pajol and Teste were some miles in the rear round Mazy. Had Grouchy formed an energetic purpose to march as quickly as possible across the Dyle, he might have had the corps of Vandamme and Gérard under arms by four in the morning of June 18; he might have directed Excelmans to cover the intended movement, and Pajol and Teste to follow Excelmans without delay. Had he taken these steps—and they were almost obvious—he might have marched to the Dyle with Vandamme and Gérard by the roads passing through Villeroux and Cortel; and if his march had been at the rate of about two miles an hour, his columns having been divided to ensure celerity, he would have reached the river between nine and ten in the forenoon at the two bridges of Moustier and Ottignies, having possibly surprised and cut to pieces the detachment of Ledebur at Mont St. Guibert—Ledebur, we have seen, was surprised in the afternoon—having certainly swept it out of his path. The bridges were of stone, and, like those on the Sambre, had, whatever the reason, been left intact. With the exception of the weak divisions of Pajol and Teste—and these would not have been far in the rear —Grouchy would have been across the Dyle and on the western bank before noon, as has been acknowledged even by the most bitter of Napoleon's detractors.*

Grouchy and the mass of his forces, being now over the Dyle, had two alternative courses to take; either would have given him an opportunity grand and decisive. At Moustier and Ottignies he was about six miles from Maransart, a village near Plancenoit, on the other bank of the Lasne, and some two miles from the main French army. At

* Jomini ('Précis de la Campagne de 1815,' 222) says that Grouchy would have reached Moustier at about ten. Charras (ii. 115) admits that he could have been over the Dylè 'before noon.'

Moustier and Ottignies, too, he was only some three miles farther from Napoleon than Bulow at St. Lambert was; he was not more than four or five miles from the flank of the corps of Bulow, now on its march from Wavre in disunited masses, and not expecting an enemy at hand. Had Grouchy, as no doubt he would have done, pushed his cavalry forward in both directions, he would have come in contact almost at once with the horsemen of Marbot sent to the two bridges, and he would have ascertained how affairs stood with Bulow. In this situation Grouchy, we are convinced, would have marched directly on Maransart in conformity with the message given by Marbot; he would have reached that place between two and three, long before Bulow had begun his attack; he would have received the Emperor's commands; in all human probability, he would have been placed either before or behind the Bois de Paris in order to cover Napoleon's right flank, and to protect it from any effort to be made by Bulow. In that event Grouchy would have interposed with complete effect between Blucher and Wellington; Bulow certainly would not have attempted to attack—at least, until he had been reinforced by Pirch, then on a march many miles in the rear; Zieten assuredly would not have stirred from Ohain; in the meantime Napoleon, left free to act with all his forces, including the Guard, would beyond question have overpowered Wellington.

Grouchy, on the march from Moustier and Ottignies, could hardly have received the despatch from Soult, sent off, we have seen, at half-past one, and directing him to fall on the flank and rear of Bulow. Conceivably, however, though not probably, he might have decided on marching against that General; in that event he would have reached the lines of Bulow's march between two and three, but his influence would have been felt long before; the Prussians would have been surprised and caught in a perilous flank march by an enemy superior in force at the decisive point. In this position they must have hesitated and paused for a time; his was inevitable, from the nature of the case; if so, Bulow's attack would have been delayed some hours. We must bear in mind that even Blucher would not run the risk until he had ascertained that his flank and rear were safe. The attack might not have been made at all, and Pirch, in all probability, would not have moved towards Bulow with the two divisions— all he had in hand. He would, it is all but certain, have waited for his two divisions in the rear. Bulow and Pirch, in a word, would have been paralysed by the apparition on their flank of an unexpected enemy—at least not less than 30,000 strong. They could not have acted with effect for some hours. Zieten, of course, would not have stirred a step. Grouchy would have prevented Blucher from joining Wellington, and secured for Napoleon time to gain the day at Waterloo. It should be added that, had Grouchy marched against Bulow in the position in which the Prussians were, he might very possibly have annihilated part of their forces, scattered as these were, and most dangerously exposed.

These conclusions, however, as sound, we believe, as is possible in a case of the kind, have been assailed by specious, but, we think, false sophistry. The movement of Grouchy to Moustier and Ottignies would, it has been said, have been perceived by Ledebur at Mont St. Guibert; and that officer would have carried the news to Wavre, and have reached the town perhaps by eight in the morning. In that event Gneisenau and Blucher would at once have made a complete change in the dispositions of the Prussian army, and in the arrangements which had been prepared for its advance on Waterloo. Zieten, who had been directed to stay around Wavre, would have been moved to the Dyle and the bridges of Moustier and Ottignies; Pirch, who was to second the march of Bulow, would have been turned aside from the road to St. Lambert, and ordered to hold the bridges of Limale and Limelette on the Dyle. In that case Grouchy could not have got over the river; he would have found a large army in his path; he would have at least been compelled to fight a battle, which necessarily would have detained him for hours. Under these conditions Thielmann would have been sent to support Bulow, and both would have overwhelmed Napoleon with the aid of Wellington. Nay, even if, as was not probable, Grouchy had succeeded in crossing the Dyle, the whole Prussian army would have made for Waterloo; Pirch and Zieten would have followed in the track of Grouchy; Bulow and Thielmann would have joined Wellington; Napoleon would not the less have been destroyed.*

This reasoning disregards important facts of the case, and is opposed to the natural inferences to be drawn in war. We may grant that Ledebur would have reached Wavre at about eight, and given news of Grouchy; if, as was most likely, he could not have had time to estimate the numbers of the Marshal's army, Blucher and Gneisenau, who, we must bear in mind, thought that Grouchy had not more than 15,000 men, and were making preparations to join Wellington, would assuredly have made no changes in these, and would not have sent Zieten and Pirch to the Dyle: for this, from their point of view, would have been a false movement. If, on the contrary, Ledebur had ascertained that Grouchy was at the head of some 30,000 men, and was making for the Dyle by Moustier and Ottignies, it is equally certain that not one of the movements that have been suggested would have been made. Eager as Blucher was to push on to Waterloo, Gneisenau, his strategic Mentor and master, was at this very time in hesitation as to whether the march should be made. He was craning, so to speak, like a hunter at a fence. If

* Charras, ii. 114, 116.

he had learned, to his surprise and amazement, how formidable was the power of Grouchy's force, he would very probably have detained the whole Prussian army around Wavre—the foremost column of Bulow was still at hand—and not moved for two or three hours at least, until the situation had developed itself. In that event Grouchy would have had ample time to advance across the Dyle, and to join Napoleon ; not a single division of the Prussian army would have reached Waterloo until it was far too late to give the slightest support to Wellington ; the defeat of Wellington would have been assured.

It may be admitted, however, having regard to Blucher's heroic nature and high sense of honour, that the old chief would have insisted that no change should be made in the arrangements for the march on Waterloo, and that, though made aware of the real strength of Grouchy, he would have ordered Bulow, Pirch, and Zieten to continue their projected movements. But in that case Grouchy, as we have seen, would have been able to reach Maransart, or to arrest the advance of Bulow and Pirch, and therefore of Zieten ; in other words, he would have prevented Blucher from joining Wellington ; Waterloo would have been a victory for France. As to the supposition that, when it had become known that Grouchy was close to the Dyle with a real and large army, Zieten and Pirch would have been sent to stop him upon the river, and, still more, that the whole Prussian army would have been directed to follow the Marshal, and to press on to Waterloo, it may confidently be said that such an operation was never conducted in war. Were there no other reason, the Prussian commanders would never have left Wavre without a considerable force to protect their communications and rear.*

* For an able refutation of the arguments of Charras on this subject, see Ropes, 'The Campaign of Waterloo,' 281, 283.

Had Grouchy, therefore, got over the Dyle at Moustier and Ottignies by the forenoon, he would have accomplished his master's purpose, and kept Blucher away from Wellington. Let us next consider what he might have achieved had he, giving ear to the counsels of Gérard, marched from Walhain on Waterloo on hearing the roar of the battle. At this moment—that is, not far from noon—the cavalry of Excelmans had reached La Baraque, a point about three miles from the Dyle; part of the corps of Vandamme was at Nil St. Vincent, the remaining part being not far behind. Gérard and his corps were at Walhain and Sart les Walhain ; Pajol and Teste were approaching Tourinnes. These distances were between six and eight miles from the rievr. Had Grouchy, therefore, marched to the Dyle, and crossed it at the bridges of Moustier and Ottignies, sending Excelmans and Vandamme to the nearest bridges at Limale and Limelette—these, like the others, were of stone, and not broken—he would have been over the river about four, the divisions of Pajol and Teste remaining on the eastern bank, and covering, as Gérard had proposed, the movement. At this time Bulow had not fired a shot ; two of his divisions were in the defiles of the Lasne. Only half of the corps of Pirch was much beyond Wavre ; it did not reach Plancenoit until long after eight. Zieten was still a march of two hours from Ohain. Thielmann was encamped in and around Wavre. In these circumstances Grouchy, of course, would have pushed forward, his march accelerated by the sound of the cannon ; and he would have made his influence felt at once on Bulow and Pirch, for he would be on their flank only three or four miles distant, just as Bulow made his influence felt with effect on Napoleon from St. Lambert, about as far from the French army. Bulow and Pirch must have paused and made preparations to resist an attack ; both, especially the first, were in a position that might become most critical. It may be confidently said that Bulow's attack on Napoleon would have been long postponed; and had it then been made, it would have been too late; Napoleon would have been master of the field at Waterloo. The march of Bulow, in a word, must have been arrested; that of Pirch and Zieten would have equally come to a stand. No doubt, possibly, but not probably, Thielmann would have advanced from Wavre to support Pirch; but the result would practically have been the same. Grouchy, though outnumbered, would have been able to detain the Prussians on their march sufficiently long to give the Emperor the means of defeating Wellington. It ought to be added that, as Gérard has maintained, Grouchy not improbably would have succeeded in destroying parts of the corps of Pirch and Bulow, surprised and caught in a position of no little peril.

The kind of argument, however, which has been employed to prove that Grouchy could not have kept Blucher and Wellington apart, had he crossed the Dyle by the early forenoon, has been urged to show that had Grouchy, at Walhain, followed the advice of Gérard to march on Waterloo, the result would, even more certainly, have been the same. Ledebur, it is said, would have reported to Wavre the movement of the French army to the Dyle, which he would have seen long before it reached the stream; the corps of Thielmann, and part of the corps of Pirch—these, it will be recollected, still near Wavre—would have been directed to the bridges to stop the march of the enemy. Grouchy would, therefore, be compelled to fight a battle; this must have detained him until nightfall. He could not even have drawn near Napoleon, still less have prevented the junction of Blucher and Wellington. Besides, time and distance, though no Prussians had stood in the Marshal's path, would have made it impossible for him to do anything to assist his master or to molest the allies; he could not have crossed the Dyle until about six, or have reached the field of battle until nine or ten. At that hour the French army was in complete rout; he probably would have been involved in the general ruin.*

These arguments, we think, are even more unsound than those we have already dealt with. Ledebur completely failed to perceive the movement of the French on La Baraque and Nil St. Vincent; he did not stir from Mont St. Guibert until after one. He was surprised and all but cut off; he could not have reached Wavre until between three and four. There is no reason to suppose that he would have been more vigilant, have acted differently, and have done better, had Grouchy marched to the bridges on the Dyle; if so, any report he could have made at Wavre would have been much too late to enable a large Prussian force to move to the bridges in order to stop Grouchy. Besides, Thielmann, who by this time must have ascertained that Grouchy was at the head of an army more than twice as numerous as had been supposed, and who had been just ordered to defend the town, would never have attempted to leave Wavre; and the half of the corps of Pirch, which had remained in the rear, and was even now marching to join the other half, would not have been diverted from its movement on St. Lambert to make an attempt to hold Grouchy in check on the Dyle. As to time and distance, the arguments are either false in fact or point to conclusions plainly erroneous. Grouchy would have been over the Dyle long before six; once he was across, the question would not have been at what hour his army would have reached Waterloo, but when it would have made its power so felt by the Prussians as to arrest and prevent their attack on Napoleon. That influence would have told, and told with effect, almost as soon as the Marshal had crossed the Dyle. An army threatening another upon a hazardous flank march, especially as affairs stood with Bulow and Pirch, would paralyse it long before

* Charras, ii. 117, 124.

it could strike it ; and that being so, Grouchy could have stopped his enemy. We fully acknowledge, however, that Grouchy's movement in the afternoon could not have had the decisive effect his movement in the morning would have had; it might have enabled Napoleon to employ the whole Imperial Guard, but could not have prevented the wasteful and unsuccessful cavalry attacks.*

It is unnecessary to notice the idle remark that, as Grouchy was ordered to march to Wavre, he is not to be blamed for not making a different movement, however better this might have been. Napoleon and perhaps Soult are alone to blame.† Writers who take this position are blind to the facts, or worse. Apart from the interpretation to be put on Soult's letters, Grouchy did not receive these until the afternoon of the 18th; his instructions were those given by Napoleon on the 17th, either in person or through the message of Bertrand. He was perfectly free to march to Moustier and Ottignies from four in the morning of the 18th to four in the evening ; he is solely responsible for not having taken this course. Another criticism on Grouchy of very different value is of real importance, and deserves close attention. Since the publication of Marbot's 'Memoirs,' Napoleon, we know, expected Grouchy to cross the Dyle at Moustier and Ottignies, and to be on the field of Waterloo at an early hour, whether in compliance or not with orders received

* As to the operations of Grouchy and to what he might have accomplished, the reader may be referred to Jomini, 'Précis de la Campagne de 1815,' 219, 224 ; Thiers, 'Histoire du Consulat et de l'Empire,' vi. 504, 510, 515, 517 ; Van Loben Sels, 322, 323, 340 ; La Tour d'Auvergne, 'Waterloo,' 315, 343; Ropes, 'The Waterloo Campaign,' 243, 262, 281, 288 ; H. Houssaye, 'Waterloo,' ii. 245, 248, 284, 297, 441, 451, 484, 495. The only writer who takes a contrary view, and has dealt with the subject seriously, is Charras (ii. 91, 121). He is able and plausible, but inaccurate and sophistical. No English writer has gone really into the question.

† Mr. Ropes ('The Campaign of Waterloo,' 249, 250) has treated this criticism as it deserves.

on the night of the 17th, which were given, we believe,
but never reached the Marshal. Apart, however, from
considerations of this kind, Napoleon, in his narrative of
the campaign, has pronounced a judgment on Grouchy's
conduct, and on what he might have done on June 17
and 18, which cannot be lightly passed over. Grouchy,
we have seen, had marched extremely slowly to Gembloux; had halted around the town on the night of
the 17th; had left his camp very late on the following
day, and had only reached Wavre about half-past four,
soon before he began his attack on Thielmann. The
Emperor has insisted that had his lieutenant advanced
beyond Gembloux to Wavre on the 17th, or had marched
rapidly and early on the 18th, and had been before Wavre
in the forenoon, he would either have kept the whole of
Blucher's army on the spot, or three-fourths of it—that
is, excepting the corps of Bulow; and in either event
the French would have gained Waterloo.* We may
think that, in coming to this conclusion, Napoleon underrated Blucher's energy, and that the Prussian army,
90,000 strong, or three-fourths of it, would not have been
completely held in check by Grouchy, appearing with only
33,000 men, at Wavre; the movement could not have
been as effective as that across the Dyle by Moustier and
Ottignies, which would have brought Grouchy on the
flank of Bulow and Pirch, far from each other and in
divided masses. But if we bear in mind that Blucher
and Gneisenau thought that Grouchy had only 15,000

---

* 'Comment.,' v. 182: 'Si le Maréchal Grouchy eût couché devant
Wavre, comme il le devait et eu reçut l'ordre le soir du 17, le Maréchal
Blücher y fût resté en observation, avec toutes ses forces; se croyant
poursuivi par toute l'armée française. Si le Maréchal Grouchy comme
il l'avait écrit à deux heures après minuit de son camp à Gembloux,
eût pris les armes à la pointe du jour, c'est à dire à quatre heures du
matin, il ne fût pas arrivé à Wavre à temps pour empêcher le détachement du Général Bulow, mais il eût arrêté les trois autres corps du
Général Blücher ; la victoire était encore certaine.'

men, it is very difficult to say that, when they had ascertained he had a force before Wavre of more than twofold strength, they would not have kept the greatest part of the Prussian army around the town for hours, and thus given time to Napoleon to defeat Wellington.

Had Grouchy, therefore, been worthy of his trust, the facts and the probabilities of the case show that he could have prevented the junction of Blucher and Wellington, and secured a victory for his master on June 18.* The question was not, as has been untruly said, of the superiority in numbers of the Prussian army; it was whether, as affairs stood on the scene of events, the French restraining wing had the means to stop it, and this can be answered in the affirmative with but little room for doubt. It follows that Grouchy was the real and the main author of the disaster that befell the arms of France; the Marshal's conduct, Napoleon has justly remarked, was no more to be anticipated than that an earthquake would swallow up his whole army on his march.† But it does not follow that the Emperor was altogether free from blame, though this is infinitely less than has been commonly supposed. The lethargy which made him prostrate on the morning of the 17th explains, and can alone explain, how it came to pass that the line of Blucher's retreat was not ascertained at an early hour, and Grouchy not detached with the restraining wing to hold the Prussian army so completely in check that it could not by any possibility reach that of Wellington. But for this Napoleon would deserve the severest censure; as the facts are, he is more to be pitied than condemned.

---

* Jomini ('Précis de la Campagne de 1815,' 261) pointedly says : 'Le plan d'opérations adopté était si bien le plus convenable, que . . . il eût complètement réussi . . . si l'aile droite avait pris la direction de Moustier.'

† 'Comment.,' v. 209 : 'La conduite du Maréchal Grouchy était aussi imprévoyable que si, sur sa route, son armée eût éprouvé un tremblement de terre qui l'eût engloutie.'

We believe, too, that the Emperor, on the night of the 17th, did communicate with Grouchy more frequently than has been acknowledged by most of his critics; it seems most probable that he ordered the Marshal to move on Waterloo with a detachment or with his whole army, though Grouchy never received the message. But Napoleon underrated Blucher, and was too obstinately convinced that the veteran at Wavre could not draw near Wellington —though even here we must recollect the Bertrand letter; he turned a deaf ear to the warnings of Jerôme, perhaps of Milhaud; he placed too implicit a faith in Grouchy, and refused to see that an army of 90,000 men might elude an army of 33,000 if this was not directed by an able chief. Napoleon, too, ought to have been more observant of the despatches of Soult—ambiguous, ill-worded, sent often by a single officer too late; but here again he deserves rather compassion than blame. Perhaps his chief fault was that he gave Grouchy a command, which he ought to have seen that Grouchy was not fit for, from the Marshal's own expressions on the 17th; had Gérard had the command of the restraining wing, the catastrophe that was witnessed would not have occurred.

As it was most probable that Grouchy would possess the means of separating Blucher from Wellington on June 18, it follows, too, that the movement of Blucher to join Wellington was perilous and essentially bad strategy, and of this Gneisenau appears to have been conscious. Had the Prussian Generals been aware that Grouchy was at hand with 33,000 men, very possibly they would not have stirred from Wavre—for some time, at least; but, with Wellington, they believed he had only 15,000. Yet it is astonishing they entertained this idea; they ought to have been convinced, from a study of Napoleon's campaigns, that he would detach a powerful restraining wing to keep them away from Wellington while the Emperor should fall on the army at Waterloo. Never-

theless, they made the movement, being in ignorance of
the real facts. This secured a decisive and grand triumph,
but it ought to have been rendered vain by Grouchy; and
then the errors of this combination would have become
apparent, the Prussian army would have been placed in
the gravest danger, and Wellington would have certainly
lost the battle. It has been truly said, besides, that the
projects of the allied leaders were such as ought to have
ensured their defeat. Had Grouchy had only 15,000 men
with him, Napoleon would have been able to attack the
Duke with not much less than 100,000; his army could
not have escaped a disaster at Waterloo. And this brings
us back to what we have said before—Wellington, as
affairs stood, ought not to have fought on the 18th; the
probabilities were far too distinctly against him. No
doubt he expected the Prussians to be on the field much
sooner than they were; but he believed that Napoleon
was before him with nearly 100,000 men, all excellent
troops of one nation. He had not more than 70,000 of
many races—a third, at least, not good. What chances
would he have had without the support of Blucher, on
which he could not reckon with reasonable hope? Nay,
what chances would he have had, spite of Grouchy's faults
had the Emperor attacked him in the early morning?
Beyond question, as Napoleon has proved, he ought to
have retreated beyond Brussels, and effected there his
junction with Blucher; both would then have been assured
of ultimate success, neither would have well-nigh courted
defeat. That Wellington did not adopt this obvious course
was probably because he thought the retention of Brussels
of the highest importance to the allied cause; he sacrificed
military to political ends, very seldom judicious conduct
in war.

To extol the strategy of the allies on June 17 and 18
is simply to set the plainest evidence at naught. But
national prejudice is of enormous power; the idolaters of

success, the detractors of genius, were to act according to their ignoble kind. Hence the operations of Grouchy have been misdescribed—nay, falsified—or, what is worse, have been little noticed, though obviously of supreme importance. It was necessary to justify the ill-designed movement from Ligny to Wavre, a half-measure that ought to have been disastrous. Attempts have therefore been made to prove that, whatever Grouchy could do, this made the movement of Blucher on Waterloo certain. It was necessary to maintain the absurd position that the allies outmanœuvred Napoleon on the 17th and the 18th. It has been contended, accordingly, that the great master never even suspected the plans of his enemies ; that he sent Grouchy in the wrong direction ; that he did not conceive it was Grouchy's duty to keep Blucher away from Wellington at any point in the space between Wavre and Waterloo—nay, to be in close relations with the main French army. It was necessary, in order to support these views, to make charges against Napoleon which cannot be sustained, and to make apologies for Grouchy that are utterly untrue ; to insist that the Emperor scarcely gave a thought to the position of his lieutenant, and that it was for him to do what Grouchy was bound to do—to ascertain accurately where the Prussians were ; to show that Grouchy could not on June 18 have stopped—nay, even delayed — Blucher ; to make the Emperor alone responsible for the defeat of Waterloo ; to exonerate the Marshal wholly from blame. Especially it was necessary to hurry over the facts ; to avoid a thorough investigation of them ; to jump to the conclusion that, because Blucher was largely superior in force, it was impossible that Grouchy could act with effect against him ; to deal in plausible generalities ; to avoid sound criticism. This sophistry and mystification, however, are being dispelled ; few capable writers will now deny that, but for Grouchy, Napoleon would have gained Waterloo, and that the allies, many and great as their merits were, ought not to have been victorious on June 18.*

Passing from Waterloo to the campaign as a whole, we shall try to pronounce an impartial judgment, if our knowledge is in some particulars incomplete. The supremacy of Napoleon's strategic genius has seldom, if ever, been more distinctly displayed than in this memorable passage of arms. The outlaw of Europe, the ruler of a divided France, he seizes the initiative as he seized it in 1800 and 1805. With military forces not a third of those of the allies, he sees in the wide distance between the hosts of the coalition in the north and east an opportunity of brilliant, perhaps decisive, success. The dissemination of the armies of Blucher and Wellington along a broad and deep front in Belgium; the weakness of their centre where their inner flanks met; the faulty arrangements of the allied chiefs, especially the great interval between their headquarters—all this induces him to spring on them from across the frontier of France, in the hope of dividing and defeating them in detail; and the opposite natures of the hostile commanders, correctly appreciated in a great measure, form other elements on which to found a hope of victory. At the outset the rising in La Vendée deprived the Emperor of a considerable part of his forces, which might have made his triumph assured. His calculatious are baffled, but he had made his choice; it is now too late to give up the venture. The operations leading to the invasion of Belgium were as masterly as any in that

---

* For a general review and criticism of the combinations of the allies on June 17 and 18, see the unanswerable remarks of Napoleon, 'Comment.,' v. 209, 210. The Emperor's figures are far from correct, but his reasoning and the conclusions he draws are irresistible. No real attempt has been made to refute them. Mr. Ropes ('The Campaign of Waterloo,' 235, 236, 258, 262, 280, 288) substantially accepts them. We have accepted them also, but with some reservations. German and English writers as a rule avoid a thorough examination of the subject.

extraordinary career. Four corps of the French army, their movements admirably concealed, are moved from between Lille and Metz along the northern borders of France, under the beard, so to speak, of an unsuspecting enemy; two corps are moved from Paris and Soissons to join these. On the night of June 14 the whole army, 128,000 strong, is concentrated upon a narrow front, near the Sambre and the town of Charleroy, ready in the course of a single march to pounce upon and seize the weak allied centre. Meanwhile the two hostile armies, about 220,000 strong, have scarcely stirred, and remain for the most part spread over an immense space, their centre and one of their fractions being dangerously exposed.

Napoleon's object for the following day, the 15th, is to close on and destroy the corps of Zieten, extended along and near the Sambre, to occupy the strategic points of Quatre Bras and Sombreffe on the lateral road from Nivelles to Namur, the main line of communication of the allies, and at the same time to command at Quatre Bras the great main-road from Charleroy to Brussels, an avenue into the midst of Belgium, and the line very weakly held by the allied centre. This operation was quite feasible; its success would have annihilated part of Blucher's army, and would have placed the Emperor in a position in which he could hope to strike the hostile army with effect should they move against him, and then to separate and beat them one after another, as he had done in his immortal campaign of Italy. Napoleon's march was perfectly designed, but the accident that delayed Vandamme, the desertion of Bourmont, and the mischance that kept Gérard back—this retarded the advance to Charleroy. The corps of Zieten, ably handled, escaped, and a large part of the French army, which ought to have been over the Sambre by noon, was as night fell on the southern bank of the river. Meanwhile, owing mainly to the hesitations of Ney, Quatre Bras was not seized as it might have easily been, and partly owing to the skill of *Z*ieten, and partly to disputes between Grouchy and Vandamme, the same incident occurred as regards Sombreffe. The day, it has truly been said, was incomplete, but it was not the less full of most auspicious promise. The allies were still far apart from each other, and unable to resist Napoleon with nearly their united forces; he was within easy reach of their weak centre, and might expect important success on the morrow.

The Emperor on the night of the 15th was suffering from the physical decline which affected his conduct in the campaign, but we differ from the critics who impute inactivity to him on the morning of the 16th. He thought his enemies were falling back before him, according to true strategic principles; there was no necessity, in that case, for a rapid forward movement. He expected easily to master Quatre Bras and Sombreffe, and even to reach Brussels on June 17. But his dispositions were so ably made that they assured him success in almost any event, and ought to have secured him decisive success in the events that happened. Ney was directed to occupy Quatre Bras, and to send a detachment to his right to support the main army; Grouchy was ordered to advance to Sombreffe, and even to Gembloux. But meanwhile Blucher had pressed forward to Sombreffe and Ligny with three-fourths of his army only, eager to give battle, hoping for aid from Wellington, who, however, was in no position to give it. Napoleon admirably seized the occasion, and made arrangements that ought to have destroyed the Prussian army—nay, probably brought the campaign to an end. While the Emperor should attack Blucher in front, the detachment of Ney was to fall on his rear; D'Erlon was ordered afterwards to make a similar movement. Had either attack been made, Ligny would have been another Jena. But Ney had been most remiss and irresolute on this day; he had even disobeyed his master's orders. He had not assembled his army at an early hour, as was his simple and obvious duty; as the general result, he had no body of troops to descend on the rear of the Prussians. D'Erlon failed also to make his attack, partly owing to the misconduct of Ney, partly to his own thoughtlessness and want of insight, in some degree to a mistake made by Napoleon himself. Blucher thus escaped the annihilation that had been prepared for him, but after a desperate conflict his centre was pierced through, and his army was driven, beaten, from the field. In the meantime Ney at Quatre Bras had fought an in-decisive combat with Wellington, whose forces had come up in driblets and piecemeal. The Marshal ought not only to have been able to make the detachment, which would have wrought the ruin of Blucher, but ought to have severely beaten the Duke, who largely owed his safety for a time to the Belgian Perponcher. Ney, how-ever, would not collect his forces in time; he set express orders at naught, whatever his motive. He held Welling-ton, indeed, in check, but this was a trifle to what he should have achieved. The 16th, like the 15th, was in-complete, but Napoleon had gained already most impor-tant success, and the future was big with magnificent promise.

Ligny had not blotted out the Prussian army, as the Emperor had had reason to expect, but superior strategy had wrought its effects. The French had mastered the weak allied centre; Blucher, defeated on the 16th, had been forced away from his colleague; it was impossible, had due precautions been taken, that the two chiefs could join hands in front of Brussels. An opportunity now presented itself, such as has seldom presented itself in war, to attack Wellington and to beat the enemy in detail, the great end of Napoleon's aims. The British General was isolated at Quatre Bras; Napoleon and Ney could fall upon him early on the 17th with forces far superior in numbers and strength. He could hardly have escaped a great disaster. The examples of many campaigns since the days of Turenne prove what the Napoleon of 1796 to 1809 would assuredly have done at this conjuncture. He would have made himself certain of the situation on the night of the 16th, have detached from his army a strong restraining wing to pursue and to hold Blucher in check, and then assailed Wellington quickly in overwhelming force. But all went wrong with the French army on that eventful night; the retreat of the Prussians was not even observed. Napoleon fell ill, and was overcome by the lethargy that for a time paralysed his commanding powers. He gave no orders until late on the morning of the 17th; he even contemplated a halt for a day. As the forenoon was advancing, he changed his purpose; he gave Grouchy a large restraining wing, directing him to follow Blucher and to complete his defeat, warning him that the allied leaders might try to unite, practically ordering the Marshal to stand between them. He then marched to Quatre Bras with the mass of his forces, in the hope of reaching and overpowering Wellington. This was his characteristic and perfectly correct strategy, but it was too late; the opportunity had been lost. Napoleon had again to complain of Ney at Quatre Bras, but the chance of completely defeating Wellington had passed away; the Duke had skilfully effected his retreat. Napoleon pursued his adversary, but to little purpose; military movements were almost prevented by torrents of rain. The French army on the evening of the 17th halted in front of Wellington's army before Waterloo.

The Prussian army retreated from Ligny to Wavre, defeated but not pursued, or even observed. This movement was made by the direction of Gneisenau, Blucher having been disabled for a time; it has been extolled by the idolaters of success, but it was essentially an ill-designed and feeble movement. As affairs stood on June 17, the Prussians could have made for Waterloo, and joined Wellington—the operations of the French had been so tardy and careless; this would really have been fine strategy. The retreat to Wavre left them far from their supports, and ought to have proved disastrous on June 18. Nevertheless, if we except Thielmann, who halted for several hours and much too long, the Prussian leaders showed activity and resource; the troops, beaten as they had been, were not cowed, and gave proof of remarkable energy. By the night of the 17th the four corps of Blucher's army—Bulow had come into line from Liége and Hannut—were assembled around Wavre, on both banks of the Dyle; they were about 90,000 strong. The object of their chiefs was now to join Wellington; but they were some ten or eleven miles from Waterloo, a most difficult country between, not, as at Ligny, about six or seven, with an excellent communication by the lateral road from Nivelles to Namur. Meanwhile Grouchy, in command of the restraining wing, had reached Gembloux, where he had been sent by Napoleon; but his movement had been extraordinarily slow. On the night of the 17th he was hardly beyond Gembloux—that is, from ten to fourteen miles from Wavre. This was a bad beginning; but nothing was yet endangered had Grouchy taken his measures for the next day with judgment and insight. He had ascertained long before daybreak on the 18th that the Prussian army was around Wavre; had he broken up from Gembloux at an early hour, and marched across the Dyle by Moustier and Ottignies, he would have prevented Blucher from joining Wellington, and France would not have lost Waterloo.

The morning of June 18 has come; the decisive success which might have been won on the 16th and the 17th is now hardly possible. Napoleon, indeed, might have been checkmated. Had the allied commanders fallen back

22

beyond Brussels, they could have joined hands without running risks; in that case their armies would have been greatly superior to the French in numbers. Napoleon would have been fortunate had he repassed the frontier— discomfited, baffled, his plans frustrated. But Wellington chose to make a stand at Waterloo with an army weaker than it need have been, and very much weaker than that of his enemy, on the assumption that Blucher would come to his support, about mid-day or a little after. The Duke believed that Napoleon had more than 90,000 men in his front, the whole French army, in fact, except 15,000; he could not have withstood the Emperor's attack, in that case, for any length of time with his motley army of 70,000. Nay, though Napoleon had only 72,000 men, the Duke would have been defeated before his colleague could reach him, had the attack been made in the early forenoon, as it would have certainly been made but for the state of the weather. On the other hand, neither Blucher nor Wellington had a right to suppose that a powerful restraining wing would not be employed to prevent their junction; in that position of affairs they had no right to assume that their armies would come together on the field of the battle at hand.

These calculations were in principle false; it was the insolent play of fortune that they proved successful. The great fight of Waterloo, however, begins; the tactics of the French show impatience and want of caution; the attacks are ill-conducted and ill-designed. Ney is as reckless as he was remiss at Quatre Bras; the strength of Napoleon's army is wasted. The defence of Wellington is most admirably sustained; the constancy of his British and German Legionary troops is above praise. Meanwhile Grouchy, the commander of the restraining wing, does exactly what he ought not to do; he leaves Gembloux late; his movements are slow. He does not make for the Dyle at Moustier and Ottignies; he sets at naught the counsels of Gérard, and will not march on Waterloo when he hears its thunder. He does not try to place himself between Blucher and Wellington; he advances to Wavre, keeping aloof from his master; he allows Blucher, scarcely molested, to reach the decisive scene of action. The restraining wing, in a word, is almost worse than useless. Meantime Bulow begins his attack. Napoleon is compelled to fight two battles; the French army is placed in terrible straits; and, after the defeat of part of the Imperial Guard, the irruption of Zieten and Pirch completes a disaster almost as frightful as ever was seen in war. But had Grouchy been equal to his task, the catastrophe could not have occurred; nay, Waterloo would have been a victory for the arms of France.

The splendour of the triumph achieved at Waterloo cannot hide from the sight of the true student of war the strategic errors which, so to speak, were its prelude. The superiority of Napoleon in the great combinations of his art, and the complete inferiority of his opponents, are, indeed, the salient features of the campaign of 1815; these give it its chief historical interest. With an army not much more than half in numbers that of his enemy, the Emperor outmanœuvres the allied commanders at once; but for accidents he would have routed Blucher on the 16th, and probably routed Wellington on the next day. His chances on the 18th were less; but he would have gained Waterloo had he attacked in the morning, or had Gérard had the command of Grouchy. The strategy of his adversaries, on the other hand, was essentially faulty from first to last; strategically they were not fit to cope with Napoleon. Their arrangements before the contest were ill-conceived; the dispersion of their forces, the weakness of their centre, the great distance between their headquarters, their immobility when they first heard of Napoleon's advance—all this subjected them from the outset to the gravest peril. Other and even more palpable mistakes followed. Blucher rushed into the lion's mouth at Ligny, and only escaped being swallowed up by a chance. The delays of Wellington on the 15th may be yet explained ; but they were unfortunate in a very high degree. The campaign might have been brought to an end at Ligny. Gneisenau's march to Wavre was a bad half-measure, which increased the distance between the allied armies ; the Duke ought not to have left a great detachment at Hal and Tubize, and weakened his army at the decisive point. He ought not to have offered battle on the 18th ; the flank march from Wavre ought to have failed—nay, proved disastrous. Blucher and Wellington, instead of running enormous and unnecessary risks, ought to have fallen behind Brussels, and thus have baffled their enemy, and made their ultimate success certain.

It would be unfair, however, to judge either Blucher or Wellington as strategists by their operations in 1815. They, indeed, gave each other cordial support, and acted as true companions in arms ; but their movements give proof of the divided counsels so often fatal in the case of the chiefs of a League, and, in this very instance, not without untoward results. Wellington would probably not have advanced to Quatre Bras, with portions of his army hurried up piecemeal, had not Blucher advanced to Ligny. He would not have challenged Napoleon with all the chances against him ; he probably would have fallen back on Waterloo, marked out by him as a position for a great defensive battle. Had he had the command of the two armies, they might have been assembled at that place on June 17, and had Napoleon attacked he must have been defeated. In leaving the detachment at Hal and Tubize, the Duke perhaps revealed a lurking suspicion that Blucher could not reach the field of Waterloo ; in that case the detachment would have been of the greatest use to him had he been compelled to retreat behind the Forest of Soignies ; it would probably have joined his army and made up for its losses. And Wellington, it seems likely, would not have fought at Waterloo had he not thought the possession of Brussels of supreme importance. Here he made strategy subordinate to the needs of politics; it may account for his conduct in this respect that the general gave way to the statesman.

But if the strategy of the allied chiefs cannot commend itself to impartial judges, high praise, though in different degrees, is certainly due to both as soldiers. Blucher ought not to have advanced to Ligny; he arrayed his army in the field with little judgment; he made grave mistakes in the battle. But his heroism almost redeemed his faults. The spirit he breathed into his devoted troops enabled them to rise superior to defeat, and gave them the energy we see in their retreat on the 17th. That the Prussian army, too, ever reached Waterloo, and that Bulow fell on Napoleon's flank in time, was owing to Blucher, and Blucher alone; Gneisenau and his subordinates would not have made these movements with success. Here we see Blucher in his best aspect, rash and heady, no doubt, but indomitable in adverse fortune. The conduct of Wellington was even more to be admired in many respects, and the burden and heat of the day on the 18th fell, we must recollect, on the British General. He effected his retreat most skilfully on the 16th; the disposition of his army at Waterloo, and the masterly defence he made on the field, have justly deserved the greatest eulogy. Had Blucher been in command, the old Marshal would probably have been defeated in four or five hours. But what, as always, was apparent in Wellington was his calm, stern, and invincible constancy, the grand strength of character which was his most distinctive excellence. Undoubtedly, as we survey the course of the campaign, we see that Napoleon underrated the best qualities of his antagonists on more than one occasion.

Superior strategy, nevertheless, usually prevails in war.
The superiority of Napoleon's strategy in the campaign
of 1815 is not doubtful. Why, then, was the result the
disaster of Waterloo? We may glance at the minor
causes of Napoleon's defeat, though these did not deter-
mine the final issue. The Emperor's army was too small;
128,000 men could with difficulty be pitted against
220,000; sufficient allowance could not be made for
mere mischances. The 20,000 men sent off to La
Vendée might very probably have redressed the balance
of fortune. Napoleon, too, made some positive mistakes.
He did not summon D'Erlon to the field of Ligny when
D'Erlon appeared; he refused to listen to Jerôme, and
perhaps to Milhaud, as regards the chances of a Prussian
advance from Wavre; he would not believe the movement possible; he allowed Ney at Waterloo to waste the
greatest part of his cavalry; he may have missed an
opportunity to attack with the Guard after the first
repulse of Bulow. And unquestionably he undervalued
Blucher and Wellington, and formed too low an estimate
of both the allied armies. He ridiculed the Prussian chief
as 'an old hussar'; he thought Wellington essentially a
bad General. These false calculations more than once
deceived him. And so it was with the forces opposed to
him. He declared that a French soldier was worth two
Prussians; he would not believe until it was too late that
British troops were what they have always been from
Blenheim and Ramillies to Busaco and Waterloo. All
this certainly told against him, and distinctly affected the
course of events. These, however, were not the main
causes of the catastrophe that was seen at Waterloo.
Had Ney been equal to himself—nay, had he obeyed his
orders — Ligny would have beheld the destruction of
Blucher's army, the Duke could hardly have effected his
escape, the campaign in Belgium probably would have
come to an end. The same result would have followed

had Ney not recalled D'Erlon, or had D'Erlon acted with vigour and insight; and Reille also is to blame for the delays before Quatre Bras. On the 17th, again, Napoleon must have gained decisive success had he been the General of Arcola and Rivoli. We can only ascribe the extraordinary failure of that day, when the issue of the contest was virtually in his hands, to the lethargy which occasionally made him prostrate, and simply good for nothing. He would have gained Waterloo but for the strange misconduct of Grouchy, an aberration of judgment most difficult to account for. He could even have won but for the state of the weather. The paramount causes of the result of the campaign were that Napoleon was not the Napoleon of old, and that the lieutenants in whom he trusted failed him. Soult, too, the Chief of his Staff, deserves severe censure for his inactivity, his remissness, and bad despatches. Very possibly he had much to do with the tissue of mistakes that kept Grouchy away from his master.* Except Gérard, too, the subordinate chiefs of the French army were inferior to their former selves, and this was especially the case with the chiefs in the highest command. Nor can this surprise anyone acquainted with the facts. The memory of past misfortunes weighed heavily on all these men. They were unnerved by the prospect of a struggle with Europe; they had been demoralised by the events of 1814-15; they were divided by jealousies and angry discords; they knew their officers and their troops had little confidence in them. The contest may be described in a figure of speech: the eagle was suffering, even when it made its swoop. This, at the outset, was terrible and swift; but it could not use its wings to close on its quarry; it had to fight with beak and talons only; and yet it was with difficulty over-

---

* Thiébault, we have said, disliked Soult, but says of the Marshal ('Mémoires,' v. 355): 'Bourmont major-général n'eut pas mieux fait que Soult.'

powered by the birds of prey that gathered around it at last.

The brave men who fought in 1815 have passed away; no evil phantoms should rise over their honoured graves; enough to say they nearly all did their duty. A very few words, however, may be said on the qualities displayed by the contending armies. The French soldiery gave proof of the high courage of the race; but the French army was deficient in discipline, organisation, and the power of endurance. The old Grand Army would not have been annihilated on the day of Waterloo. Many of the auxiliaries of Wellington did not stand the strain of a tremendous conflict, but many did service of real value; the British and German Legionary troops were worthy of themselves. As for the Prussian army, it was ill-directed at Ligny; but it exhibited great tenacity and stubborn valour, and its conduct in the retreat of the 17th deserves the highest praise. As regards Napoleon, it was well, perhaps, for his renown that he succumbed on his last fatal field of Waterloo. The campaign in Belgium might have ended on June 16, but the war would assuredly not have ended. The Emperor made a complete mistake in calculating that England would change her policy after a single defeat. The League of Europe was bent on destroying its still-feared enemy. Napoleon must have fallen at last, with less glory on his arms, perhaps, than that which shone on them in the campaign of 1815. For the rest, that grand passage of arms remains a model on his part of splendid conceptions marred by faulty execution from first to last, as on the part of his adversaries the reverse was the case. They carried out admirably, as a rule, conceptions essentially faulty in themselves. But Waterloo has not dimmed the fame of Napoleon any more than Zama has dimmed the fame of Hannibal. Each is supreme in modern and in ancient war.

CHAPTER XII

THE RETREAT OF GROUCHY—THE SECOND FALL OF NAPOLEON

Grouchy, as yet ignorant of the result of Waterloo, makes preparation to attack Thielmann and march on Brussels—Thielmann, who had heard of the victory, attacks Grouchy, but is repulsed—Grouchy receives the news of the complete defeat of Napoleon—He retreats to Namur, and thence to Givet—This movement was rapid and judicious, but has been unduly extolled—Partial success of the French armies on the frontier and in La Vendée—The intelligence of the rout of Waterloo reaches Paris—Unwise attitude of the Chambers and their foolish expectations—Perfidious conduct of Fouché—He schemes for the restoration of Louis XVIII.—Napoleon returns to Paris and proposes to defend France if assisted by the Chambers—These, under the influence of Fouché and Lafayette, usurp power—Napoleon abdicates—Fouché at the head of a Provisional Government—He goes on with his treacherous policy, and prevents any real efforts to make a national defence—His negotiations with Wellington, who seconds him and indicates the conditions of peace—Fouché exposed to danger—Proposal of Napoleon to attack Blucher rejected by Fouché—Indignation of the army and the population of Paris—Imprudence of Blucher—Wise and statesmanlike conduct of Wellington—The capitulation of Paris and the restoration of Louis XVIII.—Fouché's policy triumphs, but only for a short time—Great position of Wellington—The service he does to France—Reflections—Conclusion.

THE rout of Waterloo left the army of Grouchy the only organised force remaining to France in Belgium. The Marshal, ignorant of the catastrophe, cherished, we have seen, the illusion that his master had won the battle; he resolved during the night of June 18 to make good his way from Wavre to Brussels, where he expected to find and join the main French army. He ordered Vandamme to cross the Dyle and to come into line with him, and made preparations for a determined attack on the enemy in his front between Rixensart and Wavre. By daybreak on the 19th Thielmann received the news that the allies had gained a decisive victory; he detached a considerable part of his troops to the support of Zieten, who, we have said, had not reached Waterloo in force—it is difficult to understand this movement; he fell on Grouchy at an early hour in the morning, assuming that the Marshal was thinking only of his escape. Grouchy, however, had as yet heard nothing of the tragical events which had just taken place; he made a vigorous resistance, but was compelled to give way, Vandamme having disobeyed his orders, and not having come to his superior's aid. The Prussians pressed forward, Thielmann having been informed of the results of Waterloo by a despatch from Blucher himself, and having been apprised that Pirch had been sent off from the field to intercept Grouchy and to bar his retreat. But the French successfully opposed the enemy; and part of Vandamme's corps having reached the scene, Thielmann was obliged to execute a change of front, this, however, enabling him still to keep Grouchy in check, and to retain his hold on the roads from Wavre to Brussels. But Grouchy, seconded by this time by Vandamme in force, resumed the offensive and advanced. Thielmann, assailed in front, and threatened in flank by one of the divisions of Vandamme which had crossed the Dyle, with somewhat precipitate haste retreated, and, losing all contact with the allied army, fell back fully half a march towards Louvain.

It was now near eleven in the forenoon. Grouchy, still in command of more than 30,000 men—his losses at Wavre were not 3,000—pushed forward to Rosieren and La Bavette, elated with his recent success, fully expecting

that he would soon meet the Emperor.   At this moment
a haggard spectre, so to speak, came across him.   This
was one of the two messengers* sent off to inform the
unfortunate Marshal of the late catastrophe; broken down
and terror-stricken, he could hardly utter a word or report
his orders, which appear not to have been in writing.†
Grouchy, doubtless stung by conscience to the quick,
and shedding, it has been said, bitter tears to no purpose,
instantly assembled a kind of council of war.   His first
and, we must add his natural, impulse was to try to
justify his conduct on the preceding day, and especially
to explain why he had not followed the counsels of Gérard
to march on Waterloo.   His excuses were the lame and
utterly false apologies which he afterwards endeavoured
to palm off on history; he was listened to in cold and
significant silence.   The time, however, for complaining
of what had happened was passed; the terrible question
was before the French chiefs how to extricate themselves
from the midst of their victorious enemies, and if possible
to effect their retreat into France.   Grouchy thought for
a moment of making an attempt to close on the rear of
the hostile armies, and thus to attract them towards his
own; Vandamme boldly proposed to advance on Brussels,
and then, making a long circuit southwards, to reach the
frontier between Lille and Valenciennes.   These vain projects, however, were soon abandoned; Grouchy properly
resolved to adopt the only course that promised a reasonable hope of safety—to fall back on Namur, and thence
to make his way along the Meuse to Givet.   It is still
uncertain whether, in taking this step, he was acting in
conformity to his master's orders, which seem to have
indicated a movement in this direction.‡

---

* Charras (ii. 160) says there was but a single messenger. H. Houssaye ('Waterloo,' ii. 427-433) says there were two—one a spy.

† Another of the innumerable proofs of the negligence of Soult.

‡ Thiers ('Histoire du Consulat et de l'Empire,' vi. 552) relates that

The retreat began before noon on the 19th; it was conducted with praiseworthy celerity, and on this day with judgment. Pajol, a very skilful and experienced soldier, was despatched to observe Thielmann, and to feign pursuit; Excelmans pressed onwards to Namur with his cavalry, and reached the fortress before nightfall, a march from Wavre of more than twenty miles. Meanwhile the rest of the army retreated in two columns—Grouchy, with the corps of Gérard, by Mont St. Guibert and Gentinnes; Vandamme and his corps by Dion le Mont, Tourinnes, and Grand Leez. The movement was not molested; it was about twice as rapid as that from Gembloux to Wavre on June 18. By the close of the day Grouchy had attained the main lateral road from Nivelles to Namur, and had his bivouacs round Mazy and Temploux; Vandamme had advanced beyond Gembloux, and was but a few miles from the Marshal on his right. The double march was one of about twenty miles; it contrasts most strikingly with that of the day before.* Had Grouchy pushed forward to Moustier and Ottignies on the morning of the 18th, even nearly as quickly as he had fallen back from Wavre—nay, had he marched from Walhain to Waterloo at an equal rate of speed—he would have turned the scales of fortune in favour of the arms of France.

Meantime Thielmann, deceived by Pajol—he masked the retreat with remarkable skill, and successfully rejoined the mass of the army—had continued to fall back for some hours, and did not turn to pursue Grouchy until it was too late. Pirch, too, at the head of troops worn out by

---

Napoleon ordered Grouchy to retreat on Namur, but he gives no authority. Charras (ii. 160) asserts that Napoleon gave no such orders. H. Houssaye ('Waterloo,' ii. 433) says the retreat, by Napoleon's directions, was to be either on Philippeville or on Givet. This seems probable.

* Grouchy, too, had to carry his sick and wounded men with him in his retreat. This must have hampered him to some extent, and there was no such impediment on June 18.

the harassing marches of two days, only reached Mellery by the night of the 19th, still some miles from the road from Nivelles to Namur; Thielmann was as yet far away and backward. Besides, the united forces of the Prussian chiefs were not superior to those of Grouchy in numbers; they were converging, at wide distances, against a concentrated enemy; their movements were necessarily, therefore, cautious; they had hardly a chance of defeating Grouchy. On the 20th the French army resumed its movement, but this was imperilled for a time by an untoward accident. Grouchy, in command of the corps of Gérard, and encumbered by the charge of many sick and wounded men, had ordered Vandamme to cover the retreat; but Vandamme, always a bad companion in arms, had left his troops and gone off to Namur, conduct for which no kind of excuse can be made; his corps was attacked by Thielmann's horsemen on the morning of the 20th, and for a time was in some danger. Simultaneously the advanced guard of Pirch, moving from Mellery, had approached Grouchy; but the Marshal, a really good cavalry officer, succeeded in baffling Thielmann's efforts. Vandamme, hastening back from Namur, kept the enemy at bay; Grouchy and the men of Gérard reached the town in safety; Vandamme followed at a short distance. The population of Namur detested the Prussians, and felt generous sympathies with the French in their distress. They gave Grouchy every assistance in their power; his army before long was across the Sambre. Teste, another skilful and bold officer, repelled the attack made by the Prussians on the place, and beat them back with not an inconsiderable loss. Meanwhile Grouchy had continued his movement; his army, almost intact, had come under the guns of Givet by the evening of June 21.* The

---

* For the retreat of Grouchy, see Grouchy, 'Relation Succincte,' 46, 47; Ollech, 263-269; Wagner, iv. 99; Charras, ii. 157-165; H. Houssaye, 'Waterloo,' ii. 453-488. Chesney, a detractor of Napo-

intelligence and the resource he had shown in the retreat
would have saved Napoleon three days before.

By this time a revolution, marked with sinister features
and humiliating in the extreme to a great nation, was
again changing the destinies of France. For some days
after Napoleon had left Paris the intelligence that reached
the capital was of auspicious promise. The forces on the
eastern frontier were keeping the enemy in check; the
rising in La Vendée had collapsed; the victory of Ligny
was welcomed with noisy rejoicings while Waterloo was
being fought and decided. There were no tidings of the
war on June 19, but on the 20th a sudden and terrible
rumour, disseminated, no doubt, by a traitor's hand,
spread far and near that a great battle had been lost in
Belgium, and that the French army was dissolving in
complete rout. A thrill of alarm and dismay ran through
the mass of the citizens, and, save amidst the populace in
its lower orders—and these were unorganised and without
leaders—few symptoms appeared of a patriotic impulse to
rally around the Emperor and to resist the invader. In
the presence of a disaster declared to be fatal, faction,
selfish fears, and the divisions and hatreds of party began
to exhibit themselves in their worst aspects; and the
attitude of the Chambers, the depositories of power, was
from the first moment unworthy of the representatives of
the State. The deputies and the peers had, as it were,
but yesterday bowed before the Emperor and sworn
allegiance to him. Had real statesmen been among their

---

leon, and an apologist of Grouchy ('Waterloo Lectures,' 235, 236),
extols the retreat as a grand operation of war. It really was a well-
combined movement of a very ordinary kind. Thielmann lost fifteen
hours; Pirch's troops were unable to press a pursuit; and, besides,
Thielmann and Pirch had not the means of overpowering or inter-
cepting Grouchy. What is striking in the retreat was the celerity of
the march, the very opposite of the hesitations, the delays, and the
negligence of June 17 and 18. This makes Grouchy's conduct all the
more inexcusable.

ranks, they would have resolved, desperate as it might now appear, to support his cause, at least for the present. But the profound distrust they had always shown of Napoleon exhibited itself in vain and angry complaints, and in their inexperienced self-conceit they began to imagine that they could dispense with the great master of war, and save France and secure peace by their own efforts. Two sentiments at this moment possessed their minds and impelled the immense majority to break with Napoleon. They persuaded themselves that on his return from his late defeat he would lay hands on every part of the Government, and effect a second 18th Brumaire; the reign of Liberalism and of the new ideas would thus come to an end. And at the same time they cherished the idle belief that the armed League of Europe would instantly sheathe the sword should they offer Napoleon up as a sacrifice; that should they throw Jonah over the tempest would cease; as if France had not been his accomplice in recent events, and had not given him the means of challenging the world to arms.

The base intriguer, who at this conjuncture acquired a bad ascendancy in the State in France, left nothing undone to promote these opinions and to increase their force. During the brief period of the second reign of Napoleon, Fouché had been trafficking with the allied Powers; he had betrayed many most important secrets; he had even disclosed the strength of the French army, though he had ingeniously counterplotted his own plots, and had withheld the plan of operations he had promised to furnish. He had hated and feared Napoleon for months; and had the Emperor been victorious in Belgium, he would not improbably have made an example of his traitorous Minister. Fouché's object at this crisis was to overthrow his master, and to compass his ruin, whatever the means. He poured the leprous distilment of his evil counsels into the willing ears of members of both Houses, and quickened their animosities and suspicious terrors. ' He had urged the Emperor to abdicate at the Champ de Mai ; but the great gambler would throw the dice of war, and had even forgotten his old game. His army had disappeared ; France was in the extreme of peril. Napoleon was within a few miles of the capital ; he would proclaim himself a dictator, dissolve the Chambers, fight desperately to the last, and, sooner than yield, destroy Paris and let the forces of anarchy loose. He must, therefore, be compelled to abdicate, or be driven from the throne.' Fouché at the same time dropped significant hints that, the great disturber of the world having been removed from the scene, the allies might accept the infant King of Rome as the Sovereign of France. They had no wish to impose on the nation a Government not of its choice ; the arrangement would secure the permanent repose of Europe. It is certain, however, that while he made these professions he was already intriguing for the restoration of Louis XVIII., in the expectation that this would raise him, perhaps, to the highest place in the State. He was too sagacious not to see that, after Waterloo, there was scarcely a hope for the cause of Napoleon or his son, and that the allies would place the Bourbons on the throne again. He had resolved to follow and direct the set of an irresistible current. His services to the coalition and to Louis XVIII. would enable him, he hoped, to play in 1815 the part played by Talleyrand the year before ; he would be the master of the situation —nay, of the restored monarchy. Treachery and deception were the elements in which Fouché lived ; but here he stifled any scruples he may have felt by the reflection that, when he had gained his ends, it would be in his power to mitigate the White Terror which he foresaw might become the policy of the new Government of France.

Meanwhile Napoleon had arrived in Paris in the early

morning of June 21. On his way from Philippeville he
had passed through Laon, where he had given some
orders, and drawn up an account of the campaign. He
had scarcely uttered a word during the long journey.
When he reached the palace of the Elysée, he rebuked
one of his affrighted followers by the remark that honour
at least was not lost. After giving a few hours to much-
needed repose, he met his ministers in Council ; explained
what, in his view, had been the cause of the great reverse
for his arms ; set forth, at some length, the resources that
still remained to France; and insisted that if the nation
would earnestly second his efforts—' would be the Rome
of Cannæ, not the Carthage of Zama '—the war might be
prolonged and an honourable peace secured. Whatever
may be thought of the soundness of this judgment—and
we cannot forget the marvels of 1814, though the result,
we are convinced, must have been the same—it deserves
notice that Napoleon did not entertain the designs attributed to him by the Chambers and Fouché. He saw,
indeed, that the only prospect of safety for France was to
concentrate in his hands all the powers of the State for
the moment; he expressed a hope that the Houses, of
their own accord, would make him a dictator during the
existing contest. But he knew that the days of the
18th Brumaire had passed away ; he never contemplated
a *coup d'état*. He felt that the representatives of France
must rally around him, and give him loyal and undivided
support, if he was to steer the vessel of the State through
an appalling sea of troubles. ' In the close union between
the Chambers and myself,' he emphatically said, ' is our
only chance of success.'

These true and noble words made a profound impression
on men already trembling for themselves and their master,
but still yielding to the spell of the genius of a great ruler.
Carnot, simple-minded, but a sincere patriot, was convinced that the Chambers would comply with Napoleon's

23

request, and would make him the absolute head of the
State for the time. But Lucien Bonaparte, the abettor
of the 18th Brumaire, and Davoût, a soldier who not
wrongly dreaded what a popular assembly might attempt,
pronounced for a dissolution of the Chambers at the
present crisis; this was within the Emperor's constitutional rights, as these had been declared by the Acte
Additionnel. One minister, however, more sagacious or
better informed, denied that the proposed dictatorship
would be ever conceded; he hinted, not obscurely, that
the Houses wished to get rid of Napoleon, and to negotiate
with the allies on behalf of the infant King of Rome.
Fouché, who had stammered out a few ambiguous phrases,
perfidiously let the deputies and the Peers know that the
dissolution of the Chambers was being prepared; he
added that measures would be taken to put down resistance by force. The assembly of the representatives broke
out into frenzied passion, and was ready to declare
Napoleon an enemy of the State. Lafayette, a stiff-
necked constitutional pedant, blind to the real situation
of affairs, carried by an almost unanimous vote a solemn
resolution to the effect that it would be a crime of high
treason to dissolve or to prorogue the Chambers, and
that the ministers of the Emperor must appear at their
bar. This stickler for forms and legality did not perceive
that what he was doing was a violation of the Acte
Additionnel, and was really in itself a flagrant *coup d'état*.
The Chamber of Peers acted after its kind; composed as
it was for the most part of Napoleon's creatures, it
followed simply in the wake of the lower House.

Had Napoleon at this crisis dissolved the Chambers
and appealed to Frenchmen to rally round his throne, he
would have been justified by the letter of the Constitution
and the law. But of what avail were considerations such
as these, when armed Europe was upon the frontier;
when an immense disaster had already occurred; when

the Acte Additionnel had no real hold on the nation; when the Legislature and the Government were in conflict; when revolution was plainly already at hand? Detractors of Napoleon have charged him with culpable weakness—nay, with pusillanimity at this conjuncture. He ought, they have said, to have braved everything, seized supreme power and involved the nation in a desperate struggle. It is no doubt true that, as was seen, even on the 18th Brumaire he dreaded a contest with the representatives of France. Like most soldiers, familiar chiefly with material force, he felt embarrassed in the presence of moral power, and he had not indomitable constancy in the extreme of misfortune. As had been manifest, too, in the campaign in Belgium, he had lost much of the energy and decision of his prime; and certainly few great men have been placed in the terrible situation he had now to confront. Yet these were not the paramount causes that prevented him from defying the Chambers and insisting on a dissolution that must have been worse than useless. In the expressive language he used on another occasion, he felt that he had become a mark for the animosities of faction in France, and that he had been placed under the ban of the great powers of Europe. To have broken up the Legislature under these conditions, to have grasped at a dictatorship, and made an appeal to the sword, would have only led to civil war and anarchy, and caused universal national ruin. He would have, perhaps, had the support of millions of Frenchmen, of the remains of the armies, of part of the peasantry, of the populace of the towns; but he would have been resisted by the great bodies of the State, by a majority of the upper classes, by the intellect and the good sense of the nation. What would have been his chances, in these circumstances, in a struggle with Europe? Once France refused to support him as a united people, Napoleon rightly judged that his occupation was gone,

23—2

and that he could not turn aside the coming strokes of Destiny.

The dissolution of the Chambers, therefore, was not to be thought of, though they had really usurped supreme power in the State. Napoleon, after hearing what had taken place, declared that he was ready to abdicate—Fouché circulated the remark with malignant delight—but he endeavoured for a few hours to avert and retard fate, and to see if a compromise was not possible. He proposed that two Commissions, partly selected by himself and partly by the Houses, should be formed, and should report on the existing condition of affairs, and on the measures required for the public safety. The Commissions agreed that a great national effort should be made, and that, if necessary, France should defend herself; but the representatives of the Chambers—their leader was Lafayette—insisted that negotiations should be set on foot to obtain peace; and that this would be impossible were Napoleon to remain at the head of the State, as the Coalition would have no dealings with him. This was virtually a declaration that the Emperor must abdicate, or be deprived of his crown. After some hesitation and angry complaints in the Chambers, Napoleon reluctantly consented that commissioners should repair to the camp of the allies to treat, not in his own name, but in that of the two Houses. It was time that equivocation and deception should end. The Emperor, seeing that he had been practically deposed, announced his abdication in the dignified words he knew how to make use of on great occasions. He implored the nation and its representatives to unite with the noble object of preserving France; while he declared that his political existence had come to an end, he proclaimed his son his successor to the imperial throne. This was a last tribute, perhaps to pride, perhaps to paternal feeling, but he had no illusions as to what was about to happen. ' I abdicate in favour of the Bourbons,' he bitterly said ; ' not of a child kept at Vienna an imprisoned hostage.'

The Chambers, with a sentiment of respect for fallen greatness, passed a vote of thanks to Napoleon for the abdication they had, in fact, extorted. It was otherwise with many of the followers of the discrowned Emperor. The scenes of 1814 were witnessed again. Ney, deeply responsible for the issue of the late campaign, but recklessly lending an ear to the counsels of Fouché, spoke against his great master in the House of Peers ; courtiers and servitors fell away from the benefactor to whom they owed everything. Napoleon, really by the orders of Fouché, was removed to Malmaison from the Elysée, for there were fears that he might attempt a *coup d'état*. Davoût, with singular want of feeling, urged him to quit the soil of France.* History compassionately throws a veil over the great victim, as he remained for a few days in almost deserted loneliness. Napoleon was alive, but within the Inferno of Dante ; there could be no hope for him, whatever might happen ; he was the proscribed outlaw of Europe and France ; Marius sitting amidst the ruins of Carthage, Hannibal after the catastrophe of Zama, might look forward to a change of fortune he could not contemplate. He had been unjustly treated by the allies ; France had abandoned him, in defeat, with weak and unwise levity. But if we calmly look back at what he had been in the past, we can hardly feel surprise that he was made a sacrifice to the animosities and fears of the civilised world. The blood of Danton had choked Robespierre ; the tyranny of the Emperor, who had bestrode the Continent, the violence of a despot who had exhausted France, not unnaturally brought about the second fall of Napoleon. It was as nothing that he had protested, when he had regained his throne, that he was a

* Thiébault ('Mémoires,' v. 369, 370) describes this scene, probably with exaggeration.

changed being, and had no thought but of peace; he had ruled for years by the sword; he was struck down by it.

The question of the succession of the young King of Rome was adroitly eluded by the Chambers. A Provisional Government was appointed; Fouché contrived with cynical audacity to have himself named President. He had got rid of the master he dreaded and had betrayed, but the obstacles to his policy were great and might be fatal to him. The Chambers were opposed, almost to a man, to the return of the Bourbons; one of their first acts was to vote supplies for continuing the war, and to issue Decrees, parodies of those of the Convention of 1793, though it is questionable if they thought resistance possible, for they sent envoys to the allies without delay. The Provisional Government, too, was largely composed of regicides; their interests and feelings forbade them to seek for a restoration of Louis XVIII. But Fouché had his arrangements made, and though events seconded him in almost every way, he played his unprincipled part with characteristic skill. One of his first expedients was to release from Vincennes, where he had been imprisoned, the royalist agent Vitrolles, who, we had seen, had tried to stir up the South against Napoleon; through him, and other obscure messengers, he entered into fresh relations with the exiled Court in Belgium. At the same time, while he made great professions of strengthening the defences of Paris, and calling the nation to arms, and while he still talked about a regency, and the Duke of Orleans, he steadily went on with his work of intrigue, and manœuvred to place the King again on his throne. He laboured dexterously to paralyse every attempt to resist, or even to check the invader; he kept down the population of the capital, passionately eager to take up arms, and enlisted against them the timid fears of the upper classes and the bourgeoisie. The selections he made for the highest commands were significant, and showed his sagacious cunning. He placed a great name, Masséna, at the head of the National Guard of Paris; but Masséna was the shadow of the Chief of Zurich, and was thinking only of self-enjoyment and repose; he made Davoût the commander of all the forces around the capital; and Davoût had declared that, after Waterloo, the coalition would not be opposed with success. As events progressed, and no doubt could remain that Paris was in a state of formidable defence, Fouché assembled a great Council of War, composed of Marshals and Generals of high degree. Such a Council proverbially never fights; and it offered irresistible reasons that Paris could not keep out the enemy with any assurance of permanent success; and that, in any event, the allies were at hand, and would soon have the fortunes of France in their power.

Meanwhile Blucher and Wellington with their victorious forces had crossed the northern borders of France, and were marching on Paris by the western bank of the Oise. They had employed themselves for a few days in capturing strong places upon the frontier, but at the intelligence of the fall of Napoleon they advanced rapidly, hoping to bring the war to an end, Blucher, as was his wont, pressing forward with imprudent want of caution. The negotiators despatched by the Chambers had reached the camp of the old Marshal, and giving too easy credence to vague expressions dropped by Prussian officers had sought an interview with the allied Sovereigns on the Rhine, in the hope that they would not insist on a return of the Bourbons. Fouché sent a second set of envoys to treat with Wellington, the real master of the situation at this moment. The victory of Waterloo had immensely increased the influence in the Councils of Europe the Duke had already acquired by his calm-minded wisdom, and he was almost supreme in the little Court of Louis XVIII., while through Fouché he controlled the Chambers. The conduct of Wellington at this juncture was worthy of his statesman-like and well-balanced judgment. He sincerely thought that the restoration of the House of Bourbon would be in the interest of Europe and of France herself; but, above all, he was desirous of securing peace without further effusion of blood, of avoiding a desperate struggle round the walls of Paris, the consequences of which he could not foresee with certainty, and of establishing Louis XVIII. on his throne with as little delay as possible. With these objects in view he had advised the King to make his entry into France, and to issue a proclamation pledging himself to maintain the Charter, and the rights and interests created by the Revolution and what had flowed from it, and even holding forth a prospect of future reforms, and he spoke freely to Fouché's envoys, knowing perfectly well they would serve his purpose. He said very plainly that in his judgment the Bourbons ought to be restored to the throne, though he admitted the claim of France to choose a Sovereign for herself; but he insisted that the immediate and most urgent question was to avert a conflict, which the negotiators must know would inevitably be in the long-run hopeless, and could only lead to further woes for their country. He gradually obtained their assent to the conditions he laid down as the necessary preliminaries to a suspension of arms: the military forces employed in the defence of Paris must evacuate their positions and retreat to a distance; the allied armies should occupy certain points in the capital, but the police of the city should be entrusted to the National Guard. It was understood that the restoration of the Bourbons would follow as a matter of course.

It was the strange irony of fate that one of the greatest men of his time was associated with one of the very basest at this moment for a common object, although with completely different motives. The countenance of Wellington gave immense support to Fouché—in fact,

almost placed in his hands the immediate future of
France. Yet the position of the arch-intriguer, dexterous
as he was, was not without real danger, and his Machia-
vellian policy was more than once not far from failing.
By the last days of June Grouchy, who had been made
the commander of all the military forces which had in-
vaded Belgium, had brought his own corps and the
remains of the Waterloo army with little loss under the
walls of Paris; a considerable number of troops were
within the city, and Paris was in a good state of defence
along its northern front. At this moment the Prussian
army, diminished by the corps of Pirch detached in the
rear, and now not more than 60,000 strong, was around
Gonesse, a few miles from the capital; the army of
Wellington was near Gournay, at least two marches
distant. This separation of the hostile forces gave an
opportunity to Napoleon's genius. From his retreat at
Malmaison he proposed to fall on Blucher with 70,000 or
80,000 men, who could have been assembled; he pledged
himself to gain a signal victory; he promised that when
this had been won he would instantly lay down his command. The project was certainly attractive in a military
sense; it could not ultimately have changed the course of
events, but it might have revived the glories of Montmirail and Vauchamps. Blucher would, not improbably,
have been defeated. Fouché, however, curtly rejected
proposals which ran counter to his treacherous schemes.
From his point of view he was consistent and in the
right. The slightest temporary success of Napoleon
might have blown into air the intriguer's web of duplicity,
and might, it is not unlikely, have cost Fouché his head.

This, nevertheless, was not the last of the troubles
which beset the head of the Provisional Government.
Blucher, setting Wellington's counsels at nought, marched
across the Seine to the southern front of Paris, in the
hope, perhaps, of storming the city on its unprotected

side. He gave out that he would take the life of Napoleon
should the fallen Emperor come into his hands, and that
he would occupy, not impossibly sack, the capital of
France. This insolence and arrogance stirred Paris to
wrath, made even the half-hearted Chambers indignant,
provoked the population to assume an attitude as vehe-
ment as that of 1792-93, and turned against Fouché the
colleagues he had hitherto mastered and deceived. An
insurrectionary movement seemed impending, and the
army in and around the capital clamoured for a last
appeal to the sword and for a last effort against the
detested invader. Meanwhile the military situation had
become hazardous for the allies ; part of Blucher's cavalry
had fallen into a snare and had been destroyed. The
army of Wellington had, indeed, reached the northern
front of Paris, but it was divided from that of Blucher by
the Seine and the great city ; and the French army, from
80,000 to 90,000 strong, not to speak of irregular levies
not to be despised, stood in a kind of vast fortified camp
between the two hostile masses. At this grave conjuncture the wisdom of the Duke was conspicuously made
manifest ; it averted events that must have been calamitous. He persuaded Blucher to adopt more moderate
language ; he candidly wrote to him that he thought their
two armies were by no means certain of success should
they attack Paris, or even be involved in a great battle.
He pointed out that it was only common prudence to
wait until the other armies of the coalition should appear
on the scene. At the same time he continued in close
relations with Fouché, and through him with his still
numerous partisans, and he reiterated to the negotiators,
who had returned to his camp, the arguments he had
employed with a view to put an end to the war. These
appeals, which as affairs now stood were irresistible to
reflecting and sound-thinking men, and were supported
by accomplished facts with overpowering force, proved

successful, and gained for Wellington his end. The pride
of Blucher was judiciously soothed by making him appear
the arbiter of the proposed arrangements; but Wellington
was their real author, and the conditions he had laid
down from the first were, in the main, accepted. Within
a few days the French army was retiring beyond the Loire,
the capitulation of Paris was signed, and Louis XVIII.
was on his way to the Tuileries. The policy of Fouché,
seconded as it had been by a succession of overmastering
events and by the wisdom of the Duke, had triumphed;
but Fouché had risked his life in a dangerous game. As
for the army and the population of Paris, they expressed
their indignation in angry and widespread complaints;
but the army found no leaders to make its power felt.
The population was almost unarmed; both had no option
but to submit with reluctance.

After Waterloo France played an ignoble part, and
appeared to be unworthy of her great place in history. It
was a sorry spectacle, but this must be mainly ascribed to
the condition to which she had been brought by events,
and to the peculiar circumstances of the time. Had the
nation rallied around Napoleon, and put forth its still
immense strength, it would have ultimately succumbed to
the hosts of Europe; but it might have made a resistance
as grand and heroic as it made after the disasters of 1870,
and this effaced the ignominy of Metz and Sedan, and
restored France to her true position as a leading State in
the world. But France was enervated by revolution and
despotic rule; she was exhausted and worn out by long
years of war; above all, she was a house divided against
itself. Such an effort at this juncture was not possible,
and no one knew this better than Napoleon himself. The
nation, on the other hand, might have openly deposed
Napoleon, taking care that his safety should be assured,
and have frankly invited Louis XVIII. to return to the
throne under conditions he would, no doubt, have

accepted.   This compromise would have made it very
difficult for the allies to insist on the spoils of conquest;
they might have been satisfied with an indemnity for the
losses caused by the war; the dignity of France would
have been preserved.   But a policy of this kind required
real statesmen, and a Parliament versed in political
affairs; above all, a determined and united people; and
France at this crisis had none of these elements of power.
The result was humiliating and to be deplored; a base
intriguer, thinking almost wholly of his low ambition,
cajoled the weak and inexperienced Chambers; compelled Napoleon to abdicate by making false pretences;
laid his hands on the resources of the State; made an
attempt at a national defence well-nigh impossible;
dragged a feeble Government artfully in his wake; and
then trafficked with the chiefs of the coalition for a restoration which virtually placed France at the mercy of
the allies, and obtained peace indeed, but peace under
evil conditions.   It is significant of what revolution and
despotism can effect, that the France which in 1794 defeated Europe, and from 1800 to 1812 was the Queen of
the Continent, should in 1815, after a single reverse for
her arms, have bowed under the disgraceful yoke of
Fouché.

The end of this episode in the history of Europe was at
hand; it was calamitous for France, but what might have
been expected.   Fouché, like Judas, obtained his reward;
he was placed high in the councils of Louis XVIII.; but
he was soon disgraced and relegated to obscurity for the
rest of his life.   The Chambers verified the bitter words
of Napoleon; they were the Greeks of the Lower Empire
discussing abstract theories while the battering-ram of
the invader was at their gates.   They were summarily
suppressed in the midst of debatings about, forsooth, a
new Constitution for France.   The King accepted the
Charter, and promised reforms, but he was swept away by

a royalist reaction of extreme violence; his Government was stained by deeds of proscription and blood. A White Terror rioted for many months in France. Meanwhile the coalition held the vanquished country in its grasp; it cannot be truly said that it was unnecessarily exacting and severe, but its armies occupied the territory of France for years. It made the nation pay heavily for the results of the venture of 1815. It was well for France that Wellington at this crisis held a commanding position in the allied councils, and that the great Army of Occupation was entrusted to his hands. He did not indeed try to control the Government of Louis XVIII., though he disapproved, we know, of many of its acts; he did not interfere to save Ney and Labédoyère, for his was a stern and not a sympathetic nature; but if he may have committed mistakes in this matter, they were mistakes due to an excellent quality, a dislike to meddle with affairs not within his province, and his position besides was difficult and delicate in the extreme. On the other hand, within the limits of his military rule he maintained order, and kept lawlessness down; his treatment of the country was a model of humanity and well-directed discipline. And he did France an inestimable service she did not forget at the time; his far-sighted prudence saved her from a dismemberment he rightly thought unwise; it was due to Wellington, and to Wellington alone, that she was not deprived of Alsace and Lorraine, torn from her in 1871 by conquerors of a very different type.*

The world was soon to enter into a new phase of existence—a phase of little apparent promise for the estate of

---

* Thiers is not an admirer of Wellington, and, like a patriotic Frenchman, naturally feels bitter regret for the events of 1815. But he is an historian and a statesman, and he has done full justice to the great qualities exhibited by Wellington at this time ('Histoire du Consulat et de l'Empire,' vi. 567 *et seq.*).

man. Napoleon, like Prometheus, was to appeal in vain to humanity from a barren rock; he was to offer to mankind a spectacle mournful indeed, but not without a profound moral lesson. The Holy Alliance was to deceive and keep down the Continent; the sceptre of Metternich with its deadening weight of oppression was to be supreme for a series of years. The whole period of 1815 is one in which history finds much to deplore and condemn, and but little on which it can bestow praise. That period and its results have long passed away; its grand military events alone give it permanent interest. We have endeavoured to describe these with an impartial hand, and to present them in their true historical aspect.

APPENDIX

I.

NAPOLEON'S ADDRESS TO HIS ARMY.

À l'Armée.

AVESNES,
14 *juin*, 1815.

SOLDATS !

C'est aujourd'hui l'anniversaire de Marengo et de Friedland, qui décidèrent deux fois du destin de l'Europe. Alors, comme après Austerlitz, comme après Wagram, nous fûmes trop généreux ; nous crûmes aux protestations et aux serments des princes que nous laissâmes sur le trône ! Aujourd'hui, cependant, coalisés contre nous, ils en veulent à l'indépendance et aux droits les plus sacrés de la France. Ils ont commencé la plus injuste des agressions. Marchons donc à leur rencontre : eux et nous ne sommes-nous plus les mêmes hommes ?

Soldats ! à Jena, contre ces mêmes Prussiens aujourd'hui si arrogants, vous étiez un contre trois ; à Montmirail, un contre six.

Que ceux d'entre vous qui ont été prisonniers des Anglais vous fassent le récit de leur pontons et des maux affreux qu'ils ont soufferts !

Les Saxons, les Belges, les Hanovriens, les soldats de la Confédération du Rhin, gémissent d'être obligés de prêter leurs bras à la cause des princes ennemis de la justice et des droits de tous les peuples. Ils savent que cette coalition est insatiable.

Après avoir dévoré douze millions de Polonais, douze millions d'Italiens, un million de Saxons, six millions de Belges, elle devra dévorer les États de deuxième ordre de l'Allemagne. Les insensés! Un moment de prospérité les aveugle. L'oppression et l'humiliation du peuple français sont hors de leur pouvoir. S'ils entrent en France, ils y trouveront leur tombeau.

Soldats! nous avons des marches forcées à faire, des batailles à livrer, des périls à courir : mais, avec de la constance, la victoire sera à nous : les droits, l'honneur et le bonheur de la patrie seront reconquis.

Pour tout Français qui a du cœur, le moment est arrivé de vaincre ou depérir!

NAPOLÉON.*

(D'après la copie. Dépôt de la Guerre.)

II.

SOULT TO D'ERLON.

À Monsieur le Comte d'Erlon.

(Extrait du registre du Major-Général.)

EN AVANT DE CHARLEROI,
15 *juin,* 1815, *à trois heures du soir.*

MONSIEUR LE COMTE D'ERLON,

L'Empereur ordonne à M. le comte Reille de marcher sur Gosselies, et d'y attaquer un corps ennemi qui paraissait s'y arrêter. L'intention de l'Empereur est que vous marchiez aussi sur Gosselies, pour appuyer le comte Reille et le seconder dans ses opérations. Cependant, vous devez toujours faire garder Marchienne, et vous enverrez une brigade sur les routes de Mons, lui recommandant de se garder très-militairement.†

---

* Napoleon Correspondence, xxviii. 281.
† 'Documents inédits,' No. 5, Paris, 1840.

III.

Soult to D'Erlon.

(June 15.)

(Cet ordre fut réitéré après le passage du Maréchal Ney, c'est-à-dire, vers quatre heures et demie.)

À Monsieur le Comte d'Erlon, Commandant de 1ᵉʳ Corps.

CHARLEROI,
15 *juin*, 1815.

MONSIEUR LE COMTE,

L'intention de l'Empereur est que vous ralliez votre corps sur la rive gauche de la Sambre, pour joindre le 2ᵉ corps à Gosselies, d'après les ordres que vous donnera à ce sujet M. le Maréchal Prince de la Moskova.

Ainsi, vous rappellerez les troupes que vous avez laissées à Thuin, Solre et environs; vous devrez cependant avoir toujours de nombreux partis sur votre gauche pour éclairer la route de Mons.

LE MARÉCHAL D'EMPIRE, MAJOR-GÉNÉRAL
DUC DE DALMATIE.*

IV.

Napoleon to Ney.

(June 16.)

*Au Maréchal Ney, Prince de la Moskowa, Commandant l'Aile
Gauche de l'Armée du Nord.*

CHARLEROI,
16 *juin*, 1815.

MON COUSIN,

Je vous envoie mon aide de camp le Général Flahault, qui vous porte la présente lettre. Le major-général a dû vous donner des ordres, mais vous recevrez les miens plus tôt, parce que mes officiers vont plus vîte que les siens. Vous recevrez l'ordre de mouvement du jour, mais je veux vous en écrire en détail, parce que c'est de la plus haute importance.

* 'Documents inédits,' No. 6, Paris, 1840.

24

Je porte le Maréchal Grouchy avec les 3ᵉ et 4ᵉ corps d'infanterie sur Sombreffe : je porte ma Garde à Fleurus, et j'y serai de ma personne avant midi. J'y attaquerai l'ennemi si je le rencontre, et j'éclairerai la route jusqu'à à Gembloux. Là, d'après ce qui se passera, je prendrai mon parti ; peut-être à trois heures après midi, peut-être ce soir. Mon intention est que, immédiatement après que j'aurai pris mon parti, vous soyez prêt à marcher sur Bruxelles. Je vous appuierai avec la Garde, qui sera à Fleurus ou à Sombreffe, et je désirerais arriver à Bruxelles demain matin. Vous vous mettriez en marche ce soir même, si je prends mon parti d'assez bonne heure pour que vous puissiez en être informé de jour et faire ce soir trois ou quatre lieues et être demain à sept heures du matin à Bruxelles.

Vous pouvez donc disposer vos troupes de la manière suivante :

Première division, à deux lieues en avant des Quatre-Chemins, s'il n'y a pas d'inconvénient : six divisions d'infanterie autour des Quatre-Chemins, et une division à Marbais, afin que je puisse l'attirer à moi à Sombreffe, si j'en avais besoin ; elle ne retarderait d'ailleurs pas votre marche.

Le corps du Comte de Valmy, qui a 3,000 cuirassiers d'élite, à l'intersection du Chemin des Romains et de celui de Bruxelles, afin que je puisse l'attirer à moi si j'en avais besoin. Aussitôt que mon parti sera pris vous lui enverrez l'ordre de venir vous rejoindre. Je désirérais d'avoir avec moi la division de la Garde que commande le Général Lefebvre-Desnoëttes, et je vous envoie les deux divisions du corps du Comte de Valmy pour la remplacer. Mais, dans mon projet actuel, je préfère placer le Comte de Valmy de manière a le rappeler si j'en avais besoin, et ne point faire de fausses marches au Général Lefebvre-Desnoëttes, puisqu'il est probable que je me déciderai ce soir à marcher sur Bruxelles avec la Garde. Cependant couvrez la division Lefebvre par les divisions de cavalerie d'Erlon et de Reille, afin de ménager la Garde : s'il y avait quelque échauffourée avec les Anglais, il est préférable que ce soit sur la ligne que sur la Garde.

J'ai adopté comme principe général, pendant cette campagne,

de diviser mon armée en deux ailes et une réserve. Votre aile sera composée des quatres divisions du 1er corps, des quatres divisions du 2e corps, de deux divisions de cavalerie légère et de deux divisions du corps de Comte de Valmy. Cela ne doit pas être loin de 45 à 50,000 hommes.

Le Maréchal Grouchy aura à peu près la même force et commandera l'aile droite.

La Garde formera la réserve, et je me porterai sur l'une ou l'autre aile selon les circonstances.

Le major-général donne les ordres les plus précis pour qu'il n'y ait aucune difficulté sur l'obeissance a vos ordres lorsque vous serez détaché, les commandants de corps devant prendre mes ordres directement quand je me trouve présent.

Selon les circonstances, j'affaiblirai l'une au l'autre aile, en augmentant ma réserve.

Vous sentez assez l'importance attachée à la prise de Bruxelles. Cela pourra d'ailleurs donner lieu à des incidents, car un mouvement aussi prompte et aussi brusque isolera l'armée anglaise de Mons, Ostende, etc. Je désire que vos dispositions soient bien faites, pour qu'au premier ordre vos huits divisions puissent marcher rapidement et sans obstacles sur Bruxelles.

NAPOLÉON.*

V.

NAPOLEON TO GROUCHY.

(*June* 16.)

Au Maréchal Comte Grouchy, Commandant l'Aile Droite de l'Armée du Nord.

CHARLEROI,
16 *juin*, 1815.

MON COUSIN,

Je vous envoie Labédoyère, mon aide de camp, pour vous porter la présente lettre. Le major-général a dû vous faire connaître mes intentions ; mais, comme il a des officiers mal

* Napoleon Correspondence, xxviii. 289-291.

24—2

montés, mon aide de camp arrivera peut-être avant. Mon intention est que, comme commandant l'aile droite, vous preniez le commandement du 3ᵉ corps que commande le Général Vandamme, du 4ᵉ corps que commande le Général Gérard, des corps de cavalerie que commandent les Généraux Pajol, Milhaud, et Exelmans ; ce qui ne doit pas faire loin de 50,000 hommes. Rendez vous avec cette aile droite à Sombreffe. Faites partir en conséquence, de suite, les corps des Généraux Pajol, Milhaud, Exelmans, et Vandamme, et sans vous arrêter, continuez votre mouvement sur Sombreffe. Le 4ᵉ corps, qui est à Châtelet, reçoit directement l'ordre de se rendre à Sombreffe sans passer pas Fleurus. Cette observation est importante, parce que je porte mon quartier-général à Fleurus et qu'il faut éviter les encombrements. Envoyez de suite un officier au Général Gérard pour lui faire connaître votre mouvement, et qu'il exécute le sien de suite.

Mon intention est que tous les généraux prennent directement vos ordres ; ils ne prendront les miens que lorsque je serai présent. Je serai entre dix et onze heures à Fleurus : je me rendrai à Sombreffe laissant ma Garde,' infanterie et cavalerie, à Fleurus ; je ne la conduirais à Sombreffe qu'en cas qu'elle fût nécessaire. Si l'ennemi est à Sombreffe, je veux l'attaquer ; je veux même l'attaquer à Gembloux et m'emparer aussi de cette position, mon intention étant après avoir connu ces deux positions, de partir cette nuit, et d'opérer avec mon aile gauche, que commande le Maréchal Ney, sur les Anglais. Ne perdez donc point un moment, parce que plus vite je prendrai mon parti, mieux cela vaudra pour la suite de mes opérations. Je suppose que vous êtes à Fleurus. Communiquez constamment avec le Général Gérard, afin qu'il puisse vous aider pour attaquer Sombreffe, s'il était nécessaire. La division Girard est à portée de Fleurus ; n'en disposez point à moins de necessité absolue, parce qu'elle doit marcher toute la nuit. Laissez aussi ma jeune Garde et toute son artillerie à Fleurus.

Le Comte de Valmy, avec ses deux divisions de cuirassiers, marche sur la route de Bruxelles : il se lie avec le Maréchal Ney, pour contribuer à l'opération de ce soir, à l'aile gauche.

Comme je vous l'ai dit, je serai de dix à onze heures à Fleurus. Envoyez-moi des rapports sur tout ce que vous apprendrez. Veillez à ce que la route de Fleurus soit libre. Toutes les données que j'ai sont que les Prussiens ne peuvent point nous opposer plus de 40,000 hommes.

NAPOLÉON.*

VI.

SOULT TO NEY.

(June 16.)

À Monsieur le Maréchal Prince de la Moskowa.

MONSIEUR LE MARÉCHAL,

L'Empereur ordonne que vous mettiez en marche les 2e et 1er corps d'armée, ainsi que le 3e corps de cavalerie, qui a été mis à votre disposition, pour les diriger sur l'intersection des chemins dits les Trois-Bras (route de Bruxelles), où vous leur ferez prendre position, et vous porterez en même temps des reconnaisances, aussi avant que possible, sur la route de Bruxelles et sur Nivelles, d'où probablement l'ennemi s'est retiré.

Sa Majesté désire que, s'il n'y a pas d'inconvénient, vous établissiez une division avec de la cavalerie à Genappe, et elle ordonne que vous portiez une autre division du côté de Marbais, pour couvrir l'espace entre Sombreffe et les Trois-Bras. Vous placerez près de ces divisions la division de cavalerie de la Garde Impériale commandée par le Général Lefebvre-Desnoëttes, ainsi que le 1er régiment de hussards, qui a été détaché hier vers Gosselies.

Le corps qui sera à Marbais aura aussi pour objet d'appuyer les mouvements de Monsieur le Maréchal Grouchy sur Sombreffe, et de vous soutenir à la position des Trois-Bras, si cela devenait nécessaire. Vous recommanderez au général qui sera à Marbais de bien s'éclairer sur toutes les directions, particulièrement sur celles de Gembloux et de Wavre.

Si cependant la division du Général Lefebvre-Desnoëttes

---

* Napoleon Correspondence, xxviii. 271-292.

était trop engagée sur la route de Bruxelles vous la laisseriez et vous la remplaceriez au corps qui sera à Marbais par le 3e corps de cavalerie aux ordres de Monsieur le Comte de Valmy et par le 1er régiment de hussards. J'ai l'honneur de vous prévenir que l'Empereur va se porter sur Sombreffe, où, d'après les ordres de Sa Majesté, Monsieur le Maréchal Grouchy doit se diriger avec les 3e et 4e corps d'infanterie et les 1er, 2e et 4e corps de cavalerie. Monsieur le Maréchal Grouchy fera occuper Gembloux.

Je vous prie de me mettre de suite à même de rendre compte à l'Empereur de vos dispositions, pour exécuter l'ordre que je vous envoie, ainsi que de tout ce que vous aurez appris sur l'ennemi.

Sa Majesté me charge de vous recommander de prescrire aux généraux commandant les corps d'armée, de faire réunir leur monde et rentrer les hommes isolés, de maintenir l'ordre le plus parfait dans la troupe, et de rallier toutes les voitures d'artillerie et les ambulances qu'ils auraient pu laisser en arrière.

LE MARÉCHAL D'EMPIRE, MAJOR-GÉNÉRAL
DUC DE DALMATIE.*

VII.

SOULT TO GROUCHY.

(*June* 16.)

Au Maréchal Grouchy.

MONSIEUR LE MARÉCHAL,

L'Empereur ordonne que vous vous mettiez en marche avec les 1er, 2e et 4e corps de cavalerie et que vous les dirigiez sur Sombreffe, où vous prendrez position. Je donne pareil ordre à Monsieur le Lieutenant-Général Vandamme pour le 3e corps d'infanterie, et à Monsieur le Lieutenant-Général Gérard pour le 4e corps, et je préviens ces deux généraux qu'ils sont sous vos ordres, et qu'ils doivent vous envoyer immédiatement des officiers pour vous instruire de leur marche et prendre des instructions. Je leur dis cependant que lorsque Sa Majesté

* 'Documents inédits,' No. 8, Paris, 1840.

sera prése.te, ils pourront recevoir d'elle des ordres directs, et qu'ils devront continuer de m'envoyer des rapports de service et les états qu'ils ont l'habitude de me fournir.

Je préviens aussi Monsieur le Général Gérard que dans ses mouvements sur Sombreffe il doit laisser la ville de Fleurus à gauche, afin d'éviter l'encombrement. Ainsi, vous lui donnerez une direction pour qu'il marche, d'ailleurs bien réuni, à portée du 3e corps, et soit en mesure de concourir à l'attaque de Sombreffe, si l'ennemi fait résistance.

Vous donnerez aussi des instructions en conséquence à Monsieur le Lieutenant-Général Comte Vandamme.

J'ai l'honneur de vous prévenir que Monsieur le Comte de Valmy a réçu ordre de se rendre à Gosselies, où, avec le 3e corps de cavalerie, il sera à la disposition de Monsieur le Prince de Moskova.

Le 1er régiment de hussards rentrera au 1er corps de cavalerie dans la journée. Je prendrai à ce sujet les ordres de l'Empereur. J'ai l'honneur de vous prévenir que Monsieur le Maréchal Prince de la Moskova reçoit ordre de se porter avec le 1er et le 2e corps d'infanterie et le 3e de cavalerie à l'intersection des chemins dits des Trois-Bras, sur la route de Bruxelles, et qu'il détachera un fort corps à Marbais pour se lier avec vous sur Sombreffe et seconder au besoin vos opérations.

Aussitôt que vous vous serez rendu maître de Sombreffe, il faudra envoyer une avant-garde à Gembloux, et faire reconnaître toutes les directions qui aboutissent à Sombreffe, particulièrement la grande route de Namur, en même temps que vous établirez vos communications avec Monsieur le Maréchal Ney.

La Garde Impériale se dirige sur Fleurus.

LE MARÉCHAL DUC DE DALMATIE.*

VIII.

SOULT TO NEY.

MONSIEUR LE MARÉCHAL,

Un officier de lanciers vient de dire à l'Empereur que l'ennemi présentait des masses du côté des Quatre-Bras.

---

* 'Brochure du Général Marquis de Grouchy,' Paris, 1864.

Réunissez les corps des Comtes Reille et d'Erlon, et celui du Comte de Valmy, qui se met à l'instant en route pour vous rejoindre ; avec ces forces, vous devrez battre et détruire tous les corps ennemis qui peuvent se présenter ; Blücher était hier à Namur, et il n'est pas vraisemblable, qu'il ait porté des troupes vers les Quatre-Bras ; aussi, vous n'avez affaire qu'à ce qui vient de Bruxelles.

Le Maréchal Grouchy va faire le mouvement sur Sombreffe, que je vous ai annoncé, et l'Empereur va se rendre à Fleurus ; c'est là où vous adresserez vos nouveaux rapports à Sa Majesté.*

IX.

WELLINGTON'S FIRST MEMORANDUM OF ORDERS.

(*June* 15, 1815.)

Memorandum for the Deputy-Quartermaster-General—Movements of the Army.

BRUXELLES,
June 15, 1815.

General Dornberg's brigade of cavalry and the Cumberland Hussars to march this night upon Vilvorde, and to bivouac on the high-road near to that town.

The Earl of Uxbridge will be pleased to collect the cavalry this night at Ninhove, leaving the 2nd Hussars looking out between the Scheldt and the Lys.

The first division of infantry to collect this night at Ath and adjacent, and to be in readiness to move at a moment's notice.

The third division to collect this night at Braine le Comte, and to be in readiness to move at the shortest notice.

The fourth division to be collected this night at Grammont, with the exception of the troops beyond the Scheldt, which are to be moved to Audenarde.

The fifth division, the 81st Regiment, and the Hanoverian brigade of the sixth division, to be in readiness to march from Bruxelles at a moment's notice.

* ' Documents inédits,' No. 9, Paris, 1840.

The Duke of Brunswick's corps to collect this night on the high-road between Bruxelles and Vilvorde.

The Nassau troops to collect at daylight to-morrow morning on the Louvain road, and to be in readiness to move at a moment's notice.

The Hanoverian brigade of the fifth division to collect this night at Hal, and to be in readiness at daylight to-morrow morning to move towards Bruxelles, and to halt on the high-road between Alost and Assche for further orders.

The Prince of Orange is requested to collect at Nivelles the second and third divisions of the army of the Low Countries; and, should that point have been attacked this day, to move the third division of British infantry upon Nivelles as soon as collected.

This movement is not to take place until it is quite certain that the enemy's attack is upon the right of the Prussian army, and the left of the British army.

Lord Hill will be so good as to order Prince Frederick of Orange to occupy Audenarde with 500 men, and to collect the first division of the army of the Low Countries and the Indian brigade at Sotteghem, so as to be ready to march in the morning at daylight.

The reserve artillery to be in readiness to move at daylight.

WELLINGTON.*

X.

WELLINGTON'S 'AFTER ORDERS.'

(10 p.m., *June* 15, 1815.)

Movement of the Army—After Orders, 10 *o'clock, p.m.*

BRUXELLES,
June 15, 1815.

The third division of infantry to continue its movement from Braine le Comte upon Nivelles.

The first division to move from Enghien upon Braine le Comte.

* Despatches, xii. 472.

The second and fourth divisions of infantry to move from Ath and Grammont, also from Audenarde, and to continue their movements upon Enghien.

The cavalry to continue its movement from Ninhove upon Enghien.

The above movements to take place with as little delay as possible.

WELLINGTON.*

XI.

WELLINGTON'S CONVERSATION WITH THE DUKE OF RICHMOND.

(*June* 16, 1815.)

Captain Bowles to Lord Fitzharris—Original Memorandum by the Writer.

At the Duchess of Richmond's ball at Brussels the Prince of Orange, who commanded the first division of the army, came back suddenly, just as the Duke of Wellington had taken his place at the supper-table, and whispered some minutes to his Grace, who only said he had no fresh orders to give, and recommended the Prince to go back to his quarters and go to bed.

The Duke of Wellington remained nearly twenty minutes after this, and then said to the Duke of Richmond, ' I think it is time for me to go to bed likewise'; and then, whilst wishing him good-night, whispered to ask him if he had a good map in his house. The Duke of Richmond said he had, and took him into his dressing-room, which opened into the supper-room. The Duke of Wellington shut the door and said, ' Napoleon has *humbugged* me, by G——! He has gained twenty-four hours' march on me!' The Duke of Richmond said, ' What do you intend doing?' The Duke of Wellington replied, ' I have ordered the army to concentrate at Quatre Bras; but we shall not stop him there, and if so I must fight him *here*'—at the same time passing his thumb-nail over the position of

* Despatches, xii. 474.

Waterloo. He then said adieu, and left the house by another way out. He went to his quarters, slept six hours and breakfasted, and rode at speed to Quatre Bras, where he met Hardinge, and went with him to Blucher, who took him over the position at Ligny. The Duke of Wellington suggested many alterations, but Blucher would not consent to move a man.

The conversation in the Duke of Richmond's dressing-room was repeated to me, two minutes after it occurred, by the Duke of Richmond, who was to have had the command of the reserve, if formed, and to whom I was to have been aide-de-camp. He marked the Duke of Wellington's thumb-nail with his pencil on the map, and we often looked at it together some months afterwards.*

XII.

WELLINGTON'S LETTER TO BLUCHER.

(10.30 a.m. *June* 16, 1815.)

SUR LES HAUTERS DERRIÈRE FRASNE,
16 *Juin*, 1815, *à* 10 *heures et demi.*

MON CHER PRINCE,

Mon armée est situé comme il suit :

Le Corps d'Armée du Prince d'Orange a une division ici et à Quatre Bras ; et le reste à Nivelles.

La Reserve est en marche de Waterloo sur Genappe ; où elle arrivera à midi.

La Cavalerie Anglaise sera à la même heure à Nivelles.

Le Corps de Lord Hill est à Braine le Comte.

Je ne vois pas beaucoup de l'ennemi en avant de nous ; et j'attends les nouvelles de votre Altesse, et l'arrivée des troupes pour décider mes opérations pour la journée.

Rien n'a paru du côté de Binche, ni sur notre droite.

Votre très obéissant serviteur,

WELLINGTON.†

* 'Letters of First Earl of Malmesbury,' ii. 445.
† Ollech, opposite p. 124 in his work.

XIII.

Soult to Ney.

(*June* 16.)

En avant de Fleurus,
16 *juin, à deux heures.*

Monsieur le Maréchal,

L'Empereur me charge de vous prévenir que l'ennemi a réuni un corps de troupes *entre Sombreffe et Bry*, et qu'à deux heures et demie Monsieur le Maréchal Grouchy, avec les 3ᵉ et 4ᵉ corps, l'attaquera :

L'intention de Sa Majesté est que vous attaquiez aussi ce qui est devant vous, et qu'après l'avoir vigoureusement poussé, vous rabattiez sur nous, pour concourir à envelopper le corps dont je viens de vous parler.

Si ce corps était enfoncé auparavant, alors Sa Majesté ferait manœuvrer dans votre direction pour hâter également vos opérations.

Instruisez de suite l'Empereur de vos dispositions, et de ce que passe sur votre front.*

XIV.

Soult to Ney.

(*June* 16.)

En avant de Fleurus,
16 *Juin*, 1815, *trois heures un quart.*

Monsieur le Maréchal,

Je vous ai écrit, il y a une heure, que l'Empereur ferait attaquer l'ennemi à deux heures et demie dans la position qu'il a prise entre le village de Saint-Amand et de Bry ; en ce moment l'engagement est très-prononcé.

Sa Majesté me charge de vous dire que vous devez manœuvrer sur-le-champ, de manière à envelopper la droite

* ‘Documents inédits,’ No. 13, Paris, 1840.

de l'ennemi et tomber à bras raccourcis sur ses derrières ; cette armée est perdue si vous agissez vigoureusement, le sort de la France est entre vos mains.

Ainsi n'hésitez pas un instant pour faire le mouvement que l'Empereur vous ordonne, et dirigez-vous ' sur les hauteurs de Bry et de Saint-Amand, pour concourir à une victoire peut-être décisive. L'ennemi est pris en flagrant délit au moment où il cherche à se réunir aux Anglais.'*

XV.

Captain Bowles' Story of Wellington at Quatre Bras.

(June 17, 1815.)

Captain Bowles in Lord Malmesbury's Letters, vol. ii., p. 447 :

On the morning of the 17th, my company being nearly in front of the farmhouse at Quatre-Bras, soon after daybreak the Duke of Wellington came to me, and being personally known to him, he remained in conversation for an hour or more, during which time he repeatedly said he was surprised to have heard nothing of Blucher. At length a staff officer arrived, his horse covered with foam, and whispered to the Duke, who, without the least change of countenance, gave him some orders and dismissed him. He then turned round to me and said, ' Old Blucher has had a d——d good licking and gone back to Wavre, eighteen miles. As he has gone back, we must go too. I suppose in England they will say we have been licked. I can't help it ; as they are gone back, we must go too.'

He made all the arrangements for retiring without moving from the spot on which he was standing, and it certainly did not occupy him five minutes.†

---

* ' Documents inédits,' No. 14, Paris, 1840.
† ' Letters of First Earl of Malmesbury,' ii. 447.

XVI.

SOULT TO NEY.

(*June 17.*)

À Monsieur le Maréchal Prince de la Moskowa.

FLEURUS,
17 juin, 1815, entre sept et huit heures du matin.

MONSIEUR LE MARÉCHAL,

Le Général de Flahault, qui arrive à l'instant, fait connaître que vous êtes dans l'incertitude sur les résultats de la journée d'hier. Je crois cependant vous avoir prévenu de la victoire que l'Empereur a remportée. L'armée prussienne a été mise en déroute; le Général Pajol est à sa poursuite sur les routes de Namur et de Liége. Nous avons déjà plusieurs milliers de prisonniers et trente pièces de canon. Nos troupes se sont bien conduites: une charge de six bataillons de la garde, des escadrons de service et de la division de cavalerie du Général Delort, a percé la ligne ennemie, porté le plus grand désordre dans les rangs et enlevé la position.

L'Empereur se rend au moulin de Bry, où passe la grande route qui conduit de Namur, aux Quatre-Bras; il n'est donc pas possible que l'armée anglaise puisse agir devant vous; si cela était, l'Empereur marcherait directement sur elle par la route des Quatre-Bras, tandis que vous l'attaqueriez de front avec vos divisions, qui, à présent, doivent être réunies, et cette armée serait dans un instant détruite. Ainsi, instruisez Sa Majesté de la position exacte des divisions, et de tout ce qui se passe devant vous.

L'Empereur a vu avec peine que vous n'ayez pas réuni hier les divisions : elles ont agi isolément : ainsi vous avez éprouvé des pertes.

Si les corps des Comtes d'Erlon et Reille avaient été ensemble, il ne réchappait pas un Anglais du corps qui venait vous attaquer.

Si le Comte d'Erlon avait exécuté le mouvement sur Saint-Amand, que l'Empereur a ordonné, l'armée prussienne était totalement détruite, et nous aurions fait peutêtre trente mille prisonniers.

Les corps des Généraux Gérard, Vandamme, et la garde

impériale, ont toujours été réunis ; l'on s'expose à des revers, lorsque des détachements sont compromis.

L'Empereur espère et désire que vos sept divisions d'infanterie et la cavalerie soient bien réunies et formées, et qu'ensemble elles n'occupent pas une lieue de terrain, pour les avoir bien dans votre main et les employer au besoin.

L'intention de Sa Majesté est que vous préniez position aux Quatre-Bras, ainsi que l'ordre vous en a été donné ; mais si, par impossible, cela ne peut avoir lieu, rendez-en compte sur-le-champ avec détail, et l'Empereur s'y portera ainsi que je vous l'ai dit ; si, au contraire, il n'y a qu'une arrière-garde, attaquez-la, et prenez position.

La journée d'aujourd'hui est nécessaire pour terminer cette opération, et pour compléter les munitions, rallier les militaires isolés et faire rentrer les détachements. Donnez des ordres en conséquence, et assurez-vous que tous les blessés sont pansés et transportés sur les derrières : l'on s'est plaint que les ambulances n'avaient pas fait leur devoir.

Le fameux partisan Lutzow, qui a été pris, disait que l'armée prussienne était perdue, et que Blücher avait exposé une seconde fois la monarchie prussienne.

LE MARÉCHAL D'EMPIRE, MAJOR-GÉNÉRAL
DUC DE DALMATIE.*

XVII.

SOULT TO NEY.

(June 17.)

EN AVANT DE LIGNY,
17 juin, 1815, *midi.*

MONSIEUR LE MARÉCHAL,

L'Empereur vient de faire prendre position, en avant de Marbais, à un corps d'infanterie et à la garde impériale : Sa Majesté me charge de vous dire que son intention est que vous attaquiez les ennemis aux Quatre-Bras pour les chasser de leur position, et que le corps qui est à Marbais secondera

* 'Documents inédits,' No. 7, p. 45, Paris, 1840.

vos opérations ; Sa Majesté va se rendre à Marbais, et elle attend vos rapports avec impatience.

Le Maréchal d'Empire, Major-Général
Duc de Dalmatie.*

XVIII.

Wellington to Lord Hill.

To General Lord Hill.

June 17, 1815.

The second division of British infantry to march from Nivelles on Waterloo at ten o'clock.

The brigades of the fourth division, now at Nivelles, to march from that place on Waterloo at ten o'clock. Those brigades of the fourth division at Braine le Comte, and on the road from Braine le Comte to Nivelles, to collect and halt at Braine le Comte this day.

All the baggage on the road from Braine le Comte to Nivelles to return immediately to Braine le Comte, and to proceed immediately from thence to Hal and Bruxelles.

The spare musket ammunition to be immediately packed behind Genappe.

The corps under the command of Prince Frederick of Orange will move from Enghien this evening and take up a position in front of Hal, occupying Braine le Château with two battalions.

Colonel Estorff will fall back with his brigade on Hal, and place himself under the orders of Prince Frederick.

Wellington.†

XIX.

Wellington's Orders.

June 17, 1815.

The army retired this day from its position at Quatre Bras to its present position in front of Waterloo.

---

* 'Documents inédits,' publiés par le duc d'Elchingen, No. 16, p. 44, Paris, 1840.

† Despatches, xii. 476, quoted by Siborne, 263, *et seq.* Ed. 1895.

The brigades of the fourth division at Braine le Comte are to retire at daylight to-morrow morning upon Hal.

Major-General Colville must be guided by the intelligence he receives of the enemy's movements in his march to Hal, whether he moves by the direct route or by Enghien.

Prince Frederick of Orange is to occupy with his corps the position between Hal and Enghien, and is to defend it as long as possible.

The army will probably continue in its position in front of Waterloo to-morrow.

Lieutenant-Colonel Torrens will inform Lieutenant-General Sir Charles Colville of the position and situation of the armies.

WELLINGTON.*

XX.

NAPOLEON TO GROUCHY.

(June 17.)

MONSIEUR LE MARÉCHAL,

Rendez vous à Gembloux avec le corps de cavalerie du Général Pajol, la cavalerie légère du 4ᵉ corps, et le corps de cavalerie du Général Exelmans, la division du Général Teste dont vous aurez un soin particulier, étant detachée de son corps d'armée, et les 3ᵉ et 4ᵉ corps d'infanterie. Vous vous ferez éclairer sur la direction de Namur et de Maëstricht, et vous poursuivrez l'ennemi. Éclairez sa marche et instruisez-moi de ses mouvements, de manière que je puisse pénétrer ce qu'il veut faire. Je porte mon quartier général aux Quatre-Chemins, où ce matin étaient encore les Anglais. Notre communication sera donc directe par la route pavée de Namur. Si l'ennemi a évacué Namur, écrivez au général commandant la deuxième division militaire, à Charlemont, de faire occuper Namur par quelques bataillons de garde nationale et quelques batteries de canon qu'il formera à Charlemont. Il donnera ce commandement à un maréchal de camp.

* Despatches, xii. 476.

25

Il est important de pénétrer ce que l'ennemi veut faire : ou il se sépare des Anglais, ou ils veulent se réunir encore pour couvrir Bruxelles et Liége, en tentant le sort d'une nouvelle bataille. Dans tous les cas, tenez constamment vos deux corps d'infanterie réunis dans une lieue de terrain, et occupez tous les soirs une bonne position militaire, ayant plusieurs débouchés de retraite. Placez des détachements de cavalerie intermédiaire, pour communiquer avec le quartier général.

Dicté par l'Empereur, en l'absence du Major-Général.

Le Grand Maréchal Bertrand.*

XXI.

Grouchy to Napoleon.

(Written at 10 *p.m. on June* 17.)

Sire,

J'ai l'honneur de vous rendre compte que j'occupe Gembloux et que ma cavalerie est à Sauvenière. L'ennemi fort d'environ trente-cinq mille hommes continue son mouvement de retraite ; on lui a saisi ici un parc de quatre cents bêtes à cornes, des magasins et des bagages.

Il parait, d'après tous les rapports, qu'arrivés à Sauvenière, les Prussiens se sont divisés en deux colonnes ; l'une a dû prendre la route de Wavre en passant par Sart-les-Walhain ; l'autre colonne paraît s'être dirigée sur Perwez.

On peut peut-être en inférer qu'une portion va joindre Wellington, et que le centre, qui est l'armée de Blücher, se retire sur Liége ; une autre colonne avec de l'artillerie ayant fait son mouvement de retraite par Namur, le Général Exelmans a ordre de pousser, ce soir, six escadrons, sur Sart-les-Walhain, et trois escadrons sur Perwez. *D'après leur rapport, si la masse des Prussiens se retire sur Wavre, je la suivrai dans cette direction, afin qu'ils ne puissent pas gagner Bruxelles, et de les séparer de Wellington.* Si, au contraire, mes renseignements prouvent que la principale force prussienne a marché sur Perwez, je me dirigerai par cette ville à la poursuite de l'ennemi.

Les Généraux Thielmann et Borstell faisaient partie de

* Cette dépêche a été publiée pour la première fois dans une biographie du Maréchal Grouchy, par Pascallet. Paris : Octobre, 1842.

l'armée que Votre Majesté a battue hier ; ils étaient encore ce matin à dix heures ici, et ont annoncé que vingt mille hommes des leurs avaient été mis hors de combat. Ils ont demandé en partant les distances de Wavre, Perwez et Hannut. Blücher a été blessé légèrement au bras, ce qui ne l'a pas empêché de continuer à commander après s'être fait panser.

Il n'a point passé par Gembloux.

Je suis avec respect,

Sire,

de Votre Majesté

le fidèle sujet,

Signé : Le Maréchal Comte De Grouchy.*

XXII.

Soult to Ney.

(*June* 18.)

A Monsieur le Maréchal Prince de la Moskowa.

L'Empereur ordonne que l'armée soit disposée à attaquer l'ennemi à neuf heures du matin : Messieurs les commandants des corps d'armée rallieront leurs troupes, feront mettre les armes en état, et permettront que les soldats fassent la soupe ; ils feront aussi manger les soldats, afin qu'à neuf heures précises chacun soit prêt et puisse être en bataille que l'Empereur a indiquée par son ordre d'hier soir. Messieurs les lieutenants généraux commandant les corps d'armée d'infanterie et de cavalerie enverront sur-le-champ des officiers au major-général pour faire connaître leur position et porter des ordres.

Au quartier général impérial, le 18 Juin, 1815.

Le Maréchal d'Empire, Major-Général

Duc de Dalmatie.†

Expedié :

Monsieur le Lieutenant-Général Comte Drouot, commandant la Garde Impériale.

---

* La Tour d'Auvergne, ' Waterloo,' 232 : ' Certifié conforme à l'original qui nous a été remis par l'Empereur Napoléon, et qui est entre nos mains.' —Signé, le Général Gourgaud.

† ' Documents inédits,' No. 18, p. 52 ; Paris.

XXIII.

SOULT TO NEY.

(*June* 18.)

PARIS,
21 juin, 1815.

Une fois que toute l'armée sera rangée en bataille, à peu près à une heure après midi, au moment où l'Empereur en donnera l'ordre au Maréchal Ney, l'attaque commencera pour s'emparer du village de Mont-Saint-Jean où est l'intersection des routes. A cet effet, les batteries de douze du 2e corps et du 6e se réuniront à celle du 1er corps. Ces vingt-quatre bouches à feu tireront sur les troupes du Mont-Saint-Jean, et le Comte d'Erlon commencera l'attaque, en portant en avant sa division de gauche et la soutenant, suivant les circonstances, par les divisions du 1er corps.

Le 2e corps s'avancera à mesure pour garder la hauteur du Comte d'Erlon.

Les compagnies de sapeurs du 1er corps seront prêtes pour se barricader sur-le-champ à Mont-Saint-Jean.

Au crayon et de l'écriture du Maréchal Ney, ajouté par le Maréchal Ney.

' Le Comte d'Erlon comprendra que c'est par la gauche que l'attaque commencera au lieu de la droite. Communiquer cette nouvelle disposition au Général en Chef Reille.

Au dos.—' Ordre dicté par l'Empereur sur le champ de bataille de Mont-Saint-Jean, le 18 vers onze heures de matin, et écrit par le Maréchal Duc de Dalmatie, Major-Général.

' LE MARÉCHAL PRINCE DE LA MOSKOVA.'[*]

XXIV.

SOULT TO GROUCHY.

(*June* 18.)

EN AVANT DE LA FERME DU CAILLOU,
Le 18 *juin, à dix heures du matin.*

Monsieur le Maréchal, l'Empereur a reçu votre dernier rapport, daté de Gembloux : *vous ne parlez à Sa Majesté que*

---

[*] ' Documents inédits,' No. 19.

de deux colonnes prussiennes qui ont passé à Sauvenière et à Sart-les-Walhain; cependant des rapports disent qu'une troisième colonne, qui était assez forte, a passé a Géry et à Gentinnes, se dirigeant sur Wavre. L'Empereur me charge de vous prévenir qu'en ce moment Sa Majesté va faire attaquer l'armée anglaise, qui a pris position à Waterloo, près de la forêt de Soignes; ainsi Sa Majesté désire que vous dirigiez vos mouvements sur Wavre, afin de vous rapprocher de nous, *vous mettre en rapport d'opérations, et lier les communications;* poussant devant vous les corps de l'armée prussienne qui ont pris cette direction et qui ont pu s'arrêter à Wavre, où vous devez arriver le plus tôt possible.

Vous ferez suivre les colonnes ennemies, qui ont pris sur votre droite, *par quelques corps légers,* afin d'observer leurs mouvements et ramasser leurs trainards. Instruisez-moi immédiatement de vos dispositions et de votre marche, ainsi que des nouvelles que vous avez sur les ennemis, *et ne négligez pas de lier vos communications avec nous.* L'Empereur désire avoir très-souvent de vos nouvelles.

Le Duc de Dalmatie.*

XXV.

Grouchy to Napoleon.

(June 18.)

Gembloux,
18 juin, 1815, trois heures du matin.

Sire,

Tous mes rapports et renseignements confirment que l'ennemi se retire sur Bruxelles, pour s'y concentrer ou livrer bataille après s'être réuni à Wellington. Namur est évacué, à ce que me marque le Général Pajol.

Les 1er et 2e corps de l'armée de Blücher paraissent se diriger, le 1er sur Corbais et le 2e sur Chaumont. Ils doivent être partis hier au soir, à huit heures et demie, de Tourinnes et avoir marché pendant toute la nuit; heureusement qu'elle a été si mauvaise qu'ils n'auront pu faire beaucoup de chemin.

---

* 'Le Maréchal Grouchy, du 16 au 19 juin, 1815,' par le Général de Division Sénateur Marquis de Grouchy; Paris, 1864.

Je pars à l'instant pour Sart-les-Walhain, d'où je me porterai à Corbais et à Wavre. J'aurai l'honneur de vous écrire de l'une et l'autre de ces villes.

Je suis, etc.,

LE MARÉCHAL GROUCHY.*

Dans sa brochure de 1864, le Général de Grouchy fait figurer cette dépêche, comme étant celle que son père aurait adressé a l'Empereur.

XXVI.

SOULT TO GROUCHY.

(*June* 18.)

Au Maréchal Grouchy.

DU CHAMP DE BATAILLE DE WATERLOO,

Le 18 *juin, à une heure après midi.*

MONSIEUR LE MARÉCHAL,

Vous avez écrit, ce matin à deux heures, à l'Empereur, que vous marcheriez sur Sart-les-Walhain ; donc votre projet était de vous porter à Corbais ou à Wavre. Ce mouvement est conforme aux dispositions de Sa Majesté, qui vous ont été communiquées. *Cependant, l'Empereur m'ordonne de vous dire que vous devez toujours manœuvrer dans notre direction. C'est à vous de voir le point où nous sommes pour vous régler en con-séquence et pour lier nos communications, ainsi que pour être toujours en mesure de tomber sur les troupes ennemis qui chercheraient à inquiéter notre droite et de les écraser.* Dans ce moment, *la bataille est engagée* sur la ligne de Waterloo ; le centre ennemi est à Mont-Saint-Jean : ainsi manœuvrez pour joindre notre droite.

P.S.—Une lettre qui vient d'être interceptée porte que le Général Bulow doit attaquer notre flanc. Nous croyons apercevoir ce corps sur les hauteurs de Saint-Lambert ; ainsi, ne perdez pas un instant pour vous rapprocher de nous et nous joindre, et pour écraser Bulow, que vous prendrez en flagrant délit.

LE MARÉCHAL DUC DE DALMATIE.

LE MARÉCHAL GROUCHY.

* La Tour d'Auvergne, ' Waterloo,' 318.

XXVII.

GROUCHY TO NAPOLEON.

(June 18.)

SART-LES-WALHAIN,
18 juin, 1815, onze heures du matin.

SIRE,

Je ne perds pas un moment à vous transmettre les renseignements que je recueille ici ; je les regarde comme positifs, et afin que votre Majesté les reçoive le plus promptement possible, je les lui expédie par le Major de la Fresnaye, son ancien page ; il est bien monté et bon écuyer.

Les 1er, 2e et 3e corps de Blücher marchent dans la direction de Bruxelles. Deux de ces corps ont passé à Sart-les-Walhain, ou à peu de distance, sur la droite ; ils ont défilé en trois colonnes, marchant à peu près en même hauteur. Leur passage a duré six heures sans interruption. Ce qui a défilé en vue de Sart-les-Walhain peut être évalué à trente mille hommes au moins, et avait un matériel de cinquante à soixante bouches à feu.

Un corps venant de Liége a effectué sa jonction avec ceux qui ont combattu à Fleurus (ci-joint une requisition qui le prouve). Quelques-uns des Prussiens, que j'ai devant moi, se dirigent vers la plaine de la Chyse, située près de la route de Louvain, et à deux lieues et demie de cette ville.

Il semblerait que ce serait à dessein de s'y masser, ou de combattre les troupes qui les y poursuiveraient, ou enfin de se réunir à Wellington, projet annoncé par leurs officiers, qui, avec leur jactance ordinaire, prétendent n'avoir quitté le champ de bataille, le 16, qu'afin d'opérer leur réunion avec l'armée anglaise sur Bruxelles.

Ce soir, je vais être massé à Wavre, et me trouver ainsi entre Wellington, que je présume en retraite devant votre Majesté, et l'armée prussienne. J'ai besoin d'instructions ultérieures sur ce que votre Majesté ordonne que je fasse. Le pays entre Wavre et la plaine de la Chyse est difficile, coupé et marécageux.

Par la route de Wilvorde, j'arriverai facilement à Bruxelles avant tout ce qui sera arreté à la Chyse, si tant il y a que les Prussiens y fasse une halte.

Daignez, Sire, me transmettre vos ordres : je puis les recevoir avant de commencer mon mouvement de demain.*

XXVIII.

WELLINGTON'S REPORT OF WATERLOO.

To Earl Bathurst.

WATERLOO,
June 19, 1815.

Buonaparte, having collected the 1st, 2nd, 3rd, 4th, and 6th corps of the French army, and the Imperial Guards and nearly all the cavalry, on the Sambre, and between that river and the Meuse, between the 10th and 14th of the month, advanced on the 15th, and attacked the Prussian posts at Thuin and Lobbes on the Sambre at daylight in the morning.

I did not hear of these events till in the evening of the 15th; and I immediately ordered the troops to prepare to march to their left, as soon as I had intelligence from other quarters to prove that the enemy's movement upon Charleroi was the real attack.

The enemy drove the Prussian posts from the Sambre on that day, and General Ziethen, who commanded the corps which had been at Charleroi, retired upon Fleurus, and Marshal Prince Blucher concentrated the Prussian army upon Sombref, holding the villages in front of his position of St. Amand and Ligny.

The enemy continued his march along the road from Charleroi towards Bruxelles, and on the same evening, the 15th, attacked a brigade of the army of the Netherlands, under the Prince de Weimar, posted at Frasne, and forced it back to the farm-house on the same road, called Les Quatre Bras.

The Prince of Orange immediately reinforced this brigade with another of the same division under General Perponcher, and in the morning early regained part of the ground which had been lost, so as to have the command of the communica-

* Brochure du Général de Grouchy, p. 54; Paris, 1864.

tion leading from Nivelles and Bruxelles with Marshal Blucher's position.

In the meantime I had directed the whole army to march upon Les Quatre Bras; and the fifth division, under Lieutenant-General Sir T. Picton, arrived at about half-past two in the day, followed by the corps of troops under the Duke of Brunswick, and afterwards by the contingent of Nassau.

At this time the enemy commenced an attack upon Prince Blucher with his whole force, excepting the 1st and 2nd corps, and a corps of cavalry under General Kellermann, with which he attacked our post at Les Quatre Bras.

The Prussian army maintained their position with their usual gallantry and perseverance against a great disparity of numbers, as the 4th corps of their army, under General Bulow, had not joined; and I was not able to assist them as I wished, as I was attacked myself, and the troops, the cavalry in particular, which had a long distance to march, had not arrived.

We maintained our position also, and completely defeated and repulsed all the enemy's attempts to get possession of it. The enemy repeatedly attacked us with a large body of infantry and cavalry, supported by a numerous and powerful artillery. He made several charges with the cavalry upon our infantry, but all were repulsed in the steadiest manner.

In this affair H.R.H. the Prince of Orange, the Duke of Brunswick, and Lieutenant-General Sir T. Picton, and Major-Generals Sir J. Kempt and Sir Denis Pack, who were engaged from the commencement of the enemy's attack, highly distinguished themselves, as well as Lieutenant-General C. Baron Alten, Major-General Sir C. Halkett, Lieutenant-General Cooke, and Major-Generals Maitland and Byng, as they successively arrived. The troops of the fifth division, and those of the Brunswick corps, were long and severely engaged, and conducted themselves with the utmost gallantry. I must particularly mention the 28th, 42nd, 79th, and 92nd Regiments, and the battalion of Hanoverians. Our loss was great, as your Lordship will perceive by the enclosed return; and I have particularly to regret H.S.H. the Duke of Brunswick, who fell fighting gallantly at the head of his troops.

Although Marshal Blucher had maintained his position at Sombref, he still found himself much weakened by the severity of the contest in which he had been engaged, and, as the 4th corps had not arrived, he determined to fall back and to concentrate his army upon Wavre; and he marched in the night, after the action was over.

This movement of the Marshal rendered necessary a corresponding one upon my part, and I retired from the farm of Quatre Bras upon Genappe, and thence upon Waterloo, the next morning—the 17th—at ten o'clock.

The enemy made no effort to pursue Marshal Blucher. On the contrary, a patrole which I sent to Sombref in the morning found all quiet, and the enemy's vedettes fell back as the patrole advanced. Neither did he attempt to molest our march to the rear, although made in the middle of the day, excepting by following, with a large body of cavalry brought from his right, the cavalry under the Earl of Uxbridge.

This gave Lord Uxbridge an opportunity of charging them with the 1st Life Guards upon their *débouché* from the village of Genappe, upon which occasion his lordship has declared himself to be well satisfied with that regiment.

The position which I took up in front of Waterloo crossed the highroads from Charleroi and Nivelles, and had its right thrown back to a ravine near Merke Braine, which was occupied, and its left extended to a height above the hamlet Ter la Haye, which was likewise occupied.

In front of the right centre, and near the Nivelles road, we occupied the house and gardens of Hougoumont, which covered the return of that flank; and in front of the left centre we occupied the farm of La Haye Sainte. By our left we communicated with Marshal Prince Blucher at Wavre, through Ohain; and the Marshal had promised me that, in case we should be attacked, he would support me with one or more corps, as might be necessary.

The enemy collected his army, with the exception of the 3rd corps, which had been sent to observe Marshal Blucher, on a range of heights in our front in the course of the night of the 17th and yesterday morning, and at about ten o'clock he commenced a furious attack upon our post at Hougoumont. I had occupied that post with a detachment from General Byng's Brigade of Guards, which was in position in its rear, and it was for some time under the command of Lieutenant-Colonel Macdonnell, and afterwards of Colonel Home; and I am happy to add that it was maintained throughout the day with the utmost gallantry by these brave troops, notwithstanding the repeated efforts of large bodies of the enemy to obtain possession of it.

This attack upon the right of our centre was accompanied by a very heavy cannonade upon our whole line, which was destined to support the repeated attacks of cavalry and infantry —occasionally mixed, but sometimes separate—which were made upon it. In one of these the enemy carried the farm-house of La Haye Sainte, as the detachment of the light battalion of the German Legion, which occupied it, had expended all its ammunition, and the enemy occupied the only communication there was with them.

The enemy repeatedly charged our infantry with his cavalry, but these attacks were uniformly unsuccessful; and they afforded opportunities to our cavalry to charge, in one of which Lord E. Somerset's brigade, consisting of the Life Guards, the Royal Horse Guards, and 1st Dragoon Guards, highly distinguished themselves, as did that of Major-General Sir W. Ponsonby, having taken many prisoners and an eagle.

These attacks were repeated till about seven in the evening, when the enemy made a desperate effort with cavalry and infantry, supported by the fire of artillery, to force our left centre, near the farm of La Haye Sainte, which, after a severe contest, was defeated; and, having observed that the troops retired from this attack in great confusion, and that the march of General Bulow's corps, by Frischermont, upon Planchenois and La Belle Alliance, had begun to take effect, and as I could perceive the fire of his cannon, and as Marshal Prince Blucher had joined in person with a corps of his army to the left of our line by Ohain, I determined to attack the enemy, and immediately advanced the whole line of infantry, supported by the cavalry and artillery. The attack succeeded in every point.   The enemy was forced from his positions on the heights, and fled in the utmost confusion, leaving behind him, as far as I could judge, 150 pieces of cannon, with their ammunition, which fell into our hands.

I continued the pursuit till long after dark, and then discontinued it only on account of the fatigue of our troops, who had been engaged during twelve hours, and because I found myself on the same road with Marshal Blucher, who assured me of his intention to follow the enemy throughout the night. He has sent me word this morning that he had taken sixty pieces of cannon belonging to the Imperial Guard, and several carriages, baggage, etc., belonging to Buonaparte, in Genappe.

I propose to move this morning upon Nivelles, and not to discontinue my operations.

Your Lordship will observe that such a desperate action could not be fought, and such advantages could not be gained, without great loss, and I am sorry to add that ours has been immense.   In Lieutenant-General Sir T. Picton, His Majesty has sustained the loss of an officer who has frequently distinguished himself in his service, and he fell gloriously leading his division to a charge with bayonets, by which one of the most serious attacks made by the enemy on our position was repulsed.   The Earl of Uxbridge, after having successfully got through this arduous day, received a wound by almost the last shot fired, which will, I am afraid, deprive His Majesty for some time of his services.

H.R.H. the Prince of Orange distinguished himself by his gallantry and conduct, till he received a wound from a musket-ball through the shoulder, which obliged him to quit the field.

It gives me the greatest satisfaction to assure your Lordship that the army never upon any occasion conducted itself better.   The division of Guards, under Lieutenant-General Cooke—who is severely wounded—Major-General Maitland, and Major-General Byng, set an example which was followed by all, and there is no officer nor description of troops that did not behave well.

I must, however, particularly mention, for His Royal Highness's approbation, Lieutenant-General Sir H. Clinton, Major-General Adam, Lieutenant-General C. Baron Alten (severely wounded), Major-General Sir C. Halkett (severely wounded), Colonel Ompteda, Colonel Mitchell (commanding a brigade of the 4th division), Major-Generals Sir J. Kempt and Sir D. Pack, Major-General Lambert, Major-General Lord E. Somerset, Major-General Sir W. Ponsonby, Major-General Sir C. Grant, and Major-General Sir H. Vivian, Major-General Sir J. O. Vandeleur, and Major-General Count Dornberg.

I am also particularly indebted to General Lord Hill for his assistance and conduct upon this as upon all former occasions.

The artillery and engineer departments were conducted much to my satisfaction by Colonel Sir G. Wood and Colonel Smyth, and I had every reason to be satisfied with the conduct of the Adjutant-General, Major-General Barnes, who was wounded, and of the Quartermaster-General, Colonel De Lancey, who was killed by a cannon-shot in the middle of the action. This officer is a serious loss to His Majesty's service and to me at this moment.

I was likewise much indebted to the assistance of Lieutenant-Colonel Lord Fitzroy Somerset, who was severely wounded, and of the officers composing my personal staff, who have suffered severely in this action. Lieutenant-Colonel the Hon. Sir A. Gordon, who has died of his wounds, was a most promising officer, and is a serious loss to His Majesty's service.

General Krüse, of the Nassau service, likewise conducted himself much to my satisfaction, as did General Trip, commanding the heavy brigade of cavalry, and General Vanhope, commanding a brigade of infantry in the service of the King of the Netherlands.

General Pozzo di Borgo, General Baron Vincent, General Müffling, and General Alava were in the field during the action, and rendered me every assistance in their power. Baron Vincent is wounded, but I hope not severely, and General Pozzo di Borgo received a contusion.

I should not do justice to my own feelings, or to Marshal Blucher and the Prussian army, if I did not attribute the successful result of this arduous day to the cordial and timely assistance I received from them. The operation of General Bülow upon the enemy's flank was a most decisive one, and, even if I had not found myself in a situation to make the attack which produced the final result, it would have forced the enemy to retire if his attacks should have failed, and would have prevented him from taking advantage of them if they should have unfortunately succeeded.

Since writing the above, I have received a report that Major-General Sir W. Ponsonby is killed, and in announcing this intelligence to your lordship I have to add the expression of my grief for the fate of an officer who had already rendered very brilliant and important services, and was an ornament to his profession.

I send with this despatch three eagles taken by the troops in this action, which Major Percy will have the honour of laying at the feet of His Royal Highness. I beg leave to recommend him to your Lordship's protection.*

XXIX.

The Prussian Report of Waterloo.

Bataille du 18.

Au point du jour l'armée prussienne se mit en mouvement; les quatrième et deuxième corps marchèrent vers Saint-Lambert, où ils devaient rester en position, couverts par une forêt près de Frichermont, pour prendre l'ennemi par derrière quand le moment paraîtrait favorable. Le premier corps devait opérer par Ohain sur le flanc droit de l'ennemi; le troisième corps devait suivre lentement, afin de porter du secours en cas de besoin. La bataille commença environ à dix heures du matin: l'armée anglaise occupait les hauteurs de Mont-Saint-Jean, celle des Français était sur les hauteurs en avant de Planchenoit. La première était forte d'environ quatre-vingt mille hommes, l'ennemi en avait à peu près cent trente mille. En peu d'instants l'action devint générale sur toute la ligne.

---

* Despatches, xii. 478 *et seq.*

Il paraît que Napoléon avait le dessein de rejeter l'aile gauche sur le centre, afin d'effectuer entièrement la séparation des Anglais de l'armée prussienne, qu'il croyait en retraite sur Maëstricht.

Dans cette intention, il avait placé la plus grande partie de la réserve au centre, près de son aile droite, et il attaqua avec fureur sur ce point. L'armée anglaise combattit avec une valeur qu'il est impossible de surpasser. Les charges répétées de la vielle Garde échouèrent devant l'intrépidité des régiments écossais, et chacune des charges de la cavalerie française fut repoussée par la cavalerie anglaise. Mais la supériorité de l'ennemi était trop grande ; Napoléon envoyait continuellement en avant des masses énormes, et quelque fermeté que les troupes anglaises missent pour se maintenir dans leur position, il était impossible que de si héroïques efforts n'eussent enfin des bornes.

Il était quatre heures et demie. L'extrême difficulté du passage du défilé de Saint-Lambert avait considérablement retardé la marche des colonnes prussiennes, en sorte que deux brigades seulement du quatrième corps étaient arrivées à la position couverte qui leur était assignée. Le moment décisif était venu, il n'y avait pas un instant à perdre. Les généraux ne le laissèrent point échapper. Ils résolurent aussitôt de commencer l'attaque avec les troupes qu'ils avaient sous la main. Le Général Bulow, avec deux brigades et un corps de cavalerie, avança donc rapidement sur le derrière de l'aile droite ennemie. L'ennemi ne perdit pas sa présence d'esprit il dirigea de suite sa réserve contre nous, et un engagement des plus meurtriers commença de ce côté. Le succès resta longtemps incertain. Pendant ce temps-là le combat avec les Anglais continuait avec la même violence.

Vers six heures, nous reçumes la nouvelle que le Général Thielmann, qui commandait le troisième corps, était attaqué à Wavre par un corps ennemi très-considérable, et que déjà on se disputait la possession de la ville. Le Feld-Maréchal ne s'inquiéta pas de ce rapport ; c'était où il était, et non ailleurs, que l'affaire devait être décisive. Un combat continué avec ténacité et soutenu continuellement par des troupes fraîches pouvait seul assurer la victoire, et si on l'obtenait ici, un revers éprouvé à Wavre était de peu de conséquence. Les colonnes continuèrent leurs mouvements. A sept heures et demie, l'issue de la bataille était encore incertaine. Tout le quatrième corps et une partie du deuxième, sous le Général Pirch, s'étaient successivement engagés. Les troupes françaises se battaient avec une rage désespérée ; cependant on apercevait quelque incertitude dans leurs mouvements, et on observa que quelques pièces de canon battaient en retraite.

A ce moment, la première colonne du Général Ziethen arriva sur les points d'attaque, près du village de Smohain, et chargea aussitôt le flanc gauche de l'ennemi. Ce moment décida de sa defaite. L'aile droite fut enfoncée en trois endroits et abandonna ses positions. Nos troupes marchèrent en avant au pas de charge, et attaquèrent les Français de tous côtés, tandis qu'au même moment toute la ligne anglaise avançait.

Les circonstances furent entièrement favorables à l'attaque de l'armée prussienne. Le terrain s'élevait en amphithéâtre, de sorte que notre artillerie pouvait librement diriger ses feux du sommet de plusieurs hauteurs qui s'élevaient graduellement au-dessus les unes des autres, et dans les intervalles desquelles les troupes descendaient dans la plaine, formées en brigades et dans le plus grand ordre, pendant que des troupes fraîches se développaient sans cesse en sortant de la forêt, qui était derrière nous sur la hauteur. Cependant l'ennemi conserva quelques moyens de retraite jusqu'au moment où le village de Planchenoit, qui était sur ses derrières, et qui était défendu par la Garde, fut, après plusieurs attaques sanglantes, emporté d'assaut. Dès ce moment la retraite devint une déroute qui se répandit bientôt dans toute l'armée française, qui dans son affreuse confusion entraînait tout ce qui tentait de l'arrêter, et finit par présenter l'aspect de la fuite d'une armée de barbares.

Il était neuf heures et demie ; le Feld-Maréchal fit assembler tous les officiers supérieurs et donna ordre qu'on envoyât à la poursuite de l'ennemi jusqu'au dernier homme et au dernier cheval. L'avant garde de l'armée précipita sa marche. L'armée française, poursuivie sans interruption, fut entièrement désorganisée. La chaussée offrait le tableau d'un immense naufrage ; elle était couverte d'une quantité innombrable de canons, de caissons, de chariots, de baggages, d'armes et de débris de toute espèce.

Ceux des ennemis qui avaient essayé de prendre quelque repos et ne s'attendaient pas à être poursuivis si vivement, furent chassés de plus de neuf bivacs. Dans quelques villages ils tentèrent de se maintenir, mais aussitôt qu'ils entendaient le battement de nos tambours et le son de nos trompettes, ils se précipitaient dans les maisons, où ils étaient taillés en pièces ou faits prisonniers. Ce fut la clarté de la lune qui favorisa grandement la poursuite ; car toute cette marche n'était qu'une chasse continuelle dans les champs et dans les maisons.

À Genappe, l'ennemi s'était retranché avec des canons et des voitures renversées ; à notre approche, nous entendîmes tout à coup dans la ville un grand bruit de mouvement de voitures ; en y entrant, nous fûmes exposés à un feu de mousqueterie fort vif auquel nous ripostâmes par quelques coups de canon, suivis d'un *hurrah*, et dans un instant toute la ville fut à nous. Ce fut là que, parmi d'autre équipages, la voiture de Napoléon fut prise ; il l'avait quittée pour monter à cheval, et cela avec tant de précipitation, qu'il avait oublié dedans son epée et son chapeau. L'affaire se continua ainsi jusqu'au point du jour. Environ quarante mille hommes, restes de tout l'armée, et dans le désordre le plus complet, se sont sauvés en opérant leur retraite par Charleroi, une grande partie sans armes, n'emmenant avec eux que vingt-sept pièces de leur nombreuse artillerie. Dans sa fuite, l'ennemi a passé toutes ses forteresses, seules défenses de ses frontières qui maintenant sont dépassées par nos armées.

À trois heures, Napoléon dépêcha de dessus le champ de bataille un courrier à Paris, avec la nouvelle que la victoire n'était pas douteuse ; peu d'heures après, il n'eut plus que son aile gauche. Nous n'avons pas encore un état exacte des pertes de l'ennemi ; il suffit de savoir que les deux tiers de son armée sont tués, blessés ou prisonniers ; parmi ces derniers se trouvent les Généraux Du Hesme et Compans. Jusqu'à ce moment, environ trois cents pièces de canon et cinq cents caissons sont tombés entre nos mains.

26

Peu de victoires ont été si complètes, et il n'y a certainement pas d'exemple qu'une armée se soit, deux jours après la perte d'une bataille, engagée dans une telle action, et s'y soit soutenue aussi glorieusement. Il faut rendre honneur aux troupes capables d'autant de fermeté et de valeur. Dans le milieu de la position occupée par les Français, et tout à fait sur la hauteur, se trouve une ferme appelée la Belle-Alliance. La marche de toutes les colonnes prussiennes fut dirigée vers cette ferme, qui se voyait de tous les côtés ; ce fut là aussi que Napoléon se tint pendant la bataille ; ce fut la aussi qu'il donnait ses ordres, qu'il se flattait de l'espoir de la victoire, et que sa ruine fut decidée. Ce fut encore là que, par un hasard heureux, le Maréchal Blücher et le Lord Wellington se rencontrèrent dans l'obscurité et se saluèrent mutuellement comme vainqueurs.

En mémoire de l'alliance qui régne maintenant entre les nations anglaise et prussienne, de l'union des deux armées, et de leur confiance réciproque, le maréchal désire que cette bataille porte le nom de la Belle-Alliance.

Par un ordre du Feld-Maréchal Blücher,

LE GÉNÉRAL GNEISENAU.*

XXX.

NAPOLEON'S REPORT OF WATERLOO.

Bataille de Mont-Saint-Jean.

À neuf heures du matin, la pluie ayant un peu diminué, le 1ᵉʳ corps se mit en mouvement, et se plaça, la gauche à la route de Bruxelles et vis-à-vis le village de Mont-Saint-Jean, qui paraissait le centre de la position de l'ennemi. Le second corps appuya sa droite à la route de Bruxelles, et sa gauche à un petit bois à portée de canon de l'armée anglaise. Les cuirassiers se portèrent en réserve derrière, et la Garde en réserve sur les hauteurs. Le 6ᵉ corps, avec la cavalerie du Général Domon, sous les ordres du Comte Lobau, fut destiné

* La Tour d'Auvergne, 'Waterloo,' 401-411.

à se porter en arrière de notre droite, pour s'opposer à un corps prussien qui paraissait avoir échappé au Maréchal Grouchy, et être dans l'intention de tomber sur notre flanc droit, intention qui nous avait été connue par nos rapports et par une lettre du général prussien que portait une ordonnance prise par nos coureurs.

Les troupes étaient pleines d'ardeur. On estimait les forces de l'armée anglaise à quatre-vingt mille hommes. On supposait que le corps prussien, qui pouvait être en mesure vers le soir, pouvait être de quinze mille hommes. Les forces ennemis étaient donc de plus de quatre-vingt mille hommes; les nôtres étaient moins nombreuses.

À midi, tous les préparatifs étant terminés, le Prince Jérôme, commandant une division du 2e corps, destinée à en former l'extrême gauche, se porta sur le bois dont l'ennemi occupait une partie. La cannonade s'engagea; l'ennemi soutint par trente pièces de canon les troupes qu'il avait envoyées pour garder le bois. Nous fîmes aussi de notre côté des dispositions d'artillerie. À une heure, le Prince Jérôme fut maître de tout le bois, et toute l'armée anglaise se replia derrière un rideau. Le Comte d'Erlon attaqua alors le village de Mont-Saint-Jean, et fit appuyer son attaque par quatre-vingts pièces de canon. Il s'engagea là une épouvantable cannonade, qui dut beaucoup faire souffrir l'armée anglaise. Tous les coups portaient sur le plateau. Une brigade de la 1re division du Comte d'Erlon s'empara du village de Mont-Saint-Jean; une seconde brigade fut chargée par un corps de cavalerie anglaise, qui lui fit éprouver beaucoup de pertes. Au même moment, une division de cavalerie anglaise chargea la batterie du Comte d'Erlon par sa droite, et désorganisa plusieurs pièces; mais les cuirassiers du Général Milhaud chargèrent cette division, dont trois régiments furent rompus et écharpés.

Il était trois heures après midi, l'Empereur fit avancer la Garde pour la placer dans la plaine, sur le terrain qu'avait occupé le 1er corps au commencement de l'action, ce corps se trouvant déjà en avant. La division prussienne, dont on avait prévu le mouvement, commença alors à s'engager avec les tirailleurs du Comte Lobau, en plongeant son feu sur tout notre flanc droit. Il était convenable, avant de rien entre-prendre ailleurs, d'attendre l'issue qu'aurait cette attaque. A cet effet, tous les moyens de la réserve étaient prêts à se porter au secours du Comte Lobau et à écraser le corps prus-sien lorsqu'il se serait avancé. Cela fait, l'Empereur avait le projet de mener une attaque par le village de Mont-Saint-Jean, dont on espérait un succès décisif ; mais, par un mouve-ment d'impatience si fréquent dans nos annales militaires et qui nous a été si souvent funeste, la cavalerie de réserve, s'étant aperçue d'un mouvement rétrograde que faisaient les Anglais pour se mettre à l'abri de nos batteries dont ils avaient déjà tant souffert, couronna les hauteurs de Mont-Saint-Jean et chargea l'infanterie. Ce mouvement, qui, fait à temps et soutenu par les réserves, devait décider de la journée, fait isolément et avant que les affaires de la droite fussent terminées, devint funeste.

N'ayant aucun moyen de le contremander, l'ennemi montrant beaucoup de masses d'infanterie et de cavalerie, et les deux divisions de cuirassiers étant engagées, toute notre cavalerie courut au même moment pour soutenir ses camarades. Là, pendant trois heures, se firent de nombreuses charges qui nous valurent l'enfoncement de plusieurs carrés et six drapeaux de l'infanterie anglaise, avantage hors de proportion avec les pertes qu'éprouvait notre cavalerie par la mitraille et les fusillades. Il était impossible de disposer de nos réserves d'infanterie jusqu'à ce qu'on eût repoussé l'attaque de flanc du corps prussien. Cette attaque se prolongeait toujours et perpendicu-lairement sur notre flanc droit. L'Empereur y envoya le Général Du Hesme avec la Jeune Garde et plusieurs batteries de réserve. L'ennemi fut contenu, fut repoussé et recula ; il avait épuisé ses forces et l'on n'en avait plus rien à craindre. C'est ce moment qui était celui indiqué pour une attaque sur le centre de l'ennemi.

Comme les cuirassiers souffraient par la mitraille, on envoya quatre bataillons de la moyenne Garde pour protéger les cuirassiers, soutenir la position, et, si cela était possible, dégager et faire reculer dans la plaine une partie de notre cavalerie.

On envoya deux autres bataillons pour se tenir en potence sur l'extrême gauche de la division qui avait manœuvré sur nos flancs, afin de n'avoir de ce côté aucune inquiétude ; le reste fut disposé en réserve, partie pour occuper la potence en arrière de Mont-Saint-Jean, partie sur le plateau, en arrière du champ de bataille qui formait notre position de retraite.

Dans cet état de choses, la bataille était gagnée ; nous occupions toutes les positions que l'ennemi occupait au commencement de l'action, notre cavalerie ayant été trop tôt et mal employée, nous ne pouvions plus espérer de succès décisifs. Mais le Maréchal Grouchy, ayant appris le mouvement du corps prussien, marchait sur le derrière de ce corps, ce qui nous assurait un succès éclatant pour la journée de lendemain. Après huit heures de feu et de charges d'infanterie et de cavalerie, toute l'armée voyait avec satisfaction la bataille gagnée et le champ de bataille en notre pouvoir.

Sur les huit heures et demie, les quatre bataillons de la moyenne Garde qui avaient été envoyés sur le plateau au delà de Mont-Saint-Jean pour soutenir les cuirassiers, étant gênés par la mitraille de l'ennemi, marchèrent à la baïonnette pour enlever ses batteries. Le jour finissait ; une charge faite sur leur flanc par plusieurs escadrons anglais les mit en désordre ; les fuyards repassèrent le ravin ; les régiments voisins, qui virent quelques troupes appartenant à la Garde à la débandade, crurent que c'était de la Vieille Garde et s'ébranlèrent ; les cris : ' *Tout est perdu ! la Garde est repoussée !*' se firent entendre. Les soldats prétendent même que sur plusieurs points des malveillants apostés ont crié : ' *Sauve qui peut !*' Quoi qu'il en soit, une terreur panique se répandit tout à la fois sur tout le champ de bataille ; on se précipita dans le plus grand désordre sur la ligne de communication ; les soldats, les canonniers, les caissons se pressaient pour y arriver ; la Vieille Garde, qui était en réserve, en fut assaillie et fut elle-même entraînée.

Dans un instant, l'armée ne fut plus qu'une masse confuse, toutes les armes étaient mêlées, et il était impossible de reformer un corps. L'ennemi, qui s'aperçut de cette étonnante confusion, fit déboucher des colonnes de cavalerie ; le désordre augmenta; la confusion de la nuit empêcha de rallier les troupes et de leur montrer leur erreur.

Ainsi une bataille terminée, une journée finie, de fausses mesures réparées, de plus grands succès assurés pour le lendemain, tout fut perdu par un moment de terreur panique. Les escadrons de service même, rangés à côté de l'Empereur, furent culbutés et désorganisés par ces flots tumultueux, et il n'y eut plus d'autre chose à faire que de suivre le torrent. Les parcs de réserve, les bagages qui n'avaient pas repassé la Sambre et tout ce qui était sur le champ de bataille sont restés aux pouvoir de l'ennemi. Il n'y a eu même aucun moyen d'attendre les troupes de notre droite; on sait ce que c'est que la plus brave armée du monde lorsqu'elle est mêlée et que son organisation n'existe plus.*

* Napoleon Correspondence, xxviii. 295-298.

INDEX

A

ABDICATION, The, of Napoleon, 356

Acte Additionnel, The, 41, 42

Adam, British General at Waterloo, 211

Allies, The: they proscribe Napoleon as an outlaw, 23, 24; gigantic preparations of, to overthrow him, 36, 37

Allix, French General: his division commanded by Bourgeois and Quiot at Waterloo, 243; their attack fails, 243, 244; they take part in the final attack, 287

Alten, General, commander of Wellington's third division, 92-94; at Quatre Bras, 137; at Waterloo, 210; his division suffers terribly, 287

Angoulême, The Duc de, at the Restoration, 5; he endeavours to raise a part of the South of France in favour of the Bourbons, 22; is made prisoner and released by Napoleon, 22

Angoulême, The Duchesse de: she endeavours to retain Bordeaux for Louis XVIII., 21

Arentschild, General of the German Legion at Waterloo, 210

Army, The French, at the Restoration of Louis XVIII., 4; discontent in, 4; unwise policy of the Bourbons to, 7; the army turns its eyes to Napoleon at Elba, 11; it declares for Napoleon soon after he had landed in France, 15, 17; it is reorganised by Napoleon, 29-35; distribution of the army on

the northern frontier of France, 55; concentration of, 128,000 men near Charleroy on the night of June 14, 1815, 56; admirable skill shown in this operation, 56; numbers and characteristics of the army, 57-60; its march on June 15 retarded, and the causes of this, 79, 80; the positions it holds on the night of June 15, 87; the army does not move at an early hour on June 16, 103; movement of the right and centre of the army, excepting the corps of Lobau, in the forenoon of June 16, 112; the army is victorious at Ligny, 128, 129; its conduct in the battle, 150; exultation of the army after Ligny, and want of proper precautions, 159; the whole French army is divided into two groups on June 17, one group to hold Blucher in check, the other to pursue Wellington, 168; part of the army reaches Waterloo on the night of June 17, 188; feelings of the army on the morning of June 18, 199, 200; magnificent appearance of the army before the attack at Waterloo, 220-225; its probable numbers, 221; its exultation and confidence, 226; defeat and rout of the French army, and its flight, 295; its supposed losses, 306

Army, The Prussian, in Belgium: it is divided into four corps d'armée under Zieten, Pirch, Thielmann, and Bulow, 50; like that of Wellington, it is widely disseminated, 50; the positions it holds in June, 1815, 50, 51; numbers and characteristics of the Prussian army, 63, 64; positions of the army on the night of June 15, 99; positions of the corps of Zieten, Pirch, and Thielmann at the Battle of Ligny on June 16, 114, 116; the army is defeated at Ligny, 128, 129; its conduct on June 16, 151; its position critical in the night, 152; retreat of the army after Ligny, 173 - 175; its positions around Wavre on the night of June 17, and its numbers, 174, 175; delays in the advance of the Prussian army from Wavre on June 18, 215, 216; losses of the Prussian army at Waterloo, 306

Army, The, of Wellington in Belgium, 49; it is divided into three corps d'armée under Hill, the Prince of Orange, and Wellington, 49; like Blucher's army, it is widely disseminated, 49, 50; the positions it holds in June, 1815, 49, 50; numbers and characteristics of Wellington's army, 60-62; its positions on the night of June 15, 99; its conduct at Quatre Bras on June 16, 151; its position critical, 152; feelings of the army before Waterloo, 201, 202; its order of battle, 207-212; its probable numbers, 209; its appearance before the attack on June 18, 226; it is moved forward by Wellington after the defeat of the French army, 295; its losses at Waterloo, 306

Artois, The Comte de, at the Restoration, 5; his fruitless efforts at Lyons, 15

B

Bachelu, French General at Quatre Bras, 133, 135, 136; at Waterloo, 272

Baudus, officer of Soult, carries Napoleon's message to D'Erlon on June 16, 122; remonstrates with Ney, 142

Belgium, Topography of, 47, 49; positions of the armies of Blucher and Wellington in June, 1815, 49, 51

Belle Alliance, Heights of, 181, 226; meeting of Blucher and Wellington at, 298

Berri, Duc de, 5

Bertrand, one of Napoleon's most trusted officers, conveys a very important despatch of Napoleon to Grouchy on June 17, 171

Best, Hanoverian General at Waterloo, 209

Blucher, Marshal, colleague of Wellington in 1815: he arrives in Belgium, 36; his faulty dispositions and those of Wellington before hostilities begin, 51-53; characteristics of Blucher in war, 70, and of his lieutenants, 71; Blucher on June 14 directs that his army is to move on Sombreffe, 88, 89; imprudence of this strategy, 90; he had not received a promise of assistance from Wellington on June 16, 90; his operations and those of Wellington up to this time faulty, 100-102; Blucher assembles the corps of Zieten, Pirch, and Thielmann around Sombreffe on June 16, and arrays his army for a great battle, 113; his conversation with Wellington before Ligny, 117; his conduct during the battle, 120-127; he is thrown from his charger at the end of the day, 128; his strategy and tactics on June 16, 147-150; Blucher resolves to lead his army to join Wellington on June 18, 192; he is entitled to the whole credit, 193; his messages to Wellington, 192, 193; his plans and those of Wellington for June 18 bad strategy, 194; Blucher on the march from Wavre to Waterloo, 213; his orders to his army for June 18, 214; he presses on the march of his columns, 214; his energy in urging the attack of Bulow from St. Lambert, 264; he promises to assist Wellington with part of the corps of Pirch, 283; he meets his colleague at La Belle Alliance, 298; he advances on Paris with Wellington, 359; his march imprudent, 359; he crosses the Seine, and places himself in a dangerous position, 361; his violent threats, 362; he is persuaded by Wellington to become more moderate, and is soothed by being made to appear the arbiter of events, 363

Bordeaux holds out for the Bourbons under the Duchesse d'Angoulême, 21

Bourmont, French General: his desertion of the army, 78

Braine l'Alleud, Village of, 208

Brussels, Wellington's headquarters in, 1815, 52; he attaches great importance to it, 50, 52

Bulow commands the 4th corps of the Prussian army, 64; he is directed on the night of June 14 to move towards Sombreffe, 88, 89; he is prevented by distance from doing this, 89; he joins the Prussian army after Ligny, 175; Bulow is delayed on June 18 when on the march from Wavre, 215, 216; he reaches St. Lambert with half of his forces only, 264; the other half comes up at three in the afternoon of June 18, 264; his first attack repulsed, 265; his attack renewed and again repulsed, 277; with the support of Pirch he storms Plancenoit, 297

Bylandt, Dutch-Belgian General at Waterloo, 209; defeat of his troops, 243, 244

Byng, British General at Waterloo, 210

C

Cambacérès, Minister of Napoleon in 1815, 19

Carnot, Minister of Napoleon in 1815, 19; his advice to Napoleon after Waterloo, 353

Caulaincourt, Minister of Napoleon in 1815, 19

Chambers, The French, of 1815: their composition and qualities, 43, 44; they declare themselves the sole representatives of the State after Waterloo, 350; their illusions, 351; they pronounce against being dissolved by Napoleon, 354; they vote thanks to Napoleon when he abdicates, 357; they are strongly opposed to the restoration of the Bourbons, but are made the dupes of Fouché, 358; they are suppressed on the return of the King, 364

Champ de Mai, The, 44, 45

Charleroy: the French army enters the town on June 15, 79; passes through it after the rout of Waterloo, 301

Chassé, Dutch General, gives Wellington valuable assistance, 69; at Waterloo, 211; he breaks the first column of the Imperial Guard, 292

Church, The French, at the Restoration, 5

Clinton, British General at Waterloo, commands the second division, 211

Colville, British General: the greatest part of his division left at Hal and Tubize, 211

Constant, Benjamin, consulted by Napoleon, and the author of the Acte Additionnel, 41

Cooke, British General, commands the first division British Guards, 94; at Quatre Bras, 142; at Waterloo, 210

D

Davoût, Minister of Napoleon in 1815, 19; his advice after Waterloo, 354; his unfeeling conduct to Napoleon, 357; is made commander of the French army around Paris, and declares that resistance is hopeless, 359

Delcambre, chief of D'Erlon's staff, informs Ney that D'Erlon has been summoned to Ligny, 137; Ney orders him to recall D'Erlon, 138

D'Erlon, commander of the 1st corps of the French army in 1815, 57; his operations on June 15, 77-80; D'Erlon moves his corps to Jumet early on June 16, 104; he is remiss and backward on June 16, but receives only one order from Ney, 138; he turns aside with his corps towards Ligny, but in the wrong direction, 139; he is recalled by Ney, and joins the Marshal, 139; this was grave misconduct, 139; he detaches Durutte to observe the Prussians at Ligny, 139; what he might have accomplished, 139, 140; his conduct on June 16 deserves censure, 146; at Waterloo, 220; he conducts the first great attack, 241; vicious formation of his columns, 241, 242; he takes part in the final attack, 287.

Desnoëttes, Lefebvre-, commands the light cavalry of the Imperial Guard : his operations on June 15, 80, 84; at Waterloo, 220; he takes part in the great cavalry attacks, 259

Domon, French cavalry General at Waterloo, 220; detached with Subervie and Lobau to hold Bulow in check, 232

Donzelot, French General at Waterloo, 241, 242, 245; his attack fails, 245; he takes part in the final attack, 287

Dornberg, General of the German Legion at Waterloo, 210

Duhesme, commander of the Young Guard, not slain by the Prussians in cold blood, 299

Duplat, one of Wellington's Generals at Waterloo, 211

Dupont, General, made Minister of War at the Restoration, 8

Durutte, French General detached by D'Erlon on June 16, 139; his attack at Waterloo fails, 248; his conduct in the final attack, 287

E

Émigré party, The extreme, at the Restoration of Louis XVIII., 3

Emperor. See Napoleon

Empire of Napoleon quickly restored in 1815, 21

Excelmans, French cavalry General: his operations on June 17, 159; he is remiss and overconfident, 183; he reaches Sauvenière, 183; his conduct on June 18, 303, 304, and on June 19, 348

F

Forbin-Janson carries Napoleon's message to D'Erlon on June 16, 122

Fouché : his objects at the Restoration; he sets a military conspiracy on foot, 11; is made Minister of the Police by Napoleon in 1815, 20; at the Champ de Mai, 45; his intrigues during the second reign of Napoleon, 351; his perfidy, 354; he persuades the Chambers that Napoleon is about to dissolve them, 354; he is made head of the Provisional Government of France, 358; his subsequent intrigues, 358, 359; he paralyses every effort to resist or to check the invaders, 358; he sends envoys to Wellington, 359; he releases Vitrolles, and negotiates with the exiled Court of Louis XVIII., 358, 359; he acquires great influence from the support of Wellington, 360, but is placed in a position of real danger, 360; his crooked policy succeeds, 363; he obtains a high place in the councils of Louis XVIII., but is disgraced, 364

Foy, French General at Quatre Bras, 132, 134, 136; joins in the attack on Hougoumont, 231

France, State of, at the Restoration of Louis XVIII., 1-11; accepts the Empire after Napoleon's return from Elba, 19, 22; parts of, gradually fall away from Napoleon, 24, 25; attitude of, after Waterloo, 363

Frischermont, 207

G

Gaudin, Minister of Napoleon in 1815, 19

Gembloux, Grouchy at, 183

Generals, Feelings of the French, at the Restoration, 9

Gérard commands the 4th corps of the French army, 17; his operations on June 15, 78, 81, 85; his conduct at the Battle of Ligny, 121, 123; remark of Napoleon to, at Fleurus, 119; Gérard's operations on June 17, 182, 183; at Walhain he urges Grouchy to march on Waterloo, 238; the means he proposes to effect this, 238; Grouchy rejects his wise counsel, 240; indignation of Gérard at Grouchy's conduct, 304; he takes part in the attack on Wavre, and is severely wounded, 306

Ghigny, Dutch-Belgian General at Waterloo, 209

Girard, Conduct of, at Ligny, and death of, 120, 123

Gneisenau, chief of Blucher's staff, directs the Prussian army after

Ligny to Wavre, 174; this movement a bad half-measure, 177; what might have been accomplished, 177; Gneisenau hesitates on the night of June 17 and the morning of June 18, 214; his distrust of Wellington 214; he presses the pursuit after Waterloo, but not energetically, 298, 299

Government of Louis XVIII. at the Restoration: its bad policy and many errors, 5-7; it breaks faith with Napoleon when at Elba, 13; Government of Napoleon in 1815 inevitably feeble, 26, 27

Grant, British cavalry General at Waterloo, 210

Grouchy made a Marshal of France, 22; at first commands the cavalry reserve of the French army, with Pajol, Kellermann, and Milhaud as subordinates, 57; he informs Napoleon of the retreat being made by Pirch II. on Gilly, 86; Vandamme refuses to comply with his request to march on Sombreffe, 86; Grouchy receives Napoleon's orders for June 16, 111; he shows energy and attention, 111; his report to Napoleon, 111; his conduct at Ligny, 121, 123, 127; Grouchy accompanies Napoleon to Ligny on June 17, 165; he receives Napoleon's orders, 169; their true purport, 169, 170; he remonstrates with Napoleon, and is rebuked, 171; he receives another order of the first importance through Bertrand, 171; Grouchy denied for many years the existence of this order, 171; his operations on June 17, 181; his march to Gembloux extraordinarily slow, 182; 183; positions of his army around Gembloux on the night of June 17, 184; his despatch to Napoleon at ten at night, 184; what he ought to have done on June 18, 186; he does not even think of this operation on the night of June 17, 187; his despatch to Napoleon at three in the morning of June 18, 217; he does not make for Moustier and Ottignies on June 18, and does not try to interpose between Blucher and Wellington, 217; he

marches on Sart les Walhain, 218; he moves at a late hour and slowly towards Wavre, 218, and sends out no reconnoitring-parties, 218; he reaches Walhain near eleven in the morning of June 18, 236; his despatch to Napoleon from Walhain, 236, 237; positions of his army at this moment, 237, 238; he hears the thunder of Waterloo, and is urged by Gérard to march to the scene of the battle, 238; he rejects this advice, 239; marches on Wavre by the eastern bank of the Dyle, and keeps far away from Waterloo, 240; positions of his army, 303; he receives Soult's despatch of ten in the morning of June 18, 304; he is indignantly censured by Gérard, 304; he reaches Wavre at about half-past four, 304; he attacks Wavre, 304; he receives Soult's letter of one in the afternoon, and the postcript to it, 305; he sends Pajol and Teste to the Dyle, and continues the attack on Wavre, 305, 306; Grouchy resolves to march on Brussels on June 19, 346; he receives the news of the rout of Waterloo, 347; his excuses to his lieutenants, 347; he retreats on Namur, 348; celerity of this movement in marked contrast with his operations on June 18, 348; Grouchy reaches Namur on June 20, and Givet on June 21, 349, 350; he is given the command of the French army that had fought in Belgium, and leads its remains to Paris, 361

Guard, The Imperial: conduct of at Ligny, 127, 128; it is at Waterloo, 220; the Young Guard and part of the Old detached to oppose Bulow on June 18, 265, 276; part of the Guard attacks Wellington's line, 289; it is wrongly directed, 291; attack of the Guard in four echelons, 291, 204; it is completely defeated, 294; the part of the Guard left in Napoleon's hands makes a fine resistance, but is overwhelmed, 297; retreat of another part of the Guard from Waterloo, 297, 300

Guilleminot, chief of Jerôme's staff, disapproves of the reiterated attacks on Hougoumont, 230

Guyot commands the heavy cavalry of the Imperial Guard at Waterloo; Napoleon always denied that he allowed him to take part in the great cavalry charges, 263

H

Halkett, C., British General at Waterloo, 278, 291

Halkett, W., one of Wellington's Generals at Waterloo, 211

Heymès, aide-de-camp of Ney, 82; not a faithworthy witness, 83; sent by Ney at Waterloo to ask Napoleon for infantry, 275

Hill commands the 2nd corps of Wellington's army, 49; commands the right wing at Waterloo, 211

Hougoumont, important outpost of Wellington at Waterloo, 211; description of, 224

J

Jacquinot, French cavalry General at Waterloo, 220

Jerôme Bonaparte at Quatre Bras, 134, 136; takes part in the attack on Hougoumont, 229

K

Kellermann, French cavalry General, 143; conduct at Quatre Bras, 141, 142; at Waterloo, 220; his conduct in the battle, 266; he disapproves of the great cavalry attacks, 266

Kempt, British General at Waterloo: he repulses D'Erlon's attack, 244

Kilmansegge, one of Wellington's Generals at Waterloo, 278

Kruse commands the Nassau contingent at Waterloo, 210

L

Labédoyère: his defection to Napoleon, 15

Lafayette, 43; he persuades the Chambers to resist any attempts at a dissolution, 359

La Haye Sainte, important outpost of Wellington at Waterloo, 211;
first attack on, 243; fall of, at about four in the afternoon, 256; fierce attacks of the French from, 278, 287

Lambert, British General at Waterloo, 209

Ledebur, Prussian officer at Mont St. Guibert, charged to observe Grouchy, 238; he is surprised and nearly surrounded, 303

Liberal party in France at the Restoration, 4, 9

Ligny: description of the battlefield, 113, 114; the battle of, 114-129; the attack of the corps of Vandamme, 120; the attack of the corps of Gérard, 121; Blucher reinforces the point assailed, 120, 121; continuation of the battle, 123, 126; furious counter-attack of Blucher, 126, 127; defeat of the Prussian army, 128, 129

Lobau commands the 6th corps of the French army, 57; his operations on June 15, 78; he reaches the field of Ligny at the close of the battle, 128; at Waterloo, 220; he is detached with Subervie and Domon to hold Bulow in check, 234; rout of his troops at Plancenoit after an heroic resistance, 297

M

Macdonald, Marshal: his fruitless efforts at Lyons to oppose Napoleon, 15

Maitland, British General at Waterloo, 210

Marbot sent by Napoleon on the morning of June 18 to communicate with Grouchy, 221, 222; finds no trace of him, 222

Marie Louise, The Empress: Fouché conspires in her behalf, 11; she is separated by the allies from Napoleon, 13

Marmont, Marshal, known as Marshal Judas, 8

Marshals, the French, Feelings of, at the Restoration, 9, 10

Masséna, Marshal: he sends a column from Marseilles to stop Napoleon, 14; he is made Commander-in-Chief of the National Guard in Paris, and declares resistance impossible, 359

Merbe-Braine, Village of, 208

Milhaud, French cavalry General : conduct of at Ligny, 128 ; at Waterloo, 220 ; his conduct on June 18, 259 ; part of his cuirassiers defeated near La Haye Sainte, 247, 248 ; he disapproves of the great cavalry attacks, but takes part in them, 259

Mollien, Minister of Napoleon in 1815, 19

Mont St. Jean, Village and ridge of, 207, 208

Murat, Fall of, disastrous to Napoleon, 39, 40

N

Namur : headquarters of Blucher in 1815, 52 ; Grouchy's army retreats through the town after Waterloo, 349

Napoleon at Elba : his attitude during the first months of his exile, 12 ; he resolves to leave the island and to regain his throne, 12 ; unjust policy of the allies to him, 13 ; projects of assassinating Napoleon, 13 ; his departure from Elba, 13 ; he lands near Cannes, 13 ; his march through Dauphiné, 14, 15 ; a regiment declares for him, 15 ; he reaches Grenoble and Lyons, 15, 16 ; he is welcomed with enthusiasm by the peasantry, the population of the towns, and the army, 15, 16 ; Ney declares for him, 16 ; vain efforts of the Bourbon Government, 17 ; Louis XVIII. flies to Lille and Ghent, 18 ; Napoleon enters the Tuileries March 20, 1815, 18 ; exultation of his partisans, 18 ; he re-establishes the Empire, 18, 22 ; he is proscribed by the allies, 23 ; he ought to have been made a dictator, 25 ; he must have failed had he played the part of a Jacobin dictator, 27, 28 ; he reorganises the army, 29, 35 ; he fortifies Paris, 36 ; his plans of operations against the allies, 37, 39 ; he resolves to attack Blucher and Wellington in Belgium, 39 ; he tries to conciliate Liberal France, 41 ; the policy and measures he adopts, 41, 43 ; he presides at the Champ de Mai, 44 ; he leaves Paris to join his army in Belgium, 46 ; he resolves to attack the centre of the armies of Blucher and Wellington, 53, 55 ; he concentrates his army on the frontier near Charleroy with extraordinary skill, 56 ; characteristics of Napoleon in war, 66, and of his lieutenants, 66, 68 ; Napoleon's address to his army, 72, 73 ; his orders for the advance on June 15, 73, 75 ; his objects in making this march, 75, 76 ; he enters Charleroy on June 15, and gives his orders, 79, 80 ; his orders to Ney to seize Quatre Bras on June 15, 82 ; Napoleon directs the combat at Gilly, 86 ; his excessive fatigue on the night of June 15, 86, 87 ; he had not accomplished all that he expected, but had gained important strategic success, 87, 88 ; Napoleon charged with inactivity on the morning of June 16, 104 ; examination of this charge — the true reasons of his delay, 105 ; Napoleon's orders to Ney for June 16, 105, 107 ; his orders to Grouchy for the same day, 107 ; his anticipations for June 16 ill-founded, but his arrangements perfectly combined to meet all that might happen, 108 ; Napoleon assembles the right and centre of his army, apart from the corps of Lobau, around Fleurus at about one in the afternoon of June 16, 112 ; his message to Ney at two to fall on the flank and rear of Blucher, 118 ; the message repeated at a quarter past three, 121 ; Napoleon's direct orders to D'Erlon to march against Blucher, 122 ; he sends an aide-de-camp to reconnoitre when informed that an enemy's column is moving on Fleurus, 124 ; the aide-de-camp reports that the column is that of D'Erlon, 125 ; Napoleon, whatever the reason, does not summon D'Erlon to the field, 125 ; he breaks Blucher's centre, and gains the Battle of Ligny, 144 ; his operations very able, but he made one signal mistake, 145 ; he had not obtained all the results he might have obtained on June 16, but his prospects are still full of promise, 151, 152; Napoleon could have gained decisive success on June 17, 155; he retires to rest at Fleurus on the night of June 16 completely exhausted, 159; he saw no one, and had no conversation on the position of affairs until the morning of June 17, 159; he believes that Blucher had been routed, and was recoiling upon his base, 159; his first orders to pursue the Prussians, 160; his despatch sent through Soult to Ney, 161; the French army, among other things, was to halt for the day, 162; the state of Napoleon's health was the true cause of his apparent remissness, 162-165; Napoleon leaves Fleurus at about nine in the forenoon of June 17, accompanied by Grouchy, 165; he reviews his army at Ligny, 166, 167; he receives messages from Quatre Bras and from the lines of the retreat of the Prussians, 167; he resolves to send a restraining wing to pursue Blucher, and with Ney to attack Wellington, 167; this was the true course to adopt, but it was adopted very late, 167; his orders to Grouchy, and their real import, 169, 170; Napoleon dissatisfied with Grouchy's remarks, 171; he sends a second order to Grouchy through Bertrand, 171; its real purport, 172, 173; it clearly directs Grouchy to keep Blucher and Wellington apart, 173; Napoleon begins his offensive movement against Wellington, 177; he reaches Marbais on his way to Quatre Bras, 179; indignant at the inactivity of Ney, he orders D'Erlon to advance, 180; he rebukes Ney and D'Erlon, 180; he conducts in person the pursuit of Wellington's army, 180; he reaches the position of Waterloo, 180; he makes a significant remark, 181; Napoleon before Waterloo on the night of June 17, 188; his leading idea is to bring Wellington to bay, 188; he does not believe that Blucher

could reach Waterloo, 189; he reconnoitres Wellington's position in the night, 189; he receives Grouchy's despatch written at ten at night, 189; this is calculated to give him complete confidence, 190; his communications with Grouchy in the night of June 17, 190; examination of the question whether Napoleon ordered Grouchy to send a detachment of 7,000 men to St. Lambert, and to second the movement with the main part of his army, 191; Napoleon has now met Wellington for the first time, 195; his confidence as to the result, 196; he had not been outgeneralled by the allies, 197, 198; Napoleon on the morning of June 18, 203; his overconfidence, 203, 204; his conversations with his lieutenants, 204, 205; he had given orders for the attack to begin at nine in the morning, but countermands these in order to gain time for the ground to harden, 206; the sun in its courses fights against him, 207; the evidence as to the state of his health on June 18 conflicting, 219; Napoleon's plan of attack at Waterloo, 219; he turns his attention to Grouchy, and directs Marbot to send reconnoitring-parties to Moustier and Ottignies in order to meet Grouchy, 221; on being informed that French troops are not at Moustier and Ottignies, he directs Marbot to search for Grouchy at the bridges of Limale and Limelette, 222; his significant conversation with Zenowicz, 222; Napoleon learns that Bulow is approaching the French army, 233; he had received Grouchy's letter written from Gembloux at three in the morning, 233; he detaches Subervie and Domon with Lobau to hold Bulow in check and to join Grouchy, 233; he does not think his army in real danger, 234, 235; Napoleon receives ominous intelligence from Grouchy at Walhain, 251, 252; he is compelled to modify his plan of attack, 254; he resolves to attack Wellington's centre and left centre only, 254; his orders to Ney, 254; Ney disobeys these, 257; Napoleon severely condemns Ney, and disapproves of the great cavalry attacks, but feels obliged to support them, 263; he detaches the Young Guard to repulse Bulow, 265; whether he made a mistake at this crisis of the battle, 273; his angry remark to Heymès, 275; he detaches part of the Old Guard to oppose Bulow, 276; fresh orders to Ney, 276; he makes preparations for the final attack, 278; he is still hopeful of victory, 279, 281; he forms the Imperial Guard for the final attack, 286-288; his energy at this crisis, 288; he sends a message to Durutte announcing the approach of Grouchy, 289; he forms four battalions of the Guard to resist the advance of the enemy, 296; he leaves the field with three battalions of the Old Guard, 297, 301; he is nearly made prisoner by the Prussians, 301; his orders to Grouchy, 302; he reaches Charleroy and Philippeville, 302; Napoleon arrives in Paris on June 21, 353; he expresses a hope to his Ministers that the Chambers will make him a dictator during the war, 353; he feels that a dissolution of the Chambers would only lead to civil war and national ruin, 355; after some hesitation, he abdicates, 356; he retires to Malmaison, 357; his proposal to fall on the allied armies, when apart, as they approached Paris, 361; this is rejected by Fouché, 361; Napoleon is exiled to St. Helena, 366

Ney, Marshal: his defection to Napoleon, 16; he joins Napoleon on June 15, 82; he receives the command of the left of the French army, 82; his operations on June 15, 83; he is quite inferior to himself, 83; he advances to Frasnes with a small body of troops, having neglected to rally the corps in his rear, and, after a mere demonstration, places his men in camp, 85; he does not seize Quatre Bras, as he might have done, 85; Ney receives Napoleon's orders for June 16, 109; he gives proof of irresolution and negligence, and disobeys his orders, 111; what he might have done, 111; he does not assemble his army and occupy Quatre Bras at an early hour on July 16, 129; his orders to Reille, D'Erlon and Kellermann late and inadequate, 129, 130; fresh proofs of hesitation and disobedience, 130; sharp reproof of Napoleon to Ney on the morning of June 16, 130; what Ney could have accomplished, 132; he attacks at Quatre Bras at two in the afternoon, 133; he receives Napoleon's message sent from Fleurus at two, 135; and the subsequent message sent at a quarter-past three, 137; Ney is informed that D'Erlon has been summoned to Ligny, and peremptorily orders his recall, 138; his indignation and want of reflection, 142; his retreat to Frasnes skilful, 143; examination of Ney's conduct on June 16, 143, 144, 146; it deserves severe censure, 146; Ney, furious at what he deemed illtreatment, sends no account to Soult of the results of Quatre Bras, 159; he is rebuked by Napoleon on June 17, 180; his remarks to Napoleon on the morning of June 18, 204; he is entrusted with the first great attack to be made by D'Erlon's corps, 232; Ney is ordered by Napoleon to seize La Haye Sainte, to establish himself there, and to await a decisive attack pressed home, 254; he disobeys his orders, and resolves to make the great cavalry attacks, 257; this most unwise and premature, 258; his conduct in the cavalry attacks reckless and precipitate, 271, 272; he sends to Napoleon to ask for infantry, 275; he conducts the final attack of part of the Imperial Guard, supported by D'Erlon and Reille, 286; he gives a false direction to the attack, 291; he fights desperately at the close of the battle,

300 ; his injudicious conduct after Waterloo, 357

Noblesse, The French, at the Restoration, 3, 9

O

Ompteda, one of Wellington's Generals at Waterloo, 278

Orange, The Prince of, commands the 1st corps of Wellington's army, 49 ; his skilful arrangements on June 16, 133 ; he is repulsed with Perponcher, but gains time, 134 ; is thanked by Wellington, 134 ; he commands the centre of Wellington's army at Waterloo, 211

Orleans, The Duke of : plots of Fouché in his favour, 11 ; his fruitless attempts in behalf of the Bourbon Government at Lyons, 15

P

Pack, British General at Waterloo, repulses D'Erlon's attack, 244

Pajol, French cavalry General : his operations on June 15, 78-80 ; and on June 17, 159, 160, 182 ; his conduct on June 18, 238, 305 ; he skilfully masks the retreat of Grouchy, 348

Paris, State of opinion in, at the Restoration, 8 ; and after Waterloo, 350

Peasantry, Feelings of the French, in 1814, 2, 11

Perponcher, Dutch-Belgian General, gives Wellington valuable assistance, 69 ; his admirable conduct on June 15, 95 ; his skilful arrangements at Quatre Bras, 133 ; is thanked by Wellington, 139

Picton, one of Wellington's best lieutenants, 69 ; he reaches Quatre Bras rather late, 135 ; his conduct in the battle, 135-137 ; he commands Wellington's left at Waterloo, 211 ; is killed in the battle, 244, 245

Pirch commands the 2nd corps of Blucher's army, 64 ; is directed on the night of June 14 to march on Sombreffe, 88 ; his corps is assembled round that place on June 16, 113 ; his conduct at Ligny, 120, 121, 123, 126 ; and during the retreat to Wavre, 174 ;

he is delayed, on June 18, in marching from Wavre on Waterloo, 216 ; part of his corps reaches Bulow at the close of the battle, 284 ; with Bulow storms Plancenoit, 297 ; he pursues Grouchy on June 19, but fails to come up with him, 348, 349

Pirch II., one of Zieten's subordinates : his operations on June 15, 77, 79 ; he makes a successful stand at Gilly, 85

Piré, French cavalry General : his conduct at Quatre Bras, 135, 136 ; at Waterloo, 220 ; his conduct in the battle, 266, 271, 286, 287

Plancenoit stormed by the Prussians at the close of Waterloo, 297

Ponsonby, cavalry General of Wellington at Waterloo, 209 ; his magnificent charge, 245 ; his cavalry get out of hand, and he is slain, 246

Q

Quatre Bras : important strategic point not seized by Ney on June 15, 85 ; battle of, 132, 144 ; description of the field, 133 ; attack of Bachelu, Foy, and Piré, 133 : Perponcher and the Prince of Orange are driven back, but have gained time for the arrival of reinforcements, 134, 135 ; Wellington arrives at Quatre Bras, and is reinforced, 134, 135 ; Jerôme's division reaches the field ; attack of Bachelu, Foy, Piré, and Jerôme, 136, 137 ; the situation for Wellington critical, 137 ; he receives fresh reinforcements, 137 ; Ney attacks again with the forces in his hands, and with one brigade of Kellermann's cavalry, 141 ; the attack fails, 141, 142 ; Wellington, largely reinforced, assumes the offensive, and compels Ney to retreat to Frasnes, 143

R

Reflections on Waterloo : Napoleon's original plan of attack the best possible, 307 ; his second plan of attack admirably conceived, 308 ; four distinct mistakes were made in the tactics of the French, 308, 309 ; question as to the delay in making the attack, 309 ; how far Napoleon is responsible for these errors, 310, 311; the attacks would have succeeded before the Prussians made their presence felt but for the conduct of Wellington and of part of his army, 311; admirable tactics of Wellington, 312; steadfastness of his British and German Legionary troops, 312; the result of Waterloo not due to mere differences of tactics, 312; it was determined by the junction of Wellington's and Blucher's forces on the field, 313; ought Grouchy to have prevented this junction? 313; examination of the question in detail, 314, 323; Grouchy could have kept Blucher away from Wellington had he got over the Dyle at Moustier and Ottignies by noon on June 18, 323; he could nearly have attained the same result had he followed Gérard's advice and marched from Walhain on Waterloo, 323; review of arguments to the contrary, 320, 326; remarks of Napoleon on the subject, 327; Grouchy the main cause of the disaster at Waterloo, 328; Napoleon not wholly free from blame, and why, 328, 329; the combinations of the allied Generals essentially faulty, 329; why Grouchy's conduct has been misdescribed and slurred over, 331

Reille commands the 2nd corps of Napoleon's army, 57; his operations on June 15, 77, 80, 83; his hesitation and delay on June 16, 131; he urges Ney not to attack at Quatre Bras, 133; his conduct on June 16 deserves blame, 146; at Waterloo he is charged with the attack on Hougoumont, 228; his conduct of the attack faulty, 228, 232; he takes part in the final attack, but the onset of his troops is feeble and slow, 286; he might have done more, 286

Restoration of Louis XVIII.: state of France under the Bourbon Government, 1-11

Résumé of the campaign of 1815, 332, 344; the supremacy of Napoleon's strategic genius fully seen, 332; his objects for June 15 only partly attained, but his position full of promise, 334; ability of his dispositions for June 16, 334, 335; the result is incomplete, but his prospects brilliant, 335; Napoleon's delays on June 17 caused by the state of his health, 336; he gives Grouchy a powerful restraining wing to pursue Blucher, but very late, 336; retreat of the Prussian army to Wavre, 337; slowness of Grouchy's march, but nothing as yet is endangered, 337; prospects of Napoleon for June 18, 338; the calculations of Wellington and Blucher not well-founded, 338; misconduct of Grouchy—he does exactly what he ought not to do, 338, 339; the strategy of the allied Generals faulty from first to last, 339; but they are not to be judged as strategists by their conduct in 1815, and why, 340, 341; high praise is due to both as soldiers, 341; the paramount causes of the result of the campaign of 1815, 343; the conduct of the belligerent armies, 344; Napoleon must have succumbed at last, 344; but his fame has not been dimmed, 344

Retrospect of the operations up to June 17, 153, 154

Rossomme, 207

S

St. Lambert, village near Waterloo, and Napoleon's lines, 208, 232, 233

Savary, Minister of Napoleon in 1815, 19

Saxe-Weimar, Bernard of, judiciously moves forward a detachment from Genappe on June 15, 84; occupies the hamlets of Papelotte and La Haye at Waterloo, 211

Sombreffe, important strategic point not seized by the French on June 15, 85

Somerset, British cavalry General at Waterloo, 211; his fine charge in the battle, 247

Soult, Marshal, succeeds Dupont as Minister of War, and becomes detested in the army, 8; he assembles 30,000 men to support the claims of France at Vienna,

14; he is deprived of his office as War Minister, 17; he is made Chief of the Staff of the French army in Belgium, 69; the appointment unfortunate, 69; Soult's letters to Ney and Grouchy on June 16, 107; his staff work bad and his despatches obscure, 139; Soult does not inform Ney of the results of Ligny on the night of June 16, and until late in the morning of June 17, 159; his important letter to Ney, 161; Soult not hopeful on the morning of June 18, 223; his letter to Grouchy written at ten on the morning of Waterloo, 204; it is obscure and misleading, 224; its real but ill-explained purport, 224; it is not contradictory to the evidence of Marbot and Zenowicz, 224, 225; Soult's despatch to Grouchy, and the postscript written at one and a quarter past one, after the news of the apparition of Bulow, 235; this is also vague and ill-worded, 235; its true meaning, 235; Soult condemns Ney for making the great cavalry attacks, 263

Steinmetz, one of Zieten's subordinates: his operations on June 15; his retreat, 84

Subervie, French cavalry General at Waterloo, 220; is detached with Domon and Lobau to hold Bulow in check, 232

Suchet, Marshal, entrusted by Napoleon with the defence of Lyons, 38

T

Talleyrand is privy to plots against Napoleon, 13

Teste, French General, commands a division of Lobau's corps, 168; with Pajol on June 18, 238, 323; he repulses the Prussians at Namur, 349

Thielmann commands the 3rd corps of Blucher's army, 65; is directed on the night of June 14 to march to Sombreffe, 88, 89; his corps assembled around Sombreffe on June 16, 113; his conduct at Ligny, 121, 123, 127; he halts too long at Gembloux, 179; he is kept back at Wavre on June 18, 215;

he defends Wavre from the attacks of Grouchy, 305, 306; he hears the result of Waterloo on June 19, 346; he is repulsed by Grouchy, and falls back towards Louvain, 346; he fails to intercept Grouchy, 348, 349

Trip, Dutch-Belgian General at Waterloo, 210

U

Uxbridge, Lord, commands the corps of the British cavalry in 1815, 50; his skilful retreat from Quatre Bras, 179; his conduct at Waterloo, 245, 247

V

Vandamme commands the 3rd corps of the French army, 57; his operations on June 15, 78 et seq.; he is delayed through an accident, 78; he refuses to march on Fleurus and Sombreffe, 86; his conduct at Ligny, 120, 123, 124; his message to Napoleon as to a supposed enemy's column, 124; his operations on June 17, 182, 183; on June 18 he takes part in the attack on Wavre, 305, 306; his operations on June 19 and June 20, 348, 349

Vandeleur, British cavalry General at Waterloo, 209; he charges Durutte's division, 249; he supports the defence at La Haye Sainte, 287; his charge at the close of Waterloo very effective, 295

Van Merlen, Dutch-Belgian General at Quatre Bras, 134; at Waterloo, 210

Vendée, La, The Duc de Bourbon tries to raise, 21; the rising in 1815 disastrous to Napoleon, 40

Vienna, Congress of: the policy of the Powers at resented in France, 10; policy of the allies at against Napoleon, 13

Vitrolles, partisan of the Bourbons, in the South of France, 21; released by Fouché after Waterloo, 358

Vivian, British cavalry General at Waterloo, 209; co-operates with Vandeleur, 249, 287, 295

W

Waterloo, Battle of: description of the positions of Wellington's army, 207, 208 ; these may be compared to a natural fortress, 209 ; how the army was arrayed in its order of battle, 209, 213 ; the attack on Hougoumont, intended to be a feint, is made a real attack, 228 ; progress of the attack, 229, 232, 233 ; success of the defence, 232 ; the attack made by D'Erlon's corps, 240, 249 ; it is completely defeated, 249 ; state of the battle at three in the afternoon, 249, 250 ; renewed attack of the French army, tremendous cannonade, 255 ; fall of La Haye Sainte, 257 ; the great cavalry attacks, 259, 269 ; they are ill-sustained and defeated, 268, 269 ; but the losses of Wellington are very great, 270 ; the attack of Bulow, 264, 276 ; it is repulsed for a time, 265 ; the Young Guard repulsed, 276 ; part of the Old Guard detached to resist Bulow, 265, 276 ; Bulow's attack apparently completely defeated, 277 ; renewed attacks on Wellington's army, 277 ; Papelotte taken by the French, and important success gained at La Haye Sainte, 277, 278 ; the battle still undecided at about seven in the evening, 278 ; state of the battle before the final attack, 280, 281 ; the crisis and the end of Waterloo, 285, 297

Wavre, Prussian army assembled around, on the night of June 17, 175 ; positions of the Prussian army around Wavre on the morning of June 18, 213 ; Grouchy attacks Wavre, 304-306

Wellington, Field - Marshal the Duke of : he arrives in Belgium in April, 1815, 36 ; he proposes to invade France, 37 ; his faulty dispositions before the campaign began, and the reasons, 51-53 ; characteristics of Wellington in war, and of his lieutenants, 68, 69 ; Wellington had received intelligence early in June that an attack was impending, 91 ; he makes no movement, 91 ; he learns from Zieten, probably in the afternoon of June 15, that Zieten's outposts have been driven in, 91 ; he still makes no movement, and the reasons, 91, 92 ; his first orders despatched between five and seven, 92, 93 ; these directed a movement essentially false, 93 ; his second orders, 94 ; these are also ill-conceived and dangerous, 95 ; the dispositions of Wellington up to this time unworthy of him, 96 ; his last orders directing a movement on Quatre Bras, 96 ; conversation of Wellington at the ball with the Duke of Richmond, 97 ; his letter to Blucher on the morning of June 16, 98 ; Wellington's strategy and that of Blucher faulty, 100, 101 ; the allied commanders in peril, 101, 102 ; Wellington's conversation with Blucher before Ligny, 117 ; he arrives at Quatre Bras in the afternoon of June 16, 134 ; his skilful direction of the battle, 134, 143 ; his strategy and tactics on June 16, 147, 150 ; conduct of Wellington on the morning of June 17, 179 ; his message to Blucher that, if supported, he would accept battle at Waterloo, 179 ; his skilful retreat from Quatre Bras, 179 ; he concentrates part of his army at Waterloo, 191, 192 ; he places a large detachment at Hal and Tubize, a grave strategic error, 192 ; his confidence as to the result on June 18, 196, 197 ; the plans of Blucher and Wellington for the Battle of Waterloo essentially bad strategy, 193, 194 ; what the allied commanders ought to have done, 194, 195 ; Wellington arrays his army on June 18, 209 ; his front extends from Smohain to Braine l'Alleud, 209 ; positions of his extreme left, his left centre, his right centre, and his right, 209, 210 ; his main battle, 210 ; his extreme right at Merbe-Braine and Braine l'Alleud, 211 ; his advanced posts, Hougoumont, La Haye Sainte, Papelotte, and La Haye, 211 ; Wellington the soul of the defence,

211; he occupies the ground admirably, 212; but there are two mistakes in his arrangements, 213; he superintends the defence of Hougoumont and the defence of La Haye Sainte, 229, 231, 247; he draws his right in on his centre to resist the great cavalry attacks, 267; his conduct in striking contrast to that of Ney, 274, 275; Wellington's hopes of victory towards the close of the battle, 281, 284; he orders Maitland's Guards to attack the Imperial Guard, 293; he makes his whole army advance after the defeat of the Guard, 295; he meets Blucher at La Belle Alliance, 298; he advances with Blucher into France after Waterloo, 359; his negotiations with Fouché, 360; his wisdom conspicuously manifest, 362: he moderates Blucher, 363; he is made commander of the Army of Occupation, 365; his great position in the councils of the allies, and his services to France, 365

Wincke, Hanoverian General at Waterloo, 209

Z

Zenowicz, a Polish officer: Napoleon's conversation with him on the morning of Waterloo, 222; he is the bearer of Soult's despatch to Grouchy written at ten in the morning of June 18, 224; he reaches Grouchy's army, 304

Zieten commands the first corps of Blucher's army, 64; his skilful retreat on June 15, 81; he directs Pirch II. to make a stand near Gilly, 85; he retreats to Fleurus and then to Sombreffe, 89; his corps assembled around St. Amand and Ligny on June 16, 112; his conduct at Ligny, 120, 123, 126; and during the retreat to Wavre, 174; Zieten detained on the morning of June 18, 215; he reaches Ohain at six in the afternoon, 284; he hesitates to support Wellington, 284, 285; his irruption on the right flank of the French army and its effects, 295

INDEX TO APPENDIX

LIST OF DOCUMENTS

I. Napoleon's address to his army, June 14, 367
II. Soult to D'Erlon, June 15, 368
III. Soult to D'Erlon, June 15, 369
IV. Napoleon to Ney, June 16, 369, 370
V. Napoleon to Grouchy, June 16, 371-373
VI. Soult to Ney, June 16, 373, 374
VII. Soult to Grouchy, June 16, 374, 375
VIII. Soult to Ney, June 16, 375, 376
IX. Wellington's first memorandum of orders, June 15, 376, 377.
X. Wellington's 'after orders,' June 15, 377, 378
XI. Wellington's conversation with the Duke of Richmond, June 15, 378, 379
XII. Wellington's letter to Blucher, June 16, 379, 380
XIII. Soult to Ney, June 16, 380
XIV. Soult to Ney, June 16, 380, 381
XV. Captain Bowles' story of Wellington at Quatre Bras, June 17, 381
XVI. Soult to Ney, June 17, 382, 383
XVII. Soult to Ney, June 17, 383, 384
XVIII. Wellington to Lord Hill, June 17, 384
XIX. Wellington's orders, June 17, 384, 385
XX. Napoleon to Grouchy, June 17, 385, 386
XXI. Grouchy to Napoleon, June 17, 386, 387
XXII. Soult to Ney, June 18, 387
XXIII. Soult to Ney, June 18, 388
XXIV. Soult to Grouchy, June 18, 388, 389
XXV. Grouchy to Napoleon, June 18, 389, 390
XXVI. Soult to Grouchy, June 18, 390
XXVII. Grouchy to Napoleon, June 18, 391, 392
XXVIII. Wellington's report of Waterloo, June 19, 392-398
XXIX. The Prussian report of Waterloo, 398-403
XXX. Napoleon's report of Waterloo, 403-406

THE END

Lightning Source UK Ltd.
Milton Keynes UK
UKHW02f0100050418

320549UK00008B/383/P